# New Technologies
# in
# Organization Development: 2

(Originally Entitled
*Theory and Method in
Organization Development:
An Evolutionary Process*)

*Edited by*
## John D. Adams

University Associates, Inc.
7596 Eads Avenue
La Jolla, California 92037
1975

ISBN: 0-88390-112-9

Printed in the United States of America

# Contents

# Contributors

CLAYTON P. ALDERFER
Associate Professor of
 Administrative Sciences
Yale University

ROBERT R. BLAKE
President
Scientific Methods, Inc.

LEE BOLMAN
Lecturer, Graduate School
 of Education
Harvard University

R. DOUGLAS BRYNILDSEN
Manager, Organization
 Development
Systems Group of TRW, Inc.

W. WARNER BURKE
Director of Executive Programs
 and Executive Director of OD
 Network
NTL Institute

WILLIAM J. CROCKETT
Vice President for Human
 Relations
Saga Administrative Corporation

MARGE DUFUR
Organizational Development
 Trainer
Saga Administrative Corporation

JAMES A. FOLTZ
Consultant
Pittsburgh, Pennsylvania

ROBERT E. GAERTNER
Organizational Development
 Trainer
Saga Administrative Corporation

ROBERT T. GOLEMBIEWSKI
Research Professor and Head,
 Department of Political Science
University of Georgia

ROGER HARRISON
Vice President for
 Overseas Operations
Development Research
 Associates, Inc.

JERRY B. HARVEY
Associate Professor of
 Management Science
George Washington University

CHARLES G. KRONE
Consultant
Cincinnati, Ohio

GORDON L. LIPPITT
Professor of Behavioral Sciences
School of Government and
 Business Administration
George Washington University

JOANNE McLAUGHLIN
Consultant
Pittsburgh, Pennsylvania

CYRIL R. MILL
Program Manager
NTL Institute

JANE SRYGLEY MOUTON
Vice-President
Scientific Methods, Inc.

PETER B. VAILL
Dean
School of Government and
  Business Administration
George Washington University

LEOPOLD S. VANSINA
International Institute for
  Organizational and Social
  Development
Kessel-Lo, Belgium

MARVIN R. WEISBORD
President
Organization Research and
  Development, Inc.
Wynnewood, Pennsylvania

D. CHARLES WHITE
Vice President
Drossler Research Corporation

# *Preface*

This book is the outcome of the second New Technologies in Organization Development Conference, held in Washington, D.C. on November 30 and December 1, 1972. As such, it is a companion volume to *Contemporary Organization Development: Conceptual Orientation and Interventions,* edited by W. Warner Burke, which resulted from the first conference, held in New York in October, 1971.

In the preface to the first volume, Dr. Burke began by pointing out that Organization Development (OD), after about a decade of growth, was just about to reach adolescence and that a clear definition of OD was not yet formulated. He also related practitioners' difficulties in keeping up with the field. While strides have been made, many of them contained in this volume, my feeling is that the field of OD, after an additional 18 months, is still pretty much in the same place. If anything, OD has become more diverse, there is still no clear definition and, at the same time, the number of practitioners has just about doubled!

There have been clear advances, however, and a quick comparison of the contents of this volume with its predecessor bears that out. The present volume contains fewer papers by academically based professionals than did the first, and reflects an increase in the number of papers from organizationally based practitioners and private consultants. While it increasingly is being remarked that major progress in OD is moving away from the university and into the field, the trend reflected here is not strong enough for me to agree—yet. Be that as it may, the contributions contained in this volume from academically based professionals reflect a stronger confrontation of their colleagues to be more rigorous intellectually than has been previously published. In addition, the papers from practitioners and consultants, by and large, reflect a strong trend towards broader perspectives and long term efforts with larger chunks of their client systems.

In general the second conference, and this book, may be

characterized as representing a strong push towards theory building and the use of the human intellect. Perhaps the main difference between the two volumes is that the present volume is strongly professional development oriented and challenges the practitioner to use his head, to build theories and to help his clients build theories. In contrast, the first volume is more client oriented and provided conceptual approaches for working with client groups. While this may be in part due to different selection criteria used by Warner Burke and by me, I do not think that it is a major factor in the difference, by any means.

The papers selected for this book are not elementary, for the most part, and the book is intended for an audience of OD practitioners and students of OD who are already knowledgeable of OD practice and methodology.

The mechanics behind the book are similar to those of the first volume. Ten months before the conference, a request for potential presentations was circulated. This resulted in well over 150 offers, of which 16 eventually were selected for presentation. Those selected submitted first drafts of their papers which were duplicated and given to conference attendees. Following the conference, second drafts were invited from the presenters and these formed the basis for this book.

I would like to thank Warner Burke and Bobbi Robertson for their support. Their experience with the first conference and book proved invaluable in developing this second round. I am also indebted to Saundra Reese for her administrative work related to the second conference and to Sheryl Ryan whose eleventh hour secretarial support finally made this book a reality.

The unique character of this volume resides in the twenty-one professionals who provided original contributions. I am certain that the readers will find that they have each made a large investment in the book. I especially appreciate these efforts and the speed with which they were made. As editor, I have tried to do very little to alter the uniqueness of each individual chapter.

John D. Adams, Ph.D.
NTL Institute
Arlington, Virginia
October 17, 1973

# Section I

# Development of the
# Organization Development Practitioner

This section of the book represents significant advances in organization development in two related areas. First, each of the chapters is related directly to the importance today of theory building and the utilization of articulate conceptualizations in the practice of OD. Second, each of the chapters has a focus on the professional development needs of current and newly arrived OD practitioners. Continued attention to both of these advances is seen in these chapters as being necessary if OD is to mature beyond what Burke (1972) has referred to as its adolescence.

In the first chapter, Blake and Mouton develop a matrix typology of interventions, including OD, intended to improve human performance. The matrix relates five different contexts for diagnosis to five different types of intervention, thereby increasing the practitioner's rational choice of interventions through providing means for categorizing and analyzing the broad array of interventions currently in use. Illustrations of each cell in the matrix are provided.

The rapidity and complexity of change in contemporary society provides the impetus for Gordon Lippitt in Chapter 2. In order to maintain proactive and influential choices in the face of the impact of such change, Lippitt builds a strong case for the need for practitioners to become model builders and to learn to select from the models and schematics available and relevant to OD activities. He describes a variety of the models currently in use and discusses their usefulness as predictors and for clarifying the thinking of practitioners.

Lippitt's concerns are shared in Chapter 3 by Peter Vaill. Vaill, however, takes a slightly different approach in that he challenges the practitioner to become more self aware of the subjective ways in which he or she views the world. He identifies twelve key properties of one's personal theories and stresses that more rigorous attention is needed by practitioners relative to the study of organizations, their problems and how to intervene effectively.

In Chapter 4, Bob Golembiewski continues the challenge to OD practitioners to become more conceptually rigorous. Drawing on perspectives derived from the first twelve or so years of OD

experience, Golembiewski projects eight groundrules which
henceforth should guide the practice of OD. These include increasing
clarity and sophistication in areas such as contracting, change and
decision making models, client choice and working with large or
multiple systems.

Clay Alderfer, Chapter 5, forsees increasing demands from clients
for higher grade intellectual work by OD practitioners and predicts
that, increasingly, the success of OD efforts will be a function of
practitioners' abilities to meet these demands. Alderfer develops a
model which he feels meets this demand; which focuses upon power
and authority relations as they affect the practitioner and his
relationships with other practitioners and clients; and which provides
professional development opportunities for new practitioners. Two
case studies are included which demonstrate the viability of the
model.

## REFERENCES

Burke, W. Warner (Ed). *Contemporary organization development: conceptual orientations and interventions.* Washington, D.C.: NTL Institute,
1972.

# The D/D Matrix*

*ROBERT R. BLAKE and JANE SRYGLEY MOUTON*

These are challenging times. So much is going on in the areas of organization diagnosis and development that it is almost impossible for anyone to keep well informed. Yet it is important to know what's going on. All of this creativity, innovation, and experimentation is opening up so many possibilities that it becomes very difficult for a person, whatever his particular career line may be, to know what his range of choices is, to know what the options are, to know what the strengths and limitations of each one might be. Training and development, as a body of knowledge for inducing planned change, is like an elephant in the dark—lets revise the anecdote so as not to speak of blind men!—where one person can feel the toe and another person an ear and another person the tail. But no one can put his and others' impressions all together. It's just that mammoth.

Now this problem didn't just arise. It's been with us for some time, but it is getting to be more bewildering day by day. It stands in need of a solution which can enable the theoretician or practitioner of planned change to master the full range of approaches and possibilities.

For some time we have been interested in this problem of getting better definition of the entire scope in systematic terms. We have been investigating to what degree the broad range of options and choices available can be compressed into some form through which their main features and likely consequences in actual use can be made more visible. We would like to present our conclusions here. In addition, we will show practical application of the Matrix through utilizing it to trace the similarities and differences among approaches depicted in other chapters in this book.**

** References to other papers in this volume are the interpretations of Drs. Blake and Mouton and do not necessarily represent the views of the authors cited (Ed.).

## The Diagnosis /Development Matrix

In the process of our studies we have come to recognize that five different kinds of interventions characterize what applied behavioral scientists do as they work with people in organizations. They intervene, in any of these five ways, in five different settings or units of change. So a matrix of twenty-five cells is necessary to describe the significant change efforts that are going on. We would like to explain what these cells are, provide a brief bibliography to pinpoint work going on in each, and summarize some examples that describe the intervention/development assumptions that each particular cell contains. Although what people *say* they do may not correspond in fact to *what* they do, the basis for categorizing approaches into the various cells is the intervention *itself*, as it has been described. In other words, interventions are coded according to what the interventionist does, or is described as doing, *as he intervenes*. It is important to note, therefore, that *consequences* of various interventions are not what are being categorized.

You will notice that Figure 1 is called the D/D (Diagnosis/Development) Matrix. This is because diagnosis and development are two aspects that are more or less interdependent in planned change efforts, although occasionally they need to be separated for purposes of analysis.

The *rows* of the matrix represent types of interventions. The row at the top contains *cathartic* interventions. The next has *catalytic* ones. A third contains *confrontation*; the fourth, *prescriptive*. The bottom row represents use of *principles, theories and models* as factors in change.

Selection of any particular intervention, of course, is a judgmental decision taken on the basis of prior diagnosis. The intervention itself is intended to promote some planned change in the particular "unit of intervention" to which it is applied. Some interventions are explicitly requested or, in some way, invited by their subjects; others are not. As a general criterion of "legitimacy" in intervention, it is assumed that there is some explicit basis of cooperation or contract of service between the interventionist and the organization or social system in which the unit of change is situated. Such links are usually evident in the examples of interventions that will be cited.

The *columns* of the matrix refer to settings within which the change occurs. The first column, on the left, takes the *individual* as a

| TYPES OF INTERVEN-TION | UNIT OF CHANGE | | | | |
|---|---|---|---|---|---|
| | INDIVIDUAL | TEAM (group, project, department) | INTERGROUP (interdivi-sional, head-quarters-field, union-management, etc.) | ORGANI-ZATION | SOCIETY |
| CATHARTIC | A | B | C | D | E |
| CATALYTIC | F | G | H | I | J |
| CONFRON-TATION | K | L | M | N | O |
| PRESCRIP-TIVE | P | Q | R | S | T |
| PRINCIPLES, MODELS, THEORIES | U | V | W | X | Y |

FIGURE 1

*The D/D Matrix*

unit of change. The next column, *team,* refers mainly to small "family" groups, projects, and departments, but it also includes interpersonal relations on a one-to-one basis. The third column is for *intergroup* relationships. Examples of intergroup diagnosis/development units are interdivisional, headquarters-field, union-management, and other relationships between any organized groupings within or semi-external to the organization. The fourth column refers to an *organization* as a whole, considered as a setting for change. The column on the right, *society,* is reserved for behavioral science based interventions that have to do with planned change of society at large.

Each of the twenty-five matrix cells is identified by a particular letter of the alphabet. Thus, we can refer to Cell A, Cell T, and so on.

### Cathartic Intervention

Now let's go along the top. What a "cathartic" intervention does is to enter into contact with the feelings, tensions, and subjective attitudes that often block a person and make it difficult for him to function as effectively as he otherwise might. The developmental objective is to enable him to express, work through and resolve these feelings so that he can then return to a more objective and work-related orientation. This is not the whole area of counseling as it relates to therapy. It is that aspect of counseling which takes place within the framework of organizations and which is intended to help a person perform better. Certainly it is a very important application of counseling.

Here is a Cell A example of cathartic interventions with in-dividuals. During the 1930's, at the Hawthorne plant of the Western Electric Company, it was discovered that many employees were blocked, taut, seething with tensions of one kind or another. Generally these tensions were either work-focused or home-focused, or an intricate combination of both. For some years Hawthorne management provided a counseling service that enabled people to be aided through counseling to discharge the emotion laden tensions. We say "to discharge" tensions, as distinct from resolving them more or less permanently. The procedure was, in effect, "Any time you feel overcome by tension, get a slip from your supervisor and go see a counselor." This is comparable—if we adopt an oil-industry analogy—to "flaring off" subterranean natural gas rather than piping it to wherever it can be productively used.

In the peak year of the program, 1948, Hawthorne's department of counseling was staffed by fifty-five people. That's a large complement of counselors. This very interesting experiment has been documented by its originators, who were able to return to the scene of their effort and to study the consequences thirty years after the program began.

An example we would like to paraphrase for you is from their book (Dickson & Roethlisberger, 1966, 225-226). The situation takes place in the counselor's office. Charlie enters. He is a semiskilled worker who has been with the company for some time but has recently been transferred to a new inspection job from another one he had formerly mastered and enjoyed. He is unhappy with his new job. After greeting the counselor, Charlie says: "Well I'm ready any time to get out of this g.d. place. *You know, you get shoved around from one place to another . . ."* The counselor responds: "You mean you don't have one steady job?" Charlie continues: "Steady, hell. When I came from the first floor I was supposed to do this particular bank job. I stayed on that for two or three weeks . . . then I got transferred up here. . . . It got me nothing, just this job here which was a cut." The counselor replies: "Then all that work didn't pay off?" Charlie responds: "There's no payoff at all."

As you can see in this brief example, Charlie is ventilating his feelings and frustrations and the counselor is "reflecting"; trying to aid Charlie to clarify them by feeding him back a summary of those tensions so that Charlie might get an understanding of what they are, rather than just feeling the hurt and distress of them. You will notice that the counselor is not attempting to help Charlie solve his "transfer with pay cut" problem.

In recent years—and "way out" from Hawthorne—the continuum of learning through experience has been extended and enriched through experimentation with action oriented, non-verbal approaches. One of the most common uses of "encountering" is in the effort to promote personal growth through individual cathartic experiences (Watson, 1972, 155-172). An advantage here is that the modalities through which an individual is able to experience himself in situations are increased. Results and experiences can be more directly *felt*, in the sense that words, to convey whatever emotions are involved, are unnecessary.

Now let's look to Cell B. This involves cathartic interventions at the team or group level. Here the idea is that before a team can do an effective job of dealing with its work problems, it may have to deal with emotional tensions and feelings that exist within and between its members.

Gibb has for a considerable time been aiding teams to discharge tensions in a cathartic way. This example is from his account of his methods (Gibb, 1972). He describes how, in the process of team building, he may begin with what he calls a "preparation meeting." He brings together the people who are going to be leaders of different teams in order to prepare them for their experience. Why does he start this way? "The primary constraint," he says, ". . . is, of course, fear. Participants are given . . . perhaps the first half-day to share and fully explore as many of their fears as they are able to verbalize." What help is this? "Fears dissipate as they are brought into awareness, shared with others, lived with, listed on the board, made public, and made acceptable. The public expression of the fear may take many forms" (Gibb, 1972, 38). So the effort begins with group exploration which aims to remove these constraints so that constructive sessions can take place.

Cell C identifies approaches to planned change utilizing catharsis at the intergroup level. For example, we are sure that many readers have experienced the tensions and emotions that sometimes underlie union-management relationships. Bickering at the bargaining table is a constant feature and, many times, the topics discussed are not the relevant issues that need to be resolved. Sometimes the latter can't even be expressed! Rather, the issues that people concentrate on seemingly are brought to the table in order to provoke a fight. Often such intergroup dynamics emerge from emotions and frustrations which never get uncovered but stay beneath the surface. Catharsis at the intergroup level has as its purpose to uncover feelings that are barriers to problem-solving interaction; to provide the opportunity for them to be made public; and, in this way, to escape from their hidden effects.

Here is an example from a union-management situation we happen to be familiar with. Contract bargaining was underway. It was hopeless. It was going nowhere. We heard management voicing its frustrations and bitching about the union, and we suggested that perhaps the needed activity was to get *away* from the union-management bargaining table and to sit down together in a special conference for the sole purpose of exploring the feelings the two groups held toward one another. This was done. The tensions discharged in those three days were destructive, deep-rooted, intense. Numerous grudges and fantasies from the past that were blocking present effectiveness finally got unloaded, and this freeing-up permitted bargainers to get back to their deliberations.

Here is one example of the many fantasies unveiled during these days. At one time, actual events which were the source of the fantasy had occurred, but now the "truth" of these events was a matter of history. At the present time the varied feelings about these events were in the realm of fantasy.

"In 1933," (this cathartic session took place in 1963) the union told the management, "you s.o.b.'s had us down and out because of the depression. And what did you do? You cut everybody's pay in half and, having done so, then you turned us out into the yard to dig up all the pipe and repack it. How do you expect us to bargain with a bunch of cutthroats who would do that to helpless human beings?"

The managers, hearing this, did a retake and said, "Oh, but golly, that was not *us*; you're harking back about five dynasties of management ago!" But this disclaimer didn't mollify the union. Eventually, 1963 management walked the 1963 union back through the time tunnel in an attempt to reconstitute the thinking that the 1933 management had undertaken. This was "We shouldn't let people go home with no job. We should keep them 'whole.' We can't employ them full time because we don't have that much production scheduled—market demand is way down. Rather than laying off people *en masse,* the humane thing to do is to keep everyone on the payroll, but to make the cost burden bearable by reducing wages. Also, we have to keep them occupied somehow. With operational activities currently at such low levels, the only thing we can do that has long-term utility to it is to dig up the yard pipe and repack it."

So the 1933 management's intentions were probably well-meant, but the union's legend regarding those intentions portrayed them as very malicious. Yet eventually the 1963 union, after reconsidering that management's dilemma, agreed that it had taken the most humane alternative open to it. So the old legend dissolved away. Only by getting this kind of emotional muck out in the open and discharged was it possible for these union and management representatives to get back to a business-like basis of working toward a contract. That's an example of catharsis at the intergroup level.

Now for an example of cathartic intervention at the organization level, Cell D.

In one emotion-blocked industrial organization, the entire management took part in a "cathartic" experience prior to bargaining. The reason was that even though management, at an intellectual level, desired to interact on a problem-solving basis with the plant's independent-union representatives, many had deep-rooted antagonistic attitudes which continually surfaced and stifled the effort. Why? The ostensibly humane attitudes of people who have received formal education sometimes only serve as a mask for deeper feelings of resentment and antipathy. Often there is a lot of hate among managerial people toward the work force. Such feelings are particularly prevalent among engineers, supervisors and foremen who have, in their own careers, only recently risen above the level of the "blue-collar stiff."

The consultant determined that to work merely with management's bargaining team would be insufficient, as these representatives could only move in a problem-solving direction if they had the support of the rest of management. So a series of conferences were held. Participants were the top 100 members of management, who represented all levels of supervision except first and second line foremen. The stated purpose of these meetings was to develop shared convictions in regard to answering the key question, "How can we create better relations between union and management?"

Participants were put into three "cross-section" groups during each conference. Quinn, the plant manager, sat in one group. Van, the operations superintendent, was in another and Wes, the personnel chief, in a third. The groups struggled with the problem of how to improve union-management relations. Their proceedings were fascinating to listen to, because a fairly substantial number of the managers considered this key question a hopeless one to answer. "There is no way to bring about improvement vis-a-vis the thugs, thieves and crooks who presently are running the union. How can you cooperate and collaborate with such a rat pack?"

Then as the question got debated and looked at from many points of view, a new concept began to appear. Consciousness dawned that one can never look forward to an improvement in union-management relations unless this deep-seated attitude—namely, that the union is composed of thugs, thieves, and crooks—is erased or at least given an experimental adjournment in the minds of management. In group after group, after the cathartic discharge of emotions was completed, it was concluded, "Regardless of what the union officers are, personality-wise, and what their history has been, the only conceivable way of bringing about a resolution of conflict is through treating the union officers as officers and according them the dignity and respect due to people who are duly elected. It is not our place to judge the people who have been chosen by their membership as lawful representatives. This is not our role. Our role is to meet with these people and to search for whatever conditions of cooperation and collaboration are possible."

As a result of this cathartic experience, it was possible thereafter for management's bargaining team to take a more collaborative stance (Blake & Mouton, 1973).

At the level of society shown in Cell E, there also are mechanisms that provide for catharsis. Religious institutions are one example. More so in American history than now, but still persisting, is the role of the clergyman as one of the persons to whom people turn when in deep emotional trouble, with the expectation of his providing the disturbed person an opportunity to talk out his feelings. In addition, the doctor, teacher, and school or private counselor are often turned to for help during periods of emotional turmoil, as indeed may be true for parents as well. Beyond these, whenever there is a trauma in society it frequently happens that *ad hoc* mechanisms are created which help people work through their distressed emotional feelings. Well remembered American examples include the two Kennedy funeral processions that were carried by television to many parts of the world. These occasions aided people to mourn. Mourning, in this sense, means working through and discharging tensions of a painful emotional character which currently are preventing people from going on living in their customary ways. As is true in the individual case, societal catharsis mechanisms may not have any direct and systematic connection to potential problem-solving steps, although they sometimes stimulate remedial action of one kind or another.

## Catalytic Interventions

Let's move to the next row down: catalytic interventions. "Catalytic" intervention means entering a situation and adding something that has the effect of transforming the situation in some degree from what it was at an earlier time. That's quite different from catharsis. When a training manager or consultant is acting to induce catharsis, he is reflecting or restating the problem—or perhaps simply listening in a fashion that gives empathic support. But when a person makes a catalytic intervention, he might provide a suggestion that causes the problem to be seen in a different and more relevant perspective. Or he might suggest a procedure that will lead to a different line of action being adopted.

Here is a catalytic intervention at the individual level, Cell F in the D/D Matrix. In one particular company they have a career-planning project. A young man who had been employed for some time came in to talk about his career hopes. The interviewer said, "What are your aspirations? Where would you like to end up in the company?"

The young man replied, "Well, I think I would like to be president or chairman."

Now then, the interviewer might have said something in a cathartic or reflective way. But he didn't. He said, "Well, that's an interesting aspiration. I would like to think it through with you. How many years of education do you have?"

"Six."

"How many promotions have you had in the last two years?"

"One small wage increase."

"Have you taken any courses on your own initiative?"

"No."

And as the discussion continued, the young man began to see the unrealism in his aspiration to be president. Currently there was *no* realistic possibility either in terms of some evidence of upward progression, or of autonomously achieved preparation, or in terms of anything else he was doing. The interviewer thereby brought him to the choice point of whether he was prepared to make the additional sacrifices necessary for him to generate upward movement, or whether he was simply content to go on projecting an unrealistic career fantasy (Gould, 1970, 227-228). That's a catalytic intervention at the *individual* level.

Another example, which uses a laboratory setting for life/career planning, is premised on catalytic intervention at the individual level (Fordyce & Weil, 1971, 131-132). Harrison's chapter in this book (chapter 6), based on values related to autonomy and initiative-taking, squares with the intervention strategies of Cell F, i.e., a catalytic-supportive approach to individual development.

Catalytic intervening at the *team* level, Cell G, is one of the most widespread applied behavioral science developments of the past twenty-five years, and has become a central intervention in industrial life. There are a whole host of names that come to mind at this point. There are people who engage in team-building sessions where the purpose of their interventions is not to direct the team or merely to reflect back members' feelings, but to facilitate the interaction process so that the team comes to have a better understanding of the problems and pitfalls it's gotten into and so on.

The following is an example of Schein, a consultant, facilitating group action by focusing attention in the Apex company on how the agenda for meetings was determined.

While sitting in on a weekly executive committee meetings, he became aware that the group was loose in its manner of operations.

This meant to Schein that the climate created a major difficulty for the group. No matter how few items were put on the agenda, the group was never able to finish its work. Consequently, the list of backlog items grew larger, further intensifying the frustration of group members.

Schein's intervention was to suggest to the group that they seemed overloaded and should discuss how to develop their agenda for their meetings. He reports that this suggestion was adopted after a half-hour or so of shared feelings.

He took an active, facilitating role by helping to sort the agenda items into several categories. Also, with his help, a decision was made to devote some meetings entirely to operational issues, with others being exclusively policy meetings (Schein, 1969, 106).

Another example of facilitative or catalytic interaction occurs between boss and subordinate as they engage in "management by objectives." Quite frequently, however, in the introduction of MbO in an organization, people other than just the boss and subordinate are used to develop and facilitate the program. In Humble's work with management by objectives he calls these internal people "company advisers" (Humble, 1967, 60). They are viewed as "educators" and "catalysts" *not* as managers. It is the latter, rather than company advisers, who state what the standards should be, what the priorities are and how the problems should be solved.

In this description we see a clear distinction between what we later on call prescriptive interventions—where the intervention is for the purpose of telling people what to do—and the facilitative or catalytic type of intervention where the goal is to aid a process of change or development to occur. Gaertner's chapter (chapter 12) presents a data survey evaluation of the impact on the organization of a catalytic approach to development, primarily focused on team-building interventions of the Cell G variety.

In the work with the Chaplaincy by the NTL Institute described in Mill's paper (chapter 13), the approach rests on sensitivity training with followup of the catalytic sort. It has features that are found in approaches that are described in both Cells F and G.

The Foltz, Harvey, and McLaughlin paper (chapter 8) presents a case study of organization development where catalytic interventions (Cells F and G) followed prescriptive interventions of the Cell S type which concentrated on organization structure.

Elsewhere in this volume Vaill (chapter 3) recognizes the importance of practitioners being aware of the assumptions that underlie their interventions. He identifies some commonly held assumptions by behavioral science practitioners. In the Matrix, we identify these as primarily catalytic and Cell G.

Data-gathering procedures frequently are used in a catalytic way. This is where data are intended to add something to the situation in order to change it (Likert, 1961). When these data are returned to their users, the expert's own personal participation is best described as catalytic. Usually he doesn't tell people what the data mean, but he does ask them questions that aid them to probe meanings more directly.

Next is Cell H, intergroup. Catalysis here denotes adding something *between* two groups, in order to enable existing difficulties to rise to the surface or be placed squarely on the examining table so that they can be dealt with.

An intergroup intervention example, where managers meet with people from a lower level of hierarchy, is described by Beckhard. The goal is to aid the lower-level people to communicate with the managers, or discuss specific problems with them, or to bring forth their feelings, attitudes, opinions and ideas regarding what actually is happening in some existing situation. Usually they have been unable, on any prior occasion, to communicate their ideas directly through organization channels.

The person who organizes and leads the meeting is acting in a catalytic way. He is inserting a procedure into the situation, one that may help develop it toward resolution. In the following description, the meeting leader gives an assignment to each of the groups—in this instance probably a top level group and a middle management group. He does not give directions as to what specifically should be discussed, but he indicates a way to get started on a facilitative discussion.

> "Think of yourself as an individual with needs and goals.
> Also think as a person concerned about the total
> organization. What are the obstacles, "demotivators,"
> poor procedures or policies, unclear goals, or poor
> attitudes that exist today? What different conditions, if
> any, would make the organization more effective and
> make life in the organization better?" (Beckhard, 1967,
> 154.)

Then each unit goes off and discusses this separately. Beckhard's instructions are sufficiently general to permit people to put into their discussion whatever it is that is specifically troubling them in their particular jobs and situations. Then the meeting leader, from there on, continues in his procedurally facilitative role by helping the two units collect their data, analyze their feelings and facts, evaluate and compare them, and generally make progress. A similar example of catalytic intervention with multiple membership groups is provided by Bennis (Bennis, 1970, 158-160). Sometimes this approach is called a confrontation meeting, but this is a misnomer, because it entails no confrontation of the sort more correctly described by Argyris (Argyris, 1971) which will be discussed later. Rather, the proceedings have a "group suggestion box" quality.

At the organization level (Cell I), intervention by an "ombudsman," who is empowered to bypass ordinary channels when he problem-solves on behalf of people who are burdened with difficulties because of some mistake or lack of response on the part of his particular company or government department, is catalytic in character, particularly in its facilitative aspects (*Commerce Today,* 1972, 29; Foegen, 1972, 289-294). Vansina (chapter 14) describes how organization development might be applied "mostly as a process consultant" in his description of work with multinational companies (Cell S).

At the level of society there are many endeavors that are essentially catalytic, as specified in Cell J. We wish it were possible to say they were being systematically implemented within comprehensive and coherent frameworks of development. But there are some that, considered individually, have become quite systematic by now. Taking a census every five or ten years, one which describes the state of the nation "as of" a given point in time and permits comparisons to be made across several decades, is one way of aiding citizens to review their situation, of aiding national leadership to formulate policy and of aiding industries to see the contemporary shape of markets, population trends and many other things. The census is a powerful force in society. So are opinion polls. These are becoming ever more significant in the eyes of the public. Unfortunately their uses are somewhat limited to political affairs, but there are many other points of application that are possible for polling mechanisms, ones that can have a catalytic effect in terms of how society sees itself conducting its affairs.

Many of the descriptions of poverty-intervention efforts instituted during the 1960s (Reissman & Popper, 1968; Spencer, 1970; Zurcher, 1970) are best characterized as illustrating societal interventions of the catalytic kind.

### Confrontation

Let us now look along the next row, which deals with *confrontation* strategies. These represent quite different intervention styles from catalysis and very different from cathartic interventions. Confrontation has much more challenge in it. It's a much more active intrusion into the life experience of other people than could possibly be implied by a catalytic approach, and certainly much more than would be implied by a cathartic one.

There's another distinction here. As you move from catharsis and catalytic approaches into the next three, what you find is that, under the first two, there is no challenge of the *status quo* by the intervener. In other words, he accepts the definition of the problem, and the associated values and attitudes usually as these are given by the client, and then helps the client to adjust better to the *status quo*. Under a confrontation mode you frequently find a shifting across some kind of "gap"—the existence of this gap having been identified in the locus of the challenge that the intervener implies.

In different ways, each of the next three approaches is much more likely to cause people to challenge the *status quo* and to reject the existing situation as being less preferable than a stronger situation that could be designed to replace it. That's a very important shift in thinking—from simply aiding people to conform or adjust, to assisting people to redesign the situations in which they live and work.

First, we'll describe a confrontation type of intervention at the individual level (Cell K). This occurred in a multinational company where the New York president visited the subsidiary president and said to him, in effect—though it was a whole day in the doing—'Look, Henry, I want you to know that we're very unhappy with how your company is operating. As we look at it, in comparison with other companies in our worldwide group, your profit performance is far below the best, and we just don't see you taking the vigorous action necessary to solve your problems.'

Henry *said*—that is, he didn't reply to the specifics of that statement: he couldn't hear them—'If you'll look at our 1949 figures and then look at our latest performance records relative to 1949 when I took over, you'll see that over the years we have made a dramatic shift for the better.'

And so they went at it, this way and that, all day, and neither heard the other. From the New York Headquarters president's point of view, this was a company they would willingly sell, because they couldn't exert influence upon it. From the subsidiary president's point of view, a valiant effort over many years that had produced betterment was being disregarded. Now the confrontation was this.

The next day, one of us said to Henry, "My hearing is that two quite different *perspectives* are being employed to evaluate this company's performance. The perspective of the New York president is a here-and-now perspective. He doesn't care what you did for him yesterday, he is asking, 'What are you doing for me today?' By comparison, your perspective is historical. You're saying, 'How much better we're doing now than yesterday and last year and five years ago.' So unless you two can get onto a common perspective and reason from there, I see very little possibility of any collaborative effort occurring." Well, they did eventually get onto that common perspective basis. Once both of them understood what the central issue was, and that they weren't just totally unresponsive to each other, then some very significant changes took place in the subsidiary company, ones which are continuing to have enlivening effects. That's a confrontation that has caused development to get underway. And the *status quo* has been radically changed from what it previously had been.

Gestalt approaches, several of which are engineered to dramatize encounter between the participant and an absent person, sometimes between strangers or sometimes between a boss and a subordinate or within a work team, or even to dramatize ambivalent feelings within the person's own personality, are confrontational in character, even though cathartic elements are present. Conflicts, contradictions, incongruencies, and so on, are focused on as the intervener structures the situation in such a way as to permit more insightful resolutions through the elimination of contradictions, rationalizations and so on. Herman seems to prefer that a conflict be acted out to its natural conclusions in a holistic way and then concentrate on critique of its process dynamics rather than interrupting it along the way for catalytic suggestions of alternative ways of relating, or to reduce tensions by cathartic release (Herman, 1972).

Now let's examine confrontation at the team level (Cell L). An example of this occurred during a team-building session conducted by Argyris. During this team-building session, and for the last several hours, members had been insisting that the company has a soft, manipulative, ineffective philosophy. Yet they had not really pinned down examples but were just talking in terms of generalities.

So he said, "It is difficult to deal with such an answer, namely that the whole company is at fault. Could you give a specific example?" Nobody could. He continued very directly, saying, "OK fellows, are you going to be soft on these issues? You speak of integrity and courage. Where is it? I cannot be of help, nor you for that matter, if all you do is accuse the company of being ineffective. You said you were ready to talk—OK, I'm taking you at your word" (Argyris, 1971, 84). He is confronting them with the discrepancies between what they can be specific about and the abstractions they have been voicing.

Confrontation at the intergroup level (Cell M) usually involves each group in coming to terms with the other. This interaction is not in terms of discharge of emotional tensions—as in the example of union and management given earlier—but in terms of gaining a shared and realistic sense of what their relationship is.

Here is an example. This one involves the headquarters' Division of Manufacturing in a large company and its major plant, which is located thirty miles away. The Division is headed by a vice president. A general manager runs the plant. These two had gotten more and more out of phase with each other over the years until they had nearly reached total impasse. It was very difficult for anyone to see how their misunderstandings had originated and grown into crisis proportions.

Eventually it was arranged for the vice president of manufacturing, and eight or ten people who reported to him, and the plant's general manager and the twelve people who reported to him, to get together to study their relationship. The task was for each group to describe what the relationship between headquarters and the plant would be like if it were really a good one. Thereafter, they were to describe what the relationship actually was, here and now. The vice president of manufacturing's group worked in one room and put on newsprint a description of what, from their viewpoint, an ideal relationship would be like. The plant manager's group did the same thing, but in another room. Then they came back together and put their newsprints on the wall so that it could be seen by all what both sides thought a sound relationship would be like. The descriptions were similar and this similarity gave a lot of encouragement. The few differences between them were discussed and resolved.

The next step, working separately, was for each group to describe the relationship as it actually existed here and now. They did this, and brought back their newsprints. Now it seemed like the relationship being described, as viewed from the headquarters point of view, was "totally" different from the relationship being pictured from the plant point of view. These dramatic divergences stimulated confrontation between the two groups on the issue of what, in fact, *did* characterize their mutual relationship. For several days, with the interventionist maintaining close management of situations and modes of interaction in order to avoid an uncontrolled explosion, they thrashed through many aspects until a more accurate picture of the present relationship emerged. Now it became possible for both groups to see the many deep problems that in fact existed. They then designed some strategies for improvement steps that could lead toward resolution.

At the organization (Cell N) level, there is a comprehensive description of confrontation (Jaques, 1951). The project was one of the innovative applied behavioral science interventions of the early post-war period and took place within the Glacier Metal Company in England. Jaques describes how he and others on his research team continually confronted the organization with the character of its internal relationships and objective performance.

At the societal (Cell O) level are found a good many in-stitutionalized as well as informal mechanisms through which problems are confronted. What these are is a function of the kind of society one is looking at. The two-party system provides a way of confronting issues by challenging what's going on. When one party publicizes its point of view, the other side is confronted with the necessity of either accepting the point of view as expressed, or identifying flaws in it. This is not to imply that in *any* political system this is done particularly well. We are only suggesting that two-party mechanisms, as these link into and work through a nation's executive branch, legislatures and public media, constitute one important way of confronting the problems of society and getting them into definition so that actions can be taken in behalf of solving them. Furthermore, the spread of the union-management confrontation mechanism into government, school, university and professional settings has resulted in this mechanism of intervention taking on societal dimensions. Beyond that, the entire legal system contains mechanisms by which confrontation with redress of in-justice is provided for.

Some efforts to "break the poverty cycle" are confrontational in character (Klein, 1967, 144-161). Other strategies, such as Synanon (Enright, 1971, 147-177), which focus on the societal malaises of alcoholism, drug addiction and so on also come within this confrontational area.

## Prescriptive

Now let's consider the *prescriptive* row. These are the most forceful types of intervention, ones which are widely practiced by training and development people as well as by outside business consultants in conjunction with managers in industry, commerce and government. Higdon describes the prescriptive approach as often used by various consulting firms such as McKinsey and Company; Arthur D. Little; Booz, Allen and Hamilton and many others (Higdon, 1969). The basic procedure is that management asks an expert in, and he and his associates study the situation and provide a recommended solution. The "mainstream" consultant is not working with emotions in a cathartic sense. He is not working catalytically. He is not confronting. He is telling. His recommendations would be directions, if he had the authority of rank. But he is certainly prescribing, and these prescriptions sometimes are very complete and fundamental. Often they involve changing an organization's structure, or getting out of one product line and into another, or applying a more efficient theory of business. Many times they involve firing or laying off people, and so they can have impactful consequences on the development of an organization.

Sometimes the consultant's prescription is rejected out of hand. Sometimes, when taken, it results in a healthful bracing up of part or all of the organization. There have been numerous instances, however, of consultant prescriptions becoming very frustrating to the organization in terms of the difficulties of implementation and side effects left in their wake. These include lowered morale, people leaving because they no longer can give their commitment and so on. Brynildsen's chapter on career planning with particular focus on strengthening the individual's achievement motivation, though theoretical in its formulation (which might indicate a Cell U placement), has a prescriptive formulation in it which suggests that the interventions are more of the prescriptive character found in Cell P. (chapter 7.)

Here's a description of another prescriptive strategy at the individual level. It is where a consultant is trying to hold up a mirror in front of a manager to help him see what he is like, and then to prescribe, in concrete and operational terms, what he'd better do. The client is a plant manager who has trouble with a rather "cold and formal" individual, his chief accountant. To obtain better results than he was presently getting from this man, the plant manager—a genial fatherly person who likes to develop warm personal relations with his subordinates—was advised to take a forceful, direct, impersonal approach with him. This, the consultant predicted, would resonate much better with the accountant's psyche than the manager's more typical approach had been doing. On the matter of delayed reports the manager was to say the following: "I want your report on my desk at nine o'clock Friday morning, complete in every detail, and no ifs, ands, or buts about it." Having delivered that ultimatum, he was to turn around and leave. The plant manager did just that, although, being the kind of person he was, it was hard for him to do. The new approach brought striking results. The report came in on schedule and it was one of the finest the plant manager had ever received (Flory, 1965, 158-159). The client had been told specifically how he should act and he followed it through in strict accordance with the consultant's plan. In this case it produced effective results. Incidentally, the developing area of "behavior modification" (Krumboltz, 1965) is a training strategy that has prescriptive qualities.

Mintz (1971, 20-21) gives an example of the use of behavioral prescription intervention in a "going around" session during a marathon encounter group. Claire had expressed the disappointment with herself that she had difficulty in attracting men. The intervention was for the leader to ask her to go around the group, speaking in a flirtatious way to each of the men. When she demurred, rather than exploring with her in a cathartic or catalytic way what her resistances were, the approach was to overcome her resistance by the leader's putting her arm around Claire's shoulder to provide reassurance and support and urging her into the activity by saying, "I'll go around with you. Come on." After completing the activity Claire's fears were reduced and she reported that, "Oh, flirting's really fun, it's not so scary!"

An example of a prescriptive intervention at the group level (Cell Q) is offered by Cohen and Smith (1972, 103). They think this kind of intervention is most suitable toward the end of a group experience. At that time the total group is divided into subgroups of four or five members who are given instructions regarding what to do by way of telling individuals how to improve.

During the time when one member of the subgroup is out of the room, the remaining members diagnose this person's typical style of

interacting and try to pinpoint definite and specifit prescriptions to
carry out; ones which, for him, are generally atypical but that can be
productive. For example, one person might be told to express anger
toward the group more directly and verbally instead of remaining
quiet. Eventually everyone in the total group is given a "behavioral
prescription."

*Robert's Rules of Order* are prescriptive rules for conduct at the
group or team level [Robert (1876), 1970]. They tell the leader how
to operate meeting procedures. This rather mechanical set of
criteria, if followed, prescribes the process parameters of the
meeting, provides for expressions of differences, and offers a voting
mechanism for resolution.

The third party arbiter is used at the intergroup (Cell R) level to
provide for the resolution of differences, and to speed thinking
toward further progress. Typically, the procedure operates in the
following way. Two groups—say, management and a union—reach
an impasse. Both agree to submit the disagreement to binding
arbitration. The arbitrator, characteristically a disinterested outsider, hears evidence or otherwise studies the case and renders his
decision. This usually takes the form of a prescription which both
sides in the dispute are obligated to take (Linke, 1968, 158-560,
Lazarus *et al,* 1965). In the description of the power laboratory by
Oshry, it begins with a deliberate prescriptive structuring of the
power and role arrangements among groups. In other words, in
order to produce the desired learning outcomes, the situation is
structured in a prescriptive manner. Thereafter, the relationships are
allowed to unfold with staff interventions that are primarily but not
exclusively catalytic, ranging from F through H.

A prescriptive approach at the organization level (Cell S) is vividly
described in a case study from *Fortune* (Thompson, 1959). Here, the
president of Philco had engaged an outside firm to study the
organization and to propose needed changes. After a six-months'
study, the consultants presented a massive reorganization plan for
Philco's marketing setup. The case study illustrates a whole range of
dynamics that can occur when a consultant prescription clashes with
an organization head's appraisal of the needs.

Levinson, operating out of a psychoanalytic tradition, has
described his model for organization diagnosis in step-by-step terms.
The approach he depicts is prescriptive in character, as
demonstrated in the sample set of diagnostician's recommendations
regarding improvement  to be made in personnel practices as

"Claypool Furniture and Appliances."

These recommendations are that the company "establish descriptions and standards and objectives for all positions" as well as to "develop orientation and training programs to properly prepare people for their jobs." Also, appraisal devices by which personnel and their superiors can assess progress and training needs. A procedure for identifying prospective managerial talent should be evolved. In addition, the present "representative council" should be eliminated, and be replaced by employee task forces appointed to solve specific intraorganizational problems (Levinson, 1972, 491).

Alderfer presents in this volume (chapter 5) the view that the relationship of external consultants to the organization as contrasted with that of internal consultants, accounts for important differences in the character of their interventions. Being less dependent on the organization, the external consultant is more apt to intervene with the organization on a confrontation basis or with prescriptive overtones, whereas the internal consultant is more likely to collaborate with the organization or even to collude with its unexpressed requirements.

The Hoover Commission was an effort to use prescriptive techniques of diagnosis and development at the societal level. It followed a customary U.S. Government procedure, which is to set up a formal inquiry into existing conditions, in the hope of bringing forth concrete recommendations with a fair chance of adoption. Ex-president Herbert Hoover and other members of the commission comprised a prestigious group. The presumption was that the voice of their authority behind recommendations would be sufficient, along with a responsive incumbent President, to bring about the recommended reformations in terms of restructuring the design and operations of the executive branch of the government.

Skinner's recent writings about society, though derived from theory and principles, also rest on a prescriptive concept (Skinner, 1971).

## Principles, Theories, and Models

The fifth row of the matrix identifies diagnostic and developmental efforts which focus upon aiding people to acquire insights derived from principles, theories, or models. The assumption is that deficiencies of behavior or performance can be resolved best when people responsible for results use relevant principles, theories, or models in terms of which they themselves can test alternatives, decide upon and take action, and predict consequences. It is an approach which emphasizes intervention by concepts and ideas rather than by people.

With regard to Cell U, the particular significance of theory, principles, and models to an individual is that they are capable of providing a map of valid performance against which actual behavior and performance can be contrasted. When gaps exist between actual behavior and theory specifications for sound conduct, then action can be taken to close the perceived gap. In this sense—and also, importantly, in the sense of removing self-deception—systematic concepts involving theories, principles, or models constitute a "theory mirror" which has the unique power of enabling people to see themselves, their present situations or future potential more clearly than if reliance is placed upon subjective notions that something feels "right," "natural," or "okay," or simply that others "approve" it. Here are some examples:

Transactional Analysis is a conceptual formulation which provides a mirror into which people can look as a way of seeing themselves. Training designs have been created which enable participants to identify "Parent," "Child," and "Adult" oriented behavior both directly and with the benefit of colleague feedback, and to study and practice ways of shifting toward more adult-like behavior (Blansfield, 1972, 149-154).

Also at the individual level, there is the Kepner-Tregoe system which provides managers with a model through which to design an analysis of any given problem and evaluate the quality of decisions they make. The objective is to reduce impulse, spontaneity and reliance on past practice and to shift to a rationality basis for problem analysis and decision making (Kepner & Tregoe, 1965).

Bolman's chapter (chapter 11), as example of a Cell U approach, pictures how he works with managers by aiding them to identify first the theory inherent in their current management, and then alternative theories that might constitute more effective approaches.

Lippitt's paper (chapter 2) discusses the importance, yet the difficulty, of producing a model at the organization level. In it, he explores issues pertinent to Cell U.

There are a variety of theories, principles or models regarding individual behavior, some of which are accompanied by intervention strategies calculated to make the models functionally useful in concrete situations. Some of the more widely known include Theories X and Y (McGregor, 1960), Grid formulations (Blake &

Mouton, 1964, 1968, 1970; Mouton & Blake, 1971), and Systems 1 through 4 (Likert, 1967). However, the approach described by Likert does not involve man-to-man feedback on actual performance. Thus provisions are unavailable for penetrating and correcting self-deception.

Examples of theory orientation at the individual level include four Grids: Managerial, Sales, Customer, and Marriage; each of which describes several alternative models—9,9, 9,1, 1,9, 5,5, and 1,1—as well as mixed, dominant and backup theories. Once a person has learned the various theories, he can use them to diagnose his own behavior. In addition, he can select any theory as a model to change toward, but the most likely endorsed one is 9,9. He can then study and practice ways of increasing the congruence between his actual behavior and the model (Blake & Mouton, 1968, 34-66).

Some approaches to team building (Cell V) use principles, theories and models as the basis for diagnosing and feedback and for implementing development activities. Central issues, which, for the top team of a large chemical plant, demonstrated the gap between a diagnosis of their present ways of functioning and a model of what they considered ideal, are shown in Figure 2. In this example, individual development of the Cell U variety, where each person has examined his personal managerial Grid styles as the basis of personal growth, has preceded team development. This actual/ideal comparative diagnosis was used for designing strategies of change to be implemented within the next four months (Blake & Mouton, 1968, 120-157).

Theory, principle and models also have proven useful in strengthening intergroup relations (Cell W). An example of using theory in a medical school setting to illuminate intergroup relationships, Cell W, is provided in this volume by Weisbord (chapter 9). Phase 3 of Grid Organization Development begins with two groups convening for the purpose of describing what would be an ideal model for their particular relationship. This ideal model is itself based on theories of intergroup conflict and cooperation (Blake & Mouton, 1964; Blake, Shepard & Mouton, 1964). It culminates with an *in situ* design which spells out the properties of a sound and effective relationship in a particular, concrete setting. The modeling stage is followed by implementation strategies for converting "what is" to "what should be." An example of the properties of an ideal management-union relationship as described by one company is shown in Figures 3 and 4.

**Actual vs. Ideal Top Team Culture in a Chemical Plant**

| Actual | Ideal |
|---|---|
| Persons only do what is expected of them. Each man runs his own shop. The boss calls the shots. | Synergism is exploited, issues are talked through, and solutions and decisions based on facts are fully thrashed through to understanding and agreement. |
| Plans come down from the boss without opportunity to review, evaluate, or recommend changes by those who implement them. | Plans based on analysis of facts permit real issues to be treated soundly; plans are produced jointly by those who should be involved; individual rresponsibilities are clear. |
| Traditional ways of doing things are rarely questioned; they represent the tried and true operating standards. | Elements of culture are continually evaluated in the light of requirements for peak performance and, if necessary, they are modified or replaced through thoughtful discussions and agreement among team members. |
| Results are what count, no matter how achieved. | Team members are fully committed to excellence, results are achieved because members are motivated to excel. |

FIGURE 2

The development of an Ideal Strategic Corporate Model in Phase 4 of Grid Organization Development is an example of the use of models at the organization level (Cell X). With prior steps of intervention involving individual, team, and intergroup development, the stage is set for a top group, particularly, to isolate itself from the *status quo* long enough to design what would be an "ideal" company, given its realistic access to financial resources. Issues considered include, "What should be the key financial objectives that the company should strive after?" "What should be the nature of the company's business, and the nature of its markets?" "What should

## The Management Would:

Maintain open communications with the union in the following areas:
- Economics of industry and company
- Goals and objectives of company
- Long range company plans
- How company profits handled and distributed
- Problems facing company
- Growth opportunities—company and individual
- Security and development of employees
- Employee induction and orientation—where person fits in total scheme of things

Participate in prebargaining discussions to:
- Identiy and clarify current economic climate
- Identify and understand company's competitive position
- Assess and evaluate indexes for productivity
- Identify and agree upon appropriate and objective cost of living standards
- Identify and understand employee attitudes and concerns
- Assess strengths and weaknesses of present contract
- Identify possible obstacles and barriers that could arise during negotiations

Adopt bargaining strategy to:
- Develop frame of reference for agenda
- Explore problem areas jointly
- Explore opportunity areas

Have more joint problem solving—e.g., on:
- Evaluating impact on employees from operational changes
- Work simplification
- Benefits and pension programs
- Techniques of training
- Job safety

Handle complaints and grievances as follows:
- First line supervisors would discharge responsibility for resolving complaints and grievances and act with dispatch
- Participate in continuing joint efforts leading to clear interpretation and uniform application of contract clauses at working level
- Maintain open door policy—union executives have free access to management executives and vice versa.
- Establish and maintain open, upper level labor-management dialogue—ongoing critique
- Endeavor to understand problem confronting union officers within their frame of reference in their relationship with membership.

FIGURE 3 *(continued on next page)*

---

**The Union Would:**

Develop comprehensive understanding of specific nature of the business and concern for it

Understand and consider nature of competition as it relates to company performance and needs for change

Develop understanding of relationships of productivity to wages and benefits

Because of peculiar nature of industry, understand long range impact on both company and employees from work stoppages.

Recognize implications of taking fixed positions in approaching problems—win-lose trap

Recognize harm in intragroup (within union) conflict resulting in company and employee backlash

Subdue personal interests in favor of overall company and union objectives

Accept responsibility to communicate facts to employees without prejudice.

---

Source: Blake, R. R. & Mouton, J.S. *Corporate excellence through grid organization development: A systems approach.* Houston: Gulf Publishing. 1968, 181-182. Not to be reproduced without permission.

FIGURE 3 *(continued)*

*What a Sound Union-Management Relationship Would Be as Described by Management*

its structure be?" "What policies should it operate under?" Finally, "What are development requirements for getting from where it is to where it would go if it were to approach the ideal model?" An example of the change in thinking about financial objectives at the corporate level during Phase 4 is shown in Figure 5.

A model of business performance which presents seventy-two windows through which to diagnose concrete operations within an enterprise is afforded by the Corporate Diagnosis Rubric shown in Figure 6. It identifies six functional areas of organization: Operations (Manufacturing), Marketing and Sales, R&D, Personnel Management, Financial Management and Corporate Leadership. Also, it specifies three perspectives through which corporate functioning can be viewed. These include *current effectiveness,* the enterprise's degree of *flexibility* for meeting unanticipated re-

---

**The Management Would:**

Exercise authority on complaints, grievances, questions, decisions needed, etc., without needless delay, particularly first level managers

Adopt uniform education program for all supervisors, vertical and horizontal, on understanding, interpreting, and applying the contract
Interpret the contract in an honest and aboveboard way

Consult employees on changes in working schedules, shifts, transfers, location, etc.

Apply a system of seniority and rotation without favoritism, e.g., assigned overtime, easy jobs, time off, vacations, best working schedules, etc.

Rate employees' performance on a uniform, systematic, and fair basis and with employees told where they stand

Coordinate and communicate effectively between department supervisors to prevent needless work by employees and cut down costs and wasted effort.

---

**The Union Would:**

Represent all employees fairly

Communicate problems, complaints, contract infractions to management

Have access to top management without runaround at lower levels

Be concerned with costs and amount of production

Insure employee has correct rating for skills he has and that he is paid for job he does, not the classification he has.

(Union had insufficient time remaining to complete this activity.)

---

Source: Blake, R. R. & Mouton, J. S. *Corporate excellence through grid organization development: A systems approach.* Houston: Gulf Publishing, 1968, 183. Not to be reproduced without permission.

FIGURE 4

*What a Sound Union-Management Relaionship Would Be
as Described by the Union*

quirements and strategies of long term *development.* Each of these eighteen cells is further subdivided into four orientations toward action: "internal aggressive," "internal defensive," "external aggressive," and "external defensive." *Internal* and *external* refer to the scope of action, while *aggressive* and *defensive* refer to purpose (Blake & Mouton, 1972).

| From | To |
|---|---|
| Maintain or increase market share while living within a budget.<br><br>Dollar profit should improve and not fall behind last year. Return on investment computed and discussed on an after-the-fact calculation which exerted little or no influence on operational decision making. | Optimal 30, minimum 20 percent pretax return on assets employed with an unlimited time horizon.<br><br>Each business should have a specified profit improvement factor to be calculated on a business-by-business basis. The objective should be an earnings per share level which would within five years justify a price-earnings ratio of 20 to one or better.<br><br>Share of market objectives should be established within the framework of return on assets and cash generation objectives. |

Source: Blake, R. R. & Mouton, J. S. *Corporate excellence through grid organization development: A systems approach.* Houston: Gulf Publishing, 1968, 233. Not to be reproduced without permission.

FIGURE 5

*Genuine Concern with the Organization's Earning Capacity
Results from Designing an Ideal Strategic Model*

The use of principles, models and theories also can be seen at the level of society (Cell Y). The Magna Charta is a well-known historical example. The U.S. Constitution describes the kind of behavior, freedom and control which American society was expected to be modeled after. Over nearly two centuries, several constitutional amendments have updated the model in the light of contemporary perspectives. Legislative and executive actions are always being tested against the Constitution.

Lilienthal's work in Iran can be viewed as intervention at the societal level to bring about change through assisting the eventual users to design models of "what should be" as the basis of specific implementation plans. Lilienthal is a notable industrial statesman

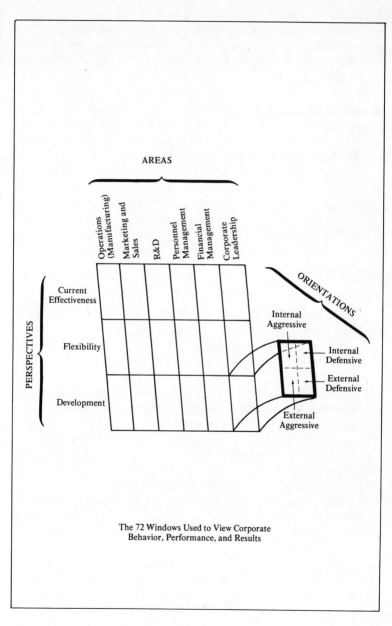

The 72 Windows Used to View Corporate
Behavior, Performance, and Results

**FIGURE 6**

*The Corporate Diagnosis Rubric*T.M.

who led first the Tennessee Valley Authority and then the U.S. Atomic Energy Commission in their beginning years. He has described his later consulting work (Lilienthal, 1969) when, with his own and his colleagues' vast knowledge of hydro-electric engineering, community rehabilitation, and agri-business, they helped the Iranian government design a model for water and electric-power resources for the future of its then undeveloped Khuzestan province. That model is being systematically implemented through the building of dams, power irrigation systems, and so on, as well as infrastructure developments such as agricultural advisory programs, health and educational facilities, etc. This is an example of how a consultant can work, not in a prescriptive mode, but as a skillful teacher in aiding people to learn to design and implement complex models. Lilienthal thus has enabled a vast development to occur, one that otherwise would have been piecemeal, suboptimizing, and possibly impractical.

## Summary and Conclusions

The D/D Matrix provides a way of encompassing a wide range of activities now underway for strengthening human performance through diagnosis and development. Illustrations of each approach have been provided without trying to be inclusive.

Using this matrix, anyone who wishes to do so can identify the assumptions underlying his own work, and evaluate their probable consequences for increasing the effectiveness of individuals, groups, groups in relationships with one another, organizations and society. The cathartic approach of emotional barrier-reduction and the catalytic approach of helping people to make progress in dealing with given situations are most likely to aid individuals and groups to do a better job within the existing *status quo*.

Confrontation and prescription are useful in a "fixed" or "frozen" situation. They provide alternatives to those currently present in the *status quo*. Both rely heavily on outside expertise.

The history of society and its capacity to identify and grapple with complex and interrelated problems of the physical environment, new technologies, and community development is significantly linked with the production and use of principles, theories and models for understanding, predicting—and therefore, managing—natural and human environments. Approaches to diagnosis and development which rely on the use of principles, theories, and models for understanding emotional, intellectual and operational events provide the most powerful and impactful approach to the implementation of planned change.

It is highly unlikely that any single approach will be based solely on one intervention mode. Rather, the likelihood is that several intervention modes will be included, with one of them central or dominant. For example, the Dickson-Roethlisberger counseling program appears to have been a very "pure" individual-cathartic approach, with minor reliance on counseling as catalytic intervention. Process consultation, as depicted by Schein, relies heavily upon catalytic intervention, with some use of cathartic interventions and very infrequent use of the confrontation mode. Schein makes practically no use of the prescriptive mode, and makes theory interventions only after the fact.

The intervening in T-Groups is mainly catalytic, with secondary reliance on the cathartic mode. "Encounter," as well as behavior modification (Wolpe, 1968), relies almost exclusively on prescriptive interventions with the primary difference between them being the social setting. Grid OD concentrates on theory, principles and models; but it also provides at key points for confrontation, catalytic intervention, and cathartic release. Other approaches can be analyzed in a similar manner.

No one can say, in an abstract sense and without regard to a particular situation, that there is "one best way." While principles, theories, and models constitute the strongest approach, they may lack feasibility until emotional blockages have been reduced through cathartic intervention. Or, perhaps, opening up the possibilities of systematic OD may take little more than a timely catalytic intervention which enables managers to see possibilities not previously envisaged. Statements of a similar character can be made with regard to confrontation and prescription.

In the final analysis, however, catharsis, catalysis, confrontation or prescription constitute means to an end, rather than ends in themselves. The ultimate goal is that people become capable of effective living through utilizing sound principles, theories and models as the basis of human enrichment.

## REFERENCES

Matrix
Cell
L      Argyris, C. *Organization and innovation.* Homewood, Ill.: R. D. Irwin, 1965.

L    Argyris, C. *Intervention theory and method.* Reading, Mass.: Addison-Wesley, 1970.

L    Argyris, C. *Management and organization development.* New York: McGraw-Hill, 1971.

H    Beckhard, R. The confrontation meeting. *Harvard Business Review,* March-April, 1967, 149-155.

H    Bennis, W. G. Organization development: What it is and what it isn't. In D. R. Hampton (Comp.) *Behavioral concepts in management* (second edition). Encino, Calif.: Dickenson, 1972. Pp. 154-163.

U    Blake, R. R. & Mouton, J. S. *The managerial grid: Key orientations for achieving production through people.* Houston: Gulf Publishing, 1964.

W    Blake, R. R., Shepard, H. A. & Mouton, J. S. *Managing intergroup conflict in industry.* Houston: Gulf Publishing, 1964.

C    Blake, R. R., Sloma, R. L. & Mouton, J. S. The union-management intergroup laboratory: Strategy for resolving intergroup conflict. *Journal of Applied Behavioral Science,* 1965, *1,* 1, 25-57.

U, V    Blake, R. R. & Mouton, J. S. *Corporate excellence through grid organization development: A systems approach.* Houston: Gulf Publishing. 1968.

U    Blake, R. R. & Mouton, J. S. *The grid for sales excellence: Benchmarks for effective salesmanship.* New York: McGraw-Hill, 1970.

X    Blake, R. R. & Mouton, J. S. *How to assess the strengths and weaknesses of a business enterprise.* Austin, Tex.: Scientific Methods, Inc., 1972. 6 vols.

D, I    Blake, R. R. & Mouton, J. S. *Journal of an OD man.* Forthcoming.

U, V    Blansfield, M. G. Transactional analysis as a training intervention. In W. G. Dyer (Ed.), *Modern theory and method in group training.* New York: Van Nostrand Reinhold, 1972. Pp. 149-154.

Q    Cohen, A. M. & Smith, R. D. The critical-incident approach to leadership in training groups. In W. G. Dyer (Ed.), *Modern theory and method in group training.* New York: Van Nostrand Reinhold, 1972. Pp. 84-196.

I    *Commerce Today,* 2, April 3, 1972, 29.

A    Dickson, W. J. & Roethlisberger, F. R. *Counseling in an organization: A sequel to the Hawthorne researches.* Boston: Division of Research, Graduate School of Business Administration, Harvard University, 1966.

O    Enright, J. B. "On the playing fields of Synanon," in L. Blank, G.

B. Gottsegen, and M. G. Gottsegen (Eds.) *Confrontation: Encounters in self and interpersonal awareness.* New York: Macmillan, 1971.

P   Flory, C. D. (Ed.) *Managers for tomorrow.* New York: The New American Library of World Literature, 1965.

I   Foegen, J. H. Ombudsman as complement to the grievance procedure. *Labor Law Journal,* May 1972, 289-294.

F   Fordyce, J. J. & Weil, R. *Managing with people: A manager's handbook of organization development methods.* Reading, Mass.: Addison-Wesley, 1971.

B   Gibb, J. R. TORI theory: Consultantless team building. *Journal of Contemporary Business,* 1972, *1, 3,* 33-41.

F   Gould, M. I. Counseling for self-development. *Personnel Journal,* 1970, *49, 3,* 226-234.

K   Herman, S. M. A Gestalt orientation to organization development. In W. Burke (Ed.) *Contemporary organization development: Approaches and interventions.* Washington, D.C.: NTL Institute for Applied Behavioral Science, 1972.

S   Higdon, H. *The business healers.* New York: Random House, 1969.

G   Humble, J. W. *Improving business results.* Maidenhead, Berks.: McGraw-Hill, 1967.

N   Jaques, E. *The changing culture of a factory.* London: Tavistock, 1951.

U   Kepner, C. H. & Tregoe, B. B. *The rational manager.* New York: McGraw-Hill, 1965.

O   Klein, W. L. "Training of human service aides," in E. L. Cowen, E. A. Gardner, and M. Zax (Eds.) *Emergent approaches to mental health problems.* New York: Appleton-Century-Crofts, 1967.

P   Krumboltz, J. D. (Ed.) *Revolution in counseling: Implications of behavioral science.* Boston: Houghton Mifflin, 1965.

R   Lazarus, S. *et al. Resolving business disputes: The potential of commercial arbitration.* New York: American Management Association, 1965.

S   Levinson, H., with Molinari, J. & Spohn, A. G. *Organizational diagnosis.* Cambridge, Mass.: Harvard University Press, 1972.

G   Likert, R. *New patterns of management.* New York: McGraw-Hill, 1961.

U   Likert, R. *The human organization, its management and value.* New York: McGraw-Hill, 1967.

Y   Lilienthal, D. E. *The journals of David E. Lilienthal.* Vol. IV. *The road to change,* 1955-1959. New York: Harper & Row, 1969.

R    Linke, W. R. The complexities of labor relations law. In R. F. Moore (Ed.), *Law for executives*. New York: American Management Association, 1968.

U    McGregor, D. *The human side of enterprise*. New York: McGraw-Hill, 1960.

P    Mintz, E. "Marathon groups: Processed people." In Blank, L., Gottsegen, G. B., and Gottsegen, M. G. (Eds.), *Confrontation: Encounters in self and interpersonal awareness*. New York: Macmillan, 1971.

U    Mouton, J. S. & Blake, R. R. *The marriage grid*. New York: McGraw-Hill, 1971.

R    Oshry, B. "Power and the Power Lab." In W. W. Burke (Ed.) *Contemporary organization development: approaches and interventions*. Washington, D.C.: NTL Institute for Applied Behavioral Science, 1972, 242-254.

J    Riessman, F., & H. I. Popper (Eds.) *Up from poverty: New career ladders for nonprofessionals*. New York: Harper & Row, 1968.

Q    Robert, H. M. *Robert's rules of order* (newly revised). Glenview, Ill.: Scott, Foresman, 1970. First published, 1876.

G    Schein, E. H. *Process consultation: Its role in organization development*. Reading, Mass.: Addison-Wesley, 1969.

Y    Skinner, B. F. *Beyond freedom and dignity*. New York: Knopf, 1971.

J    Spencer, G. *Structure and dynamics of social intervention: A comparative study of the reduction of dependency in three low-income housing projects*. Lexington, Mass.: Heath Lexington Books, 1970.

S    Thompson, E. T. The upheaval of Philco. *Fortune,* February 1959, 113-116+.

A    Watson, G. Nonverbal activities—why? when? how? In W. G. Dyer (Ed.), *Modern theory and method in group training*. New York: Van Nostrand Reinhold, 1972, Pp. 155-172.

T    Willson, F. M. G. Government departments. *Encyclopaedia Britannica*. Vol. 10. Chicago: Encyclopaedia Britannica, Inc., 1968.

P    Wolpe, J. "Some methods of behavior therapy." In A. B. Mills (Ed.) *Behavior theory and therapy*. Department of Mental Hygiene, State of California, 1968.

J    Zurcher, L. A., Jr. *Poverty warriors: The human experience of planned social intervention*. Austin: The University of Texas Press, 1970.

# 2

# Model Building:
## An Organization Development Technology

### GORDON L. LIPPITT*

By our everyday experiences, stresses, and conflicts, and by modern learning and mass media we are continuously reminded that we are living in a world characterized by rapid social and technological change. The multiple revolutions that typify the transition from an industrial to a post-industrial society make the need for coping with organization change a task for all managers, but particularly for those persons who proclaim to provide organization development leadership for the social systems of man.

We are given a choice. We may plan in advance for the impact of change, or we may wait until change forces us to react. The latter has ever been a losing game. It is, or should be, the role of the concepts, research and technology of the OD practitioners to help us to plan for organization change, to go past reaction to anticipation. Effective OD technology should allow us to influence the course of the revolutions progressing all about us so as to enable us to become proactive in our leadership of social systems. Coping with change through the creative use of the applied technology of the behavioral sciences can contribute to the process of initiating and creating needed organization changes—and confronting changes that come, needed or not—so as to make it possible for individuals, groups, and organizations to become or remain viable, to adapt to new conditions, to learn from experiences, to move toward greater maturity and, most importantly, to solve problems.

In this context, therefore, the subject at hand is models—models that further the conceptualization of a problem or situations through the use of abstract symbols, and more particularly models of human behavior in a very restricted area of concern—for planned organizational change.

The use of models as an aid to understanding is almost as old as civilization itself, and the ability of the ancients to engage in visual

---

* This paper is a partial digest of a book manuscript and is not to be quoted or duplicated without consent of the author.

thinking was not much less developed than ours is today. Visual thinking in the sense of what we now call model-building has been more or less a necessary adjunct to man's reasoning and communication, rather than an end unto itself. At least, model-building has not heretofore had a strong, probing light thrown on it in an attempt to see to what extent it has, does, and will be able to advance the applied and theoretical scientific approaches of the study of organization behavior in the last quarter of the 20th century.

As man has progressed into and through the industrial era, with its concomitant good and bad technologies, and is now emerging into a post-industrial era, research reveals a wild proliferation of kinds of models and of what are called models, many of which ultimately are concerned with some degree of change. Some large, basic categories of real models have been developed for use strictly by practitioners in certain limited fields. Examples of these are the models produced by computer programmers and theoretical mathematicians which, while sometimes involving planned change, are generally so complex and bewildering to the uninitiated as to discourage their use by most change agents. By my own choice, and certainly with the concurrence of other OD practitioners with whom I have consulted, the three key dimensions of the typology for models discussed here are: graphic, two-dimensional, and non-mathematical. I have not so far found that these obvious parameters lessen the applicability of the discussion for either the professional or the non-professional person involved in an orderly process of bringing about planned organization change.

Alike, students and practitioners in OD, as well as managers and leaders of all types, have benefitted from the opportunity to use models to grasp or convey concepts. One can readily imagine a Caesar drawing for one of his subordinates a model which made clear with only two rectangles their military relationship: the upper box contained the word ME and the lower box contained the word YOU (both in contemporary Latin, of course). It may well have been impossible to develop the sciences of chemistry and astronomy without the availability of models and someone who knew how to create them.

It may be that in the field of human behavior, Maslow's pyramidal diagram of human needs has given birth to more comprehension and believability than could ever have been possible with any number of pages of text or hours of learned lecture.

Although it supports a discipline in the field of science, model-building probably now is most accurately classified as an art. And, for the moment it is a highly individualistic art. In time, of course, it may qualify as a science in and of itself; but before this can happen there is much that must be done in the way of standardization, particularly of symbols, so that the import of any model created by any model-builder may be easily understood anywhere, any time by any other model-builder, regardless of languages.

In this paper I have dealt with models for planned change at the organization level. The examples shown are deliberately selected to be relevant to Organization Development.

In my book *Visualizing Change: Model Building and the Change Process\**, I present models for education processes, individual, group and organizational change.

The OD practitioner is dealing with multiple aspects of a complex event or situation, and their interrelationships. OD involves the varied forces at work in an organic system. A model is by nature a simplification and thus may or may not include all the variables. It should include, however, all of those variables which the model-builder considers important and, in this sense, models serve as an aid to understanding the event or situation being studied. The true value of a model lies in the fact that it is an abstraction of reality that can be useful for analytical purposes. In a way, models are analogies which problem-solvers use to clarify their thinking about a relatively complex presentation. Through the use of a model, they can predict performance under predetermined conditions or evaluate the consequences of various alternatives before committing themselves to a particular change plan or course of action.

To help us understand the essential function of modeling in organization change situations, we need to remember that the basis of behavorial responses of man are initiated by stimuli interacting with the needs of the person, thus affecting how he perceives each stimulus and environmental force.

The primary concern of persons trying to change the behavior of others, or solve a complex organization problem is the motivations of the people involved. It is imperative to consider both the needs and perceptions of people in an analysis of a change situation. Only when the perceptual picture speaks clearly to the eye can it expect to do the most for the problem-solving mind that records the message. The ability and skill to make a model sharpens the ability to perceive

* Published by Learning Resources Corporation, Fairfax, Va. 1973.

a situation. For the most part, perception is a visual process. Since we tend to think visually, modeling is a logical means to reinforce the perceptual process so essential to man's thinking and acting. This is particularly relevant when we are trying to visualize the many complexities that are usually present in any OD effort, activity or process.

*A model is a representation of a phenomenon which displays the identifiable structural elements of that phenomenon, the relationships among those elements, and the processes involved.*

Such a description, however, is not enough to make a person feel comfortable about creating an organization model. Some people feel that there is no effective way to learn the skill of modeling, that it comes by an intuition that some people possess and others do not. The present lack of systematic and descriptive information about the modeling process contributes to this feeling. If we approach the subject from different directions, however, we can hopefully eliminate any feeling that the required skill is an inherent capability possessed only by a select few.

Actually, model building is a pervasive activity of man. As already indicated, they have long provided a means of abstraction which aids communication and problem solving. They are analogies which we use to clarify our thinking about relatively complex situations. The process of using analogies is not, however, applicable only to the modeling process. Different kinds of analogies have been ranked along a continuum of differing degrees of abstraction from the real world (See Figure I).

Here we see that the farther removed we are from the real world the more caution should be exercised in the collection of input data and in the output generalization made from the model. It does not attempt to duplicate all the characteristics of the real world. When developing an organization change model, for example, it is necessary to determine first, the principal characteristics of the change and, second, what factors laid bare by analysis can appropriately be ignored. In this process—largely trial and error—it is almost always necessary also to make more than one model. One that does not effectively and accurately analyze what goes on in the real world may not be very helpful, or may be harmfully inaccurate. A model, therefore, should be validated against its applicability to the circumstances at a number of situations. As we see in the Figure 2, it is good first to draft a model and test it, and then to revise and test it again before finally accepting it as an appropriate analogy of an OD effort.

Real world
Observation & measurement
Field studies
Training, simulation, & simulators
Laboratory experiments
Psychological tests
Game simulation
Monte Carlo models
Analytic models
Mathematical models

The above figure appears on p. 97 of Systems Psychology, Kenyon B. DeGreene (Ed.), New York, McGraw Hill Book Co., 1970.

FIGURE 1

*Degrees of Abstraction*

But it would be difficult in OD applications to use *physical models* such as an astronomer's planetarium, or a physicist's reproduction of molecular structure, or an architect's replica of a new building to portray a change situation. In the physical model we are representing physically some aspect of a general problem. In a *graphic model* we are able to represent variables in two-dimensional space by length of time and configuration of symbols. Where the physical relationships are not important, we can use *schematic models*—also graphic in presentation—to show such things as information flow, current flow, and interpersonal relationships. An organization chart is a schematic model of the authority relationships within an organization*.

* It is by choice that I do not here advocate or deal with *mathematical models* in which the symbolism of mathematics is used to depict factors in the real world. Mathematical models are useful in studying interrelationships of situations where complex symbolic manipulations must be carried out. They are most commonly used in the physical sciences and have only recently begun to be used in the behavioral sciences. I feel that the use of mathematics would be too complicated and time consuming, and perhaps also too impractical for most change agents.

Symbolic World

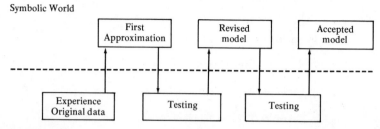

Real World

Figure 2 is from p. 383 in *Organization and Management: A Systems Approach*, New York, McGraw-Hill Book Co., 1970.

FIGURE 2

*The Modeling Process*

A blueprint is a graphic model. Graphs and charts are graphic models based on specific data. A number of schematic models have been developed which are useful in managing, planning, and controlling organizational activities. The Gantt Chart is such a schematic model. So, too, is the Critical Path Method, which is a network diagram of the scheduling of activities and events necessary to complete a project. The essential advantage of either a schematic or graphic model is that they present relative positions, directions, and relationships. Once such a model is understood, it presents complex events and concepts visually. It is easily possible, however, to so badly clutter up a graphic model as to make it incomprehensible. Some schematicized concepts can be more clearly explained in words alone. And while some models may stand by themselves, visually complete, most change models require a combination of narrative and graphic presentation.

It is possible to differentiate graphic change models into two categories: *static* and *dynamic*. The major difference between these two typologies is that a static model is a graphic representation of a situation at a given point in time, whereas a dynamic model illustrates the interaction of forces and subforces, takes into the account the dimension of time, and has built into it feedback loops that affect the input/output elements of a situation. For example, an ordinary flow-chart is a static model. It becomes dynamic in Figure 3, where we see the use of feed back loops in a model of consultant entry on a training design intervention.

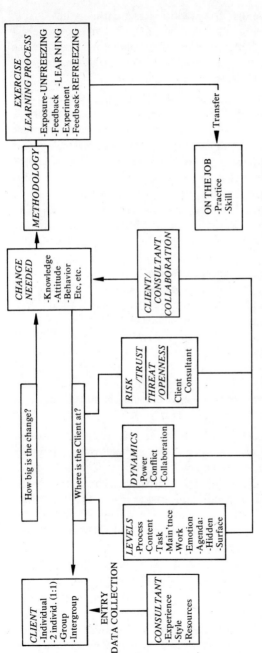

Source for Figure 3 is from take home packet of NTL Consulting Skills Workshop, Summer 1969, Bethel, Maine.

FIGURE 3

*Model for Intervention/Training Design*

While it may be true that OD practitioners are usually involved in change, and therefore are mostly concerned with dynamic models, I think it is important to identify that on a number of occasions the OD specialist may want to use a model to define the *parameters* in which on OD effort is taking place.

A responsible OD practitioner should require those in the management of any particular organization to develop a theory, a value system, or philosophy of organization and management that can become the frame of reference for the organization development activities and processes of that organization. Many organizations adopt any new management techniques, methods, or procedures hoping it will help manage their complex systems. Frequently, these methods conflict in their value implications and cause confusion to the employees. The parameter might be a commitment to MacGregor's Theory "X" or Theory "Y"; a belief in Herzberg's concept of "satisfiers" or "dissatisfiers" in motivation; a conviction about Rokeach's values of an open vs. closed system; or dedication to the teamwork management (9.9) concept of Blake's "Managerial Grid". While these represent some behavioral science parameters, one also finds parameters based on such economic beliefs as "10% profit and 10% growth" each year or consumer commitments of lessening our product recall by 50% through improved quality controls. These values are reflected in what management advocates, who they reward, kinds of development and training activities, profit goals, attitudes toward the work environment, management-labor relations, and relationship to the larger society.

What I am advocating is that an organization development activity help management identify a theory and philosophy that they find valuable, will practice, and will encourage. This provides a character structure to the organization, provides a consistency to the management methods utilized, and makes clear the important variables for management to diagnose and implement in OD. As indicated by Kurt Lewin, the famous psychologist: "There is nothing so practical as a good theory."[1]

Let me present a frame of reference that I have advanced that provides a frame of reference for organizational life. As illustrated in the model in Figure 4, it is built upon the concept that an organization is a living organism with stages of growth. An organization may begin as "the lengthened shadow of a man", but it soon takes on a life of its own. It goes through phases of development. It encounters a sequence of problems which are not entirely unpredic-

| Developmental stage | Critical concern | Key Issues | Consequences if concern is not met |
|---|---|---|---|
| Birth | 1. To create a new organization | What to risk | Frustration and inaction |
| | 2. To survive as a viable system | What to sacrifice | Death of organization Further subsidy by "faith" capital |
| Youth | 3. To gain stability | *How to organize* | Reactive, crisis-dominated organization Opportunistic rather than self-directing attitudes and policies |
| | 4. To gain reputation and develop pride | How to review and evaluate | Difficulty in attracting good personnel and clients Inappropriate, overly aggressive, and distorted image building |
| Maturity | 5. To achieve uniqueness and adaptability | Whether and how to change | Unnecessarily defensive or competitive attitudes, diffusion of energy Loss of most creative personnel |
| | 6. To contribute to society | Whether and how to share | Possible lack of public respect and appreciation Bankruptcy or profit loss |

FIGURE 4

*Stages of Organizational Development*

Figure 4 is from p. 109 in article "Crisis in a developing organization", by G. L. Lippitt and Warren Schmidt, Harvard Business Review, Nov./Dec. 1967.

table. It experiences needs and concerns which begin to fall into a recognizable, if not altogether specific, pattern.

Like an organism, an organization moves from birth to maturity. Along the way, it is likely to respond to the concerns and issues presented in Figure 4.

These six stages of growth do not come about automatically, nor does it mean that once the organization has achieved a particular stage it might not slip back into an earlier stage. For example, an organization at the fifth stage can slip back to the need to survive (the second stage) if a competing organization comes into existence or a crisis hits a particular industry. If organization development and renewal is to become a reality, organization leaders must understand their present stage of functioning. It is essential that they analyze the stages of growth through which their organizations have passed and that they relate these six stages to fundamental management functions.[2]

Thus, the model becomes a frame of reference which serves as an OD parameter, giving a *value* to the importance of social responsibility, being adaptable, and achieving uniqueness in operating. It says to the management of an organization that they should not be satisfied with merely stabilizing their functioning. In this way it provides a "raison d'etre" for the objectives of the organization.

Organizations reflect different orientations to their management values and behavior.

One of the ways of illustrating different managerial systems of organization is presented by George Rice and Dean Bishoprick.[3] In their book the authors present seven organizational models distributed along a continuum from autocracy to democracy. The models they present are as follows: Machine Model, Bureaucracy, Systems, Decentralization, Collegialism, Federations, and Egalitarianism. (See Figure 5)

These authors feel that the trend in management is from the left hand side to the right hand side of the continuum to meet the changing needs of the post-industrial society.It would seem apparent, then, as we look at models for organizational management, that many of the change efforts would be in that direction. However, I think it is appropriate to observe that management practices in organizations are not as clear cut as might be communicated by such listings or terminology. In addition, in large organizations, some segments of the organization may be operating on one basis and other segments on another. In addition, while these multiple approaches to organization management present a trend toward more participation, it is important to recognize that the organic and growth concepts of organizations imply that at different stages of growth, different kinds of structure and managerial leadership might be appropriate. That is, in the early stages of an organization some degree of autocracy may be appropriate while it might be inappropriate for the later stages of uniqueness and maturity. It is also relevant to point out that as different crises emerge in an organization and when the organization is confronted with a recession, competition from overseas, or waning interest in their product or service, it may need to revert to different styles of management to "see it through" a particular period of time.

When a management has a frame of reference of what it wants to achieve it can more likely agree on the means toward achieving its future. In management conferences, fact finding procedures, training programs, and other organization development processes the focus

| Autocratic | Democratic |
| --- | --- |
| Autority Concentrated | Authority Distributed |
| McGregor's Theory X | MacGregor's Theory |
| Machine Model | Homeostatic Cooperation |
| Boss' Will | Members' Will |
| Concentrated Knowledge | Distributed Knowledge |
| Hierarchy | Egalitarianism |
| Command | Custom |
| Coercion | Self-Discipline |

Characteristics of the Continuum

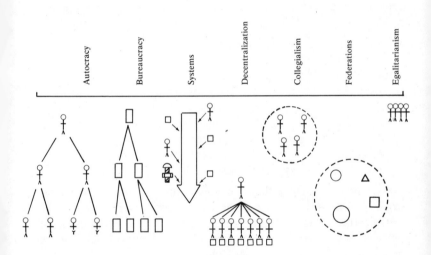

Distribution of Organization Forms

### FIGURE 5

*Organization Forms*

Figure 5 is from *Conceptual Models of Organizations* by G. Ride and D. Bishoprick. Appleton-Century-Crofts. 1971

will be clear in light of the commitment of management to a meaningful frame of reference for that particular organization.

My plea is that whether using the frame of reference suggested above or another, that some visual parameter by way of a model is needed to guide the choice of organization development efforts.

## MODELS OF ORGANIZATION CHANGE

OD is frequently defined in terms of a planned change effort that affects the total organization. As OD practitioners are modeling the process with their client they will be using dynamic models in which change, problems, forces and goals can be visualized.

Robert Chin talks about three categories of such change models: developmental, system, and intersystems.[4] Chin points out that development models center around the concept of growth or directional change toward a particular state of affairs that will lead to a major goal on the part of an individual, group or organization. They assume change in that there are noticeable differences in the organism at different times in its life state. He feels that development models have been more helpful to practitioners of change than the social scientists' new emphasis on systems models:

> The development model has tremendous advantages for the practitioner. It provides a set of expectations about the future of the client-system. By clarifying his thoughts and refining his observations about directions, states in the developmental process, forms of progression, and forces causing these events to occur over a period of time, the practitioner develops a time perspective which goes far beyond that of the more here-and-now analysis of a system-model, which is bounded by time.[5]

It is in this context that the presentation of the six stages of organization growth is relevant as a development model. The organization change agent can be helpful to the organism at particular times in this chronology of change and models can be helpful at different stages in the change process.

Chin refers to his second model as the system model. During the past decade, the behavioral sciences have been using the general systems concept much more frequently. One of the appeals is the idea that various disciplines and sciences can use the same models, and that some comparability and integration of the different sciences might take place. One key element of a system is that there are factors that interrelate with each other and establish boundaries within which the interrelationship takes place. In everyday life we frequently hear political system, legal system, payroll system, and penal system. These tend to be *social systems* that exist in order to get work done. An organization is itself a system of sub-systems.

In using models as a frame of reference with which to diagnose change potential in organization development, the change initiator should remember that each sub-system has elements that are common to all social systems and that need to be considered in making the change diagnosis and action plan.

A rather inclusive approach to organizational change has been presented by Warren Bennis. In Figure 6, we see a framework Bennis has developed for taking a look at three approaches to organization change. The first he entitled *equilibrium model*. In this context the major goal is that of keeping an organization free from conflict, i.e. the change efforts should be directed toward reducing the defensive social structure within the organization by releasing anxiety and tension throughout the organization. The change agent would use various data collection methods, feedback methods, group discussion, and situational confrontation to stabilize the functioning of the organization so that the various ups and downs of crisis, conflict, and stress are minimized.

Another method of organizational change is shown as the *organic model*. Here, the target of change is to develop team management and total system problem solving throughout the organization so that organization effectiveness is increased. Organizational change is achieved by redistribution of the power in the organization so that more effective group action might take place. The change agent uses various problem-solving exercises, system analysis methods, team building, and other approaches that will affect the organic operation and cultural operation of the total system.

A third concept for organizational change is the *developmental model*. The major thesis of this approach is the development of authentic relationships so as to further the interpersonal competence of the people in the organization. To develop such relationships the change agent would use T-groups, problem-solving activities, confrontation sessions and other opportunities to change values from efficiency and productivity to a more humanistic frame of reference.

Bennis feels that the equilibrium model was the earliest used by OD practitioners in which psychiatric and psychological application was made to organizational change. In the 1950's and early 1960's, use of the development model, with the emphasis on sensitivity training, was greatly increased by the behavioral scientists' evolving of laboratory methods. In the mid-1960's, we saw more of the organic model in which restructuring of the system, redistribution of the power, and more confrontation of operating systems came into play. These tend to be some of the major derivations of organization development activities in the 1970's.

| Selected Aspects of Change Induction / CHANGE MODEL | A Mechanism for Change | B Target of Change | C Normative Goals | D Functions of Management | E Roles of Change-Agent | F Instrumentation or Programs | G Leverage for Change |
|---|---|---|---|---|---|---|---|
| I. EQUILIBRIUM MODEL (Sofer, Jacques, Menzies, et. al.) | Tension release through anxiety reduction | Defensive social structures | Conflict-free ("realistic") social structures | Reality-tester | Consultant Researcher Trainer Counselor | Data-collection & feedback Group discussion "situational confrontations" Reconceptualization | Role model: Identification |
| II. ORGANIC MODEL (Blake, Shepard, et. al.) | Power redistribution Conflict resolution | Problem solving activities | Team Management | Adaptation, collaboration | Trainer Teacher Consultant Researcher | Problem-solving exercises T-Groups Theory (Managerial grid) 6 phase approach | "Cognitive map," acquiring new concepts |
| III. DEVELOPMENTAL MODEL (Argyris, et. al.) | Transformation of values | Interpersonal competence | Authentic relationships | Develop and maintain authentic relationships | Research trainer consultant counselor | T-groups Problem-solving activities | Valid communications new symbolic devices |

A. *Mechanism for change* refers to ways client-system unfreezes.—

B. *Target of change* refers to locus, the effect of A.

C. *Normative goals* refer to action-imperatives of change-agent.

D. *Functions of management* refer to some key elements in the manager's role as viewed by change-agent.

E. *Roles of change-agent* are listed in order of priority. (Very rough estimate)

F. *Instrumentation* refers to programs and techniques employed by change-agent.

G. *Leverage for change* refers primarily to the ways instrumentation is employed in order to manipulate A... Mechanism for change.

FIGURE 6

*Framework for Planned Organizational Change*

Figure 6 is from handout by Warren Bennis at ASTD Conference, Washington, D.C. 1964

An example of two models of organization change that fit the organic approach would be situational.

In using the word "situations" as a focal point in these two models, it is intended that the multiple and complex nature of such words as "problem-solving," "confrontation," "crisis," and "everyday decision" be included. There will be differences in the various degrees of situational intensity, but it suffices to recognize that "situations" may refer to such things as the death of the leader of the organization, inadequate cash flow to maintain financial stability, high employee turnover, sabotage by the work force, a merger, or the pickets posted at the main gate when a strike is in progress.

As a derivation of the stages of growth and the crucial crises concept, Figure 7 illustrates a conceptual framework for describing the reactions to organizational crisis. This four-stage model is based on the assumption that a human system passes through several phases as it adapts to a crisis situation, beginning with the initial period of shock of a particular crisis, followed by defensive retreat, acknowledgment of the crisis and, finally, a process of adaptation and change. These four phases are represented as common to individuals in crises but they may be extended to the organization.

Such a model could prove invaluable in helping an OD specialist and his client system to understand some of the reactions in the organization to a drastic cutback in personnel, for example.

It is through working directly on organic situations and examining the subsequent failures and successes that organizational systems discover the worth of their selection procedure, interfacing process, training programs, communication efforts, and development activities. This to me is the essence of OD. It is relatively foolish, even in theory, to believe that all responses to situations can be based on predetermined plans, conscious strategy, or objective action. There are occasions when a situation calls for an effective but unplanned response. While a great deal of the recent writing on behavioral science and organizational theory has focused on planned change, there is a place for spontaneous action, the seemingly instinctive response, or emotional reaction. It would seem that some of the experts in organization development wish that all situations could be approached with the kind of rational and unemotional behavior once advocated by a founder of organizational theory - Max Weber.

In my concept of Organization Renewal indicated in the model depicted in Figure 8, the key element is the ability to *respond*

| PHASE | INTER-PERSONAL RELATIONS | INTER-GROUP RELATIONS | COMMUNI-CATION | LEADERSHIP AND DECISION MAKING | PROBLEM HANDLING | PLANNING AND GOAL SETTING | STRUCTURE |
|---|---|---|---|---|---|---|---|
| Shock | Fragmented | Disconnected | Random | Paralyzed | None | Dormant | Chaotic |
| Defensive Retreat | Protective Cohesion | Alienated | Ritualized | Autocratic | Mechanistic | Expedient | Traditional |
| Acknowledgment | Confrontation (supportive) | Mutuality | Searching | Participative | Explorative | Synthesizing | Experimenting |
| Adaptation and Change | Interdependent | Coordinated | Authentic Congruent | Task-Centered | Flexible | Exhaustive and Integrative | Organic |

TIME ⟶

FIGURE 7

*Phases of Organizational Crisis*

Figure 7 is from p. 26 in article, "Organizational crisis and change", by S. Fink, J. Beak, and K. Taddeo, *Journal of Applied Behavioral Science.* Vol. 7 #1, 1971

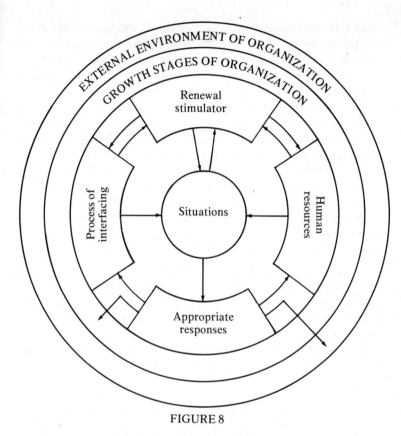

**FIGURE 8**

*Organization Renewal Model*

Figure 8 is from p. 19 of the book ORGANIZATION RENEWAL by Gordon L. Lippitt. Published by Appleton-Century-Crofts, New York. 1969.

*appropriately* to situations. Whether the response is appropriate will depend on whether an action does the following four things:

1. Optimizes the effective utilization and development of the *human* resources in the organization;
2. Improves the *interfacing process* in the organization;
3. Contributes to the *growth* of the organization; and
4. *Is responsive to the environment* in which the organization exists.

An OD practitioner, to effectively help an organization to achieve an appropriate response, therefore would initiate actions which will contribute to improved interfacing in the organization and effective utilization of human resources, contribute to the maturation process of the organization and positive adaptation to the environment.

This circular model of organizational functioning emphasizes the need for the organizational system to re-examine its goals, evaluate its performance, and renew its spirit; and it demonstrates that the ability of the socio-technical system to cope is an essential element. The quality of situational coping, therefore, may be aided by a renewal stimulator—an organization development office, training director, group manager, or some other kind of change agent. (Note arrows in figure). This model has been the basis for developing an organization renewal program that has been used by a number of organizations to initiate the OD process.*

Two colleagues, Frank Laverty and Herb Gabora, have been using this program with a number of government and private organizations in Canada where they have evolved a model for the needed follow up and feedback processes that relate to the initiating of OD (See Figure 9).

Having briefly illustrated the nature of models and their relevance to OD, it might be appropriate to take an evaluative look at the use of models.

### Advantages and Disadvantages of Models

As related to the planned organization change process, the advantages of models may be summarized in this manner:

*Models allow experimentation without risk.* We can determine with a model the effects of dozens of alternate interventions for change without actually tampering with the system. Were it possible, all planned change efforts

---

* Called "Implementing the Organization Renewal Process" or more popularly "ITORP," it was developed by my associate, Leslie E. This, and myself primarily to enable client organizations to plan in advance for the impact of multiple social, economic, and technological revolutions, to go beyond reaction to anticipation, and to influence the effect of change. Started in the winter of 1969-70, it has now been evaluated and tested, creating the beginning of a fact finding and action planning process that if adequately followed up has produced some meaningful organization change.

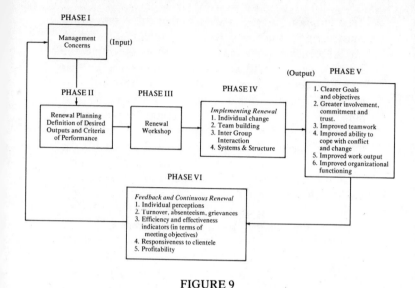

**FIGURE 9**

*Systems Approach to Organization Renewal Model*

Figure 9 was developed by F. Laverty and H. Gabora, of Management
Renewal, Ltd., of Ottawa, Canada, in an unpublished manuscript. 1972

should involve real life experimentation, but the
problems of the change agent involve not only trial and
error but also, sometimes, trial and disaster. Occasionally, the disaster is measured in terms of lowered morale or
extreme cost. The advantage of abstract experimentation
is even more pertinent when dealing with planned change
which is primarily measured not in dollars and cents, but
in human lives.

*Models are good predictors of system behavior and
performance.* Although many proponents claim that
models provide the most effective means yet developed
for predicting performance, Forrester advances the argument that whereas models are excellent in their ability to
reproduce or predict the *behavior characteristics* (e.g.,
stability, oscillation, growth) of a system, they cannot be
expected to predict *specific* conditions far enough into the
future to be helpful for long range planning of change.

*They promote deeper understanding of a system.* In constructing a model of a real world situation or system, careful consideration must be given to selecting the essential elements and eliminating the non-essential. This mental exercise develops greater insight into the problem, and the model-builder is forced to commit himself with respect to the relative importance of various factors. Some of his fondest prejudices are thus often found to be involved. Models are used as a basis for learning experiences and training activities. For these reasons both industry and business colleges have found models and model-building to be a basis for learning experiences and training activities, and valuable in teaching management trainees, middle managers, and business college students about phases of organizational behavior. In addition, model-building can identify where and how total involvement and the learning process might be helpful in effecting change.

*The relative significance of various factors can be determined.* We are able to change one factor in a change model while holding all other factors constant, and this enables us to determine the sensitivity of the system to a particular factor. Using the information thus obtained, we can make decisions on which factors are key to the planned change effort and, perhaps, even to redesign the system so as to minimize or emphasize certain factors. Also, an appropriate change model provides a means of separating facts from assumptions and of foreseeing logical consequences.

*Indicates the type and amount of data which should be collected and analyzed.* In spite of the information initially possessed or believed to be possessed and its accuracy and relevance it frequently occurs that the design and study of an applicable model will reveal the need for additional information or discredit that in hand.

*Permits consolidation of the change problem as a whole.* Here the advantage lies in displaying and considering simultaneously all of the chosen aspects of the change problem—and in then indicating what aspects might have been either overlooked or unduly emphasized.

The OD practitioner and, for that matter, all change agents have inherited the act of modeling from the physical scientists and, therefore, as a technique for prediction, models for change approximate the scientific method. Thus, while model building is partly an art and partly a science, the essential consideration in both of these aspects and, not unimportantly, the skill and difficulty lies in properly abstracting from the real life situation those elements required to analyze, synthesize, and conceptualize. And, even after all of this is done and we have a model for organization change, we may encounter pitfalls and *disadvantages* resulting from both its creation and its subsequent use:

1. A model may induce one to overgeneralize a situation.
2. The temptation arises to make the situation fit the model rather than trying to fit the model to the situation.
3. The relationships between the variables in a model, or the nature of the constraints, may be incorrect or misleading, whereby the model could lead to unproductive research or conclusions.
4. A model may not be properly validated or understood. As such, some work or effort could be expended to an invalid model or certain factors may be overlooked.
5. Model building may divert useful energy into nonproductive activity.
6. Modeling might produce over-simplification.
7. A model may have no intrinsic means of evaluation.
8. Modeling requires conceptual ability and a modest degree of sophistication, neither of which are always readily available.

In light of these advantages and disadvantages, the creation of a model should hardly be a casual matter, nor is the creation and use of a model simple, a science, or the answer to all problem-solving efforts. The danger of model-building for OD lies in the nature of its abstraction. The important principle is to keep the change model in workable form and, therefore, possibly to oversimplify. If those making change models attempt to be too literally true to the real change situation, the result may be cumbersome and so expensive in the use of time it is impracticable. The final guide to the validity of any change model is, of course, its test in the real change situation. If it is able to predict the results of difference change interventions, it is a good model. If it cannot, its major value might lie merely in providing additional insight into the nature of the problem.

## Steps in Developing a Change Model

The construction of a two dimensional graphic-schematic model requires specific, orderly steps. While these steps have chronological implications, it is not critically necessary that the sequence of presentation below be exactly followed:

*Step No. 1:* Prepare a description of the situation or system under study and identify the essential variables which can influence that situation or system. For each variable the following data should be listed:

### Relevance

All variables which might have an important effect on the intended change should be listed and where there is some possibility of confusion, they should be carefully defined.

### Relationships

Indicate how these variables interrelate with each other. This is an extremely important aspect of a model and yet it is often overlooked.

### Relative Importance

Weigh the variables—graphically, numerically, by precedence, or however—according to the effect they might exert with respect to the intended change. For example, in Lewin's force field analysis model, the relative importance of the variables is given by the length of arrows.

### Quantitative Relationships

Quantitative Relationships between variables often cannot be determined but when available, these should be included in the list.

### Outside Constraints

This is sometimes referred to as the boundary of the problem. Not only should the limits of the analysis be shown but also any outside forces which act upon the situation or system (or limit it) should be identified.

### Internal Constraints

These are generally limitations which arise out of the nature of the system or situation, or problem being studied. For instance, certain procedures may have to follow prescribed patterns. These should be included in the data.

*Step No. 2:* Establish the symbols to be used. It really makes little difference what symbols are used as long as they are commonly and correctly understood by all who are to use or be affected by the model.

*Step No. 3:* Analogies should be developed. At this stage of the model building process, using available data and the fully identified variables, the model builder should try to develop an analogy between the change problem under consideration and some previous experience. Such an analogy will sometimes occur intuitively. Is this a change problem wherein a confrontation method might be appropriate? Is this change situation similar to one that is modeled by someone else? Is this change situation similar to one which I have encountered previously? Does this change situation lend itself to a collaborative effort? These and other questions can make possible analogies that might be considered in the analysis of a situation. Such analogies may well suggest the way in which the change situation might be approached. The process of discovering analogies is not easy or well understood. It is, however, an important part of being able to "picture" the model in a helpful way.

*Step No. 4:* Establish criteria for measurement of the effectiveness of a change process. An essential early step in the modeling process would be the development of a clear statement of the criteria used to judge the success of a change endeavor. Do you want the model to predict the consequences of various interventions? Do we want the model to suggest an optimal solution to the problem? Is the model going to be successful if a certain quantitative measure of change is achieved? Some reality of the measure of effectiveness of a change endeavor is necessary for us to be able to make a model. Such a statement of objectives would provide the criteria for determining the success of a change enterprise. In establishing such an objective, however, one should keep open the possibility that it might prove unachievable or that different objectives may occur after the process of change is initiated. This might mean that the model should have certain feedback loops to provide for substitute goals, if such should occur.

*Step No. 5:* Determinations of the values of sub-parts of the change problem. A change model should be made up of simple parts where the values of those parts (whether they be factors, variables, or sub-achievements) can be determined. When we are able to understand the subparts of a problem or a change endeavor, it is easier to subsequently combine these into a total client system change model.

*Step No. 6:* Identify alternatives and looping relationships. Make the model dynamic, if at all possible. This requires examining the inter-relationship of different parts of the problem and introducing input/output loops that might affect the model. This done, it should be possible to envision how an intervening action might affect the change phenomenon, or the predicted result of alternative action. The identification of the alternative causes of action is a primary benefit to be gained from an appropriately developed model.

*Step No. 7:* Validate the model empirically. Until such validation is performed, the model represents the model builder's concept of a system or situation, but nothing more. It might be tested in consultation with the people involved, by comparing it with another model independently prepared, or by applying it to the real world situation or system through simulation or role playing.

These steps are seen as descriptive but do not necessarily need to evolve in exactly this manner as an OD practitioner works with his client system.

### Skills of the Model Builder

The means by which an OD change agent uses a model to plan change must again be described as both a science and an art. Model building is a science to the extent that it is based on recognition of the scientific process and that it has certain standards related to the development of the model. At the same time, model building is also an art because it is to a large extent "intuitive." While some rules may apply to developing models, they generally have limited usefulness. Rigid adherence to rules might to some extent impede creativity. If one assumes that modeling is both a science and an art, the interesting educational question is: How do you develop modeling skills? What can be done for the inexperienced person who wishes to be able to use the model building process in planning change? What, for that matter, can be done for the professional change agent?

Skill in modeling is an essential part of the planned change effort. It involves a sensitive and selective perception to the change situation. It also will demand a conceptual structure that will bring clarity and simplification out of conceptual complexity. Unfortunately, it is relatively infrequent that we discover a model that is already available in a satisfactory form for a given planned change situation. There is considerable evidence, therefore, of a need for increasing the number and capabilities of persons conceptually able to use the modeling process in planned change efforts.

In many ways the skills that we are trying to achieve in the modeler are related to some of the key dimensions of a creative individual. Research conducted on the characteristics of creative persons suggests that such people differ significantly from those who are not creative. Most of the attributes useful to the modeler, however, do not seem to be related to intelligence, which heretofore frequently has been assumed to be the key trait of creative people:

### A Degree of Personal Security

It requires a certain amount of poise and courage for an individual to back off from a complicated change situation and develop a simple conceptual scheme. It requires the individual to admit and even distort certain aspects of the change situation and consciously to assign values to forces. Such an approach requires a degree of confidence in his own assessment of the situation that, in turn, arises out of confidence in his own self concept.

### Situational Sensitivity

This skill is related to one's ability to see things which other persons might not perceive. It is the capacity to stretch the perceptual powers of an individual to see, hear, and feel more about forces and factors in the change situation than would ordinarily be the case. It is the ability to be "tuned in" to the complexity of the system or situation.

### Independence of Judgment

An effective modeler of change will have enough strength to ensure adequate evidence is at hand to insert a variable into a model. Such an individual will also have the courage of his own convictions when he strongly believes something about the plans calls for a change situation. An effective modeler will have the ability to experiment in the modeling process, knowing that success is not guaranteed.

## Ability to Abstract

The ability to abstract is an essential facility in modeling. The ability to separate a problem into its component parts is a prerequisite. It is an ability to take a look at many variables and to comprehend the relationships between them so as to achieve holistic understanding through the development of a model.

## Mental Flexibility

One essential skill of the modeler is flexibility, the ability to adjust quickly to new developments in the change situation, to go beyond the obvious boundaries of the change problem to see factors that may not be apparent on the surface. In addition, there is required an ability to add new dimensions to a problem rather than adjusting analysis to old ideas, concepts, and assumptions, and to abandon old assumptions and try out new approaches.

## Tolerance for Ambiguity

A creative modeler is able to tolerate a certain amount of disorder while bringing meaning out of the contradictions, complexity, and maladjustments in a change situation. He will be adept at implementing a problem-solving approach and modeling technique, and will be able to withstand pressure for immediate answers or solutions.

## Ability to Analyze and Synthesize

The process of analysis is an essential part of model building, breaking down the whole into its parts and showing the relationships of the parts to each other. The skill of synthesizing is the ability to identify, relate, combine, and limit different elements into a total holistic process or system. The interrelationship of these two fundamental skills is a key factor in effective model building.

In summary, I suppose, the effective model builder will develop a sense of dissatisfaction with the narrative approach normally used to describe an OD situation or process. He will look at the planned change problem as a challenge to be mastered by new and creative approaches, including modeling.

Like other human skills, it is obvious that the more comfortable one becomes with modeling, the more it becomes a part of one's total functioning as a change agent.

As we discuss the skill of modeling, perhaps one last point should be mentioned. The goal of modeling in the context of a planned change effort is to achieve the change goal. Modeling is not an end in itself. As Cardinal Newman has stated, "Life is for action. If we insist on proof for everything, we shall come to no action. To act you must assume, and the assumption is faith."[6] Modeling is not yet a science and neither you nor anyone else will be able to prove that all aspects of your model are correct or incorrect. The necessary balance between the science and the art of modeling is the OD practitioner's mature confidence in its proper place in the total effort.

## In Summary

Most action for organizational change will require the manifestation of power by key individuals or groups in the organization. In Gardiner's Survey of a large number of organizations and how successful changes evolved, he found that more came from shared power than from unilateral or delegated approaches. If the shared approach is going to work, however, a particular sequence of phases appears necessary, as shown in the model illustrated in Figure 10. This is the typical pattern: some key power figures in the organization become concerned from external or internal pressures, they then seek help from an outside and/or inside resource person or group, followed by their willingness to engage in some "shared" problem-solving process with associates and subordinates. Then they support some experimental attempts at organization change, and finally reward and reinforce those managers and subsystems who adopt the new behavior patterns.

These studies plus shared experiences in the OD field can identify more failure than success experiences in inducing significant changes in organization that really affect the total system culture.

> "Strangely enough, large-scale organization development is rare, and the measurement of results is even rarer. Even though management has sought for years to grasp and implement the important findings of behavioral science research, the task has proved more difficult than it first seemed. Many findings are subtle and complex. Other findings relate to individual insights

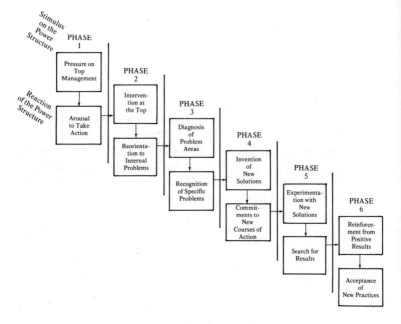

### FIGURE 10

*Organization Change & Development*

Figure 10 is from *Organization Change and Development* by Dalton, Lawrence and Greiner; Richard Irwin Co. 1970

or knowledge which is hard to build into the organization's life stream. In addition, most behavioral scientists do a better job of communicating technical findings to each other than they do of communicating the relevance of their research to practicing managers. There have been many earnest attempts to make the behavioral sciences useful to business, government, and service institutions. But because of the complexities, success has been elusive.[7]

It is my hope that model building can help all OD practitioners to increase their chance of success. We are most often concerned in America, however, with what can be weighed, measured or counted. Such qualification has stood us in good stead in many of the scientific and industrial advances of our age. Certainly the behavioral sciences have tried to become as exact as possible, and in so doing may have lost some of the vitality that might contribute to the problem-solving processes of man. Our educational system stresses reason, logic, and abstraction, but emotion and intuition are not taught to students as supplements to reason and logic. One sees this in the world of education. I agree with John Arnold's description of students' reactions when he was trying to get them to solve on the basis of reason and logic problems that could not be solved in that fashion:

> There were either too many rules or not enough rules to guide the student in his work. He either had too many ideas as to how it should be done or none at all. One of the most disturbing features was this, that when a student asked one instructor as to how he might assemble a shaft and a gear and got one answer, he would then ask a second and third instructor the same questions and get two other answers, quite different. The students at first thought that there was something wrong with the course in which there was no right answer to each and every problem, or in which even the instructors themselves couldn't agree on what the best answer should be. However, before the term was over most of the students were beginning to see the light. They were beginning to understand what we meant by a creative problem and were becoming aware of the fact that the great majority of problems that they would have to face in later life were of this type. This really was quite an ordeal for them . . . for two and a half years of their college work they have been solving problems that have one and only one right answer. They were only analyzing given data. The only synthesis involved was gathering together the data and the formulas that were to be used. The only judgment involved was to get the right formula.[8]

It seems to me that Arnold's observation is a classic description of many of the values we instill from education. These tend to be cultured values that have been established through centuries of putting priority on the rational side of human nature. I do not mean to imply that model building is an irrational process, but rather that modeling can help free the model-builder and those involved in a situation to see alternatives and forces that might not have been seen without the model. The very nature of the visual medium is superior to words because it offers substitution and structural equivalence for objects, events and relationships. The variety and impact of visual stimuli is as great as that of speech sounds or words. What is important is that in modeling these visual stimuli can be organized into patterns that are easily sensed or perceived by the viewer, regardless of the language he uses. I have always admired the work of cartoonists. In The Washington *Post* we see "Herblock" in one picture describe a complicated political event, social issue, or human frailty. The principal virtue of the visual medium is that it can represent shapes in two and three dimensional space as compared with verbal language. As indicated previously, the model for change should have three major characteristics:

1. *The model should clearly define the change target and goal.* One of the major obstacles to developing any good model is achieving definition of a goal or problem.

2. *The model must be simple and facilitate communication between the parties involved in the change situation.* Any model should, of course, help to simplify our understanding of the complications of the change situation. In much of the current literature I have felt that model builders feel compelled to increase the complexity of the models under the assumption that intricacy, preciseness, detail, and all inclusiveness is necessary to usefulness. Although such a premise might be occasionally valid, I believe it is of prime importance for a model builder to keep his model as simple as possible when working with a change process. Elaborate, technical, or mathematical models are likely to be useful when they are the result of a long-term process, and the persons using such models are familiar with the terminology and symbolism. In most cases, this is not the case and we must recognize the feasible limits of complication. This is one of the reasons why I have not discussed mathematical models. Most people involved in an OD change situation will not see the mathematical model as simplifying their understanding of the change process as technical and selected professional people do. I tend to sympathize with Jean-Jacques Rousseau:

> I never got far enough to truly grasp the application of algebra to geometry. I did not like the way of operating without seeing what one is doing, and it seemed to me that to solve a geometrical problem by equations was like playing a tune by turning a crank.[9]

3. *An effective change model should serve as a guide, enabling those in the real-life situation to develop a course of action.* By its very nature, change is a dynamic process of causing disequilibrium and creating new stabilization. The model should be more helpful to those involved than just to understand the situation. What to do and how to do it depends on the existing phenomena, i.e., a model needs to go beyond description to be suggestive of alternative actions. A graduate student made the following comment about his effort to design a change model:

> I encountered some initial difficulty in conceptualizing a suitable change model. My concern in devising the model lay in the fact that I discovered most change models to be descriptive rather than predictive; static rather than dynamic. I wanted to depict change as a dynamic process, taking place in a dynamic environment. Since my concern was *planned* change, I wanted to provide for some element of prediction and control.[10]

This is a typical difficulty encountered by many people when they engage in the process of model building. It is interesting that the many assumptions and predispositions that are a part of the experience of all of us affects our ability to construct models.

A graduate student with whom I was working undertook to examine an undesirable interpersonal relationship in a typical office and, as a change agent, to help one of the persons involved effect a different relationship through planned change. We thought this particular change project would lend itself to modeling as a computer-oriented "programming flow chart." After his preliminary model he found it necessary to go beyond his simplistic model by developing a more complex one in illustrating the change effort launced by the client system and his role as a change agent. After completing three models during the change consultation, the graduate student had this to say:

> Perhaps the greatest difficulty I had to overcome in constructing the model for my change project was my inability to understand models. It has always been easier for me to understand a written explanation than to read a chart, for example. I can't say that I really got the feel of models and their application until I was quite far along into the construction of my own.

I found that stating the problem was the hardest part. After the principal elements have been identified and quantified, and their relationships to each other established, the answer to the problem will have been identified. This happened in my case. This, however, although the most difficult, was only the preliminary, or descriptive phase.

The concept of change implies going from some present state, X, to some future state, Y—in this case, from an unsatisfactory work situation to a satisfactory work situation. In planned change what interests us is *how* we get from point X to point Y, the "crosswalk." The foundation upon which this crosswalk results is knowledge about human behavior, and the crosswalk itself is the process by which this knowledge is applied.

In the construction of a crosswalk from X to Y, we must naturally attempt to build in elements of prediction, and we must be concerned with the controllability and relative efficiency of different variables in producing the desired change.

In an ideal situation, the construction of a model of a crosswalk should follow immediately after the descriptive or problem identification stage. In this particular instance, however, the ultimate model was not developed until the actions for change were well underway. As a result, less revision of the model was necessary than would normally be expected. The first segments were, in fact, descriptive of what had actually taken place rather than predictive.

I discovered, however, that even at that point the entire exercise in model building was extremely helpful—not so much in casting light upon the process of change in the abstract as in clarifying and simplifying the issues and relationships of this particular case. I was thus able to clear away a lot of unnecessary undergrowth (i.e. relationships, personalities, factors which did not bear directly on the problem and tended to obscure it), and to structure further action in a logical rather than merely intuitive way.[11]

Such a learning experience will be encountered by most people when they use the modeling process in OD work.

This paper does not present a set of rigid model building criteria. It is important, however, that the guidelines that have been suggested in this document be recognized by any model builder. We are going through a decisive reordering of the energy nature of human existence as we move from the industrial to the post-industrial society. The ability to cope with organization change is a challenge for both laymen and professionals. It is my theory that in coping with organizational change, the nature of one's own conceptual models will, of course, affect one's action, but that a more precise attention to the attributes of a two-dimensional schematic model can be helpful to test one's plans for OD as well as assess the dynamic inter-relationships of the many forces of change.

Someone might want to comment that model building is merely proof of the statement:"A picture is worth a thousand words." This is only partly true. A picture that does not adequately take into consideration the forces that pertain to the situation may be a false picture. Likewise we can have false and inadequate models. However, it has been the goal of this paper to present something of the technology of model building as an important tool for OD professionals to use in confronting in a meaningful way the complex reactive or pro-active change they are working with in the organization. It is a technology that advantageously can be used by those who wish to expand the use of logical and visual thinking for effective organization development.

## FIGURES

Figure 1   *Degrees of Abstraction*
The above figure appears on p. 97 of Systems psychology, Kenyon B. DeGreene (Ed.), New York: McGraw-Hill Book Co., 1970.

Figure 2   *The Modeling Process*
Is from p. 383 in *Organization and Management: A Systems Approach,* New York: McGraw-Hill Book Co., 1970.

Figure 3   *Model for Intervention/Training Design*
Source is take home packet of NTL Consulting Skills Workshop, Summer 1969, Bethel, Maine.

Figure 4   *Stages of Organizational Development*
Is from p. 109 in article "Crises in a Developing Organization", by G.L. Lippitt and Warren Schmidt, Harvard Business Review, Nov./Dec. 1967

Figure 5    *Organization Forms*
            Is from *Conceptual Models of Organizations* by G. Rice and D.
            Bishoprick. Appleton-Century-Crofts. 1971.
Figure 6    *Framework for Planned Organizational Change*
            Is from handout by Warren Bennis at ASTD Conference,
            Washington, D.C. 1964
Figure 7    *Phases of Organizational Crisis*
            Is from p. 26 in article "Organizational Crisis and Change" by S.
            Fink, J. Beak, and K. Taddeo, *Journal of Applied Behavioral
            Science.* Vol. 7 #1. 1971.
Figure 8    *Organization Renewal Model*
            Is from p. 19 of the book "Organization Renewal" by Gordon L.
            Lippitt. New York: Published by Appleton-Century-Crofts,
            1969.
Figure 9    *Systems Approach to Organization Renewal Model*
            Was developed by F. Laverty and H. Gabora, of Management
            Renewal, Ltd., of Ottawa, Canada, in an unpublished
            manuscript. 1972.
Figure 10   *Organization Change & Development*
            Is from *Organization Change and Development,* by Dalton,
            Lawrence and Greener; Richard Irwin Co. 1970.

## REFERENCES

1.  Quoted on page VIII of the life of Kurt Lewin entitled *The Practical
    Theorist,* written by Alfred Marrow, Basic Books, Inc. 1969.
2.  For fuller treatment see Chapte II of Lippitt, G. *Organization Renewal,*
    New York: Appleton-Century-Croft. 1969.
3.  Rice, G. & Bishoprick, Dean, *Conceptual Models of Organization,* New
    York: Appleton-Century-Croft. 1971.
4.  R. Chin, "The Utility of Systems, Models and Development Models for
    Practitioners," Section 6.3 in book *The Planning of Change* by W.
    Bennis, K. Benne, R. Chin; New York: Holt, Rhinehart & Winston,
    Inc. 1969.
5.  *Ibid.,* p. 308.
6.  Quoted for *Matrix of Man* by S. Moholy-Navy, Praeger Publisher.
    1969.
7.  R. Blake in *Organizational Change and Development* and J. Mouton,
    *Breakthrough in Organization Development,* edited by Barnes and
    Greiner.
8.  P. 344 in proceedings of Seminar on Creative Engineering, Mechanical
    Engineering, Department of MIT noted in Alabama School Journal,
    1962.
9.  *Confessions* by Jean-Jacques Rousseau.
10. J. Joslin in unpublished paper at George Washington University. 1971.
11. *Ibid.,* p. 12.

# 3

# Practice Theories
# In Organization Development*

*PETER B. VAILL*

## INTRODUCTION

In the past few years, I have spent a good deal of time talking with managers and other action-takers, trying to understand what they think they are doing.[1][2][3] In particular, I have found the situation of the Organization Development practitioner an interesting one, worthy of the most careful investigation.

In the process of trying to understand how Organization Development (OD) practitioners look at their world, I have discovered that there is very little descriptive material available on the subject. For that matter, there is little available on how *any* action-takers in organizations view their world. Some writers, like Boulding and Vickers, have sought to erect broad, almost philosophical frameworks to guide inquiry into the point of view of the action-taker.[4][5] The psychology of perception, especially the work of the Gestalt school, is certainly relevant.[6] Another thread can be found in a school of sociologists who seek to understand how we are able to behave rationally in the eyes of those around us.[7] And in the 'forties and 'fifties the General Semanticists made a number of important contributions to our understanding of how man "abstracts from" or "maps" reality.[8]

This material is scattered and fragmentary. I know of only one major text in the management field that makes the action-taker's own frame of reference the basic thing to be understood.[9] With respect particularly to the OD practitioner as a special kind of action-taker, I have recently tried to describe how such men seem to view their organizations following a series of open-ended interviews.[10]

In the development to date of the OD field, two other subjects have received a great deal more attention than has the OD

---

* An earlier version of this paper was read before the Annual Meeting of the Academy of Management, Atlanta, Georgia, August, 1971.

practitioner's own frame of reference. The first area is the study of organizations, and particularly of what is wrong with them in terms of their effects on the people who work in them. Evidence gathered in this large set of studies forms the basic underpinning of OD: it establishes that there is indeed "organization development" that needs to be done.

The second major area is the study of how the OD practitioner, the agent of organizational change, *should* act if he wants to influence the system. This is primarily normative material; it is an evolving body of prescriptions for effectively influencing organization events. Research and theory is not yet as voluminous in this area as it is in the first, but more and more material is appearing, and there is no question that this second major focus is on the rise.[11]

The basic thesis of this paper, however, is that these two areas of OD should not continue to develop without being tempered and tested against the practical realities of the OD practitioner's situation. That is, against how the organization seems to be *to him*. The problems and opportunities he is able to perceive in the organization may or may not be the ones diagnosed by academic theories about organizational ills. This is why the study of organizations must be tempered by the practitioner's frame of reference. The ways and means he employs to deal with problems and opportunities may or may not be the ways and means specified in normative theories about how he "should" behave. This is why the theories of how he should behave must be tempered by his frame of reference. If such tempering does not occur, the risk is that OD will metamorphose into a body of idealistic and unrealizable goals which are to be sought by impractical means.

This paper seeks to identify some of the key properties of the OD practitioner's subjective view of his organization. The phrase "practice theory" is employed to talk about the models of situations and his relation to them which the practitioner develops in his mind. His practice theory is, literally, a personal theory guiding his practice, bearing some relation to public, objective theories about organizational situations, but in no sense identical with them.[12]

Twelve characteristics of these "practice theories" are hypothesized below. Then in a concluding section, some further comments are made about the impact of the OD field on the OD practitioner.

## SOME CHARACTERISTICS OF PRACTICE THEORIES

1. *Practice theories are kaliedoscopic.* In the canons of Science, a good formal theory always has its *ceteris paribus*, its other things which are assumed equal. When these "other things" change beyond some limits, the theory is no longer applicable. Such is not the case with practice theories. Rather than being tight statements of clearly defined variables and hypothesized interrelationships, practice theories are malleable textures of ideas and concepts which can be bent and twisted in various ways to fit various situations. To the extent that a practice theory asserts anything to be "true," the assertion is not with a *ceteris paribus* implied, but instead with a *mutatis mutandis,* that is, ". . . with the necessary changes." Practice theories are "fudgeable," as it were. That is their great utility. Formal theories, ideally at least, are not so malleable.

Thus it is that the OD practitioner's conceptual world, which from the outside may appear somewhat vague and disorganized, in fact rarely is. The practice theory does not have sharpness and clarity except in relation to some real world situation.

2. *Practice theories operate through multiple media.* One of the most delightful but baffling properties of practice theories is the way they help an OD practitioner learn and convey meanings in a variety of media. The practice theory makes it possible for him to talk and listen in words, in body language, in a language of physical symbols (e.g., the way he furnishes his office), in a language of things-not-done, in a language of timing, pace, and rhythm, and always, of course, at various levels from the most lighthearted and trivial to the most moving and personal. Furthermore, these channels and levels are never utilized one at a time. Instead, they are used together to reinforce and illuminate each other.

The richness of the media the practice theory utilizes is not matched by the published material in the behavioral sciences that the practitioner has available to him. The behavioral sciences that underly OD are mainly sciences of verbal behavior. Thus, the OD practitioner's problem in using such material is to discover what the appropriate media are for applying a particular concept. There are many ways to *be* accepting of others, for instance. To say, "I accept what you are saying" is only one such way which, in fact, is often not a very effective one. Conversely, when attempting to describe his practice to others, the OD practitioner is often at a loss as to how to convert the richness of what he *does*, i.e., the richness of the media he actually uses, into a sensible verbal account.

3. *Practice theories are multi-functional.* It seems apparent in the way OD practitioners describe their projects that a given course of action must be responsive to several needs. Roethlisberger has provided a remarkable analysis of the "multidimensional world" of the action-taker.[13] He says that action must somehow take account of the formal purpose for engaging in it, of the informal norms which exist in the situation, of the culturally-defined ideals for such behavior, of the personal needs of the action-taker himself, and of scientific prescriptions about the content and consequences of various possible actions in such circumstances. Mixes of these dimensions, varying from man to man and from situation to situation, are found in all practice theories. The need for a multi-dimensional mix is a commonplace matter from the point of view of the action-taker, despite our tendency from an external point of view to reduce his action problem to just one dimension or another.

4. *Practice theories blend phenomena of heterogeneous qualities.* This feature is closely related to the preceding one. It says that no matter how diverse the elements of a situation, no matter how "logically non-comparable", the OD practitioner finds some way with his practice theory of dealing with them together. An example would be a practitioner who was able to consider dollar resources, past history, personal feelings of members, time deadlines, and his own psycho-physiology "all at once" with respect to some course of action. Subjectively, it is as if the OD practitioner, or any action-taker for that matter, has a personal calculus which enables him to work with the apples and oranges of his everyday experience.

5. *Practice theories create events.* This characteristic is nicely illustrated in the old story of a debate that was raging in a baseball umpire training school. The trainees were heatedly debating the exact definition of a "ball" and of a "strike" when the discussion was interrupted by a senior umpire who observed: "Just remember one thing, you guys. That pitch ain't *nuthin'* until *you* call it."

The OD practitioner's practice theory helps him abstract from everything that is going on around him in the organization that set of events which have happened *for him*. Different practice theories, of course, produce different sets of events, for an organization is, at a minimum, a mixture of economic, technical, social, and psychological phenomena. The twin facts that (1) a practitioner needs some concrete definition of "what is happening," but that (2) that definition is not the only possible one, places the practitioner in a curious bind: he must be committed to a version of reality, but he is constantly vulnerable to being second-guessed by others in the organization or by people external to it.

The existence of competing versions of reality within the organization is nothing new to the practitioner, but in the OD field the influence of external consultants and theorist/researchers with more sophisticated behavioral science models of reality poses an additional set of problems for the practitioner. How does he avoid being continually discredited, continually getting the feeling that his version of organizational reality is not quite complete, not quite consistent with the latest theory, not quite right? How does he remain open to new ideas, but remain sufficiently closed, so to speak, that he can create a coherent version of reality on which he can act? We will return to this point in the concluding section of this paper.

6. *Practice theories are clusters of evaluations.* The conventional interpretation of theory is that it is value-free, that it can be used to investigate a variety of phenomena in a variety of ways, depending on the investigator's interests and values. Furthermore, it is held that a usage of a theory which is in some way harmful is not an indictment of the theory but rather of the values of the person applying it.

No such distinctions are true of practice theories. The practitioner does not hold his practice theory independent of applications for it and then choose (evaluate) what it is he wants to become involved in. His "appreciation," in Vickers' phrase, of a situation is a blend of "reality judgment" and "value judgment," of what is true in the situation and of what is important.[14] The practice theory is a coalescence of the practitioner's knowledge and of his interests vis-a-vis a particular situation: knowledge and interests (values) are intertwined and interdependent.

Thus it is no simple matter for a practitioner of OD or of anything else to "change his values," despite the ease with which outsiders are able to advise him to do so. The conditions under which practitioners are able to make changes in their "appreciations" of situations are not well understood. Yet the fact that more than a simple change in values is involved has far-reaching implications for the process by which practitioners are trained and retrained.

7. *Practice theories are exclusionary.* An important implication of the last two properties is that practice theories help the OD practitioner ignore a great deal of material. By defining some events

as having "happened" other events occurring at the same time and place are not subjectively noticed. In another modality of thought, the practitioner is certainly able to imagine that other events might have occurred than those he has experienced. But when it comes to the practice theory, i.e., the means by which the action-taker bridges himself in action to some set of phenomena outside himself, *imagination is suspended.* Any course of action contains a commitment to some definition of the situation. The need for such a definition is often mistaken by outsiders for some pathology on the practitioner's part. Negative lables have been created by theorists about the practitioner's need for such a definition, lables like "lack of tolerance for ambiguity," "need for certainty," "dependency," "rigidity," and so forth. These evaluations may be clinically accurate, but they tend not to take account of the realities of the practitioner's situation.

8. *Practice theories satisfice.* Popular as the concept of "satisficing" is in the literature on goal-seeking and performance evaluation, it is rarely noted that the concept refers to the subjective frame of reference of the person *doing* the goal-seeking. In the subjective world, *satisficing is all the action-taker can do!* This does not mean that he cannot fall short of or exceed the goals he held for a particular course of action. Rather, it is to say that whatever the outcome, *that* is satisficing. "Satisficing" is a retrospective evaluation of what has turned out to be possible in a situation. For something else to have happened, the action-taker knows that some change in the conditions surrounding the project would have had to be made. As the sociologist, George Homans, has put the matter, when accounting for events in a social system, " . . . whatever should have happened is what did happen."

9. *Practice theories are political.* The great debate in OD over the role of power and politics in organizational life is only a debate so long as we are concerned with how men *should* behave. In the subjective world, the problem does not exist. *No one acts with the aim of impairing his effectiveness in a situation.* To be "practical" in an organization is to take account of the reality that there are scarce resources, that there are conflicting interests, and that in the scramble for the resources the men behind the various interests will evolve techniques for getting ahead of each other. The constant operation of these techniques, whether they are benign and diplomatic or punitive and naked, is what makes the situation subjectively "political."

Practice theories take account of these realities. OD practitioners' practice theories tend to stress the importance of openness and authenticity, but they are no less political for that. Openness and authenticity, OD men have often found, can be quite politic modes of connecting the realities of the organization to the aspirations that are wrapped up in the practice theory. That openness and authenticity are not usually ends in themselves is evidenced by the many practitioners who at one time or another have found themselves using more devious means to influence events.

10. *Practice theories are key-person-oriented.* Whoever first observed that management (i.e., taking action in organizations) is "getting things done through people" grasped an essential truth about the practitioner's frame of reference. Practice theories direct the OD practitioner toward others in the organization who can increase his influence, that is, who occupy positions and have resources and personal outlooks which make them likely collaborators. As one OD man was heard to say: "I don't create the best program I can and then sell it. I create the best program that I can sell."

The opposite process also occurs: elements of practice theories which consistently fail to be transferable to key persons in the organization tend to disappear from the practice theory. If they are projects which are particularly dear to the practitioner's heart he may put them on a kind of mental backburner until the time is more ripe for them. But they cease to be projects which, for the moment he is pushing.

Because practice theories are key-person-oriented, the practitioner will react to a suggestion that he change his behavior in some way by immediately beginning to consider the proposal *in the eyes of the key people* he knows he will have to work with if the action-in-question is to be performed. He may conclude that it will not upset his relations with them, and he is thus freed to consider the intrinsic merits of the suggestion more closely. If he does conclude that the suggestion will upset his relationship with various key people, however, or that there are no key people to pick up on the idea, he is likely to dismiss the suggestion as "impractical" or "unrealistic."

11. *Practice theories register negative feedback.* Practice theories alert the practitioner to some occasions when the world is not behaving the way the practice theory said it would or should. The multi-media character of the practice theory is one of its great strengths in registering negative feedback, for messages that do not

get through on one channel may well get through on others. The kaleidoscopic property of practice theories permits adjustments to be made in response to the appearance of negative feedback.

Academic theory about management and other forms of action-taking in organizations has paid much more attention to *failures* to respond to negative feedback than to the much more common occurrence of responding appropriately. Thus, an enormous literature has arisen about the nature of the practitioner's "insensitivity," about the reasons for it (e.g., "Theory X"), and about how to teach him to be more sensitive. Certainly the practitioner is not omniscient. He cannot notice all negative feedback all the time. He cannot be flexible beyond the limits set by the need to know what he is doing. The problem for the OD practitioner is how to gradually improve his ability to notice and respond to negative feedback from the organization without going so far or so fast as to impair his capacity to *initiate* action in the organization.

12. *Practice theories control the reflexivity of action and its manifest reasonableness.* The comments above about key people and about negative feedback can be generalized to reveal a crucial property of practice theories. In the practical circumstances of everyday life, as Garfinkel has so thoroughly documented, we can't stop to explain why we do what we do apart from doing it.[15] The nature of everyday relationships is such that one's behavior must answer the question, "Why are you doing that?" *before it is asked.* We have all learned the techniques of, as Garfinkel calls them, "practical reasoning" so that we can answer the question in our behavior fairly consistently and so that we can determine whether another person has answered it in his.

By trying to change situations, the OD practitioner is particularly vulnerable to being asked the question that should not have to be asked: "Why are you doing that?" or, as it is often more bluntly phrased: "What the hell do you think you're doing?" The more occasions on which one behaves "strangely," such that one's behavior doesn't account for itself but instead has to be explained, the more difficult it is to influence others in intended ways. OD practitioners talk a great deal about the need to establish "credibility" in the organization, and I think it is this process of learning to behave reasonably in the eyes of others while remaining influential that they are talking about. Elsewhere, I have described this same process as the skill of "correlating self and system."[16] The root of the debate among practitioners over how hard to push for change in the organization is precisely the problem of trading off credibility and strangeness. Different practitioners strike different balances on the question, but for all of them their own practice theories help them manage the particular balance they find comfortable.

## *IMPLICATIONS OF PRACTICE THEORIES*
## *FOR THE OD FIELD*

In the Introduction to this paper it was pointed out that the OD field has been developing without reference thus far to the subjective outlook of the OD practitioner. It was noted that theories are being spun about organizations and about how to influence them which run the risk of gross impracticality if they do not take account of the situation in which the OD practitioner really finds himself.

In the last few pages, an excursion has been taken into the subjective world of the OD practitioner. Implicity, the question has been: "If OD theorist/researchers took a look at the way OD practitioners experience their situations, what might they find? In particular, what might the theorist/researchers discover about the kind of help practitioners need and the kind they don't need?"

The idea of a "practice theory" has been used as a way of talking about the apparent nature of the internal, personal versions of themselves-in-situations which OD practitioners develop. (I have also suggested that the ideas about practice theories hold for other action-takers besides OD practitioners, but generalization of the practice theory idea is beyond the scope of the present paper.) At various points, it has been pointed out that the OD practitioner's personal version of himself-in-situation, of his subjective appraisal of what is possible and desirable, can be at considerable variance with the external research findings, theories, and prescriptions found in the OD literature. It remains now to summarize and crystallize some of these variances, and to suggest a process by which the OD field might find a more useful stance toward the OD practitioner. *If* the fundamental importance of the OD practitioner's subjective frame of reference is granted, then some current trends in the OD field become "fallacies," i.e., practices and processes which tend to deny the reality and importance of the practitioner's subjective world. Here are a few of the more prominent fallacies:

1. *The fallacy of misplaced coherence.* It is a mistake to expect the practitioner to be able to give a satisfactory verbal account of the

motives, content, and consequences of his practice. Yet the norms of
the OD field are that he be able to do this, via "case studies,"
presentations before peers, program descriptions, and the like. It is a
mistake to assume that everything about his practice which the OD
practitioner cannot make verbally coherent is therefore *in*coherent
or, more charitably, part of the mysterious, ineffable "art" of doing
OD work which can never be spelled out. The richness of what
practitioners do is understandable and communicable, albeit perhaps
not by the known techniques of research and theorizing. The idea of
a practice theory has been advanced as a new place to look for
coherence, a place that is different from those which have thus far
been so thoroughly searched.

2. *The fallacy of organizational change.* If the basic importance
of the OD practitioner's subjective view is granted then the thing to
be studied is not "organizational change," it is "organization
changing." The unit of analysis cannot be at the social level in which
all parties are treated "objectively" and externally, for the outcome
of such a focus cannot be about anyone nor for anyone in particular.
Such studies form the bulk of all the work that underpins OD and
the difficulty everyone has in determining what such studies mean
for practitioners is testimony to their impersonality. The more
fruitful focus is to take the frame of reference of those trying to
create change and then to try to understand from their point of view
how motives and action are related.

3. *The fallacy of unintended consequences.* Not just OD research,
but all research on men's actions in organizations has tended to pay
much more attention to men's mistakes than to their successes, to
their production of unintended *rather than intended* consequences.
The OD field is merely the most recent one in which interest in the
pathology of action-taking has overshadowed interest in its health.
The OD field, like the management field before it, is documenting
discrepancies between what practitioners think they are doing and
what they are actually doing, a process which Garfinkel has
pinpointed in a memorable phrase as "collecting ironies."[17]

If an independent researcher sets out to discover what is *really*
happening in a situation, he will *always* discover a discrepancy
between his findings and what the people in the situation think is
happening. When he then makes the assumption, as academic
researchers are wont to do, that his findings have more validity
("truth," "objectivity") than the subjective versions of involved
parties, he has effectively cut himself off from ever understanding

why the situation evolved as it did for he is out of touch with the real nature of the human energy that produced it. In this state, the stage is set for the commission of the next three fallacies.

4. *The fallacy of the condescension syndrome,* and
5. *The fallacy of the gut feel syndrome,* and
6. *The fallacy of retraining the discredited practitioner.*

Faced with a continuing stream of discrepancies, ironies and paradoxes between the fruits of formal research and the subjective versions of reality held by involved parties, theorist/researchers can tend to go any one of three ways. Each way starts from the assumption (masquerading as a research finding) that practitioners tend to kid themselves and that in significant ways they often don't know what is happening, that in particular they are often ignorant of the effects they are having on the system they are trying to influence.

Cynical theorist/researchers can become condescending toward the practitioner. They state their theories simply and colloquially so the practitioner can understand. If he has difficulty understanding it is because of his needs for (security) (certainty) (a quick and dirty solution) (independence) (etc.) and so forth. In the condescension syndrome the reason for keeping one's theory related to practice is because that is how to get it implemented. The reason is *not* because (a) there is anything intellectually interesting about the practitioner's experience of his situation, or because (b) the practitioner might have anything fundamental to contribute *to the theory.* The essence of the condescension syndrome is to view the practitioner as a vehicle for the realization of one's own ideals for society, for organizations, and for the condition of man.

More charitable, perhaps romantic theorist/researchers, experiencing the same puzzlement about what the practitioner is all about, may adopt the "gut feel syndrome" instead of becoming condescending. In the 1930's and 1940's, the gut feel syndrome took the form of a fascination with the "art" of practice. Much of what was said about the mythical "generalist" implied that he had awesome and ineffable qualities which could not be spelled out, reduced to formulae, dissected and analyzed. The gut feel syndrome has had a modern resurgence in the Knownothingism we call "doing one's thing." When a person is doing his thing his behavior just "is": talk, analysis, thought, delineation regarding what he is doing are viewed as inhibitory to understanding him. The gut feel syndrome says behavior is to be approached as a work of art: the only way to know the practitioner is with one's gut.

There is a third sort of stance toward the practitioner which tries not to over-simplify him as the condescending style does, nor to over-complicate him as the gut feel syndrome does. This third approach consists of honestly attempting to retrain the practitioner in more effective ways of behaving. For OD practitioners, such training has meant a good deal of work at both the knowledge and emotional levels. Seminars, case analyses, "action-learning" exercises, sensitivity training experiences and the like have been some of the more common techniques. Yet within the OD field such training and retraining of practitioners still is often based on the fallacious assumption that the trainer knows what the practitioner-trainee needs. Where the trainer does not know what the practice theories of his group of trainees are like, where he does not know in detail what their organizations are like and what kinds of situations they have confronted, it is hard to understand how training experiences which materially strengthen the trainees' practice theories can occur. To make matters worse, many trainers not only do not know these things about their trainees, they do not consider it necessary to find out. They assume instead that problems are common enough across organizations and that practitioner deficiencies are similar enough that no process of checking these things with a particular group of practitioner-trainees needs to be carried out.

Where the trainee senses that his own organization and the practice theory he has developed for functioning in it is not well understood by the OD trainer, he may do a number of things. He may ask for examples of the principles which are being presented. He may note that his organization isn't quite ready for some of these ideas. He may become preoccupied with the problem of how exactly to apply a particular concept or technique. He may become overly compliant and dependent on the OD trainer. These are all manifestations of a growing feeling within the practitioner-trainee that he is not well understood, that he has been discredited.

The future of the OD field depends to a great extent on OD trainers learning to make more of these questions raised by practitioner-trainees. There is a considerable danger that trainers will become inured to them, as noted above, and lose interest in the idiosyncracies of the practitioner's situation. This has happened in other professions: the practitioner's role, responsibilities, and opportunities have become standardized, taken as given, and attention has shifted to the further study of the client systems the particular profession deals with.

If such a process of standardization of what we *think* the practitioner's role is occurs in the OD field, the key element in the complex process of organizational change will be lost. That element is the OD practitioner: what he is experiencing and what he thinks he is doing in all its fascinating variability. Many years ago Elton Mayo spoke of "efficacy at the point of action" as any practitioner's continuing challenge. This paper has tried to show that the nature of the OD practitioner's efficacy is a challenge not just to him, but to OD theorist/researcher/trainers as well. A joint attack on the nature of efficacy is still possible in OD work, and is most certainly worthwhile.

## REFERENCES

1. Vaill, Peter B., "Management Language and Management Action," *California Management Review,* Fall, 1967.
2. Vaill, Peter B., "An Informal Glossary of Terms and Phrases in Organization Development," American Society for Training and Development Organization Development Division, 1970 (mimeo).
3. Vaill, Peter B., "Organization Development: Ten New Dimensions of Practice," a chapter in Lippitt, Gordon, Leslie This, and Robert Bidwell, *Optimizing Human Resources,* Reading, Mass.: Addison-Wesley, 1971.
4. Boulding, Kenneth, *The Image,* Ann Arbor: University of Michigan Press, 1963.
5. Vickers, Sir Geoffrey, *Value Systems and Social Process,* New York: Basic Books, 1968.
6. Combs, A. W., and D. Snygg, *Individual Behavior,* New York: Harper, 1959, rev. ed.
7. Garfinkel, Harold, *Studies in Ethnomethodology,* Englewood Cliffs, N.J.: Prentice-Hall, 1967.
8. See, for example, Johnson, Wendell, *People in Quandries,* New York: Harper, 1946.
9. Turner, Arthur N., and George F. F. Lombard, *Interpersonal Behavior and Administration,* New York: Free Press, 1969.
10. Vaill, Peter B., *The Practice of Organization Development,* Madison, Wisconsin: American Society for Training and Development, 1971.
11. See, for instance: Argyris, Chris, *Intervention Theory and Method* (1971), Schein, Edgar, *Process Consultation* (1969), and Walton, Richard, *Interpersonal Peacemaking* (1969), all publications of Addison-Wesley, Reading, Mass.
12. I first heard the phrase "practice theory" in conversation with Professor Douglas Bunker of the State University of New York, Buffalo. The phenomenologist, Alfred Schutz, spoke of the action-taker as a "practical theorist."

13. Roethlisberger, F. J., "Learning in a Multi-Dimensional World," pp. 515-534 in Turner and Lombard, *op. cit.*
14. Vickers, *op. cit.*
15. Garfinkel, *op. cit.*
16. Vaill, Peter B., "Organization Development: Ten New Dimensions of Practice," *op. cit.*
17. Garfinkel, *op. cit.*

# 4

# Some Guidelines for Tomorrow's OD

## *ROBERT T. GOLEMBIEWSKI*

The thrust here is toward moving OD theory and practice from what they have become toward what they might still come to be. Specifically, the focus is on eight guidelines which are seen as emergent from the early experience with OD. That early OD experience is a crucible for testing initial notions, as well as for mothering more useful concepts where the old are found wanting. Note that guidelines below are intentionally prescriptive, and reflect both value considerations as well as pragmatic judgments about what seem useful perspectives and approaches.

There are three major reasons for this attempted synthesis from early OD experience. First, some stock-taking is in order, given the flurry of recent research and comment.[1] Second, even some obvious points may be restated with profit, if only to reinforce them. Third, this paper is incorrigibly optimistic that past experience can help us all do significantly better. Some incremental leapfrogging clearly seems possible.

### Eight Guidelines for Tomorrow's OD*

1. *Paramountly, OD efforts must be imbedded in an appropriate concept of man,* "man" meant in the generic sense of humankind, of course. This is a matter of avoiding extremes, and also of leaning more in one direction than another. Attaining and maintaining this in-tension view of man will be no easy matter, if only because a widely-swinging pendulum tends to symbolize man's romances with guiding concepts.

Specifically, the appropriate view of man is boundedly optimistic. Thus optimism is appropriate that man can become less imperfect, that most people can look at themselves and their behavior almost all of the time in an open way without disintegrating or being grievously shaken as persons. Similarly, optimism is appropriate that some things *can* be done to facilitate satisfying growth in all but

---

* This paper develops part of a chapter from Robert T. Golembiewski, *Renewing Organizations* (Itasca, Ill.: F.E. Peacock, 1972).

the most frozen persons and in the most reactionary organizations. This is to say that the boundaries for optimism are quite broad indeed.

But boundaries do exist for this optimism. That is, it is more or less clear what the appropriate concept of man should not be. On the one hand, the appropriate concept of man must clearly reject a view of man as basically bad and incorrigible. "When people are seen as bad," Tannenbaum and Davis sketch the underlying rationale, "they need to be disciplined and corrected" on specific issues and are otherwise left alone. Dynamically, this is perverse. "Avoidance and negative evaluation can lead individuals to be cautious, guarded, defensive," they conclude. "Confirmation can lead to personal release, confidence and enhancement."[2] On the other hand, there are dangers in assuming too much about man's perfectability, and especially about his existing perfection.

An appropriate concept of man, then, seeks to avoid the traps of two simple definitions of human nature, of man as "good" or as "bad." Greening frames the issue well, and reflects the in-between concept of man emphasized here. He notes:[3]

> One school of thought holds that man is basically good, self-actualizing, and cooperative, if only we can help him let down his barriers. On the other hand, there are those who argue that man is basically an amoral, irrational animal who must be kept in check by external restraints and a self-deluding veneer. Personally, I prefer the position I once heard Martin Buber take in a discussion with Carl Rogers: "Man is basically good — and bad."

OD ideologists fell into one of the two ultimate traps-to-be-avoided, en masse. The common view of man was boundlessly optimistic, even perfectionistic. For example, a dominant OD view held that bureaucracy was the basic blight in what could otherwise be man's garden of paradise, which blight loving and trusting man would overcome in 25-50 years at the outside. Indeed, Bennis and Slater informed us, "democracy is inevitable."[4]

The brilliance of the initial OD vision dimmed quickly, and the disappointment no doubt both added impetus to and gained momentun from a trend in managerial thought toward a darker view of man.[5] Not long after his proclamation of the inevitability of democracy, for example, at least Bennis has changed his mind. Basically, Bennis seems now to recognize the profound limitations on man's existing and future states of perfection, especially deriving from what Winn called "the irrational and destructive impulses in man."[6] For example, Bennis observes that the issue is no longer whether democracy is inevitable, but whether it is sexy enough to attract and retain enthusiastic support in competition with authoritarian alternatives. He believes that democracy is not sexy enough, on balance. Specifically, Bennis emphasizes these four factors as new limits on his earlier vision of the organizational tomorrow.[7]

- the recent widespread dislocations, if not breakdowns, in the perceived legitimacy of a broad range of traditional authority figures and institutions

- the growing evidence of tension between the elitist and populist functions of our institutions, as in universities which can be conceived as elite centers of disinterested inquiry and/or as populist centers of mass education, service, socialization, and politization

- the heightened awareness to Bennis of "the discontinuities between microsystems and macrosystems," which he notes was a painful discovery for him

- the recognition of a basic "structural" weakness of democratic ideology, especially as applied to large aggregates of people, in that it is strong on individual rights but ambiguous as to collective obligations.

The sense of Bennis' new view is illustrated by a response to a letter in which Carl Rogers stressed that an increased concern with human relationships was perhaps *the* prerequisite for managing our institutions. The letter-writer was of two minds:[8]

Though I agree with [Rogers] heartily, I have some very strong questions about whether, indeed, this kind of future is in the cards for us. I raise this primarily because out of my experiences working in the U.S. Department of Housing and Urban Development and out of experiences working in and with cities, it is clear that in the basic decision-making that takes place, the values Dr. Rogers and I hold so dear have an extremely low priority. Indeed, the old-fashioned concerns with power, prestige, money and profit so far outdistance the concerns for human warmth and love and concern that many people consider the latter extremely irrelevant in the basic decision-making. Sadly, it is my feeling that they will continue to do so.

This first concern has a quantum significance, both theoretic and practical, for the laboratory approach to OD. For example, a heroic concept of man encourages learning designs of maximum impact, like wide-open, no holds-barred, anything-goes encounters in temporary stranger groups. They proclaim that immediate experience is sovereign and that the momentary encounter is where it's all at. Relatedly, that heroic concept would require no special concern about transfer of any learning into various back-home situations. The concept of man as "good and bad" as having "irrational and destructive impulses" and other frailties that set real limits to his existing perfection if not necessarily to his ultimate perfectability, encourages concern about both learning designs and transfer of learning.[9] Such an in-between concept of man implies the need for designs with a margin of safety. Such a concept also suggests the value of family groups, which highlight the long-run responsibility of the individual for the specific and continuing impact of his contributions. As Parlour details the trade-offs:[10]

> The people in the organization have to live with what they do. It is true that in some ways people will be cautious in self-expression in such situations because of possible repercussions from the other group members who have the power to do harm. Each person also has a vested interest in making the organization successful and reducing the unnecessary obstacles to smooth cooperation resulting from faulty self-evaluations and misunderstandings between the members. Reality cannot be well-confronted without including the power factor....
>
> *We cannot know a person until we see what he does in real-life situations where he must bear the responsibility for his actions.*

For stranger experiences, the balanced concept of man urges the expenditure of considerable energy in both design and training to raise the probability that desired outcomes do occur. For example, feedback and disclosure processes in T-Groups might be variously structured to raise the probability that desired outcomes will occur. Laboratory experiences would give substantial emphasis to cognitive inputs and skill-practice, more broadly, as in work on specific skills and attitudes appropriate for helpful feedback.

To complete the point, the choice of a concept of man as basically bad also has a direct implication for the laboratory approach. That implication: forget about the laboratory approach. Given that concept of man, it would be mischievous if not dangerous.

2. *OD activities or programs should be imbedded in a social contract of reciprocal obligations appropriate to the situation.* Two kinds of social contracts can be distinguished.[11] Each has profoundly different implications for the character of the commitment required of participants, as well as for the details of the learning design. Generally, social contracts underlying OD efforts can be placed somewhere along a limited comprehensive continuum, depending upon a range of factors:

- the private vs. public character of the arena for learning
- the intended emotional/technical/cognitive mix of the learning
- the number and levels of organization of the participants involved
- the degree of boundedness of the issue-area, in terms of time, subject matter, structure of the search process, and the intended "depth" of the learning.

A. *Comprehensive social contract.* The prevailing ethos in which most OD efforts are imbedded can be characterized as a "comprehensive social contract." The contract is a pervasive and binding one, as can be suggested from two points of view. First, the typical definition of OD emphasizes planned change within a total system which has substantial influence over a considerable life-space. Hence the prototypic OD locus is a management team, often toward or at the top of a sizable organization. The common OD goal is to create a social order so as to change and guide behavior, and perhaps even contribute to "personal development." The definite bias is toward macro-system environmental change as a reinforcement for changes by individuals.

Second, the comprehensive nature of the typical OD contract is also implied by the network of values underlying such efforts. One example is sketched in Figure 1, whose basic postulate is that OD should work away from "a view of man as essentially bad toward a view of him as basically good." The authors qualify their effort in significant terms. "We clearly recognize that the values to which we hold are not absolutes," Tannenbaum and Davis note:

"that they represent directions rather than final goals. We also recognize that the degree of their short-run application often depends upon the people and other variables involved. We feel that we are now in a period of transition, sometimes slow and sometimes rapid, involving a movement away from older, less personally meaningful and organizationally relevant values toward these newer values."[12]

B. *Limited exchange social contracts.* Alternatively, OD efforts can rest on a strictly bounded rationale. Every relationship implies an exchange, goes that generic rationale; each exchange has a certain balance of benefits/costs for individuals and for their organizations;

away from avoidance, or negative evaluation, of individuals, and toward confirming them as human beings—this does not refer "to the excessively neurotic needs of some persons for attention and response, but rather to the much more pervasive and basic need to know that one's existence makes a difference to others. . . . Confirmation can lead to personal release, confidence and enhancement."

away from a view of individuals as fixed, and toward seeing them as in the process of becoming

away from resisting and fearing individual differences, and toward accepting and utilizing differentiated people

away from suppressing the expression of feelings, and toward making their expression appropriate and their use effective

away from maskmanship and game-playing, and toward greater mutual authenticity

away from the use of status for maintaining power and personal prestige, and toward the use of status for organizationally-relevant purposes, such as intervening when lower levels are in conflict as to a course of action

away from distrusting people, and toward trusting them

away from the avoidance of facing others with relevant data, and toward confrontation

away from the avoidance of risk-taking, and toward a greater willingness to risk

away from a view of interpersonal and intergroup processes as being non-relevant, and toward seeing them as essential to effective performance

away from a primary emphasis on competitive or distributive strategies, and toward a growing emphasis on collaborative or integrative strategies.

From Robert Tannenbaum and Sheldon A. Davis, "Values, Man and Organizations," pp. 132-44, in Warren H. Schmidt, editor, *Organizational Frontiers and Human Values* (Belmont, Calif.: Wadsworth, 1970).

FIGURE 1
*Some Basic Values in a Comprehensive OD Social Contract*

and at least some of these exchanges can be singled out for attention without doing major violence to the truism that every exchange is related to every other exchange in a huge nest of ever-more comprehensive systems. Assume that in the case of relationship A, the costs are too great relative to the benefits. Is there something that can be done to make the ratio more favorable? And without creating appropriate superordinate systems? The commitment to find out is a far-narrower one than Figure 1 requires.

No general rules apply, but designs can commonly be developed that express the sense of limited exchange contracts. The point applies in at least three senses. First, many OD designs based on the laboratory approach can be limited as to participants and subject-matter. For example, third-party consultation requires a deep commitment but it involves only the pair, and thereby avoids some sticky issues.[13] Similarly, some varieties of process observation or team development—such as a "mirror" exercise—can be useful while intentionally limited in subject matter, time, and so on.[14]

Second, many OD designs following the limited exchange contract can be designed so as to be relatively or even substantially private.[15] Many Career Planning designs have such a character, for example, as do many designs for eliciting feedback from large cadres of organization members.

Third, for a wide range of organizationally relevant issues, even public OD designs can be limited in ways that avoid the comprehensive social contract implicit in a design that (for example) uses T-Group training in family groups. Such designs focus on work relations in terms of the values of the laboratory approach, rather than on the personal impact of the experience. Friedlander's "organizational training laboratories" use such a design,[16] as does some innovative OD work in schools.[17] The logic and thrust of such an OD design can be illustrated usefully and economically. At the level of broad strategy, we are told that:[18]

> In designing this intervention we made strong use of the laboratory method. . . . The training often called for conscious observation of the group processes of the faculty. The design required the actual practice of new behaviors before using them in daily work. Although the design made use of the school as its own laboratory, we made use of laboratory groups in ways very different from those associated with sensitivity training or the T-Group. Personal development was not our target. We did not attempt to improve the interpersonal functioning of

individuals directly; when this occurred, it was incidental. Our targets were the faculty as a whole and several subgroups within it. We sought to increase the effectiveness of groups as task-oriented entities. We tried to teach subgroups within the school and the faculty as a whole to function more effectively as working bodies carrying out specific tasks in that particular job setting.

Somewhat more specifically, the entire faculty and staff constituted the total training population, and the design used learning units of such sizes and memberships that each participant worked with every other participant in at least two sub-groups. Early on, sub-groups worked on a variety of games, such as the NASA Trip-to-the-Moon exercise. The games were chosen so that they emphasized the role of clear and effective communication and decision-making. The initial thrust of the design was from an analysis of the results of each game-play, to a search for similarities or differences between the game dynamics and real-life experiences at school. A number of such exercises followed the same pattern, with consultants encouraging adherence to laboratory values and planning supplementary learning experiences in listening, in describing the behavior of another, and so on. The concluding two-thirds of the training experience (four days) completed the thrust of the training design. The focus was on "a problem-solving sequence, working on real issues that were thwarting the organizational functioning of the schools" Several reinforcing experiences were also held later. A broad range of indicators strongly suggests the value of such a design, using three other schools as comparison groups.[19]

By way of overview, Figure 2 provides some perspective on the range of available OD designs. That figure, more or less straightforwardly, arrays a number of OD designs along the horizontal continuum of limited exchange—comprehensive social contracts. Perhaps less straightforwardly, Figure 2 also ranks each design vertically in terms of its anticipated impact, given personal experience and a rough-and-ready interpretation of central tendencies in the available research literature. Detailed treatments of the several designs are available in a convenient source.[20]

C. *Factors affecting choice of social contract.* The thrust here is toward an obvious point. The nature of the problem, the learning goal, and the characteristics of participants as well as their environment, should interactively determine the appropriate social contract.

**Higher Impact**

| Phase I Grid Laboratory | stranger T-group | assessment center design | demotion experience | | intra-team feedback via videotape observation | family T-group | merger design |
|---|---|---|---|---|---|---|---|
| | | travel as a work/family interface | | | | | designs seeking change in organization values and climate |
| | | | | | intra-team organizational training laboratory | interface team-building | structural reorganization |
| consulting-pair design | career planning design | | third-party consultation | interview-cum-feedback by external consultant to workteam re failure | | Inter-group confrontation design | |
| | | manager's diagnostic meeting | | interview-cum-feedback by external consultant to workteam re success | team diagnostic meaning | | interface goal-setting |
| one-way mirror design | | feedback to organizational superiors from ad hoc groups | | intra-team feedback via survey data | | | |

**Lower Impact**

Limited Exchange Contracts        Comprehensive Social Contracts

FIGURE 2
*A Classification of Some Available OD Designs*

This "rule" is often breeched, however. The general appropriateness of a comprehensive social contract is often assumed, and the T-Group is commonly prescribed as the learning vehicle appropriate to that contract.[21] To illustrate, consider a small public agency experiencing some run-of-the-mill adjustments, even though the work was still being done efficiently and effectively. The supervisor's goal was "to quickly get over the hump" of these adjustments, a sentiment shared by all. These adjustments centered around: a new head, a young and attractive female who was somewhat unsure of her new role; a previously all-male group, on the older and somewhat stodgy side, a little threatened by several recent personnel changes; and several new male and female employees who were definitely mod-squad aspirants if not aficionados. The overkill prescription for this new group was three weekends of family T-Grouping, basically organized around such non-verbals as trust walks and fantasy designs. The result: the revelation of non-work material that would have tested even a far more stable group that was certain of its relations. The long-run outcome: strong cross-pressures involving peak work-demands and the humanitarian impulse to provide emotional support at work to several colleagues. The demands of work tended to win out, but at substantial cost of feelings of guilt for most members and of abandonment for a few. This seems a case of design overkill, for a range of limited exchange designs were more appropriate to the modest initial learning goals. The design chosen rested on a comprehensive social contract of obligations, for which the group was ill-prepared and whose necessity was at least questionable.

There is evidence of substantial recent recognition, in both theory and practice, of the need for caution in the choice of a social contact and designs appropriate to it,[22] fortunately, but powerful forces still induce a major bias toward the comprehensive social contract. Three points suggest the broader argument. First, the attractiveness of values such as listed in Figure 1 can be so great as to encourage a neglect in practice of the reasonable and critical qualifications that Tannenbaum and Davis detail. The highest artform is a delicate moving balance: to distinguish where you are from where you wish to be, the ultimate vision from "short-run applications;" and at the same time to move toward where you would like to be, based on a judicious estimate of what the existing culture can support. In a basic sense, early insistence on a comprehensive social contract implies that an OD program initially be what it might only eventually become.

Second, and this is a powerful  and complex issue, limited exchange contracts can be regarded as (and might actually be) sell-outs in which the OD practitioner serves merely as a cooling-out functionary for some establishment or other.[23] OD interventions provide topical relief in this view, as it were, but they do little or nothing about systemic diseases or their carriers.

Third, insistence on a comprehensive social contract can have an insidious attraction. Failures of OD programs at any level may be explained in terms of unpreparedness or unwillingness of some more inclusive system to support and nurture the program. That is, any specific OD disappointment may be dismissed as evidence only that the contract was not comprehensive enough. If you can change the broad system, goes this compelling argument, it will be easier to change its subunits. This position is at once patently true and at least potentially treacherous. One is reminded of the early history of Scientific Management, in which unsuccessful applications were not failures but rather only proof of the need to change the world so that there could only be successful applications. In one version, it was explained that Scientific Management could not really be in place anywhere until it had been applied successfully everywhere. Such a position can become a convenient rationalization for failure, an excuse. And it could also undercut the development of the increasingly-precise theory and practice that can guide changes in sub-systems without the requirement that all superordinate systems have somehow or other already experienced a similar and prior change.

3. *Whatever the specific social theory of obligation bounding any OD activity or program, the consistent bias should be toward participant choice and not necessarily change.* The value of this bias is multidimensional, and is suggested perhaps most forcefully by the greater rate of psychiatric casualties in T-Groups apparently attributable to trainers who demand change rather than offer choice.[24] Friedlander eloquently explains his emphasis on choice in this way:[25]

> . . . OD provides for the organizational member the opportunity for exploration and choice—of his values, of the structures in which he is living, and of the tasks upon which he is working. I am personally far more concerned with providing people with

an awareness of who they are, of what they are doing with who they are, and of the choices they have in these areas—than I am with changing them in some way. My own energies, then, are directed toward helping the individual encounter or experience his own values, needs and skills; the kinds of tasks to which he is devoting his organizational career; the structures and relationships he has with his work and with the people with whom he works; and finally how these all interact upon his sense of fulfilment and task competence.

This view clashes head-on with charges that the laboratory approach and especially the T-Group are engines for conformity, group-think, and lock-step. And that clash is intentional. In its broadest sense, the laboratory approach seeks to blend groupiness and individuality. The essence of the blend is straightforward. Group contexts can be useful, even indispensable, for a variety of purposes. They can facilitate the cross-validation of perceptions of individual behavior, as well as the development of norms that may persist after a group's membership has changed many times over. Moreover, group contexts can provide an important locus for exchanging emotional support. In any case, individuals are variously involved in group contexts, and indeed no small part of the self is defined and tested in group situations. Elementary common sense urges recognizing those ubiquities. Even in the T-Group it is nonsense to argue that "the group" always makes better decisions, although various group contexts can bring out the best (or the worst) in any collection of individuals. No group can make a decision for an individual, however, even though a group's members can coerce or cajole apparent ownership in other members.

The laboratory approach seeks to provide group environments that facilitate decision-making by individuals, who as a consequence can psychologically own the decision and its consequences. Ideally, the laboratory approach uses groupiness to foster individual growth and responsibility. Klaw captures much of this essence in his account of a T-Group experience. He observes:[27]

> . . . it is a fact that, for better or worse, many people do have to spend a lot of time working with groups. And it can be argued that someone who has been in a T-Group is likely to find his ability to resist group pressures strengthened rather than weakened. Furthermore, even though T-Grouping tends to emphasize such qualities as modesty, sensitivity and group

mindedness, members of a T-Group may also gain some notion as to why many people are *not* sensitive and modest and group-minded—and thereby become more ready to listen to the arrogant boor who nevertheless happens to know what he's talking about.

4. *OD activities and programs must be appropriately adjusted to various possible models of change.* The point can be approached in terms of the contrast between mechanical and organic systems in Figure 3. The development of organic systems is the *summum bonum* of OD, and the "truth-love" model is the accepted vehicle for achieving that highest good. As Winn notes: "Most of the organization development practitioners rely almost exclusively on . . . the 'truth-love' model, based on the assumption that man is reasonable and caring and that once trust is achieved the desired social change within the organization will take place with no other sources of influence required."[28] The "power-coercive" model is seen as the base technique of the contra-ideal, the mechanical system.

| *Mechanical Systems emphasize:* | *Organic Systems emphasize:* |
|---|---|
| *Individual* skills | Relationships between and within groups |
| Authority-obedience relationships | Mutual confidence and trust |
| Delegated and divided responsibility rigidly adhered to | Interdependencies and shared responsibility |
| Strict division of labor and hierarchical supervision | Multigroup membership and responsibility |
| Centralized decision making | Wide sharing of control and responsibility |
| Conflict resolution through suppression, arbitration, or warfare | Conflict resolution through bargaining or problem solving |

From Herbert A. Shepard and Robert R. Blake, "Changing Behavior Through Cognitive Change," cited in Robert T. Golembiewski and Arthur Blumberg, editors, *Sensitivity Training and the Laboratory Approach* (Itasca, Ill.: F. E. Peacock, 1970), p. 309.

### FIGURE 3.

*Some Points of Comparison Between Mechanical and Organic Systems*

There can be too much definitional tidiness about such distinctions and, in any case, the central question is perceived here as an incremental one. Where power-coercion does exist, can its patterns be modified enough to permit some movement toward truth-love while enhancing or preserving other values? The question is of enormous moment. For power-coercion is everywhere, and it is very likely to be for an extended time to come. The relevant concerns are: where is it reasonable to increase the incidence of truth-love, when, and how much? Everywhere, all the time, and to the maximum extent, are not meaningful responses to these central concerns.

If the central question is an incremental one, OD efforts must be adjusted to various models of change. Four emphases suggest the supporting argument:

- a variety of forces urge situational flexibility in many or all cases
- the dominant "tender" model of change may be inappropriate in some cases
- a "tender" model of change may induce major unanticipated consequences in many cases
- the gentle nurturance model of leadership associated with a "tender" model may be conceptually and practically naive.

Each of the emphases will be discussed briefly.

a. *Forces urging situational flexibility.* A broad range of illustrations of this point are possible, but here consider only that mechanical systems in the sense defined above will be with us for a very long time indeed, because much work is such that mechanical approaches to organizing are at least convenient and may in fact be necessary. The relevant issues must be stated in relevant terms. How big a dent can be made in the more extreme varieties of power-coercion, given specific technologies and environmental challenges? And what departures from the mechanical system are at once possible and at least comparable to it in overall outcomes, again given specific technologies and environments?

This is not to argue that OD efforts are necessarily out of the question in, for example, the cardboard carton industry, whose market structure and technology seem to encourage and may even require more of a mechanical system than the plastics industry.[29] But the considerations above do imply that limited-exchange contracts for OD efforts with cardboard carton producers might be initially more reasonable, at least, than comprehensive social contracts that seek to change basic values and structures.

b. *Inappropriateness of the dominant "tender" model.* The value of situational flexibility also can be illustrated by sketching some of the senses in which the dominant OD model can be inappropriate. That is, OD designs have strongly tended to be based on the truth-love model, to the neglect of alternative models. Schmuck and Miles develop the point persuasively:[30]

> Such a "tender" model states that shared expectations in-volving trust, warmth, and supportiveness are formed as the members of a working team gain confidence and skill in communicating clearly and openly. These norms and skills, in turn, support collaborative problem-solving and the rational use of information in making decisions. This model assumes . . . that the work of schools is carried on through interpersonal interactions and that heightening abilities for problem-solving must commence with new norms for interper-sonal openness and helpfulness.

So dominant has been the truth-love model, and so powerful have T-Groups been in inducing positive affect and strong loyalty, that OD often has been strongly associated with (if not actually viewed as the same as) T-Grouping or sensitivity training. Such association is reinforced by ideological factors. For example, most OD programs assume comprehensive social contracts with organic systems as their ultimate goal. The truth-love model well fits those critical assump-tions.

Despite such pleasing symmetries, however, the focus on truth-love may discourage emphasis on alternative models that may be as technically attractive, and which may also have a sequential priority. Schmuck and Miles direct preliminary attention to one such alternative model of OD, power-conflict. To them, early stages of OD programs in schools are in major senses:[31]

> . . . centrally a matter of clarifying and strengthening ex-pressions of the conflicting interests of diverse groups, and of radically redistributing decision making prerogatives so that low-power groups can have more influence over an organization's fate . . . those low-power clients who are usually somehow allotted the back seat in educational OD programs.

> The authors, in effect, argue not only that students ought to
> have more power in schools, but that they are in a much better
> position than educational professionals to transform schools in
> desirable ways.

This implies an advocacy role for OD, in which the truth-love
strategy may reasonably follow the "clarifying and strengthening
[of] expressions of the conflicting interests of diverse groups."[32]

The emphasis on truth-love may imply more about who is the
usual OD client than about an optimal change-strategy. Typically,
organizational power-wielders sponsor OD efforts,[33] so as to improve communications, or whatever, with and among the less
powerful. Hence a "tender" model of change is appropriate, given
that the original problem often is traceable to managerial ob-
tuseness, or insensitivity, or even to bad luck after taking a foreseen
risk of polluting interpersonal and intergroup relations. If the client
is the student population rather than the school administrators, by
way of illustrative contrast, other approaches to "radically
redistributing decision-making prerogatives" may be appropriate,
especially if management resists playing according to the truth-love
scenario.

The point is not a quibble. If all the bases really are touched,
truth-love will do the complete job. In practice, however, where one
starts tends to make a critical difference. A rough contrast illustrates
the broad point. The position here is that, given a continuing
commitment to approach the values of the laboratory approach, the
key issue is the design of diverse learning experiences that are
sensitive to where the client-system is initially. If the client-system is
characterized by blatant self-interest, narrowly defined, or coercive
power, or whatever, that is where the OD program must start. And
the appropriate initial design may be to openly counter that self-
interest with other involved self-interests to force the issue of the
kind of system that would result if all parties sought to marshall their
forces for win-lose games. The stage might also be set for bargaining
about mutual adjustments, even if no major changes in the opposed
self-interests are possible due to persisting differences in class,
status, formal power, and so on.

A contrast expresses the sense of the point, if perhaps simplistical-
ly. The basic OD commitment is to an open consideration of the
factors influencing interpersonal and intergroup relations, whatever
those factors are. With only a little qualification, more or less

oppositely, much OD work has used the T-Group as a standard learning design consistent with where an organization should ideally be: trusting, problem-solving, moving to consensus. It does make a profound difference, whichever approach one chooses. The former approach risks compromising the ideal; and the latter approach might effectively demand that the system in responding to an early design be what it only might potentially become.

c. *Unanticipated consequences of dominant truth-love model.* A third variation on the theme of the limit of applications of the truth-love model is perhaps most impactful. Especially in the early stages, for a wide variety of reasons, an OD program is likely to stress love somewhat more than truth; and thereby are induced some significant unintended consequences, or at least some awkward ones.

That substantial mischief may inhere in this tendency to give unbalanced emphasis to truth-love can be suggested from two points of view. First, OD designs have emphasized integration far more than separation, even though both are organizational truths that require confronting. Dealing with separation—as in an OD design involving demotees[34]—is still unusual and almost unique in OD efforts. Separation is not a rarity in organizational nature, however, as in the case of mergers or reorganizations. Too much emphasis on the latter theme of the truth-love model can complicate dealing with that ubiquitous reality. In one case, to illustrate, conditions required differentiating parts of a large industrial firm in which T-Groups had been widely used. Reality proved very difficult to accept, and one observer credits the earlier training for part of that difficulty. Two distinct sets of operations were reorganized out of the original whole, but the "departure was perceived as 'abandonment' with ensuing feelings of resentment and guilt. They were leaving the 'one big family,' ' which the prior reliance on the extensive T-Group strategy had helped to foster.[35]

Second, that OD programs typically accent the latter theme of the truth-love model also can be suggested in a less obvious way. OD programs are likely to be triggered by a superior's concern about his *responsibility toward subordinates.* Occasionally, the stimulus is a dramatic and tragic one. Consider the subordinate who collapses and dies outside his boss' office after a "chewing out," and the superior who blames himself and his insensitivity for that tragic consequence. More than one OD program had its proximate beginning in a deeply-felt resolve never to allow 'such a tragedy' to occur again.

Most often, the stimuli triggering a superordinate's sense of responsibility are less momentous but still troublesome. Thus superordinates might reflect on how easily they can turn-off subordinates, constipate upward channels of communication, or bind subordinates into ineffectiveness.

Accepting what Herman calls the "myth of omnipotence," the superordinate takes total responsibility and thereby overdoes it. A manager may spearhead an OD program to omnipotently undo the dysfunctional consequences of his own omnipotence, as he views it. Immediately thereafter, the manager typically keeps himself under tight rein so as to preserve the delicate new relationships that early OD activities often help induce. Under such circumstances themes of warmth, support, and positive identification tend to dominate. At the same time, some aspects of truth—those related to differences in formal authority and power—are likely to be de-emphasized. A kind of gentle nurturance model of leadership is implied. To put the point in a related way, initial OD efforts are likely to be characterized by a strategy of Attitudinal Change, which keeps a more-or-less equivalent distance from two other basic strategies, Power and Problem-solving. Figure 4 sketches some differences between these strategies.

Diverse evidence supports the aptness of the characterization above. Note, for example, the contemporary swing of the pendulum back toward the needs and concerns of superordinates as well as subordinates. One version of the "gestalt orientation" urges the instability of the binds into which superordinates can place themselves with the help of their subordinates. Assume that subordinates are doing the "poor, little, powerless me" role-play, for example. The superordinate who has recently 'got a little religion', laboratory style, but who still fancies his own omnipotence, is likely to take the easy way out. Such a superordinate will hold a tight rein on himself, and in the process will induce a variety of dysfunctional effects. These effects include: the superordinate's own nagging discomfort; a condescending or paternalistic attitude toward his subordinates, whom he basically perceives as too fragile to confront with his power, which they probably are not; and concern among subordinates that their superior is withholding data from them, which he is. Herman encourages an emphasis on this variety of "truth," even at some potential cost to "love". He concludes:[36]

> I believe it is worthwhile to urge ourselves and others to take new risks—risks of greater self assertion, more spontaneity,

*power,* in which A variously seeks to bias outcomes in his favor, as by:

a. making B more dependent on A;
b. threatening B with "harm, loss, inconvenience, or embarrassment";
c. confusing B as to A's needs or preferences;

*attitudinal change,* in which A seeks to induce desired attitudinal change in B as:

a. when A takes the initiative to minimize the actual or perceived differences between the goals of A and B, the characteristics of A and B, etc.;
b. when A takes the initiative to increase the actual or perceived mutual attractiveness of A⟶B;
c. when A takes the initiative to minimize the actual or perceived threat of A⟶B, playing down actual or perceived differences in legitimate authority, etc.

*problem-solving,* in which the potential exists that arrangements can be developed such that both A and B can gain or at least not suffer loss, or such that either A or B can gain but not at the expense of the other, as:

a. when A and B isolate and acknowledge actual differences in their goals, recognize where commonality does not exist or is not possible, and seek solutions that accommodate those differences;
b. when A and B isolate and acknowlege the bases of mutual attractiveness and unattractiveness, and where it is not possible or is not considered desirable to change the latter, seek solutions that accommodate the differences; and
c. when A and B isolate and acknowledge differences in legitimate authority, skills, etc., and seek solutions that accommodate those differences.

Based on Richard E. Walton, "Two Strategies of Social Change and Their Dilemmas," *Journal of Applied Behavioral Science,* Vol. 1 (April, 1965) pp. 167-770.

FIGURE 4

*A Sketch of Three Alternative Strategies for the Interaction of Superior A and Subordinate B.*

and more willingness to experiment with power and aggression as well as trust and love. If we in OD do indeed believe in a wider distribution of power it would be well for us to stop trying to deny power's existence, muffle it, wish it away, or disguise it under velvet wrappings. Rather we can encourage as many people as possible at *all* levels of the organization from highest manager to lowest subordinate to discover his own power and use it.

The point may be put briefly. Later stages of OD programs should tend toward the Problem-Solving strategy, as defined above. But early OD efforts often get hung-up on the Attitudinal Change strategy, often at some cost to "truth."

d. *Naivette of nurturance model of leadership.* The nurturance model of leadership reasonably associated with an Attitudinal Change strategy may be naive. Two emphases will suggest the value of situational flexibility in the choice of a model for change and its associated leadership style.

First, rather than prescribing *a* leadership model, the laboratory approach to OD may be more usefully conceived as seeking a heightened sense of, and skill with, contingencies in the matter of leadership style. Thus the goal is to make the manager more aware of his behavior and style from case to case; to sharpen his ability to sense the reactions of others to his behavior; and to deal with those reactions, whether they are positive or negative, and whether they are expected or unexpected. Similarly, the OD goal is to move toward a greater tolerance of differences, reinforced by an ability to recognize and cope with them. Again, only early honeymoon phases of development in OD programs are characterized by a homogenized and undifferentiated togetherness and sameness.[37] Moreover, organizations seem to go through stages that require or encourage different styles of supervision.[38]

Second, conceptually, the nurturance model implies serious inadequacies, as in seeking to make 'unidimensional' a reality that seems stubbornly 'multidimensional'. To explain, the nurturance model argues for behaviors, attitudes and values that would approach the gentle extreme of such continua:

Rejecting of Others, _____ Accepting of Others,
Threatened by Them                                Receptive to Them

There is no apparent problem in this, as far as it goes, for most people like to be accepted and to have others openly receptive to them.

In organizations, however, two major questions can be raised about such a one-way concept. To be truly nurturant of his employees, a manager needs other qualities. For example, he often will have to be dominant enough among his peers to accumulate the physical and financial resources his employees need to really operate. Once you introduce such other qualities, as in Figure 5, it is at least possible to argue that the prescription to move toward Accepting of Others on the continuum above is unspecific in significant ways, and perhaps gravely misleading.[39] As Buzzota, Lefton, and Sherberg argue, managers who are high on acceptance of others can be shown to differ among themselves in profound ways when the dominant-submissive dimension is introduced.[40] The manager bent on acceptance will behave in profoundly different ways than the manager seeking growth, although both are accepting of others and receptive to them.

It may also be argued that efforts to increase a manager's acceptance of others may do him a disservice, if his approach for doing so is to mask or suppress his dominance. OD specialists not uncommonly hear of Quadrant I→III changers, for example, whose personal and organizational effectiveness is compromised by the conversion experience and its attendant fixation on accepting others and being accepted by them.

These brief comments can hardly be conclusive, except about one limited but significant point. There is substantial reason to suspect

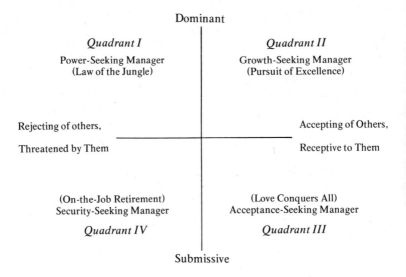

Based on V. R. Buzzota, R. E. Lefton, and Mannie Sherberg, "Train Managers to Handle Power" *Sales Management* (May, 1972), esp. p. 71.


FIGURE 5

*Managerial Styles in Two-Dimensional Space*

the adequacy of the concept of leadership that underlies many OD formulations. This issues a warning rather than supplies an answer, of course. Since that answer is still beyond our competence to provide at this time, the warning will have to do.

5. *OD activities and programs must be appropriately adjusted to various organizational conventions for making decisions.* Consensus has been the implicit or explicit ideal convention for decision-making in much OD ideology, and the underlying rationale is plain. Consensus as a decision-making convention increases the probability that participants will internalize the decision because of their involvement in it. Once internalization occurs, self-controls can be basically relied on to produce behavior consistent with the decision. In such a case, systemic controls are congruent with personal freedom. This is an attractive state of affairs, as Rousseau told us long ago. This vision-of-the-possible has proved a powerful reinforcer for consensus as the ideal convention for decision-making.

Some finer discriminations seem necessary, however. As vital as consensus may be in the case of comprehensive social contracts, and as much as widening involvement is desirable in all OD efforts, both may still be counter-productive for many OD activities. At their worst, they may imply that no action will occur until risk $=0$, or thereabouts, which means that not much is likely to happen. At their best, most formulations of consensus or near-consensus emphasize expert power, referent power, or value power.[41] And useful they are, but it is unrealistic to neglect legitimate authority or coercive power, for these still exist. And although the nurturance model of leadership is a significant one, there are times when very direct roles also are appropriate.

This is no call for the emergence of organizational Genghis Khans. Rather, it directs attention to a base reality that is neglected only at one's peril.

The vision of consensus as a kind of social Holy Grail has faded, moreover, which merely adds urgency to the present point that OD activities should be sensitive to various conventions for making decisions. Consider the recent change reported by Warren Bennis, perhaps *the* early ideologist of Organization Development. "There was a time when I believed that consensus was a valid operating procedure, " he recently explained. "I no longer think this is realistic, given the scale and diversity of organizations. In fact, I have come to think that the quest for consensus, except for some micro-systems where it may be feasible, is a misplaced nostalgia for a folk society as chimerical, incidentally, as the American search for 'identity'."[42]

What is meant by "appropriate adjustment" of OD activities to conventions for decision-making other than consensus is not always clear, of course. But some examples come to mind. Consider an organization reknowned for its unrelenting use of the power-coercive model. A number of limited-exchange OD interventions still could be useful in it: various privatized interview-cum-feedback designs[43], a wide range of Career Planning designs with minimal public sharing; and even such confrontive designs as third-party interventions, which are public but narrowly so. Other OD designs which implied comprehensive social contracts, such as a family T-Group, might be disastrous in an organization with a dominant power-coercive model. The disaster could take at least two forms: a closed, suspicious, "nothing" experience; or an ill-advised openness that might later be punished because the system had only a temporary tolerance for it.

6. *The level at which any specific OD intervention is made—at the level of interaction or behavior, task, or macro-structure of the organization—will be a critical variable in determining the appropriate contract, model of change, and appropriate set of conventions for making decisions.* This point is intimately related to the three points above, and Herman's concept of OD as dealing with an "organizational iceberg" will help develop the point. As Figure 6 suggests, OD should deal with both formal and informal aspects of organization. As with icebergs, much of the bulk of organizational phenomena is below the surface and usually is examined only in part. This neglect implies a practical priority for OD, of course. As French notes: "Organization development efforts focus on both the formal and the informal systems, but the initial intervention strategy is usually through the informal system in the sense that attitudes and feelings are usually the first data to be confronted."[44]

The reasonable priority accorded the covert aspects of the iceberg in the early development of OD programs, however, has tended to become an *idée fixe* of OD applications. This is true in two related senses. The basic OD focus has been micro-level: on interpersonal vs. intergroup phenomena, on interaction vs. structure, and so on. Relatedly, the favored learning design has been the T-Group or sensitivity training group, which of course highlights interpersonal interaction. As Winn concludes:[45]

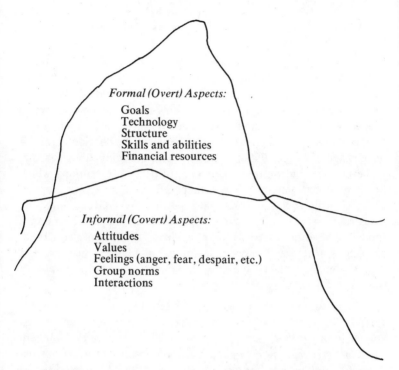

This illustration is based on an address by Stanley N. Herman, of TRW Systems, at an organization development conference sponsored jointly by the Industrial Relations Management Association of British Columbia and NTL Institute for Applied Behavioral Science, Vancouver, B.C., Canada. 1970.

FIGURE 6

*The "Organizational Iceberg"*

...far too many consultants confuse organization development with T-Group or sensitivity training. Thus, they limit their intervention almost exclusively to the interpersonal model. They pay lip service to some of the important variables of organizational effectiveness, like work flow, basic organizational design, task technology and environment.

It is not surprising then that many organization development programs based exclusively on the T-Group strategy fell short of the expected objectives, just as "Human Relations" training programs did some twenty years earlier.

The underlying assumption of this strategy is the belief that what the classical theorists missed, i.e. the motivational and collaborative issues, should get prominence in the consultant's intervention. Thus, the T-Group approach aims at organizational climate, the "ambiance", a system of beliefs, values and attitudes which determines the way people relate to each other and to authority figures. The emphasis is on openness, authenticity and confrontation.

The bias toward the interpersonal and toward interaction has numerous reinforcers. For example, the truth-love model and consensus are clearly more applicable at the level of interpersonal interaction than in larger systems. Given the broad commitment to truth-love and consensus, it is not surprising that many OD practitioners chose a congenial context for emphasis. Applications to intergroup and structural issues also are more complex and chancy.

Despite the comfortable attractions of the interpersonal and of interaction, however, phenomena of crucial interest to OD are found at other levels of organization. At these other levels, as insensitive emphasis on truth-love and consensus not only may be less appropriate, it might be seriously counterproductive. Three illustrations suggest the fullness of the point.

a. *Some awkward consequences of multiple membership.* All organizations are wheels-within-wheels, and typically an individual has memberships in several simple systems. In the sketch below, for example, X is a subordinate of A and member of A's team. But he is also the superordinate as well as the delegate of the P's, in complex and shifting senses. Consequently, any intensification of collaboration at Team Level I may bring mixed results, when one begins to consider Team Level II.

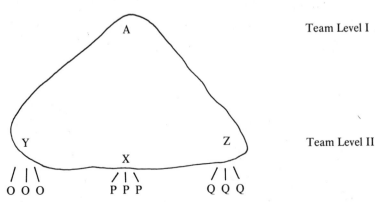

More effective short-run performance may result at Level I. But that intensified collaboration at Team Level I may be perceived as a threat by the P's. That is, the intensification may suggest that X is being co-opted. This is an implied encroachment on the autonomy of Team Level II, and may also be seen as a dilution of its legal or traditional prerogatives. The situation is perhaps clearest in university administration, involving deans and department chairmen. But most supervisors are variously "in the middle" as superordinate/delegate/subordinate, which condition is perhaps most complicated in the case of orthodox line/staff relationships.[46]

The moral should be clear. Truth-love and consensus at one level may inspire power-coercive reactions and dissensus or opposition at other levels. Powerful designs oriented toward truth-love and consensus at one level, then, might inspire equal but opposite reactions at other levels. Hence OD programs—which should typically deal with interaction, task, or macro-structure in complex combinations—have to be sensitive to different models of change and different conventions for decision-making. And all this while seeking to more closely approach OD values!

b. *Micro-level interventions and macro-level problems.* Perhaps *the* generic OD difficulty is that the typical design involves initial learning in conveniently small aggregates, which learning subsequently must be transferred to other loci, often of great size and complexity. And there's a major rub. Designs for micro-level interventions may have serious unanticipated consequences when the focal issue really resides at another level of organization. Winn gives the example of a multi-national corporation. Considerable unrest existed in the plant, due to a volatile mixture: native blacks and expatriate whites in an environment of obvious and sharp status differences, against the backdrop of a vivid history of "colonial" practices. The design to reduce the unrest emphasized interpersonal interaction. A series of T-Groups were to be formed, each with 6 black and 6 white supervisors, and with one white and one black North American trainer. Winn comes down hard on the design and its inappropriate level of focus:[47]

> The consultant obviously did not even attempt to diagnose the situation. Had he done so, he would hopefully have questioned the usefulness of the T-Group strategy in the situation. The pathology was evident on the macro-social level, and the major problems were only tangentially related to the interpersonal or inter-group issues. The T-Group strategy would have set the

stage for frustration and have been perceived as a manipulation, an attempt to have the Negro supervisor accept that his White colleague should have special privilege in terms of salary, home leaves, etc.

c. *Constraints on truth-love and consensus.* The strong possibility exists that substantial and perhaps unavoidable constraints inhibit building truth-love and consensus into at least some organizations. Consider the "contigency theory" developed by Lawrence and Lorsch. Attempting to build extensive opportunities for consensus into a plant organized to produce cardboard cartons may be disingenuous, or even counterproductive. As Lawrence and Lorsch describe them, the cardboard carton market and technology are such as to make high degrees of centralization convenient, and perhaps indispensable.[48] Somewhat the same argument might be made concerning such specialized agencies as the Strategic Air Command and other public agencies.[49]

Whatever the example, the generic point is that at least some organizations may require mechanical systems, or the functional model of organization. Inducing lofty aspirations about consensus in such organizations, consequently, may be foolhardy. Or inducing such aspirations may even be cruel, if compelling considerations require structure within which only centralized conventions for decision-making are realistic.

This is not to say that OD interventions are impossible in such organizations. Rather, such interventions will be limited in at least two basic ways. First, such OD interventions may be palliatives, to help moderate the effects of some technology or organization mission or decision, whether the effects are truly unavoidable or whether management merely considers them as acceptable on balance. This is a limited role, and fraught with "cow sociology" potential; but it often is a necessary role.[50] Second, such OD interventions also would tend to be consistent with the initial style of the host organization, while working toward laboratory values. An appropriate OD intervention in an organization with a highly centralized pattern of decision-making might be elitist in thrust. For example, at the outset such interventions might deal primarily with the structure of the organization or with the design of tasks, rather than with interaction. The prime OD challenge would be to demonstrate that alternative "organic" structural arrangements consistent with the values of the laboratory approach generate results equal to or better than the "mechanical system" or the functional model, as in the guided-participation job enlargement programs at AT & T.[51] Highly-technical and interdependent operations, or those requiring experimental verification of effects, however, may have to be approached differently. In such cases, job enlargement may need to take on an even more elitist character.[52]

In either case, the desired outcome is the same. The structural changes in both cases are intended to encourage or permit patterns of behavior and interaction more consistent with the values of the laboratory approach, while they also raise output and motivate effort.

The issue may be framed more broadly by considering the full range of possible OD interventions. Blake and Mouton provide a convenient place to start in their list of the major kinds of interventions that can facilitate OD programs. Interventions can stress:[53]

*discrepancy,* which calls attention to contradictions in actions or attitudes

*theory,* which highlights research findings or insights that might help the client system gain perspective

*procedures,* with the purpose of analyzing methods or processes of problem-solving

*relationships,* so as to focus attention on the quality of interpersonal, intragroup, and intergroup life

*experimentation,* which involves testing several alternative actions before a decision is made

*dilemmas,* which seeks to point up choice-points and potential conflicts between alternative sets of assumptions and potential solutions

*perspective,* so as to provide situational or historical understanding of problems

*organization structure,* which seeks the sources of problems in structural arrangements of tasks of organizations

*culture,* which focuses on traditions, norms, and values

OD activities with an emphasis on interaction would stress these interventions: discrepancy, relationships, dilemmas, and culture. OD activities with an emphasis on structure would focus on: theory, procedures, experimentation, perspective, and organization structure. The latter interventions incline more toward elitist modes and formulations; the former incline far more toward the participative and consensual.

7. *Whatever the level an OD activity or program initially stresses—behavior or interaction, the task, or macro-organization structure—all levels need to be integrated to reinforce lasting change.* Preaching in this regard is easy enough, but the practice has been most uneven. As Friedlander notes, the issue is less whether the initial level of intervention should be interaction, task, or structure. The critical need is to follow through on the other two levels, whatever the level of initiation. He observes that this follow through is a rarity, however:[54]

> The assumption of the behavioral scientists, for example, would seem to be that behavior change (derived from training sessions) will automatically lead to structural change in the organization. Similarly, the assumption of the technology based change-agent seems to be that changes in the task processes will automatically lead to structural change as well as change in the individual's behavior. And finally, those who would change the structure of the task and human processes will conveniently follow structural change.

There is no magic that guarantees such reinforcement. Perhaps the major initial step is the equanimity to acknowledge what should be done, even if it is conceptually treacherous and practically out-of-reach in a specific case.

8. *OD activities and programs should stress integration, but to degrees that are consistent with such factors as the nature of the problem situation, the specific social contract of reciprocal obligations, and the level of the intervention.* The point can be put bluntly. The thrust of OD typically is integrative, and should remain so. Commonly, however, a good thing has been overdone. Each conclusion will be considered, in turn.

The overwhelming bias of OD activities is to integrate that which is disparate. That is meant in social, technical and moral senses. For example, the underlying model of OD is an organic system, an on-going process of bringing together people and responsibilities. The people and responsibilities are continually changing and evolving; but they are being brought together nonetheless, even if in the very effort they become quicksilver that ultimately defies the bringing together. Similarly, at a moral level the OD bias is toward what Walton has called integrative social situations, as distinguished from distributive situations in which what one person gains, some others must lose.

The integrative bias of OD usually comes on very strong. Perhaps *the* base-objective of most OD has been to bring at least major qualities of "primary groups" into the many "secondary groups" of which people are members. In this view, large organizations sometimes come perilously close to being conceived as big T-Groups. The emphasis in OD programs on comprehensive social contracts, consensus, and truth-love reflects the same bias, if in a less extreme way.

It is all too easy, however, to make too much of even a good thing. More or less clearly, varying degrees of integration are appropriate from case to case. For example, the degree, kind and intensity of integration appropriate for a work team are likely to be unnecessary and probably impossible between that work team and the board of directors of their firm. OD designs appropriate for helping integrate the work team, as a consequence, will differ profoundly from the designs applicable to its interface with the board. Only a certain quality of integration is convenient or perhaps even safe between some organization roles, short of the millenium. Take auditors and line managers, for example. The degree of desired integration follows Beckhard's rule about conflict: little energy should be expended in interpersonal conflict; but the clash of ideas and perspectives and insights should remain high as a sign of a vital but functionally-limited interdependency.

In summary, some systems may (or should) overlap substantially; they might (or should) merely touch from time-to-time; or some intermediate condition might (or should) be characteristic of two systems. OD designs must be sensitive to the differences.[55]

## REFERENCES

1. For a useful summary, see W. Warner Burke, "Organization Development: Here to Stay?," pp. 170-77, in Richard B. Higgins, Paul V. Croke, John F. Veiga, editors, *Proceedings,* 31st Annual Meeting, The Academy of Mangement, August 1971.

2. Robert Tannenbaum and Sheldon A. Davis, "Values, Man, and Organization," p. 134, in Warren H. Schmidt, editor, *Organizational Frontiers and Human Values* Belmont, Calif.: Wadsworth, 1970 .

3. Thomas C. Greening, "Sensitivity Training: Cult or Contribution?," *Personnel,* Vol. 41 May, 1964 , p. 21.

4. Warren G. Bennis and Philip Slater, "Democracy Is Inevitable," *Harvard Business Review,* Vol. 42 March, 1964 , pp. 51-59.

5. Bennis' change in viewpoint suggests the sharper reaction, and both

seem motivated by the turbulence of recent years. His earlier optimism was based on his perception that large masses of men were prepared to work collaboratively for broad common goals. That perception diminished as the 1960s spasmodically were lived through, and as the focus swung toward a short-run, individualistic goals. Bennis explains: "we can observe a growing uncertainty about the deepest human concerns: jobs, neighborhoods, regulation of social norms, child rearing, law and order. . . " "A Funny Thing Happened on the Way to the Future," *American Psychologist,* Vol. 25 July, 1970 , p. 603.

6. Alexander Winn, "The Laboratory Approach to Organization Development." Paper presented to Annual Conference, British Psychological Association, Oxford, September, 1968, p. 3.

7. Bennis, "A Funny Thing Happened on the Way to the Future," pp. 509-602.

8. Quoted in *Ibid,* pp. 601-602.

9. For impressive documentation of the point in the case of one common learning design in the laboratory approach, see Irwin D. Yalom and Morton A. Lieberman, "A Study of Encounter Group Casualties," *Archives of General Psychiatry,* Vol. 25 July, 1971 , pp. 16-30.

10. Richard R. Parlour, "Executive Team Training," *Journal of the Academy of Management* Vol. 14 September, 1971 , p. 343. His emphases.

11. For one discussion of the contract motion in relation to sensitivity training, see Gerald Egan, *Encounter: Group Processes for Interpersonal Growth* Belmont, California: Brooks-Cole, 1970 , pp. 25-67.

12. Tannenbaum and Davis, *op. cit.,* p. 131.

13. Richard E. Walton, *Interpersonal Peacemaking: Confrontations and Third-Party Consultation* Reading, Mass.: Addison-Wesley, 1969 .

14. See Jack Fordyce and Raymond Weil, *Managing With People* Reading, Mass.: Addison-Wesley, 1971, esp. pp. 89-90.

15. For an especially interesting example, see a design dealing with the impact of business travel on marriages and home-life. Samuel A. Culbert and Jean Renshaw, "Coping with the Stresses of Travel as an Opportunity for Improving the Quality of Work and Family Life," *Family Processes* September, 1972 .

16. Frank Friedlander, "The Impact of Organizational Training Laboratories upon the Effectiveness and Interaction of Ongoing Work Groups," *Personnel Psychology,* Vol. 20 Autumn, 1967 , pp. 289-307.

17. Richard A. Schmuck and Matthew B. Miles, editors, *Organization Development in Schools* Palo Alto, Calif.: National Press Books, 1971 .

18. *Ibid.,* p. 52.

19. *Ibid.,* esp. pp. 59-61.

20. Golembiewski, *Renewing Organizations.*

21. Sylvia A. Joure, Roland L. Frye, Paul C. Green, and Frank P. Cassens, "Examples of Over-Use of Sensitivity Training," *Training and Development Journal,* Vol. 25 December, 1971 , pp. 24-26.

22. Jack K. Fordyce and Raymond Weil, *Managing With People* Reading, Mass.: Addison-Wesley, 1971 ; and Wendell L. French and Cecil H.

Bell, Jr., *Organization Development* Englewood Cliffs, N. J.: Prentice-Hall, 1973 .

23. Harvey Kramer, "More on More/More," *Journal of Applied Behavioral Science,* Vol. 8 September, 1972 , p. 630.

24. Yalom and Lieberman, *op. cit.,* esp. pp. 25-26.

25. Frank Friedlander, "Congruence in Organization Development," p. 6. Paper delivered at the Annual Meeting, Academy of Management. Atlanta, Ga., August 17-18, 1971.

26. For an impressive demonstration of the point, see Stanley E. Seashore and David G. Bowers, "Durability of Organizational Change," *American Psychologist,* Vol. 25 January, 1970 , esp. pp. 232-33.

27. Spencer Klaw, "Two Weeks in a T-Group," p. 37, in Robert T. Golembiewski and Arthur Blumberg, editors, *Sensitivity Training and the Laboratory Approach* Itasca, Ill.: F. E. Peacock, 1970 .

28. Alexander Winn, "Reflections on T-Group Strategy and the Role of the Change Agent in Organization Development," p. 1. Working Paper, February 1971. Published as "Reflexions sur la strategie du T-Group et le role de l'agent de changement dans le developpement organisationnel," *Bulletin de Psychologie,* Vol. 25, No. 296 1971-72 , pp. 250-56. The failure to deal directly with power, similarly, is seen as one of the major resolved conceptual issues in OD by Warren Bennis, "Unsolved Problems Facing Organizational Development," *The Business Quarterly,* Vol. 34 Winter, 1969 , pp. 80-84.

29. A classic statement of this position is the "contingency theory" of Paul R. Lawrence and Jay W. Lorsch, *Organization and Environment* Boston: Harvard University, Division of Research, Graduate School of Business Administration, 1967 . See also E. Raymond Corey and Steven H. Star, *Organization Strategy: A Marketing Approach* Boston: Harvard University, Division of Research, Graduate School of Business Administration, 1971 .

30. Schmuck and Miles, *op. cit.,* p. 234.

31. *Ibid.,* p. 185. See also in this volume, Mark A. Chesler and John E. Lohman, "Changing Schools Through Student Advocacy," pp. 185-212.

32. C. Brooklyn Derr, "Surfacing and Managing Organizational Power," *OD Practitioner,* Vol. 4 No. 2, 1972 , pp. 1-3, presents a model for such a power-oriented intervention in an OD program.

33. No one denies the point, but interpretations of its impact range from obvious necessity to blatant toadyism. Compare Samuel A. Culbert and Jerome Reisel, "Organization Development: An Applied Philosophy for Managers in Public Enterprise," *Public Administration Review,* Vol. 31 March, 1971, pp. 159-69;   and Robert Ross, "OD for Whom?," *Journal of Applied Behavioral Science,* Vol. 7 September, 1971 , pp. 580-85.

34. Robert T. Golembiewski, Stokes B. Carrigan, Walter R. Mead, Robert Munzenrider, and Arthur Blumberg, "Toward Building New Work Relationships: An Action Design for a Critical Intervention," *Journal of Applied Behavioral Science,* Vol. 8 March, 1972 , pp. 135-48.

35. Winn, "Reflections on T-Group Strategy," p. 8.

36. Stanley N. Herman, "Gestalt Orientation to Organization Development," p. 26. Paper delivered at NTL Conference on New Technology in Organization Development. New York, October 8-9, 1971.

37. The analogy at a simpler level of organization is the T-Group that remains in an early "honeymoon phase," which is sub-phase 4 in Warren G. Bennis and Herbert Shepard, "A Theory of Group Development," *Human Relations,* Vol. 9 November, 1956 , pp. 415-37.

38. Compare start-up to steady-state operations, for example. In the case of power plants, a nurturant model of leadership seems to be more characteristic of mature and stable organizations than at start-up. See Floyd C. Mann, "Toward An Understanding of the Leadership Role in Formal Organization," pp. 68-103, in Robert Dubin, editor, *Leadership and Productivity* San Francisco: Chandler, 1965 .

39. Relatedly, see Edwin A. Fleishman, "Patterns of Leadership Behavior Related to Group Grievances and Turnover," *Personnel Psychology,* Vol. 15 Spring, 1962 , esp. p. 50; and Rensis Likert, *The Human Organization* New York: McGraw-Hill, 1967 , esp. pp. 51-55.

40. V. R. Buzzota, R. E. Lefton, and Mannie Sherberg, "Train Managers to Handle Power," *Sales Management* May, 1972 , pp. 70-71, 146-56.

41. Warren G. Bennis, *Changing Organizations* New York: McGraw-Hill, 1968 , p. 168.

42. Bennis, "A Funny Thing Happened on the Way to the Future," p. 602.

43. For a limited-exchange OD design in an organization which was and basically remains fiercely destructive in its interpersonal relationships, see Golembiewski, *Renewing Organizations,* pp. 164-66.

44. Wendell French, "A Definition and History of Organization Development," p. 2. Paper delivered at the Annual Meeting, Academy of Management. Atlanta, Ga., August 17-18, 1971.

45. Winn, "Reflections on T-Group Strategy," pp. 2-3.

46. Robert T. Golembiewski, *Organizing Men and Power* Chicago: Rand McNally, 1967 .

47. Winn, "Reflections on T-Group Strategy," pp. 9-19.

48. *Op. cit.*

49. Robert T. Golembiewski, "Organization Development in Public Agencies," *Public Administration Review,* Vol. 29 July, 1969 , pp. 367-77.

50. The demotion design illustrates an effort to moderate the impact on employees of a specific management decision in which the employees had no voice and little choice. See Golembiewski, Carrigan, Mead, Munzenrider, and Blumberg, *op. cit.*

51. Robert N. Ford, *Motivation Through the Work Itself* New York: American Management Association, 1969 .

52. William Paul, Keith Robertson, and Frederick Herzberg, "Job Enrichment Pays Off," *Harvard Business Review* Vol. 47 March, 1969 , p. 75.

53. Robert A. Blake and Jane S. Mouton, "A 9, 9 Approach to Organization Development," cited in Warren G. Bennis, "The Change Agents," p. 307, in Robert T. Golembiewski and Arthur Blumberg, editors, *Sensitivity Training and the Laboratory Approach* Itasca, Ill.: Peacock, 1969 .

18 THEORY AND METHOD IN OD

54. Friedlander, "Congruence in Organization Development."
55. The interface of work and family relations as affected by travel illustrates the touching of two such systems. See Culbert and Renshaw, *op. cit.*

# 5

# The Relevance of Human Intellect and Organizational Power for Organization Development

*CLAYTON P. ALDERFER**

A friend and colleague of mine, Thomas Lodahl coined the statement, "The world is not a T-group." When I first heard him say this I was caught by the large number of complex issues that might be better managed if this simple statement were better understood, accepted, and applied by practitioners of organization development. Many of us have entered the field of applied behavioral science in part because of having had a moving and enriching experience through participation in a T-group. The warmth, the apparent leveling, the sense that more humane values are workable, and the experience of new ways of learning and working that often emerge from a T-group experience all contribute to the wish that all of one's experience should share these characteristics. Perhaps these goals are realizable, but I believe that enough data are in to say with some certainty that it hasn't happened yet and is probably unlikely to be achieved by tomorrow (Argyris, 1971). Like other innovations, the model offered by the T-group has its merits, but it is also incomplete. There are several issues in particular which I believe have been ignored, misunderstood, and misapplied as a result of the failure to appreciate that indeed the world is not a T-group. Harvey and Davis (1972) have done a nice job of identifying certain dimensions on which laboratory (T-groups) organizations differ from non-laboratory organizations. In this paper I shall identify a number of problems which my experience consistently tells me interfere with optimally effective organization development and which I believe have evolved because of a failure to come to terms fully with the reality that everyday organizational life differs in some very important ways from the last moments of an effectively functioning

* Appreciation for their constructive comments on an earlier version of the paper is extended to Robert Kaplan, Robert Neal, John Stanton, David Jenkins, John Adams, and the Conference participants who attended my session.

T-group. From the problems, I shall then turn to one model which I
have found helpful in getting around the problems that were
identified. The last section of the paper will then briefly describe the
two cases illustrating how the model can guide actions.

The T-group as a social innovation has been instrumental in
allowing many people to see the unrealized constructive potential of
human emotions. During the course of a laboratory program, people
can develop very warm feelings for one another as group members
struggle with and work through the problems of group formation
and as they learn to give and receive helpful feedback. But along with
these constructive gains from T-grouping have come certain other
losses. As members of a group learn how the use of words, the
analysis of human behavior, and other intellectual activity can
distance one human being from another, some tend to reach the
conclusion that intellectual work of all kinds is the arch enemy of
authentic relationships. It has often struck me as paradoxical how
some members of the human potential movement have failed to
accept planning, thinking, and evaluating (all human intellectual
activities) as part of the human potential to be developed and
utilized. I have no sense of being alone in making this criticism, and I
believe the whole field of applied behavioral science is now moving in
directions which will make increasing use of intellectual work in
furthering the values and social processes which the field has to offer.
A second mislearning which I believe has grown out of the T-group
experience concerns the understanding and use of power in group
and organizational settings. One stance toward T-group learning,
shared by many practitioners, is to minimize as much as possible the
power differences between staff and participants because ex-
aggerated authority tends to interfere with the kinds of personal
learning often achieved at the end of a group (Egan, 1970). Although
I believe this is an error in the conduct of group training, I am even
more convinced that it is a serious mistake when the purpose of
laboratory education is not only personal learning for individuals but
also leadership and group dynamics education for mangers, teachers,
and other professionals.

In summary, I believe that the application of laboratory methods
to the solution of organizational problems has suffered from two
classes of errors, each growing out of the otherwise extraordinarily
beneficial learnings first found in the T-group laboratory. The first
error concerns the under-utilization or, in some cases, the abandonment of human intellect. The second error pertains to flight from the

very difficult issues surrounding the use of power and authority.

My belief in the validity of these two criticisms stems from a variety of data, all of it informal, and yet all of it quite convincing to me at a personal level. The first source of data is myself. During my years as a professional I have found versions of these criticisms operating in and interfering with my own effectiveness. Little in what I say in the following pages by way of criticism of the profession do I feel immune to myself. A second source of data is in the observations of my colleagues, some toward whom I feel considerable warmth, some toward whom I have no relationship, and some toward whom I feel disrespect. I have observed colleagues when I have worked with them, and I have also followed others into systems and listened to clients describe (and evaluate) their work. A final source of data comes from the reactions I received when these criticisms were first presented orally to an audience of internal and external organization development consultants.

*Under-utilization of human intellect.* To test the hypothesis about the under utilization of intellectual resources, let me pose some questions for organization development practitioners. How many subscriptions to professional social science journals do you take? How many research journals from psychology, sociology, and anthropology could you list? How many new research books in the field of organizational behavior published in 1972 could you list? How many of you keep updated logs of the projects you are dealing with? How many of you have written planning documents to explain applied behavioral science to members of your organization?

Last summer (1972) at an N.T.L. Learning Community session, I was talking with one of our most respected woman colleagues and was surprised to learn that she did not have a Ph.D. In explaining to me why she had decided not to go back to school, she described how her son had recently finished his degree only after becoming quite angry at key faculty members. I responded that I had not known anyone who was honest who had not worked out a substantial degree of anger in the process of completing a doctorate. I knew that I had. Then she said that she was afraid that if she went back to school, she would lose her ability to communicate ideas in clear and simple language because she would become too intellectual and abstract. I asked her if she knew anyone who forgot how to speak English after they learned French. This episode provided me with additional understanding about why many people in our profession do not do more intellectual work. Some who resist it do so not because an assessment of the intrinsic merits of the activity, but because it is painful and difficlt to do intellectual work. They avoid intellectual work for emotional reasons.

Incidentally, I recently discovered a new "helpful" intervention. I was able to convince a number of clients in one organization to write some of their materials in complete sentences. As surprising as this may seem, it turned out to be instrumental for dealing with some resistances by a key set of line managers in one section of the organization. One of the managers' way of judging a person's competence was whether material they saw was presented in grammatically correct ways. They were in engineering not marketing or public relations.

I believe that another reason why so little intellectual work is done in OD is because many of us enjoy treating what we know as a kind of magic and keeping it to ourselves. (Still another hypothesis is that many practitioners in the field are dumb.) One of the best internal consultants I've known recognizes that the managers with whom he has worked cannot explain to one another how he has helped them. However, when asked what OD is, they say it is "what Pete does." "Pete" has thrived in several major budget cuts in the corporation because he has the support of several very highly regarded line managers, but the OD group in that company is not in good shape, partly, I believe, because lack of intellectual work has kept the group from arriving at consensually accepted statement of their corporate mission.

Another approach was taken by an internal consultant charged with developing a corporate plan for human resources management. His plan was written out and included a 30 page document as well as the usual complete dog-and-pony show. His first presentation was to the company president, a committed advocate of applied behavioral science. The president reacted very positively to the presentation, which was complete with human need theory, open systems theory, thirteen specific interventions, and a brief description of several projects already underway in the company. Both the president and the consultant agreed that the presentation was pretty theoretical and would be a problem for some others who would hear it. They further agreed that the way to deal with the problem was *not* to decrease the theoretical content, but to *increase* the use of concrete examples so that the managers would be better able to connect the theory to their work experience. One of the key features in the president's reactions to the program was that he found what the consultant said to be consistent with his 20 years of work experience and reading behavioral science literature. In fact, he found that the newer theoretical presentation solved some of the problems that had been troubling him over the years.

The writing is on the wall. As more people become familiar with applied behavioral science, they will demand higher grade intellectual work. One's success as an internal or external consultant will in part depend on his ability to meet these demands.

This criticism was viewed differentially by internal and external consultants at the 1972 New Technology in OD Conference. Most external consultants who spoke agreed with the validity of the problem. They felt that they themselves read less than was desirable and thought the general validity of the charge was high. Among internal consultants the responses were more varied. Some did not even "get around to dealing with the issue," others agreed with it, and still others wondered whether it was not a strength rather than a weakness. One possibility for understanding these reactions is that because they themselves are generally more secure intellectually (by virtue of holding Ph.D.'s, writing articles now and then, etc.), the external consultants are more able to accept the criticism. Support for this hypothesis was found in the remarks of one internal consultant who reported that the standing of an internal consultant in his own organization was increased substantially after he had completed the Ph.D.

*Flight from power and authority.* Problems with power and authority begin with the family. As a result, I assume that all of us by virtue of participating in the human condition arrive on the scene with considerably mixed feelings about the people who control our lives. From the standpoint of organization development, the significant kinds of power pertain to the ability (by virtue of personal characteristics) or the capability (by virtue of organizational position) to influence the availability and utilization of significant resources. Consultants always have power when they are functioning in role, although they may underappreciate the nature of the power they possess. The types of power and the extent of those powers depend heavily on the role a consultant negotiates for himself and upon his own personal characteristics. It is an occupational reality of consulting that persons operating in this role must deal with some individuals whose power is more than their own and others whose power is less than their own. I have noticed that internal and external consultants tend to evidence certain chronic problems in how they relate to their own and others' management of power in human systems.

Often an internal consultant is a person who entered the profession as a second-best career. He might have been "dumped" into personnel work after he had been less than successful in line management, or he might have entered the field directly because he had fears about his abilities to do the job of managing people when concrete results were demanded. He is often very good at empathizing with people who have been hurt and punished by organizations. Literally he knows because he has been there himself—perhaps more than many. He was latently in favor of people expressing all their emotions before ever seeing a T-group because he has so many emotions to express himself and sometimes has trouble holding them in check. So a group experience, where "we let it all hang out," is quite consistent with many of his personal needs.

The internal consultant with this sort of background tends to run into a number of predictable problems as he operates professionally. Because his career history is often known by his clients, he frequently has difficulty in gaining the confidence of operating managers who are understandably reluctant to accept the advice of someone whose competence, as they understand it, is not very high. If the internal consultant does not fully flee from questions about his own newly acquired competence, he is able to gain the confidence of some managers, especially those whose situation is so desperate that they are willing to try almost anything.

Having gained the confidence of line managers, the internal consultant is permitted to develop a role for himself. But as he works, he is particularly prone to two kinds of mistakes, arising from his own irresolution of authority problems. Both errors are connected with his wish to avoid being with an authority figure who is upset.

The *first* kind of error happens when the internal consultant is reluctant to discuss, with powerful line managers, elements of their style which are manipulative, secretive, or paternalistic and when he is slow to go toward the feelings of anger that often develop in the line manager toward the consultant. For similar reasons, he does not speak for his needs in key situations, and he is unlikely to take initiatives toward managers. From the manager's eyes this kind of behavior confirms some of his worst fears about the consultant. Not only did he fail in other careers because he lacked dynamism, but the same thing is happening again.

The *second* kind of mistake which internal consultants may make is to encourage subordinates to be especially thorough in expressing their negative and angry reactions to their supervisors. Some internal consultants find it much easier to support some one else's expression of criticism than to express their own. I have called this phenomenon among certain consultants, "fanning counterdependence." People who do it are good at empathizing with the suffering subordinates in a situation and significantly less able to empathize with the supervisor who must absorb and respond to all the criticism. Their unstated view of the supervisor is that anyone as powerful as he can easily deal with large amounts of negative feedback if he deserves his job, and if he can't, he shouldn't have the position. Such an internal consultant is slow to believe that supervisors have feelings of pain, anxiety, and anguish and that they need non-collusive support in establishing real mutuality in their work relations. Internal consultants who make this mistake are usually able to see how threatened the manager is of their services but unable to see how their own behavior contributes to this threat.

External consultants often have difficulty maintaining a committed organizational affiliation. They may be teaching at a university, operating in private practice or sharing membership in a consulting firm. Whatever the organizational connection, the external consultant often is not a *central* member of the system, if he is a member of the system at all. In part, this is because of his role in life, but it is also reflective of his personal style. A person who is busy helping others with their problems may be short of time and energy for dealing with his own problems. But I suspect that this is the smaller explanation for his behavior. More significant, I fear, is his reluctance to stay around to deal with the consequences of his actions. His specialty is unfreezing people and systems. In his armament are a number of proven techniques for stimulating people to examine their behavior, express their emotions and try new behaviors.

External consultants are usually good at gratifying their own needs. They too have been hurt by organizations, but not nearly as much as many internal consultants. After one or two experiences with being damaged in organizational life, many external consultants evolve a life role that keeps them without an organization or with many organizations. Expert at managing short-term power relationships; quick, articulate, funny and smooth, an effective external consultant is able to win the confidence of line managers who are looking for new tools for improving their organizations, motivating their people and increasing organizational commitment. Many external consultants are at their best when things are going well at the beginning of a relationship.

Many external consultants are also especially poor in developing professional relationships with others either inside or outside of organizations when it remains ambiguous as to who the star is. Many of the "top" external consultants work well alone or have a partner who is clearly always in second place in the pecking order.

Most external consultants enjoy contacts with powerful line managers, and it does not take much effort for them to tell you their list of well-known clients. One external consultant's feelings toward another are usually mixed and contain substantial elements of competitiveness. One pattern of behavior I have frequently noticed is for one person to praise another and then off-handedly identify something like a fatal flaw. "If only so-and-so were not so self-centered," or "Did you know what so-and-so just did?" In reacting to this paper at the conference, one well-known external consultant indicated that he had trouble responding because he had developed his own analysis of consultancy. Then he proceeded to tell the group what his views were even though another session was designed for him to do exactly that. Informally, another external consultant told me that I had presented too polarized a position which had turned him off and prevented him from wanting to read the rest of the paper. A different external consultant specifically identified another well known external consultant and characterized his work as "bullying the client until he buys the rationalization."

Some external consultants have predominantly negative feelings toward internal consultants. Forgetting their own difficulties in maintaining a sustained organizational commitment, they are critical of internal consultants who appear to be conservative in their attitudes and approach. They often head directly to the top man in the system without recognizing how much harm this might do to the insider's local esteem. When the external consultant relates to the internal consultant, he does so manifestly as a professional colleague but latently in a spirit of superior to subordinate. An external consultant who does not operate with this latent attitude should be able to tell you very easily, directly and admiringly what he respects and likes about the internal consultants with whom he is working, and perhaps most importantly, what the internal consultants can do better than he can.

A final feature of some external consultants is that they tend not to stay around long when flak hits. Their "gun-and-run" approach keeps them on the move. For the sake of image, an external consultant knows that it is not too smart to be closely associated with failures. His many other commitments always provide a convenient reason for exiting, and his disdain for internal consultants provides him with an easy explanation for why things did not work out well in a particular situation.

External consultants live constantly with the knowledge of how tenuous their relationship to clients is. If they play it cool, do not deal with their needs in a situation (out of strength, of course), and counter threats to continuation with readiness to leave, they may inadvertently encourage clients to use them in short-run ways. Rather than regular participation in an on-going developing program, the external consultant is used for emergencies and crises. He is brought in to handle the "impossible" situations. This approach aids his heroic fantasies. If he succeeds, it was a true conquest, and he emerges as a genuine hero. If he fails, he loses no face in being unable to manage the impossible. Similarly the internal consultant can avoid risking his local credibility by taking on high risk adventures. If the external consultant fails, it confirms the difficulty of the problem or his ineptness. Either way, the internal consultant also emerges relatively unscathed, and he may achieve a bit of retaliation for being one-down in relation to the external consultant.

Manifestly, internal and external consultants are very different. But there are ways that the "pathologies" of roles may complement each other. Unwittingly, or even consciously, internal and external consultants may collude to keep each other in business in the *short-run,* but the long-run consequence may be to have little effect on changing human systems other than to raise expectations which later will be frustrated, and therefore make change that much more difficult the next time around.

A major reason for this outcome lies with the ways both kinds of consultants mismanage authority relationships. Each tends to adopt a strategy for relating to those with real power over their lives which avoids working through the conflictful and turbulent processes that are always present when real change is taking place. Internal consultants who avoid these kinds of turbulent interactions do so at some cost to their self esteem and the careers of those they set up against the system. External consultants who avoid such conflictful interactions do so at the cost of their clients and the profession in general. When an external consultant does not publicly examine his errors, when he acts as if he has a magical formula and when he walks away when the relationship gets conflictful, he violates the values and processes that he is presumably hired to promote.

Reactions to the power and authority criticism also differed markedly between internal and external consultants at the conference. By and large the internal consultants seemed to engage the issue more fully, and to be more able to accept the parts that applied to them and to point out discrepancies in terms of their own experience. One representative response came from an internal consultant who had worked with me and with other external consultants and said, "Thought your remarks re 'Management of Power Relations'... were well handled ... a very direct acknowledgement of the problems faced by both parties." Other internal consultants said that they learned to distinguish between external consultants who were "mechanics" and undesirable and those who were "engineers" and with whom productive relationships could be established. Another reaction from internal consultants was that they did indeed frequently have problems working through issues of conflict with key line managers. It is hard to be sure what the low response frequency by external consultants meant. One possibility, however, is that they saw the issue as right enough not to disagree with and painful enough not to discuss publicly with other external consultants while potential clients (i.e., internal consultants) were present.

*Conclusion.* The two problems I have attempted to identify—the under-utilization of the human intellect and the flight from power and authority—are separate issues, but there are also ways that they interrelate. One kind of power available to both internal and external consultants stems from knowledge of the theories and findings of behavioral science research. Well integrated knowledge in this area should contribute to the understanding and effectiveness of both kinds of consultants, and the more internal consultants are able to develop their own intellectual equipment the less they will realistically be in a one-down position relative to external consultants on this dimension. I believe that the essence of the problem in both cases stems from an avoidance of frustrating, anxiety provoking activity. No human being will survive very well if he does not find ways to avoid certain stresses and tensions, but it is also disastrous to avoid all kinds of pressures. The working through of many kinds of anxieties is essential to both personal and professional growth. I believe that dealing effectively with the tensions of intellectual growth and the frustrations of power-conflicts are essential to the personal development of organizational consultants and to the field of applied behavioral science. I do not believe that it is necessary, however, to reproduce the dysfunctions of traditional education or the capriciousness and duplicity of politicians (organizational and societal) to cope with these difficulties. The following section will present one approach to effectively integrating the human support found in effectively functioning T-groups with the knowledge available through behavioral science to change constructively some of the realities of organizational life.

## The Complementary Relationship

The rhetoric of applied behavioral science is rich with the phrase "collaborative relationship." I have learned to mistrust that phrase because it has so often seemed to me to be used collusively and seductively. Some of the things that I have observed in the name of collaborative relationships include the following: 'Let's you and I agree that we have a collaborative relationship so we can avoid dealing with our differences.' 'Let's you and I form a collaborative relationship so we can forget that you have much more real power than I do, or that I have much more freedom than you do.' 'Let's you and I agree that we have a collaborative relationship so we don't have to recognize that I am better at some things than you are, and you are better at some things than I am.' 'Let's you and I form a collaborative relationship so we can forget that we have different things to gain and lose as a result of doing things together.' I know that the originators of the term collaborative relationship did not intend these misuses to crop-up, but they have. I propose the term *complementary relationship* as a way to get us thinking more concretely and realistically about what an effective professional relationship is.

*A complementary relationship exists when the relevant parties, recognizing that they have different organizational roles, personal needs and primary abilities, agree to work together blending their different contributions in such a way that the primary needs of each are met, the differential costs are shared according to each one's contribution to the problems, and the negotiations around these matters are dealt with as directly and as openly as possible.*

Watzlawick, Beavin, and Jackson (1967) point out that all human relationships may be classified according to whether they are based on equality, in which case they are termed symmetrical, or whether they are based on difference, in which case they are called complementary. The definition of complementary relationship I have proposed goes somewhat beyond the view offered by Watzlawick, et. al. because, while it is based on recognizing certain major classes of differences among professionals, it also calls for a common process for dealing with these differences. It is no accident that the problems with organization development that I have identified stem from excessive reliance on symmetrical relationship models. Intellectual work tends to produce differences in ideas, in results, and in conclusions, and many problems surrounding power in pyramidal systems begin when individuals and groups must cope with differential amounts of various resources. The present emphasis on the complementary relationship based on open acknowledgement and discussion of differences is intended to be an antidote to the various pathologies associated with excessive reliance on symmetrical models that do not adequately reflect the nature of individual, group, or organizational reality.

The specific complementary relationship which I have found to be very productive in the service of organizational change is a "professional triad" consisting of a senior internal consultant, a junior internal consultant and an external consultant. The purpose of this professional triad is to aid the normal task oriented line organization in developing more open and trusting problem-solving relationships in the service of meeting the individual and organizational needs of its members. The professional triad attempts to combine its social technology with organizational power and human support to achieve these ends. Each member of the professional triad contributes differentially to these ends as a function of his abilities, personal needs and organizational role.

*The senior internal consultant* is someone who has been successful in terms of the primary mission of the organization. For example, if the system is a school, he has been a fine teacher and is known for this. If the system is a research and development laboratory, he has made some first-rate contributions to the technical field. If the system is production oriented, he has achieved success in meeting quantity and quality goals. As a result of these achievements, this person is locally respected. Potential clients do not look at him as someone who does OD because he can't do anything else.

The more I have observed organizational behavior, the more convinced I have become that people do not get ahead just because they perform effectively, although in most realistic systems that is essential. But in addition to being effective, the successful manager learns how to make things happen that meet the needs of higher ranking members of the system. Thus, he usually has more informal influence—both upward and downward—than a formal position description would give him. He is usually seen as someone the system does not want to lose.

His ways of operating may approximate being manipulative, and if he is unable or unwilling to see this, he is not a good candidate for changing these values and practices in the system. But if he has evolved his techniques as a realistic response to the system and is not personally wedded to them, the utility of his knowledge of such things as when it is a good or a bad time to approach a certain person, how to phrase a particular issue, when to confront a particular conflict and when not to, who to talk to get certain kinds of information and so on, is simply invaluable.

Another important characteristic of the senior consultant is that he is substantially dissatisfied with how the system operates. He sees and abhors the human wreckage that is created by the organization, and though he is discrete about who he says this to, his own behavior in achieving his task success includes a number of examples where he intervened to aid substantially the human condition of people in the system. In short he is committed to humane values in more than a verbal way.

All of these characteristics make the senior internal consultant a person who is conceptually equipped, emotionally prepared and organizationally situated for his job. But these assets do not complete the picture; the ideal senior internal consultant also has some liabilities. Just as he is helped with some relationships because he has power in the organization, he is feared in other contexts. Some members of the system may hold back information from him because they believe he can make a difference. Most often these fears are tied to career aspirations, but there may also be people who are competing with the senior consultant for other resources and don't trust him not to use their information against them.

Another liability of the senior internal consultant is that he has felt relatively little of the pain associated with failing within the system because he has failed so little. While he readily recognizes that he could not have succeeded without the help and support of others, he also justifiably gives himself credit for achieving what he did. He is a little blind to the things that have come to him as a result of chance or the benevolent attitudes of a particular person early in his career. As a result he is somewhat inclined to blame others in the sytem who have not done as well as he has. While he is critical of the system, it is often very hard for him to believe that a particular person's plight is not more the results of his efforts than what he has been dealt by nature. All of this adds up to the senior man's possibly being short of empathy for people who have suffered the most in the system.

Most organizations have their own theory to explain why certain events happen. This view is communicated through company training programs, messages from the president and the implicit messages that are communicated by who is and is not promoted. Much of this theory becomes true by virtue of its self-fulfilling nature. People act as if it were true, and it becomes true. A person who has succeeded in the system is especially prone to accepting the local explanations for organizational life, and anyone who stays for a long time is bound to accept unknowingly certain assumptions about why things happen as they do.

The senior internal consultant and the junior internal consultant both may suffer from the blinders which spending a long period of time in a system create.

*The external consultant's* contributions begin because he is outside the system. By virtue of keeping up with the literature and consulting with other systems, he is usually familiar with many systems, not just that of his present client. He thus carries several theories for explaining things, and has watched many different prophecies fulfilled, not just the particular ones of the given system. He should be a source of new ideas and approaches and a resource for enabling the client to get access to novelty that goes beyond his own particular competencies. In this way he complements the particular set of blinders shared by the senior and junior internal consultants.

The external consultant is likely to try again things that have worked well for him in other settings. If he has been thorough in his understanding, he will be able to modify his techniques to the new setting, but there is often the danger that he suffers from misunderstanding why he was effective in a prior situation. Thus he, too, suffers from a potential set of blinders that are in many ways complementary to those of the internal consultants. If he is able to join forces effectively with the internal consultants, together the team should be able to adapt the offerings that have worked well in one setting to the special conditions of the new setting. For this to happen, however, the external consultant must accept the limitations of his own knowledge—both in terms of the particular situation and in terms of prior settings—and accept the influence of knowledgeable insiders.

For the external consultant to fully utilize his capacities, it is important that he have first hand access to the raw data of the organization he is consulting with. This means that he must see, interview and influence line managers and their subordinates. Otherwise he will have no first hand data base against which to check the reports of his inside colleagues. As he goes about this data collection, he should be alert to ways in which his actions may undermine the standing of the internal consultants and simultaneously do all that he can to enhance their deserved feelings of competence and esteem.

The external consultants can also add his own special kind of influence to the success of change activities. Presumably he has had different experiences, has developed several ways of thinking about things, and therefore can speak with the authority of competence on some issues. He may be able to help clients distinguish between reasonable risks, sure things and unreasonable gambles. This use of his professional power is very appropriate, provided that the consultant continually checks to be sure that it is the client who is making the choices, not he himself. A particularly difficult kind of input to handle is recommendation about another external consultant. If I really know another person's work, it usually means that we have some kind of personal as well as professional relationship. Thus I am inclined explicitly to include the outlines of that personal relationship in any assessment I make, telling the client that I am doing so, in order that he can use the information to correct for my biases. I invite the client to tell me his concerns in evaluating another consultant, so I can gear my comments to the dimensions of his thinking. After we have discussed the person in his terms, I am not reluctant to include additional information if I think important omissions are being made. They seldom are.

*The junior internal consultant* makes his primary contribution most often through his capacity to empathize with lower ranking members of the system, especially those who have been hurt and thwarted by the organization. He is usually able to gain the confidence of people at his own rank and below because of his personal warmth and the fact that he is not threatening organizationally. He is most able to find out where the problems are in the system and is likely to be alert to subtlties in the penalty system of the organization which are not seen by either the senior internal consultant or the external consultant.

Because he is liked by most people, he has easy access to many kinds of information that those who are less well known or more threatening could not obtain. People usually enjoy talking to this person because he is unlikely to make them uncomfortable and is likely to be a very good listener. The pattern of his not confronting people is likely to extend to his relations with the senior internal consultant and the external consultant. Therefore, an external consultant and a senior internal consultant who want to fully benefit from the contributions of the junior internal consultant have to discipline themselves to listen carefully. In the process, they may develop greater capacities for being empathic themselves. Thus by being a good listener himself and "requiring" his colleagues to listen carefully to him, the junior internal consultant may teach his colleagues to improve their own abilities in this area.

As this learning process occurs, it is likely that the junior internal consultant may also come to appreciate that he has more to offer than he might think. If he sees that his contributions are useful and is confronted with the consequences of his being mildly indirect or excessively tentative, the junior internal consultant may begin to modify one facet of his style which should allow him to enjoy more success in the organization. The outcome of this kind of exchange is that all parties benefit in complementary ways for the solution of the immediate problem and are stimulated to improve their short-comings in the long-run.

I have now observed a number of people who began as junior internal consultants grow in stature and esteem within their organizations, as they more fully integrated their reaction to authority figures and as they became more thoughtful in the diagnosis, design, and evaluation of their work. Others, perhaps as a sign of growth or as a signal of further flight, have turned to other activities. Some have gone back to line management positions, and others have found staff jobs that are less uncertain and tension-laden than OD work. Those internal consultants who have grown within their roles have usually moved in two ways. First, they have gained increased credibility and influence with line managers. One very high ranking corporate executive credited two significant promotions of his own to the help he received from an OD consultant and brought the consultant immediately into a new assignment of great complexity and difficulty. Another direction in which successful internal consultants have moved has been upward in their own staff groups. From a role in which they operated as "lone eagles," as one man put it, they begin to feel an increasing responsibility to supervise and coach junior consultants. Often pressures to take on this kind of role come from junior consultants who wish to learn, but there are also organizational needs that must be met. I believe that our social technology has progressed to the point where a stable group of internal consultants should be supported by most organizations. One way to insure that this possibility is realized is for the more successful internal consultants to seek and accept greater authority in their organizations.

### Illustrations

The model of complementary triads can be applied to organizations of varying sizes and complexity, but size *is* a critical variable in application. In smaller systems, the roles may each be held by a single individual. In a larger system the various roles may have several incumbents. I shall illustrate this application by describing how we have operated in two systems during the last several years. The first organization was a boys' boarding school consisting of approximately 50 faculty members and 400 students. The second system was a public utility corporation consisting of 14,000 employees.

*The Boarding School.* In the boarding school there were several critical subunits. One consisted of the headmaster and the staff members who reported directly to them, and the others consisted of the student officers of the various classes and the students over which they exercised influence. In this system there were two faculty members who combined their usual organizational role with that of being an internal change agent. The senior of these two men was the assistant headmaster and the junior man was the school chaplain. After a system diagnosis was carried out by a team of external consultants advised by a liaison committee of students and faculty, these two men were proposed for their new roles by the diagnostic team. Their new roles were negotiated first with the headmaster and then with the entire faculty.

The two men were proposed for their roles for two sets of reasons. Perhaps most important were their personal qualities. Both were deeply committed to helping the school become a more humane system, and during the diagnostic phase of the intervention had shown considerable talent in doing so. The second set of qualifications pertained to their organizational roles. The role of assistant headmaster, effectively the number two person in the school, symbolized access and possession of considerable influence in the school. The role of chaplain symbolized the values of care, concern, support, and aid with personal crises. Moreover, both men were highly committed to developing their roles in non-traditional ways. Assistant-headmaster-as-change-agent and chaplain-as-change-agent were emphases that blended very well with the personal inclinations of the two incumbents. Each man participated in off-site training through N.T.L. programs and engaged in regular consultation with a team of external consultants.

For some kinds of interventions the internal consulting pair worked alone. One particularly successful intervention consisted of their designing an activity to help reduce the amount of harrassment that first year students received from upper classmen. In planning this intervention, the internal change agents consulted with the external consultants, but the actual change effort was fully carried out by the two internal consultants. Measurements taken by the external consultants two years later showed that the interventions had had their desired consequences. Harrassment of new students had decreased. For other kinds of interventions, the internal and external consultants worked together. One of the more difficult interventions centered around understanding and changing the roles of senior class officers, who had school-wide responsibility for rule enforcing, rule changing, and penalty setting. Over several years a number of interventions were attempted with this group. Most were partially, but never fully, successful. Usually the internal and external consultants worked together in planning and executing these activities.

*The Public Utility.* In the public utility, two levels of natural functional groups were identified as intervention targets. The first consisted of units headed by upper middle managers, people who typically reported to corporate officers. The second type of unit were those headed by second level managers, those who supervised the lowest ranking management positions. There were a number of reasons for selecting these units for intervention. First, the senior internal consultant believed that these were the units around which "work was organized." Second, the levels directly above the upper middle managers and directly below the second level managers had long been sources of difficulty. The very top executives had been the target of several previous unsuccessful OD attempts and were skeptical of behavioral science as a whole. Foremen, classically people caught in the middle, were long the target of company training programs. Most people had rather mixed feelings about the outcomes of these efforts. The senior internal consultant reasoned that the corporate group might be most readily persuaded to consider OD technology if subordinates reported constructive outcomes from their involvement. Third, the senior internal consultant was an organizational peer of these managers. As a consequence he knew most of the people and was respected and trusted by a significant number. The professional triad in the public utility consisted of a senior internal consultant, six junior internal consultants, and several external consultants. The senior internal consultant had occupied several key management positions in the organization prior to entering OD work, and he was viewed by many in the organization as one of the more successful managers. Prior to making a full-time commitment to OD work, he had utilized behavioral science consultation as a line manager and had had a central role in the implementation of several innovations in the system, both technical (a new set of hardware) and social (a corporate wide program in MBO).

On entering his new assignment, the senior OD consultant took a number of key actions. He worked to increase his own self-understanding and capacity for self study by attending a number of laboratory education programs, and took part in a number of one-on-one sessions with the external consultant. He developed an extensive reading program in the applied and general behavioral sciences. Simultaneously with these activities, he began to recompose the existing internal OD group which had long suffered from a poor corporate reputation. Several members of the old group were transferred to new assignments, one man was promoted, and several new people were brought into the group. The senior internal consultant also began a series of presentations to upper middle managers throughout the corporation in which he outlined an extensive plan for organization development throughout the company. These talks brought a number of opportunities for entry, and as these were developed junior internal consultants were assigned to be project managers. The projects were developed through consultation with the relevant line managers, a junior internal consultant, and the senior internal consultant. As of this writing, a number of the projects have begun to bear fruit, although it is too early in the total program to have done the kind of evaluation that was possible in the boarding school.

*Conclusion*

I believe that it takes power, empathic support, and well formed theoretical ideas to bring about constructive organizational change. The complementary professional triad offers one approach for utilizing these resources. It recognizes that people occupy different organizational roles, participate in different occupational histories, have different primary needs and abilities and therefore have different essential contributions to make to the complex and challenging processes of organizational change. If we can explicitly recognize these differences and tolerate the pain of our personal incompleteness, we can begin to join the differences, not in the collusive rising of futile expectations, but in the hard work of changing human systems to be more rationale and more humane.

## REFERENCES

Argyris, Chris, *Management and Organizational Development.* New York, McGraw-Hill, 1971.

Egan, Gerald, *Encounter.* Belmont, California, Brooks/Cole, 1970.

Harvey, Jerry B. and Sheldon A. Davis, "Some differences between laboratory and nonlaboratory organizations: implications for group trainers who desire to be organization development consultants." In Dyer, W. G. (Ed), *Modern Theory and Method in Group Training.* New York, Van Nostrand Reinhold Company, 1972.

Watzlawick, Paul, Janet H. Beavin, and Don. D. Jackson, *Pragmatics of Human Communication.* New York, W.W. Norton, 1967.

# Section II

# Development of Individuals
# in the Client System

The two chapters in this section represent very different examples of the rapidly growing array of technologies being developed for helping individuals to plan their futures, learn skills, develop personally or as managers. The chapters each represent major trends of interest to OD practitioners: individuals' taking responsibility for their own development and the increasing occurrence of people entering second and third careers.

In Chapter 6, Roger Harrison presents a new training design which is based on the assumption that managers (and consultants), have been exposed to external pressures on how to behave, how to feel, and so on, to the extent that many no longer receive messages from themselves on these dimensions. The design provides a large quantity of varied learning resources (tapes, books, papers . . .the "training" staff...) geared to the population in training (e.g. management skills, OD trainees). Participants are asked to organize themselves for learning and to use the materials as they see fit. Harrison provides a case study to illustrate the design and follows this with an explication of the theoretical and philosophical base for the design.

Doug Brynildsen (Chapter 7) draws heavily on the motivation work of McClelland to support his interest in helping people plan their career development paths or new careers. He describes the development of two kinds of career planning workshops which have been successful at TRW Systems, and discusses how these fit into their broader OD programs.

# Developing Autonomy, Initiative and Risk-Taking through a Laboratory Design

*ROGER HARRISON*

The scene is a fifteenth century castle converted into a hotel standing in the midst of rolling countryside somewhere in Northern Europe. The characters are twenty middle managers, about half line and half of them staff, and two behavioural scientists. The time is a Sunday evening, the opening session of a Laboratory in Initiative and Autonomy. The first behavioural scientist is speaking.

"Most of us, most of the time are so bombarded with expectations, demands and influence attempts of others that it often becomes very difficult to hear messages from *inside* about what *we* would like to do, how we think the job ought to be done, what experiences *we* think would be interesting, exciting and good for our own growth. In most management development courses it's the same: we're exposed to a lot of pressure to be more sensitive to people, or more rational in our approaches to planning, to be more receptive or more proactive, and in general to follow out someone else's formula for managerial success. Everyone seems to have a slogan, a package or a formula they want to use to change our behaviour, our values, our styles.

"In contrast, this laboratory is an exercise in finding your own interests, strengths, and paths to growth and development. We don't believe there is one right way to do any job as complex as the ones you hold, not least because you all have different strengths, motivations, backgrounds. We believe neither that managers are born nor that they are made; on the contrary we think that in large part they create themselves. This laboratory will provide, we hope, a week of open time and a wide variety of resources for you to do just that. We hope that by Friday you may have a clearer idea as to some of the ways in which you would like to grow and develop and that you will have learned quite a lot about how to explore and use the environment actively to further your own growth.

"In order to facilitate listening to yourself we will place as few restrictions on you as we possibly can. In fact, the only required activity in this laboratory is a two hour meeting from four to six each afternoon for which you will be divided into two groups of ten, each meeting with one of us. These meetings are obligatory, and in them you will be expected to share with others what you have been doing. The meetings are a chance for the staff to keep in touch with everyone in the lab, and we hope that they will also be an opportunity for you to learn from one another's experiences, help each other to make best use of the learning resources here, and to deal with any of the issues which arise between you and the staff.

"There are no times which are arbitrarily assigned to work or to free time. The time is all free for you to use in your own best interests: to work, to play, to contemplate, to be responsible or irresponsible. Unfortunately, the hotel management are not as flexible as we are: The hours between which various meals can be taken are posted over there on a flip chart. So far as *we* are concerned, the only requirement that you be anywhere or do anything in particular is the two hour daily meeting.

"Before our meeting began those of you who were wandering about will have noticed that this main conference room is stocked with a large variety of learning resources. In selecting them we have tried to offer as many options as possible as to learning processes. What they all have in common, however, is that they have been selected to enrich your thinking, experiencing and understanding of yourself as a person, in relationship to other people, and in your role as a manager. On the table over there are various diagnostic instruments which you can use to assess your own management style, your blocks or difficulties in creative problem solving, your preference for one or another learning process, your dominant motives and so on. Across the room there is a collection of books and articles. We have included writings about behavioural sciences in management, humourous and serious observations on organisational life, messages on how to achieve fulfilment and personal growth, and even some fairly subversive writings about how to change organisations from the inside. The library doesn't necessarily reflect our views about what is true, good, or right; it does, however, represent our choice as to what is interesting, significant or worth thinking about.

"You will have noticed that we have also provided a variety of games and exercises. Some of these are standard management training and group dynamics exercises where we have run off all the materials you need to conduct the exercise. Others are handbooks or manuals of exercises which you may want to thumb through and try out. We have also selected a variety of psychological games which we think you may find interesting, and we have on hand some tape recorded instructions which allow you to conduct group and interpersonal learning activities without staff assistance. Lastly, we have provided a set of exercises called the Blocks to Creativity which permit you to explore in a self directed way fourteen different barriers to personal productivity and creativity, and hopefully to overcome these to some extent.

"This array of materials is far more than enough for anyone to cover during the week, and we hope you will be as selective as we have been wide ranging in choosing it. In order to give you a good start in exploring these materials we have made four lists of activities which we believe to be interesting and useful. These are posted on the walls. We suggest that between now and the beginning of the meeting at four tomorrow afternoon you complete at least one exercise from each of the four lists. There is one list of diagnostic exercies, things you can do to assess your styles, skills, or to uncover some difficulties you may have. There is one list of exercises which can be done alone, another for two person exercises, and a third consisting of learning activities which require a small group. It is part of your training in initiative that once having decided on a two person or small group exercise, you are responsible for recruiting from amongst the participants the other people required to carry out the learning activity. If you get really stuck, you will usually find that one of the staff will be glad to join in.

"In exploring the resources of the laboratory, you will find it important not to overlook those of the other participants and of the staff: That is, the human resources which are here. In any collection such as ours there is a vast array of experience and talent which can be of use to all of us in our own learning and problem solving. The problem is to find out what is there through taking initiatives to get to know the others and interact with them in various settings. As staff, we will take some responsibility for making our resources more readily available. We will try to respond to any request for help, information or even advice, and we will initiate conversations with you about your activities and learning experiences when that seems to be appropriate. We do not intend to be passive observers of the scene, but rather active participants in it. We expect initiatives from ourselves as well as from you, but if our work is to be of most use to you it had best be shaped by the actions you take towards us.

"That's about all we have to say for now. We will be glad to answer questions from those of you who feel the need for clarification; for those who don't I suggest you get started with one or another of the suggested learning activities on the four lists."

The group breaks up. Some wander a bit aimlessly about the room looking at the materials; others study the lists of suggested activities, and some ask questions of the staff about them. Gradually most of the participants find something to do: Some go off towards their rooms purposefully clutching stacks of material; others drift off to the bar to discuss this new experience....

*The scene shifts to 10:30 the next morning.* One participant is deep in conversation with a staff member who had observed that he looked a bit lost and had asked him how things were going. The problem, a common one, is that the participant has been unable to articulate any learning needs which he could see as related to any of the materials offered. The staff member is questioning him deeply about his work and career aspirations and will end by making several concrete suggestions as to diagnostic instruments or learning activities in which he might engage.

Several members are sitting about the room working on the "Personal Inventory" which is the diagnostic instrument for the Blocks to Creativity. They will identify three or four "Blocks" such as Fear of Failure, Reluctance to Let Go, Frustration Avoidance, Impoverished Fantasy Life, or Reluctance to Exert Influence. They will then take a workbook for each of the Blocks they have decided they would like to work on. Each workbook contains about a dozen exercises designed to increase awareness of the Block and provide practice in overcoming it. The exercises use a variety of media and materials. Some can be done alone, while others require a pair or a small group of people.

Other participants are not in evidence at the moment and may be in their rooms, walking in the grounds of the castle or on some errand in the village. For the most part, it appears that people are working alone. There are a couple of pairs, but they seem to be composed of people who have known each other previously. A few initiatives have been taken towards the staff to ask for information about materials, but the participants have so far treated each other rather gingerly.

*Four o'clock Monday afternoon.* In the small group meetings the staff members issue a questionnaire asking participants to rate the level of their own risk taking so far, write down the number of initiatives they have taken towards others, and estimate the proportion of time they have been truly autonomous (i.e. doing what *they* really wanted to do, rather than simply following custom, or the influence of staff and other participants, or doing what they felt their home organisation would expect them to do in this kind of learning situation). Each participant is also asked to rate his involvement in the laboratory at this moment, as well as the degree of positive or negative feelings he has about it.

These results are then tabulated and posted and discussed by the group at some length. One group is rather divided in their ratings. Some members are highly involved and see themselves as exercising a fair degree of autonomy and beginning to take some initiatives (though not so many as they would like to). Others are completely "turned off." They complain variously that they don't see the relevance of this kind of education to their work; that the materials seem disorganised and difficult to use; that when they try exercises in the Blocks to Creativity they "don't feel anything;" that even if they do learn to exercise autonomy and initiative in the laboratory, they will have little opportunity to do so in their jobs back home; and so on. The most aggressively outspoken and articulate of the "dissidents" is a former military officer now Operations Manager for a large international trucking firm. The main burden of his message is that the staff should clarify the precise objectives to be achieved in the course and should set up and conduct those activities required to reach those objectives. He is strongly supported by other members of the group and equally strongly attacked by several others who claim that he has missed the whole point of the laboratory and wishes not only to give up his own freedom but to regiment everyone else at the same time. The issues are hotly debated but are no closer to resolution at the end of the meeting than they were at the beginning.

During the meeting the staff member remarks that most of the learning activity that he has seen going on was individual or in pairs and asks the group members to explore some of the inhibitions and barriers which prevent them from approaching others and initiating activities with them. There is some fairly open sharing around this issue. The staff member also points out that the staff are willing to suggest and if necessary conduct as highly structured learning activities as the participants desire, and that if those who are experiencing a lack of direction and purpose will approach him, he will be glad to make some specific suggestions for learning activity. One or two of the participants visibly brighten at that, but the Operations Manager is not mollified. What *he* thinks the organisers should do is to establish a clear set of objectives for the course and conduct learning activities that are clearly related to these objectives. That is their job, not that of the participants.

*Moving ahead to Wednesday afternoon*, the scene has changed considerably. The main conference room where the materials are kept has a dishevelled, used look with books, articles and test papers scattered about where participants have left them. A group of four are gathered around the table playing a game of Executive Decision, a management game which emphasises judgement and risk taking in buying and selling. Another group are in a corner rolling dice. They are playing a new game invented by one of the staff members on the inspiration of Rhinehart's "The Dice Man." It is an anti-decision making game in which players experiment with how it feels to give up control of their behaviour to blind chance for an hour or two. Each of the players has listed several activities which he thinks he ought to or might like to engage in during the afternoon and they are rolling dice to see which ones they will actually carry out. The game is designed particularly for people who underuse or inhibit their own playful and creative impulses by an overemphasis on efficiency, planning and "making every minute count." At the conclusion of the dice rolling one member goes off to get the hotel's vacuum cleaner and begins to clean and straighten up the main conference room; another goes out to the back of the castle to make a sketch of an erotic bas relief set into the wall there; a third takes a book and goes to his room to read; and the fourth goes off to arrange a talk with one of the laboratory participants with whom he has spoken very little because his initial impressions of him were rather unfavourable.

Another group are having an encounter session in one of the smaller rooms. They are using a tape recorded set of instructions to guide their activities. They have had one session already, have become very enthusiastic about this (to them) new way of learning and getting closer to others, and the members are developing a certain elitist and clique-ish attitude towards themselves.

There remain some who are working as individuals or in pairs. Two or three have developed rather well articulated self development plans using the Blocks to Creativity package. The Operations

Manager is still aggressively skeptical, and although he does not resist attempts to involve him in the activities of others, he initiates none himself and professes himself to be unaffected by those in which he does participate. Another, sadder, case is presented by a middle aged bureaucrat who is simply bewildered by the proceedings. On enquiry by the staff member who has been working with him, it has developed that when he was offered a chance to attend the laboratory by his Personnel Officer he agreed without questioning what kind of a training course it was to be. Asked why, he replied that "if the company asked me to go to the seashore to dig holes in the sand for a week with all expenses paid, I'd go just for the holiday." With no objectives of his own and no daily routine to march to from morning rising to bedtime at night, he seems a rather pathetic figure. He reads a bit, walks occasionally in the countryside, but only really comes to life in the late evening in the bar. Other participants are gentle with him and invite him to join in their activities, but occasionally a little contempt shows through.

*The scene on Friday (the last day)* presents some marked contrasts. The high tide of group activity having been passed on Wednesday and Thursday, many of the participants are back to individual and pair activities. There is a renewed interest in the Blocks to Creativity and in some of the diagnostic tests. Those who are still working in groups are mostly engaged in some kind of life and career planning exercise which is intended as a bridge between the laboratory and the back home situation. Some are using a closed circuit video tape recorder which was brought in on Thursday to "see themselves as others see them" in face-to-face situations. Others are taking a renewed interest in the library materials with an eye to acquiring copies for their own use.

The closing session of one of the ten person groups proves a serious, hardworking learning experience rather than the expected round of farewells and testimonials. Instead, the group works intensively on exploring the difficulty they have had in using the resources of the staff member during the laboratory. Earlier, there had been a confrontation between some group members who asked that the obligatory afternoon sessions be shortened, and the staff member who was unwilling to do so; this had occurred on Tuesday afternoon. The staff member had subsequently felt left out and underused, while some of the participants had been determined to "show him" that they were competent to carry out their learning without his help. There now takes place an exploration of the role of authority in learning and some attempts to generalise this back to the organisations from which the participants have come. Participants try to think of ways to help themselves to maintain their new-found autonomy in a situation where authority will at best be neutral to their efforts. Deeply involved as the members are in these issues, the meeting goes overtime and eventually breaks up on a rather thoughtful and serious note.

These vignettes from actual training sessions illustrate the range of issues and activities in a cluster of training designs so new that they have not yet acquired a generally accepted name. Under various titles ("Motivation Laboratory," "Laboratory in Initiative and Autonomy," "Creativity Workshops") the basic design has now to my knowledge been used with upwards of 215 participants in some thirteen separate educational events conducted in five different countries (Belgium, England, Ireland, Netherlands and the United States).* The basic design and philosophy of the laboratories is described above in the opening remarks to the participants by the staff member. The content of the learning materials may vary quite widely, depending on the educational purpose of the event and the background of the participants. The duration of the laboratories has varied from three days to seven, with five or five and a half seeming about the most effective compromise between the ideal and the practical. Of the laboratories with which I am familiar, eleven have been judged by staff and participants to be very successful and two have been seen by the staff as failures. This is not to say that in some of the successful ones there were not individuals like the two described above who probably would have spent their time better elsewhere, or that in the failures there were not some people who felt they profited greatly from the experience. I would generally consider an experience a "success" if the community develops an *autonomous learning process* and this usually occurs somewhere in the middle of the laboratory if it is to happen at all. One recognises that an autonomous learning process has developed in the community when he begins to find it hard to discover participants who need a helping hand in finding something interesting or productive to do. At such a point, the staff member begins to feel a bit useless and out of things and can take a certain melancholy satisfaction in his loneliness in realising that things are now going well for the most part, and are largely out of his hands anyway.

* November 1972

The educational design which is the subject of this paper bears some resemblance and owes considerable debt to the work of others. Particularly notable are Richard Byrd's "Creative Risk Taking Laboratory;" "The Organisation Laboratory" developed by Jerry Harvey, Barry Oshry and Goodwin Watson; and the "Laboratory with Flexible Structures" created by Max Pages and his associates in Paris. The design which I have been using for what I shall here call the Laboratory in Autonomy, Initiative and Risk Taking, however, grew out of collaboration between Jacques Mareschal of IBM Belgium and myself during the winter of 1970-'71. My interest in new experience based learning designs came out of my rather unsatisfactory experience in conducting T groups with British and European Managers. The groups I conducted seldom seemed to develop a great deal of depth or involvement on the part of the participants, and they seemed to require an inordinate amount of energy and skill on the part of the staff in order to make them go at all. After a lot of thought upon the possible causes of these difficulties (and choosing to discard along the way the quite plausible hypothesis that I just wasn't very skillful with such groups) I concluded that possibly the differences I experienced between American and European T-groups had something to do with cultural differences in existential issues.

This mouthful of words means that I had decided that the problems or "hang-ups" which most deeply disturbed European Managers were different from the ones that were bothering the Americans I had worked with, and this difference was somehow a cause of their responses to sensitivity training. American managers seemed to me, by contrast with their British and European counterparts, to be rather more lonely and alienated, more disturbed in their family relationships, hungrier for a missing depth and intimacy in interpersonal relationships generally, and more willing to expose themselves and take personal risks to achieve rapid and satisfying connection with others. The European managers, on the other hand, seemed less geographically and socially mobile than the Americans, and they were much more likely to have worked with the same company all their professional lives. They frequently lived close to their own and their wives' parents, and they were much less often transferred between departments within their firms. They were thus securely embedded in a matrix of organisational, family and community relationships which appeared to meet their relationship needs much better than was true for most of the Americans. At the same time, the Europeans paid for their stability with a sense of immobilisation, entrapment and a degree of impotence within their organisations. They seemed more often dissatisfied with the amount of authority and responsibility they had, and they were more likely to express themselves in defeatist terms about the possibilities of initiating and carrying out change and innovation. To a person in such a situation, a group may be less a source of needed intimacy and acceptance, but rather may have the function of encapsulating the individual and frustrating his individual growth and development. In my thinking about the problem I began to look for an experience-based educational method which would not require the building of a cohesive group for its success and which would focus instead upon the development of individual creativity, initiative and action.

With my like minded colleage Jacques Mareschal, the first such laboratory was developed and conducted for a group of middle managers in Belgium in June, 1971. This first laboratory was called a "Motivation Laboratory" because we had the idea that it was necessary for a man to first understand his own needs and motives, those most basic wellsprings of energy and activity, before he could take in hand his own personal development and growth. I do not use this original term any more because it does not communicate very well to the public; but I still agree with this original principle.

The "Laboratory in Initiative, Autonomy and Risk Taking" (my current name for the experience) is too new to have been evaluated by research, and so it must be assessed at this time according to other criteria. I propose to do this by considering the method as an attempt to put into practice a number of principles or theories about learning, some of which are generally accepted and others about which there may be more controversy. I shall not rely heavily on the perceptions of staff and participants in judging the success of these laboratories, even though this is probably the basis on which the acceptance of the innovation and its use by others will depend.

The first principle against which I should like to compare the laboratory is a motivational one. *Effective training designs make maximum use of the learner's own internal motives, values, interests and "felt needs."* They facilitate the channelling of the learner's own motivation into productive learning activities. They use a minimum amount of energy on the part of the teacher or learner in overcoming "resistances" and in blocking or opposing the expression of the learner's needs. *Needed control of the learner's behaviour is*

*accomplished by positive incentives and rewards, rather than by*
*negative coercion.*

The Laboratory in Initiative, Autonomy and Risk Taking is designed to be consonant with these motivational principles, and this is one of its greatest assets. It is also a source of its greatest vulnerability. On the positive side, the learner is presented with an opportunity to follow his own interests and values wherever they may take him. The design effort is largely devoted to trying to provide materials which will be experienced by participants as interesting, useful and rewarding. The message intended to be conveyed by staff-participant interactions is well summed up by the phrase, "try it, you'll like it." Throughout the laboratory experience, a kind of high order operant conditioning appears to occur, as participants undertake activities on their own, find them rewarding, and are thereby encouraged to higher levels of independant activity and initiative. By providing a wide variety of materials, it is intended that the "felt needs" of each participant will find some outlet or connection in what has been designed to be a rich and responsive environment.

As I experience these laboratories they are the least coercive of any educational experiences which I have conducted or in which I have taken part as a participant. In this regard they come rather close to the principle of using internal motivation which I have set forth in two previous papers (Harrison, 1969, 1970). But this lack of coercion is also the Achilles Heel of the method. By contrast with the coercive and norm setting power of the small group and/or the charismatic leader in many other experiential learning methods (T-groups, Synanon, encounter groups and so on), the Laboratory in Initiative, Autonomy and Risk Taking has little to fence the learner in to the learning situation. Thus it is difficult to ensure that the participant will make initial responses which will prove rewarding and so develop a continuing increase in the desired learning behaviour. This appears in fact to have been the problem with the two groups we considered failures. In both cases the participants had not made a truly voluntary choice to attend such a laboratory. In one case it was part of a three month training package for middle managers, and in the other the participants had originally applied to come to a more traditional sensitivity training laboratory. In a number of the other, more successful programmes, there have been individuals who were sent by their organisations more or less without reference to their own wishes, who found little to generate enthusiasm in the programme, and who opted out of the action for most or all of the laboratory experience.

I have come to deal with the problem of ensuring that the participants have an initial experience of a variety of the learning materials by the lists of options which are given as assignments during the first day of the laboratory. This seems to provide needed support (or, less euphemistically, control) and participants generally respond well to it. But the method remains extremely sensitive to voluntarism and internal commitment of the learner, and this is reflected in strongly worded statements in my brochures about who should and should not come and how they should be recruited.

The second design principle against which to assess the Laboratory in Initiative, Autonomy and Risk Taking has to do with the individuation of learning. *The ideal design should permit the individual to spend time and effort on different learning activities which are appropriate to his background and preparation, his rate and style of learning, and the use which it is projected he will make of the material to be learned.* There are really two lines of reasoning involved in this principle. One is that ideally each individual should have a programme of learning tailormade to his own needs. He should be able to go into great depth on some matters which are new to him or which are likely to be particularly useful in his work or outside life, and he should be able to avoid or deal superficially with other matters in which he may be well prepared or which are irrelevant to his interests and needs.

He should be able also to choose and use his strengths as a learner. Some people learn better through concrete experience, others through abstract conceptualisation, and so on (see Kolb, et. al, 1971). While it is desirable that an individual be stretched to strengthen those learning processes which he does not use effectively, I think that people learn most effectively when they are not blocked from using those styles with which they are most comfortable. Thus, the totally experiential learning design puts formidable barriers in the way of a person who learns most effectively through abstract conceptualisation, just as a formal lecture and reading course is quite difficult for a person who learns through active experimentation to use and apply in his daily life. The learning resources gathered together to stock a learning laboratory in initiative and autonomy can easily be designed to offer a wide range of learning *processes* to participants so that individuals can both use those processes at which they are adept, and gain increased skill in those with which they are less comfortable.

The second major philosophical theme in this emphasis on individualising learning is the concept of *equifinality* in learning and problem solving. One of the best examples of the concept is in Management by Objectives. The basic idea is that once a goal has been clearly established and accepted, each individual should be free to find his own best means and paths to that goal, using his unique talents and strengths to achieve success. This is in contrast to the explicit philosophy of scientific management that there is one best way to do each job. In Management by Objectives a great deal more *trust* is placed in the capacity of the individual to attain goals without explicit programming regarding the precise steps or paths to be taken. The laboratory in initiative and autonomy makes a similar assumption about the individual as a learner and problem solver, trusting him to find the best combination of activities to his own goals, but providing him with opportunities for consultation and access to the resources of others. In carrying out this process the participant is *learning how to learn*. That is, he is learning how to establish and clarify his own learning goals and to explore the environment for resources useful in attaining the goals. In my opinion, the Laboratory in Initiative, Autonomy and Risk Taking goes a long way towards actualising the promise of learning how to learn which was often made but seldom kept by the early proponents of T-groups and sensitivity training. It was difficult for the sensitivity trainers to keep this promise because learning in the T-group depends upon the creation and utilisation of a highly specialised learning environment and technology for which the trainer's skills are very central if not indispensable. This is much less true in the Laboratory in Initiative, Autonomy and Risk Taking where the individual is encouraged to create his own learning programme individually, using materials which are available in the environment and depending upon himself to build those relationships with others which are required to utilise them effectively.

The third learning principle by which I like to assess designs has to do with the management of anxiety and stress. *The confrontation and resulting amount of anxiety and stress should be maintained for each individual at the level where he is stimulated to explore, experiment and learn in an active fashion, and it should not be permitted to rise to the point where he becomes immobilised or where his normal ways of coping become so ineffective that he regresses to earlier and less effective behaviour patterns* (Harrison, 1965, 1970). Maintaining the appropriate level of stress and confrontation has been a perennial problem in experiential learning, particularly in sensitivity training and encounter groups. When working with a small group the problem becomes almost impossibly complicated by the obvious fact that the appropriate level for one person may be too much or too little for another. Since cohesive groups tend to develop group norms about stress (e.g., they can be "deep" groups or relatively more cognitive and "talky" in their process) all the members tend to be exposed to the same fairly narrow range of confrontation. This sometimes results in psychological damage to weaker members of the group or in the opposite phenomenon of an entire group staying pretty much on the surface to protect one fragile member.

In the Laboratory in Initiative, Autonomy and Risk Taking the potentially high stress of a learning experience which is very unstructured in time, space and direction of activity is balanced by the opportunity for the individual to have access to learning activities which are very non-confronting. For example, it is not uncommon to see members who are having difficulty with the lack of structure spending a good deal of time with books and articles until they gain more confidence and are able to use more active exercises. We also find that the more adventurous, emotionally stronger participants are likely to be the first to use such potentially threatening materials as the Group Therapy Game and the Encountertapes. When the safety of this new territory has been explored and established, other members may feel free to join in, but there are always those who never take part in such exercises (and these are usually those who appear to the staff not to be so "eager" as the others).

We also find that people often choose a cycle of confrontation and withdrawal for themselves which seems to make a rather sensible rhythm of stress and recovery. Of course, groups can be observed to do this as well, but the cycle does not necessarily meet the needs of all the individual members.

It is, of course, possible that if the individual is left to seek his own level of confrontation he will tend to operate at one which produces less than the maximum possible learning. In my experience with these laboratories this seems rarely to be the case where the individual is strongly motivated to learn. What I have been impressed with, is the way in which the level of confrontation tends to be maintained by the individual at a level where his learning seems to be *integratable*. That is, most people seem to choose those experiences which take them on from where they are in a series of steps rather than in a great leap forward or "break-through."

Perhaps it is only a matter of personal values, but I think that a programme which is self moderated in level of stress in this way is not only safer for the individual but probably results in a higher degree of retained and usable learning than more dramatic methods. At any rate, I do feel that one of the major advantages of the self-directed learning design is the opportunity it presents for self-control of confrontation and stress. It is certainly true that in my experience with this design, I have seldom had cause to be concerned about the effects of psychological stress on individual participants. I could not make a similar statement regarding my experiences with sensitivity training.

When I get to about this point in the exposition of the Laboratory in Initiative, Autonomy and Risk Taking to colleagues or clients they are likely to raise a potentially embarrassing question. "It all sounds very good and quite effective" they say, "but of what real use is it likely to be? How many organisations do you know in the current economic climate who want to train their managers to be autonomous? The whole thing has a very anarchistic ring." Even those who see very readily the utility of this training to organisation improvement usually say that as far as they can see the market is far from ready for it.

Constrained as I am to making my living from my consulting and educating activities, I find this kind of feedback rather depressing. However, I don't quite agree with it. It seems to me that on the contrary the laboratory design which I have described in this paper and the many variations upon it which are possible have modest but substantial prospects for the short term, and an extremely bright future in the longer term. Where my skeptical friends and clients are right is in suggesting that this particular laboratory design has not much to offer in educating managers to perform roles or parts of roles which are essentially bureaucratic in structure and process.

Traditional management development is education for bureaucracy. It teaches the individual to look outside himself for the solutions to problems and for guidelines to action. These are amply provided by the bureaucracy in the form of job definitions, organisation charts, procedural specifications and the like.

However, bureacracy is under increasing stress from within and without. Donald Schon (1971) has very persuasively made the case in

"Beyond the Stable State" that the increasing rate of change in society, technology and in the marketplace means that bureaucratic organisations must increasingly give way to organisations which function as learning systems. And learning organisations require learning managers. The days when a highly centralised management could control or even adequately predict its environment are, I think, numbered. Attempts to deal with crisis by recentralisation and increasing tight controls from the top will in the long run give way to movements towards building more flexible, internally committed organisations which adapt, innovate and change themselves more rapidly than could have been thought possible in the old style bureaucracy. The essential processes in such an active learning system seems to be as follows:

1. Goal directedness: An awareness of own goals and the mobilisation of energy towards them;

2. Active exploration of the environment and of one's own resources, leading to an increased awareness of alternative means to goals;

3. Action upon the environment;

4. The search for feedback, for knowledge of results, and the use of such information to modify action.

In order for organisations to function as learning systems in this way it is necessary that managers be adept in the use of such processes, and this is indeed what the Laboratory in Initiative, Autonomy and Risk Taking is all about. No matter what the content of the learning resources which have been provided (and they could run the gamut from human relations to economics and production control), the self-directed learning process remains the same.

Even now, at a time when economic and social difficulties are being dealt with by an attempt to increase control and direction from the top in most private and public organisations, there are parts of each of these organisations which either are, or have a strong need to be, non-bureaucratic in their structure and functioning. These are the parts which are in contact with the rapidly shifting "turbulent" aspects of the environment, whether these be scientific and technological areas, marketing and purchasing functions, or social and governmental forces. Managers in these parts of organisations have a current and pressing need to become effective and autonomous learners.

There is also a growing category of managers who are given important job responsibilities which are essentially non-bureaucratic or perhaps anti-bureaucratic in nature. These are jobs which require one to function outside of normal channels of communication, to exercise influence without authority, and often to operate in the spaces between more traditional and highly structured subunits of the organisation. These are managers who may find themselves in coordinating and liaison work, in project management, in many kinds of technical staff work, and in organisational change roles. They too have a need for a high degree of autonomy, initiative and risk taking in learning and in working with the individuals and units with which they interact in the organisation. These people need today the kinds of education which our design makes possible in a number of content fields, and it is my hope that tomorrow they will be the ones who will help organisations find ways to change themselves from bureaucracies to learning systems.

Whether or not one shares my somewhat gloomy prediction regarding the viability of bureaucracy in the medium to long term, there is another way of looking at the initiative and autonomy design which I believe worthy of careful study by those concerned with management education (or indeed, with higher education generally). I believe that almost any *applied* subject can be adapted with profit to the same basic design that I have used in the laboratories described here.

Managers usually go to courses because they want to learn something related to their work. Typically, the educator makes some guess as to what sort of work situations most of the managers are in and selects from among the things he knows those which he feels it would be good for them to learn. The success rate of these guesses does not appear to be very high. I believe the success of such courses in providing real help to managers could be dramatically improved if the resources were presented in a format similar to the design described above.

First, the manager entering the course would need to go through some sort of diagnostic procedure which would have to be carefully designed to relate the content of the course to his own difficulties, problems, opportunities or responsibilities in his job. The preparation of such diagnostic material is not familiar to most management educators and would probably be the most difficult phase of the course redesign. Such a task does not, however, seem to me to present any very formidable technical obstacles.

Resources for the course would be made available on a random access basis to the participants. These might include materials in a variety of media: books, articles, case studies, audio or video tape recorded lectures and the educator himself. The diagnostic excercise would refer participants to particular learning resources according to the type and level of problem they presented, and the instructor would also serve as a guide to help match participant needs to learning resources. Participants could, as in the Laboratory in Initiative, Autonomy and Risk Taking, be formed into mutual help and learning groups which would exchange information about resources and perhaps assist one another in applying learning experiences in the course to individual back home problems.

Although there would doubtless be a proportion of managers who might find this kind of learning design a bit difficult to get used to and to use effectively, it is my guess that the prospective students are more ready for the design than the educators are to give it to them. Partly, this is a matter of developing the requisite technical and interpersonal skills to design and carry out such a learning experience; but perhaps more fundamentally, it is a question of the personal needs for control and participation on the part of the educator, and of his level of preferred risk taking and trust in the participants. Once a self-directed learning activity is launched, there may be very little for the educator to do. He needs to be available in case his expertise is required, but most of the time the participants are doing alright by themselves, and one feels distinctly redundant. Since many of us derive a good deal of the satisfaction that we have in education from the dependence of the students upon ourselves, this can be a rather depriving experience for some educators.

The same applies to the control of the learning process. In fact, we do not control the *learning* process in most management education, but we do control the *activities* and the materials to which participants are exposed. In a self-directed design, however, this control is given up at the outset and cannot be regained without a tremendous loss of confidence on the part of the participants, and loss of face on the part of the educator. This does mean that self directed education can be a rather risky business. If one gives up the responsibility to participants for determining their own activities, and if they are not motivated to take it over, it is possible to have a very uncomfortable situation in which no one has the power to make anything happen. I have experienced this in the two events which I classified as failures above, and it was anything but pleasant. Thus the educator must be willing to take more risks than he is normally used to in order to experiment with and perfect a self directed learning design in his own subject matter area. One is always more highly criticised for an experiment which fails than for carrying on a more traditional process which is boring and ineffective.

The above *caveats* to the contrary notwithstanding, I have considerable confidence that these methods will produce significant increases in the relevance and effectiveness of educational activities even in subject matter outside of the behavioral sciences. To me they offer the possibility of an educational process which uses the latest and most modern available educational technology and is at the same time personalised and in the best sense of the word humanistic in its emphasis upon the capacity of the individual to manage his own learning and growth.

# REFERENCES

Harrison, R. "Defenses and the Need to Know." In Lawrence, P.R. Seiler, J. A., et al. *Organizational Behavior and Administration.* Homewood, Illinois, Irwin Dorsey, 1965.

Harrison, R. "A Design Primer." In Runkel, P., Harrison, R., and Runkel, M., *The Changing College Classroom.* San Francisco, Jossey-Bass, 1969.

Harrison, R. "Choosing the Depth of Organizational Intervention." *The Journal of Applied Behavioral Science,* 6, 2, 181-202, 1970.

Kolb, D. A., Rubin, I. M., and McIntyre, J. M., *Organizational Psychology: An Experiential Approach.* Englewood Cliffs, New Jersey, Prentice-Hall, 1971.

Schon, D., *Beyond the Stable State.* London, Temple Smith, 1971.

# 7

# Motivation and Individual
# Career Achievement

*R. DOUGLAS BRYNILDSEN*

While the main intent of the paper is to describe two different and successful individual career workshops, it is important to understand the role of motivation in the achievement of one's goals. The first section will deal with the issues of motivation and motives, the second section will briefly describe the situational variables affecting motivation, and the last will concentrate on the application of those principles to individual career achievement. Most of the first two sections is my interpretation of David McClelland and his associates. I want to acknowledge McClelland's contribution and his extensive research here rather than refer to him throughout the paper.

## Motivation and Motives

Motivation is defined as "motive+situation." The situation refers to such variables as the job requirements, management style, climate, and the customer set. It is the *interaction* of these variables with the motives which *results* in the *motivation* and behavior. In one sense Organization Development is an attempt to make the variables more congruent so that each is supportive and facilitative of the other. Most OD efforts have started with the job requirements, climate, style, and in some cases, even the customer set. The work of Herzberg and others in job enrichment are attempts to change the job to provide more intrinsic satisfaction by providing opportunities to fulfill the achievement motive. McGregor, Likert, Litwin and others have done significant work in the area of climate. Blake, Tannenbaum, Shepard and others have been concerned with style and its impact on productivity and individual growth. The interaction of these key variables creates the situation, a concept very consistent with the work of Kurt Lewin (see Figure 1). The purpose here is to explore the variables of individual motives, a key to career achievement.

Motives are defined as a toned thought network. They are a network of thoughts in our heads which are value laden. It is as if our

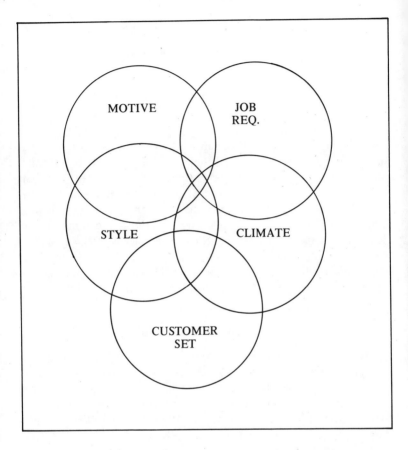

FIGURE 1

*Motivation = Motive + Situation*

mind consists of a series of clusters with links connecting them. The larger the cluster, the more "motive strength" that exists and the more tendency there will be to behave based on that motive. The less the "motive strength," the more the situation will affect the resultant motivation and behavior. Although there are many motives, those which have major impact on our organizational behavior are Achievement (N-Ach), Power (N-Pow), and Affiliation (N-Aff). It is in this area that much of McClelland's work has been done, with emphasis on the N-Ach motive. Each of these motives has a different set of thoughts within the cluster and therefore tends to create different behaviors.

Three factors virtually determine our motive network. The first factor is our *family values* and behaviors. The second is the *cultural values* (the myths, traditions, media, etc.). The last is the *opportunity structure* within the environment. Essentially, the opportunity structure provides the vehicles which can channel the motives. An extreme and simplified case would be the black-white situation. Let's say two black parents valued and behaved in achievement ways. Their son believes in these values and ways of behaving, goes to the marketplace, and finds out that there is no opportunity. This inconsistency tends to weaken the N-Ach motive and after several attempts may have the effect of depressing this motive.

Since motivation starts in the head, the mind basically controls our energy output. We each have almost unlimited amounts of energy. If one can find out how this energy is channeled in terms of the various motives, he can change the energy flow, change the way he thinks and, with a supportive environment, change his behavior.

## The Achievement Motive

The cluster of thoughts within the N-Ach motive revolve around a goal of success which requires excellent or improved performance. This kind of thinking gets translated into pictures or images, since we think in an imagery shorthand. That is, the overriding set of thoughts within this network cluster are concern for excellence. This concern for excellence has four sub-areas which account for the achievement imagery. The first is self-imposed standards of excellence. The person with high N-Ach has a built in standard of excellence which is quite high. From my experience, it's high enough to produce guilt or anxiety about not completing a task up to that standard. The second imagery is in terms of outperforming others—achievers enjoy winning. Imagery around accomplishment, the third area, refers to the thoughts around innovation, creativity and producing something unique. Last, there is a concern around advancing one's career. Therefore, the individual with high N-Ach would have a cluster of thoughts around the above areas. The greater the N-Ach motive strength, the more an individual's thoughts will revolve around these areas, and the more predictable his behavior will be because of this imagery.

This way of thinking results in certain behavioral characteristics. Individuals high in N-Ach have self-confidence and want personal responsibility for tasks they perform. They tend not to like groups, committees, task forces and so on, unless the individuals in these groups are highly relevant to the task. In a group, it's difficult to take personal responsibility and be personally accountable for results. They tend to use and seek expert help, but are not prone to work in an environment where it's difficult to take personal responsibility. High achievers want and require immediate feedback on their performance. They want to know how they're doing so they can improve and meet their self-imposed standard of excellence. The need for feedback helps to explain why many high achievers become entrepreneurs or salesmen. The feedback is built-in, as contrasted to a college professor or researchers, who have less need for such feedback and typically have lower needs for achievement. High achievers will establish challenging goals involving moderate risks. They dislike high risks or risks where they are not in control of the outcome. This explains why you don't see these individuals gambling. There is little or no control over the outcome in gambling. Moderate risk-taking is the key for the high achiever. He doesn't want to fail, but doesn't want a non-challenge, either. Money does not motivate the high achievers. They will work just as hard without the money incentive; in fact, money can produce tension among achievers. These individuals take pride in their accomplishments, and tend to be restless and innovative in establishing new goals and pursuing other accomplishments. There is a quality of impatience which surrounds many of these characteristics. This impatience changes to one being highly critical and judgemental of others (occasionally obnoxious) if the N-Ach is too high. At times overly high N-Ach people are so task-oriented they are "bores."

These characteristics, as well as others, briefly describe an individual with high N-Ach. Career implications will be discussed later, but it is important to visualize career fields where this motive is so critical for success. A few such careers are executives, entrepreneurs, and salesmen.

## The Affiliation Motive

The affiliation motive consists of a very different set of thoughts, images, and concerns than the achievement motive. The overall imagery of this motive is being with others and enjoying mutual friendship. There is high value placed around family associations and much activity takes place within the family and the social context. There is a concern around being liked and accepted. For many with high N-Aff, criticism of performance is viewed as total personal rejection. Conflict, therefore, is not perceived as a potentially growthful experience. The second kind of imagery is around separation. There is a dislike for separation, isolation, and of being alone. These individuals need others and continually want assurance of others' affection and love. The last major concern for affiliation imagery is image consciousness in social setting. Image consciousness is a way of preserving friendship and not creating undo attention to the possibility of being rejected or separated from others.

For many managerial jobs, the affiliation motive is highly critical. Thinking of others and being with and enjoying others is important for jobs requiring a lot of interfacing and coordination with others—a kind of integrating manager. It's also a key motive for many of the helping professions and some staff jobs in organizations; jobs where a premium is placed on people, teamwork, trust and concern.

*The Power Motive*

The power motive is a key to change and managerial effectiveness. The primary goals and imagery are around having impact or influence on others. It is not necessarily a need to control or manipulate, but rather a thought cluster concerned with influencing others to pursue their own ends of some superordinate goals. The first impact concern is around arousing strong positive or negative feelings in others. Individuals high in N-Pow don't like neutral reactions from others; there's no impact being created. They tend to be concerned about and think in terms of powerful actions. Such individuals want to influence others and, in fact, will provide unsolicited advice, will encourage conflict, will think in terms of debates and arguments and behave in ways which tend to result in impact or influence. Generally, there is an imagery concern for reputation or position, which is another way to have impact. Individuals high in N-Pow tend to want the organizational indications of status, prestige, and position. While the power motive is another critical dimension to management and effectiveness, to have too much can result in being very structured, bureaucratic, and non-spontaneous. The power motive is highly relevant for careers requiring impact or influence such as key executives, peace corps personnel, OD people, community development individuals and the like.

It must be understood that each motive or combination of motives can result in success and effectiveness. One is no better than the other. It depends on the way they're used, the kind of job one has, and the kind of organization and life one wants to have. Organizational effectiveness requires individuals with different motive profiles and the ability to integrate the thinking and behaviors of such individuals with the task to be accomplished.

*Changing Motives*

Programs in the area of motive change have been primarily concerned with the Achievement motive. While there have been programs to increase N-Aff and N-Pow, most of the work and research to date concentrates on increasing N-Ach. Several studies have stressed the importance of N-Ach for economic success. Others have demonstrated the potential for changing the "motive strength" of this motive. Much of McClelland's work relates the N-Ach motive to the economic growth of countries. In fact, the broad appearance of the N-Ach motive within the people of a country generally precedes the economic growth of that country by about 50 years. One of many studies indicating the importance of N-Ach to organizational success was conducted in Mexico. Motive analysis was conducted on the top executives from successful and unsuccessful companies. It was found that executives from the successful companies had far higher N-Ach scores than the less successful group. The differential was so great that the top N-Ach score for the unsuccessful company executives approximated the bottom scores for the successful company executives.

While there have been many motive change studies, two stand out as especially significant. The first involved the "India Project." With a control group of businessmen who experienced N-Ach motivation training, data were collected over a period of time. After two years, businessmen who experienced the motivation training had started up more new businesses, reinvested more capital, had larger percentage increases in the gross income of their firms, and employed more new people than the control group. (McClelland and Winter, p. 209-230.)

A study at Harvard produced similar results. High potential managers were randomly selected to attend two kinds of training programs. About one half attended a four week management development training course and the other half a ten day motivation program. Again, after two years, an analysis of results was undertaken. The group experiencing the motivation training received promotions and increases of ten percent or more at a rate significantly greater than the control group. (Aronoff and Litwin, p. 224.)

There are many other similar studies. One point which must be remembered, however, is the importance of the situation. If an individual changes his motive levels and returns to a non-supportive environment or an environment lacking in opportunity structure, the new ways of thinking and behaving will tend to diminish over time. Again it is the interaction of the situation and motives which produces the motivation and behaviors.

### A Brief Look at the Situational Variable

This section provides a brief discussion of the situational variables and their impact on motives.

One situational variable that affects organizations is the prevailing attitude set of the major customer(s). For example, if one is dealing primarily with NASA and the Department of Defense, as contrasted with a small commercial firm, the impact is quite different. The captive commercial customer may play a far less impactful role. Another factor regarding the customer is the perception and set of expectations by management regarding the customer.

While the customer can affect certain segments of the organization, the job requirements affect every individual within the system. Any given set of job requirements tends to arouse or stifle certain motives; they directly contribute to the motivation of each of us. In fact, much of the work in job enrichment and job design is an attempt to change the nature of the job to increase opportunities for satisfaction of the achievement motive. Especially at lower organizational levels, opportunities for such arousals are limited. Often, the individuals have more N-Ach "motive strength" than the job has opportunities to satisfy. Therefore, changing the job to include more "motivators" and a chance to satisfy achievement needs has produced significant results throughout the world.

The obvious need is to become skillful at matching individual motives with the motive opportunities in the job requirements. Different jobs have opportunities for arousing and satisfying any or all of the motives. All of us have seen cases where we've taken cases of high performing achievers and made them into managers requiring a high degree of interface and collaboration. The result all too often is the same; the individual is unsatisfied and the job is not satisfactorily performed. The critical need, therefore, is to understand the job requirements and the individual well enough to match these two key factors. Not all people want to achieve, have influence on others or be with others. Again it is the matching process or the process of change to provide some matching which results in increased individual satisfaction and organizational effectiveness. Figure 2 describes some of the essential job requirements for arousing and satisfying each motive.

Just as job requirements provide opportunities for arousing and satisfying different motives, so does the management style of the supervisor and the climate in which we work. The supervisor's management style and the climate norms impact on our motive profiles and behaviors. Different styles and norms arouse different motives. Figure 3 is a summary of some style and climate norms and their effect on arousing different motives.

The above discussion is intended to provide a basic knowledge of the impact of the situation on the motives. For further discussion, the interested reader is referred to the reserach by McClelland and Winter. To reiterate, the stronger the motive strength, the less the situation will affect resultant motivation and vice-versa.

### Application to Career Achievement

There are two different career workshops being conducted for personnel at TRW Systems Group: the Career Achievement

---

N-Ach
- End results of work
- High standards
- Opportunity for Creativity

N-Aff
- Expected to help others
- Opportunity to talk and joke
- Cooperation required

N-Pow
- Managing People
- Others come for decisions
- Make certain things run smoothly

---

FIGURE 2

*Job Requirements for Motive Arousal*

| Style and Climate | Motive Arousal |
|---|---|
| Conformity-constraints, rules, policies, procedures | Power |
| Responsibility-delegation of responsibility and authority | Achievement primarily, also power |
| Rewards-recognition and rewards for good work, not punishment | All three |
| Organizational Clarity—things organized, not confused or chaotic | Achievement (power under stress) |
| Tcam Spirit-Warm, trusting, good relationships | Affiliation |

FIGURE 3

*Norms and Motive Arousal*

Workshop and the Career Assessment and Achievement Workshop. The workshops recognize all the above mentioned motivation variables, but concentration is on the areas of motives and job requirements. The need for achievement is stressed in both programs. The attempt is not necessarily to create high achievers (since that motive is only critical for persons in certain career fields), but rather to help individuals understand the achievement motive and use it to become effective in planning, goal-setting, and moderate risk-taking. It is this motive which is so critical to one's becoming able to be proactive about achieving his career goals. The overall thrust is to match up motive profiles with career fields. Before discussing the Career Achievement Workshop in detail, let's take a look at presentations of successful motive profiles of different career fields as portrayed in Figure 4.

*The Career Achievement Workshop*

Socio-economic conditions which result in individuals being concerned about their careers currently prevail in many organizations, including the TRW Systems Group. While personal and career development have been a significant part of the TRW culture, the aerospace decline has resulted in a tremendous need to

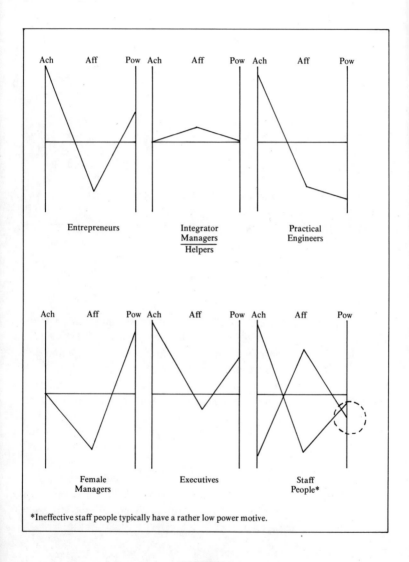

FIGURE 4

*Occupational Profiles*

develop career programs and philosophies that help the organization and individuals effectively manage these changes. To find oneself in a static condition after many years of growth is frustrating, and people don't like it. More and more, they are asking (1) Where am I going? (2) How do I get there? Management's key concern is how to utilize the strengths and motivations of individuals for maximum organizational productivity. Obviously both sets of concerns are highly interrelated. The Career Achievement Program was designed to cope with these individual and organizational career concerns. In the initial pilot programs, participants were volunteers (minorities, including women) from the Industrial Relations organization. As part of the Industrial Relations Affirmative Action Program, a memo describing the workshop and the nomination/selection process was distributed to all I. R. minorities (including women). Only women nominated themselves to attend. Twelve participants were selected for each workshop on a first come, first served basis. After the pilot workshops, they were conducted for men and women both inside and outside of Industrial Relations.

*Career Development Assumptions*

The leaders of the workshop thought it essential that the participants seriously consider four assumptions:

1. Career development is *primarily* an individual responsibility,
2. *Multiple* careers help to keep career options open,
3. Building from an individual's *strength* lessens career risk,
4. *Motivations* can be changed.

TRW's philosophy always has been that "career development is *primarily* the individual's responsibility." There have never been obvious professional  career ladders, management assessment processes, and so on. Major responsibility is on the  individual's shoulders and it's mostly up to him to advance his career in ways that make sense for him.

*Multiple* careers and *building* on *strengths* are biases of the workshop leaders. As we see it, most individuals have tremendous reservoirs of unused energy, unexplored interests and avocations not fully exploited. This energy and unused talent could be applied to develop multiple jobs or careers, a primary way for keeping career options open. With a greater number of available alternatives, individuals feel more in control of their destinies, more proactive about their careers, more fulfilled and can use more of their strengths for organizational ends without feeling bored or un-challenged.

*Building from strength* sounds simple. Unfortunately, it's a different thinking and behavior mode than most of us are used to. We have been trained and educated to spend much of our time and energy concentrating on overcoming our weaknesses, not on understanding and creatively utilizing our strengths and uniqueness. Building from strength enables one to expand his/her uniqueness, to behave with more self-confidence and self-esteem and to take more prudent risks.

*Motivations* can be changed. This principle has been demonstrated by David McClelland over many years of research and experimentation. Understanding one's motives and deciding on the most beneficial pattern is of paramount importance for one's work and life satisfactions.

## Learning to Take Risks

We have had ample experience in putting together various kinds of career programs; however, we lacked a training vehicle to encourage individuals to take more moderate risks. Risk-taking is fundamental to goal-attainment and career satisfaction. After exploring various learning models, we decided to use the Need for Achievement (N-Ach) concepts of David McClelland as discussed above. Individuals need a basic understanding of these three motives and the situational variables and need to make choices as to the kind of motive pattern and situation they desire.

Simplified, the motivation training process follows several steps:

1. The individual gains a greater understanding of some basic types of motives (achievement, power, affiliation);

2. A model of the high achiever is provided;

3. The individual decides what parts of his motive pattern, if any, he wants to change; and,

4. Practice is provided to help individuals think and behave in ways more consistent with a motive pattern the individual desires.

## Workshop Design and Process

The Career Achievement Workshop process was designed to meet the following objectives:

1. To assist individuals in exploring career alternatives,

2. To increase motivation to achieve career goals.

The process included prework, an orientation meeting, and a two and one-half day workshop, all geared toward attaining the above objectives.

## Prework

"Imagination Exercise." Participants were asked to write stories based on six different pictures. The Motivation Research Group, a Division of the Behavioral Science Center of Sterling Institute, scored the stories for the motives (achievement, affiliation, power). Each individual motive profile also contained subcomponents which form the overall motive.

## Orientation Meeting

About ten days prior to the workshop, an orientation meeting was held to distribute and discuss additional prework and to discuss the forthcoming workshop in detail. The additional prework consisted of:

1. *Strong Vocational Interest Blank*—The key elements from the "Strong" are the interests and occupational choices inventory. The Strong is perhaps the most reliable interest inventory available. Its prime use in the workshop is to expand career options, help individuals think about second careers, and explore interest combinations for career achievement.

2. *Strength Deployment Inventory (SDI)*—The SDI is a tool used to help individuals better understand their behaviors, values, and life styles. Each style has several strengths and the skill is to build on those strengths for designing a career which achieves optimum satisfaction.

3. *Career Focus*—A set of questionnaire exercises was designed to assist individuals think through the kind of career they *want* to have as opposed to what they think it will be. The set consists of the following exercises:

| | |
|---|---|
| *Career Review:* | This exercise provides an opportunity to review the individual's past career(s) or job(s) by listing key reasons he liked the job(s), the strong points the job(s) brought out in him, judging his successes on this job(s) and so on. |
| *Career Integration:* | This projection questionnaire gives the individual an opportunity to look at |

*Freedom:*

different aspects of his "ideal" career in one year, and then again in three years, as to income, responsibilities, exciting aspects, learnings, and roadblocks.

If you had the freedom to do the things you wanted, what would you do if you had one hour, one day, one week, one year? This gives the individual a better understanding of himself which he can then integrate into his career choice(s) to achieve the fullest personal satisfaction from his career. Hopefully, there would be some relation between Freedom and Career Integration. Large discrepancies indicate a lack of "being together."

*Career Focus:*

After completing the above exercise, this section is intended to help the individual focus on the career(s) he wants to pursue. Using the classified ads and other information sources, each individual is to create his own career direction, describe his uniqueness, and clearly indicate why that career choice is right for him.

4. *Readings*—Reading material by McClelland and others was distributed and discussed. These readings provided participants with an understanding of the motivation processes in the workshop.

## Workshop

The workshop had a quick pace and a climate of strength, openness, concern, and inquiry. The pace and climate contributed to the continual build-up of excitement, enthusiasm, and eagerness to pursue meaningful career directions. The following briefly covers some of the workshop elements that may not be clear from the agenda or previous discussion.

● *Ring Toss Exercise.* In this game, each individual had the choice of how far to stand from the peg and make ringers. The game has three rounds. Feedback was given to each participant as to his risk level and how he learns from feedback. Behavioral comparisons were made between high and low risk takers, especially in the area of learning from feedback.

- *Imagination Exercise Feedback.* Individual scores from the Imagination stories were distributed and discussed. These individual profiles, rating each person's need for achievement, affiliation, and power, were extremely enlightening to all the participants, and for some, it clarified their feelings toward their jobs. The subcomponent scores were especially useful. They provided individuals the specific areas to change their thinking if they wanted to adjust their overall motive profiles.

- *Business Game.* The game consisted of building several kinds of paper structures. This gave participants another look at their achievement behaviors, their ability to take risks, and behavioral comparisons between moderate, high and low risk takers. This game gives individuals feedback on their planning skills as well as a better understanding of high versus moderate risk taking.

- *Storywriting.* The storywriting is practice in thinking in ways each individual wants to change. Participants used these practices to help them think differently in areas important to them as revealed through the motive profiles and SDI analysis. One storywriting exercise was on the business game and another on their "ideal" careers. Dyads were then formed, stories shared, and feedback received from the other participants on their clarity and understanding of their motive processes. While most participants wanted to increase areas of N-Ach, some selected N-Aff, and several chose to strengthen their N-Pow. Participants also tested their understanding of the three motives by using a practice scoring for imagery exercise.

- *Work Analysis Questionnaire.* This questionnaire rated each participant's motives on his present job. The results were then compared to his personal motive profile and discussion held on what to do about discrepancies. As a result, individuals explored alternative ways to satisfy their needs by: a) changing nature of present job, b) changing careers.

- *Career Information Sources.* Lectures were given on career opportunities inside TRW Systems as well as the wealth of information on other careers, available in the library. Inputs also were provided on manpower projections inside TRW, TRW's career development philosophy, future career trends, and career projections of growing career fields. Emphasis was placed on the wealth of information provided by the Department of Labor and other agencies concerned with careers of the future.

● *Career Goal-Setting.* By this time, all the participants had a good understanding of the opportunity structure (job marketplace), a self-profile, and had a fairly clear notion of the career direction(s) they wanted to pursue. The task was now to operationalize these career aspirations into short and long range goals and action plans. As a result, each participant developed a "career roadmap." This career roadmap also included a plan to cope with potential obstacles to career goal attainment. Needless to say, this part of the workshop had high impact and value to the participant. Goals and plans were periodically tested in dyads to insure that individual "roadmaps" were clear, precise, believable, achievable, and moderately risky.

## Results and Implications

An evaluation questionnaire was sent out to the participants two weeks after the workshop. A follow-up meeting was held after three months. The responses received from the questionnaire and the follow-up sessions were overwhelmingly positive. Of the 65 male and female participants, about 85% were still focused on their career "roadmaps" and were still motivated to accomplish the goals and subgoals. A few participants had replanned their schedules because of "world blocks" (circumstances), but most were still involved in taking moderate risks to accomplish career goals and subgoals and felt optimistic about goal attainment. One fifth of the first two groups of participants received promotions within eight months after the workshop. Others had career discussions with their supervisors resulting in job restructuring; some took on additional challenging projects; still others developed second (or multiple) careers. All discussed their career plans with their supervisors and received encouragement. All participants had maintained their keen interest in setting and accomplishing career goals. Quotes expressing this attitude are:

"I know what I need to do. Now I feel like doing it instead of just thinking about it."

"Primarily, I needed the motivation to pursue my interests which I tend to place in the background in lieu of necessary things."

"Now I have started to set goals which I must reach before I am able to continue to the next plateau of goals."

"Now I have stronger motivation to accomplish my goals."

"I now have a specific action plan."

"I have accomplished all my short term goals. Only thing I have yet to do is enroll at UCLA. Supervisor very helpful. I am actively involved in project."

"I have purchased equipment to make jewelry at home and am still taking coures."

"After exploration, I have realized that environmental design is my strength, not interior decorating. I am slowly overcoming my reluctance to ask for help from others."

"Yes, motivation to achieve. Instead of saying I'd like to return to college . . . I've enrolled nights rather than waiting another year."

When the participants were asked what they had gained from the workshop, the one statement most frequently made was that they were setting realistic goals. Other frequently mentioned points included the feeling of being motivated to go ahead with their goals, an increase in self-understanding and insight into their motivation and behavior patterns.

The results of the program surpassed our expectations. Not only has the individual moved significantly toward achieving his career aspirations, but there are clear indications that productivity has increased, boss-subordinate relationships have improved, better matching between individuals and tasks has occurred and "good will" of employees has increased. Many of the workshop tools and concepts have been utilized in team-building and other OD activities. Managers and others seem to readily understand the motivation processes and other diagnostic tools, see direct relevance of these understandings to their staff and peers and are more receptive to change in their style and relationships with others.

## The Career Assessment and Achievement Workshop

This workshop basically integrates management assessment processes with the career achievement processes described previously. Participants were high potential managers having supportive environments and who wanted to commit significant time and energy to their career development. In this sense, it is a more organizationally relevant program with the potential for organiza-

**DAY I**

| | |
|---|---|
| 1:00 - 1:15 | Introduction |
| 1:15 - 2:30 | Ring Toss Exercise |
| 2:30 - 3:30 | Lecturette, Film, Discussion |
| 3:30 - 5:00 | A Deep Look at N-ACH |
| 5:00 - 5:30 | Review N-AFF and N-POW |
| | (1) Indicate extreme sub scores |
| | (2) Indicate behavior manifestations |

**DAY II**

| | |
|---|---|
| 8:00 - 8:15 | Introduction |
| 8:15 - 9:45 | Strong Analysis |
| 9:45 - 10:00 | Break |
| 10:00 - 11:30 | SDI and Career Implications |
| 11:30 - 12:00 | DYADS (Integrate Data into Career Focus) |
| 12:00 - 1:15 | Lunch |
| 1:15 - 1:45 | Practice Scoring for Imagery |
| 1:45 - 4:15 | Business Game |
| 4:15 - 5:00 | Write an 11 Point Story on the Business Game (Exchange and Score) |
| 5:00 - 6:00 | Write an 11 Point Story on your Ideal Career (Exchange and Share Reactions) |
| 6:00 - 6:15 | Close |
| | Homework—First draft at operationalizing ideal career |

**DAY III**

| | |
|---|---|
| 8:00 - 8:15 | Introduction |
| 8:15 - 9:00 | Work Analysis Questionnaire |
| 9:00 - 10:00 | Internal Career Alternatives |
| 10:00 - 10:40 | Career Information Sources |
| 10:40 - 11:00 | Career Direction |
| 11:00 - 12:00 | Sharing in DYADS |
| 12:00 - 1:00 | Lunch |
| 1:00 - 1:15 | Goal-Setting Lecture |
| 1:15 - 2:00 | Individual Career Goal-Setting |
| 2:00 - 2:30 | Testing in DYADS |
| 2:30 - 3:00 | Recycle Goals & Plans |
| 3:00 - 4:00 | Testing in DYADS |
| 4:00 - 4:30 | Total Group Sharing |
| 4:30 - 5:00 | Close/Critique |

FIGURE 5

*Career Achievement Workshop*

*Agenda*

tion impact being very high. The career assumptions are identical to the Career Achievement Workshop while the objectives are more complex:

1. To provide a diagnosis of each participant's strengths and areas needing improvement, helping him to better manage his career.
2. To train line managers in diagnostic and developmental procedures through highly involving procedures.
3. To provide a validation experience for performance perceptions of relevant organization members and provide a vehicle for meaningful career discussions.
4. To assist individuals in exploring career alternatives which optimize strengths.
5. To increase individual sense of responsibility for career growth and increase motivation to attain career goals.

The basic design incorporated many of the concepts and tools utilized by assessment centers. It is the integration of the management assessment, the developmental orientations, and the motivation training which I feel excited about and see tremendous potential for individuals and organizations.

The CAAW consists of prework, orientation meetings and a four day workshop. The first two days of the workshop consisted of somewhat typical assessment processes (in-basket interviews and simulations). One-to-one observation by senior management personnel was used for this segment of the workshop. The management assessment dimensions are: administration and planning, motivation, interpersonal relations, intellectual ability, emotional maturity and leadership.

This management assessment and other diagnostic tools (such as the Strong, LIFO, FIRO-B, motive profile, career report and career prework) provide each individual with a rather complete individual profile. Based upon the strengths of the profile, each individual explored career alternatives. After deciding on a career(s) which optimized strengths, motivation training was provided to help individuals achieve their career goals. As in the Career Achievement Workshop, a thorough career goal-setting process operationalized the proactive stance towards careers the participants had learned. Rather than describe the program in detail, the highlights are summarized:

1. The one-to-one observation by senior management has been highly useful for participants and themselves. Senior managers have developed a new way of looking at career development,

have learned how to use new diagnostic tools and have incorporated many of the learnings and tools in their own organization.

2. Participants, many for the first time, received a thorough management assessment. It is primarily the strengths in the assessment which are used to help individuals optimize their career direction.

3. Identical results regarding increased motivation, being "turned on," having meaningful career direction and increased productivity have been attained as in the Career Achievement Workshop.

4. The program has resulted in several OD applications by participants, staff and Industrial Relations Personnel. Many individuals would not get involved in OD activities prior to this experience. They now had *a set of tools and a framework* which made sense to them and they were eager to have follow-up with their organizational units.

5. The follow-up discussions between the participants, staff member, participant's boss and boss' boss have proved highly useful for the individual and the organization. Comments such as these are typical: "This is the best assessment I've ever seen—it should replace our appraisal system," "What's happened to you to get you so turned on," "I've always wanted to have career discussions with my people, but always felt uncomfortable—now we have vehicles to do this."

Participants in the CAAW were from first and second level management positions. Future workshops will have staff and participants who have been promoted within the last year above the first level of management. This criteria should maximize organizational payoff. Critiques by staff and participants indicated the workshop should remain four days with very minor design changes. The one major change is with the staff. The staff felt that it should be required to take all tests and exercises and have special training sessions conducted just for them. In the past, it was encouraged, but not required.

Results from both career programs clearly indicate their success in terms of achieving the objectives as well as several serendipitous effects. In fact, results from the CAAW surpassed results from the Career Achievement Workshop. However, these results and the motivation processes described previously generate a multitude of questions for the OD practitioner. Some of these are:

- Should individuals attend career development programs prior to other kinds of training activities?
- Should we do a more thorough analysis of job requirements and individual motive profiles prior to filling a given job?
- How can these career processes be used for career development within work teams?
- How can we analyze the task well enough to maximize the individuals and the motives required to most effectively complete the task?
- What combinations of motive profiles produce what kind of change?
- Are there differences in the motivational profiles in growth times vs. non-growth times? Should there be?
- If rewards for good work arouse all motives, don't we need more innovative and immediate reward systems?
- Many of the workshop tools are useful for organization diagnosis and team-building. What other OD applications are there?

These are just some of the questions generated from the career programs. The McClelland framework is also highly useful as an OD framework and the implications for OD are fantastic. Perhaps with more understanding, experimentation, and research, this framework may well provide a truly organic OD orientation, making it easier to implement effective planned change.

## REFERENCES

Aronoff, Joel, and Litwin, George H., "Achievement Motivation Training and Executive Advancement". *The Journal of Applied Behavioral Science,* Vol. 7 Number 2, 1971.

Litwin, George H. and Siebrecht, Adrienne, *Integrators and Entrepreneurs,* McBer and Company, copyright.

Litwin, George H. and Stringer, Robert A., Jr. *Motivation and Organizational Climate,* Division of Research Graduate School of Business Administration, Boston: Harvard University, 1968.

McBer and Company, *Summary Research Report on the Characteristics of Successful Businesswomen in the Radio-Television Industry,* Copyright, April 1971.

McClelland, David C., "Achievement Motivation Can Be Developed". *Harvard Business Review,* November/December 1965.

McClelland, David C. and Winter, David G., *Motivating Economic Achievement,* New York: The Free Press, 1969.

McClelland, David C., "That Urge to Achieve", *Think,* November-December, 1966.

McClelland, David C., *The Achieving Society,* New York: The Free Press, 1961.

McClelland, David C., "The Two Faces of Power". *Journal of International Affairs,* Vol. XXIV, No. 1, 1970.

Timmons, Jeffry A., "Black is Beautiful—Is It Bountiful?". *Harvard Business Review,* November/December, 1971.

# Section III

# Client System Technologies

Section III deals with what many practitioners consider to be the heart of OD - technologies and interventions for working with client systems. The unique aspect of this section is that nearly all of the work describes departures from the contemporary OD "routine" (data feedback, teambuilding and so on) and takes work with client systems into new and fruitful areas. As with most of the chapters in this book, the work in this section is strongly based on the development and application of theories relevant to OD.

Perhaps the most radical departure from what we have learned to refer to as OD is the first chapter in the section by Jim Foltz, Jerry Harvey and JoAnne McLaughlin. Their presentation is primarily a case review of a long term project in which OD is viewed as a line responsibility of management rather than as a series of intervention technologies performed by an OD staff. In addition, effective OD is viewed as being guided by a comprehensive theory developed and implemented by the management of the organization with advisory consultation being provided by a streamlined OD staff. A final major departure from traditional OD is that the writers advocate the authentic use of power by management as opposed to the more usual push for management by participation and consensus.

In Chapter 9, Marvin Weisbord describes his work with a complex medical center which is similar to the preceding chapter to the extent it is also a case study where the client members carry the responsibility for implementing the OD effort. In this case, however, Weisbord provides the comprehensive theory—an adaptation of the Lawrence and Lorsch research regarding appropriate levels of differentiation and integration in a complex setting where management and medical staff simultaneously must wear many different organizational hats. This case is an exceptionally good example of how research findings, to the extent that they are available, can be used to guide an OD effort.

Chapter 10, by Warner Burke, is a detailed description of an intergroup conflict management workshop. Burke wonders why more intergroup conflict interventions are not being used by practitioners and assumes that the major reason is that most practitioners do not know how to design them. Following from this assumption, he details a step by step design of an intergroup intervention, using case materials to illustrate each of the steps.

Lee Bolman (Chapter 12) agrees with Vaill's earlier chapter that there is a necessary interdependence between theory and OD effectiveness. He also is in agreement with the Foltz, et.al., chapter that the client should be helped to build his own theories of effective performance. Moving from the premise that OD practitioners can be of little help to his client's theory building efforts if his own are rudimentary or unarticulated, Bolman develops a technique for theory building which will help both clients and their consultants gain an awareness of the incongruities between their espoused theories and the ways in which they actually behave. With this awareness, greater congruity can be achieved.

The final chapter in this section, by Crockett, Gaertner, Dufur and White is one of the few reports published to date of a serious research evaluation of a large scale OD effort. The findings of the study have provided the organization with strong support to continue the expansion of its OD projects.

# 8

# Organization Development:
# A Line Management Function*

*JAMES A. FOLTZ*

*JERRY B. HARVEY*

*JOANNE McLAUGHLIN*

Organization Development is a line management function. It is not the responsibility of staff specialists. In fact, if OD becomes a staff function, it is doomed to be peripheral to the essential activities of the organization. Or, from the perspective of Bion (1959) it becomes a manifestation of the "pairing" basic assumption whereby a subgroup breaks off from the major group and searches for a messiah—with the same consequence. If a messiah is found, in the form of an idea or a person, he (or she or it) gets crucified. And if a messiah is not found, the subgroup (in this case the OD staff specialists) are basically irrelevant since they are operating, by definition, outside the mainstream of the organization and its central activities. In short, both theoretically and pragmatically, OD has to be a line activity. If it is not, it has no more impact on the basic functioning of an organization than a fundamentalist tent revival has on the operation of the Vatican.

The purposes of this paper are threefold. First, we intend to describe the OD process which was developed at The JJJ** Company headquarters in a metropolitan area of the eastern U.S. In our description we shall identify the five "essential" conditions which we feel must be present for any OD process to be successful. Second, we shall discuss the results of implementing the five "essential" conditions at JJJ in both human and economic terms. And finally,

* Appreciation is expressed to Dr. Vladimir Dupre, and Dr. Steve Ruma for their help in developing the content of the article.

** A pseudonym. The JJJ Company is in the food processing distribution business. It has gross sales of approximately 350 million dollars and employs approximately 7,500 workers.

we shall summarize the "generalizations" we feel are applicable to the practice of the OD "art" regardless of the organization, its structure or its purpose.

## The Essential Conditions

For OD to be successful in any organization, five essential conditions must be met. In brief, OD must:

1) respond directly to important organization problems;
2) be governed by a comprehensive theory which has utility for solving those problems;
3) be an extension of the chief executive officer (CEO);
4) involve the authentic use of power by all managers in the organization; and
5) be supported by an OD staff competent to provide "Socratic Consultation" assistance.

Each of these conditions will be discussed in detail in the following pages. In addition, the way they were met in the process at JJJ will be described as a means of illustrating their essentiality.

## I. The OD Process Must Respond to Important Organization Problems

Another positive way of saying it is that the process must be directly relevant to solving problems which are important to line managers. Or, the principle can be stated negatively as follows: OD must respond to the "felt" needs of the line and not the "felt" needs of the OD staff specialists.

At JJJ, the potential for responding to line organization problems was, to understate the case, considerable. For example, in July, 1970 a new President was appointed and he identified the following organization conditions which were amenable to improvement:

An extemely low level of profitability. Net profit after tax (NPAT) and return on assets (ROA) were considerably below both the prevailing norms for the industry and the expectations of management, including both "higher" corporate management and the management of JJJ.

A lack of basic managerial control over the business, the symptoms of which were:

— inventory levels were greater than acceptable;
— inventory control accountability was inadequately pin-pointed;*
— out-of-stock situations occurred at an alarming frequency and resulted in reduced sales and poor customer relations;
— accountability for the integration of sales and marketing was unclear and confused by an organization structure which made coordination of the two functions difficult, if not impossible;
— the pricing administration function was neglected;
— professional management of human resources, that is, career planning, training, and so on, was non-existent;
— headquarters personnel function neglected, to a considerable extent, the field locations;
— zero attention was given to the behavioral aspects of the organization;
— the nature of the interface with "upstairs" corporate staff was unclear;
— no adequate organization existed for the new product development function, in spite of the fact that long-term survival depended upon that function's being performed effectively;
— low productivity occurred at all levels of the organization;
— the system of cost control was inadequate;
— leadership patterns throughout the organization were essentially "passive" or "laissez faire;"
— counterproductive norms, including many which supported intergroup competition and compartmentalization, prevailed in areas where collaboration was required;
— minimal communication occurred at all levels of the organization;
— the minority hiring program was ineffective;
— management evidenced minimal concern for social responsibility;

---

* As some concrete evidence of this point, the President was unable to determine who or which Division(s) (was, were) responsible for inventories. When he attempted to "pinpoint" responsibility, he found more than ten people from several Divisions who felt they had primary responsibility for the inventory control function.

— and finally, perhaps the greatest problem was organization inertia; personnel were unwilling to make decisions and take actions for fear of contributing to the on-going failure of the organization.

Obviously, there was no lack of problems for an OD process to respond to. What was lacking was an OD process.

As a first step in developing such a process, the President determined the priority and sequence of actions he wanted to take. To assist him in implementing these actions, he appointed a Vice President of Organization (VPO) and gave him the following charge:

1) Identify the needs for *strategic business planning* and *policy development* in all areas of the business (not just the personnel function);

2) Develop an action plan for meeting those needs;

3) Develop, with the direct involvement of the President, an organization structure which would:

   a) Clarify the lines of authority and communication;
   b) Provide for the coordination and integration of the various functions of the business, e.g., sales, manufacturing and controllers;
   c) Insure that all important accountabilities were assigned either to individuals or teams;
   d) Insure that there were no "overlapping" accountabilities.

4) Whatever action plans are developed must take into account the impact of behavioral factors in the process of change.

The President's intent was to "revolutionize" the business and make it an effective* organization within two years.**

---

* Effectiveness was defined in terms of profitability, morale and contribution to the community. See the discussion of the "OD Wheel" for a more comprehensive treatment of this point.
** The "turn-around" time proved to be approximately eighteen months, a period significantly shorter than the five to six years assumed by most other OD approaches.

After considering the various dilemmas, they decided that the problem of organization structure should be attacked first since changes in that area would have both the greatest visibility and the greatest human and financial impact on the organization.

However, as they started to change the structure, they quickly discovered the interrelatedness of the various elements of the organization. For instance, a change in structure inevitably involved changes in strategic business planning, policy development, behavioral norms and administrative mechanisms. In addition, they realized that, though they understood the scope of the problems and the approach they wished to use in solving them, most other key managers in the organization did not. It also looked as if the President and VPO had a greater commitment to solving the problems than many other key managers. In fact, evidence was surfacing that some managers in the organization were both passively and actively resisting the changes which the President and VPO were trying to implement. Stated differently, change was not a part of the mores of the organization. Any change was seen as risky, because of the fear that it might result in failure and failure could no longer be tolerated.

The President and VPO realized that the organization—themselves included—was inundated with problems, changes and opportunities which threatened to crescendo into chaos at a time when the organization needed a consistent, shared, coordinated approach to solving its problems. In trying to respond to such an array of difficulties, the President and VPO gradually identified a number of organization elements which required attention and specific improvement activities. They also became aware that changing organization structure was no more critical than dealing effectively with many other dimensions of the organization such as strategy, policy and norms. In short, change of such magnitude and complexity required a conceptual scheme which was relevant to the problems, which people throughout the organization could understand and which virtually all managers could be emotionally committed to implementing.

There is an old saying that, "Necessity is the mother of invention." It was particularly true for the situation at JJJ, for it was from the necessity to develop such understanding and commitment that the "OD Wheel" was developed (see figure 1).

## II. For an OD Process To Be Successful, It Must Be Governed By A Comprehensive Theory Which Has Utility For Solving Crucial (that is, Line) Organization Problems

Theory is required for OD to be successful. Theory is the basis for implementing OD actions.* Theory is important because it describes the elements of the organization which must be influenced if the organization is to succeed. Theory dictates the process of change and the value system underlying that process. Theory provides a common language for communication. Theory identifies the output variables (such as morale and productivity) which must be influenced if the organization is to operate effectively. And, perhaps most importantly, theory defines the OD roles of the CEO and all managers in the organization.

The particular need at JJJ was for a theory which, in addition to fulfilling the above functions, also met the following criteria:

1) It must provide guidance for identifying and solving important substantive and human problems;

2) It must help anticipate problems which might arise in the future;

3) It must take into account the interrelatedness the various elements of the organization;

4) It must be easily communicated throughout the organization;

5) It must allow organization members to develop the emotional commitment necessary to implement it;

6) It must provide a continuity of effort in the face of changing personnel, business conditions, and organization dynamics; and

---

* The reader will notice that the word "intervention" does not occur in the body of the report. Instead, words such as "action," "implementation" and "problem solving" are used when to some readers, *intervention* might be more appropriate. It is not by chance that "intervention" has been discarded. "Intervention" generally refers to an intrusion into an ongoing process by some outside agent whose power within the organization is limited or non-existent. Only individuals who are outside the mainstream of an organization intervene. Line managers don't intervene. They solve problems, they act, they implement, they work. So in the line management approach to OD, "intervention" has no meaning. The manager is basically responsible for OD actions and if he intervenes, it means only that he is operating outside the mainstream of the organization and is basically irrelevant to the organization's functioning.

7) It must make managers aware of the specific organization elements which require managerial action if the organization is to succeed.

Basically, we saw the alternatives regarding the choice of theory as twofold—use someone else's or develop our own. Under the assumption that, "People support what they help create," we chose the latter alternative.

That decision led to a "sub-criterion" for a successful OD effort: *OD is facilitated when the governing theory is developed by the people who are going to implement it.* At JJJ, the theory was developed by an OD team put together by the President. That OD team included the President, the VPO, the General Manager of Organization Development, a Staff Assistant, and a consultant from a university.

Over a period of months this OD team worked to conceptualize what they were doing and wanted to do. As an integral part of the process, they met with a variety of line managers from various organization levels to test and revise their conceptualization, and eventually developed the "OD Wheel" to govern OD efforts at JJJ. The "Wheel" is portrayed graphically in figure 1.

The OD Wheel* is based on the following assumptions:

1) Line managers are basically responsible for OD.** All line managers are responsible for implementing the "Wheel" within the limits of their functional responsibilities. Or, stated in negative terms, OD staff specialists*** are not primarily responsible for the direction or implementation of OD activities.

2) Every line manager is accountable for OD as a major element of his job. That accountability *starts with the President* and continues throughout the organization.

3) The higher a manager is in the organization hierarchy, the greater the emphasis on his OD accountabilities relative to other accountabilities. For example, a VP's OD accoun-

---

* The name of the theory created some dilemma for the organization. Since JJJ is in the food business, the initial suggestion was to call it the "OD Donut." But since it looks more like a wheel than a donut we decided to "go" with graphic realism as opposed to culinary bias.
** We define line management as, "all managers, line or staff, who have direct responsibility for their own functional activities."
*** "Staff Specialists" include both "inside" and "outside" personnel.

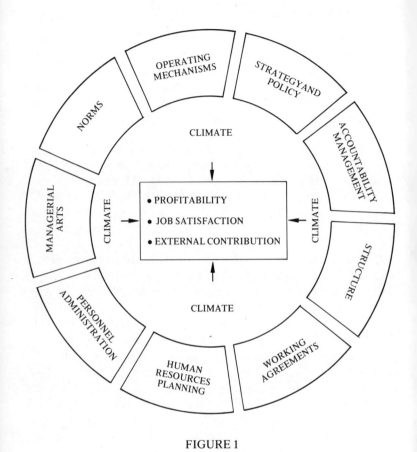

FIGURE 1

*JJJ Company—"OD Wheel"*

tabilities will require a greater proportion of his time and
energy in comparison with the OD accountabilities of a
Supervisor or a Department Head.

4) The effectiveness with which a manager discharges his OD
accountabilities is a major factor both in the evaluation of his
performance and in the determination of his compensation.

5) A major part of a line manager's job is to teach his subordinates to manage. A major part of management is OD. It is
imperative that the line managers teach their subordinates the
content of the "Wheel," its underlying assumptions, and the
processes required to implement it.

6) Goal-setting provides the means for giving systematic, organization-wide direction to the OD process.

7) The "Wheel" theory is not static. That is, it must be revised to meet changing conditions and to respond to feedback concerning results.

8) The job of staff OD specialists is to *assist* line managers in *implementing* their *OD accountabilities*.

The "OD Wheel" describes, in the nine sections of its outer rim, the elements of organization which are focal points for OD activities. Thus, each section of the "Wheel" defines a potential area for specific OD actions by managers. The nine sections are phrased as accountabilities to make them more useful as a basis for goal-setting. Managers use these nine areas as guidelines for developing annual OD goals. The specific areas are identified below as they appear in the *JJJ Organization Development Guide*:

1) *Strategy and Policy*—Assure attainment of Company objectives through the development and use of strategies and policies;

2) *Accountability Management*—Assure that division, department, and individual position accountabilities are directed at fulfillment of company objectives, through personal goal-setting;

3) *Structure*—Assure design of an organization structure that interrelates positions and departments for fulfillment of their accountabilities;

4) *Working Agreements*—Promote intergroup accomplishment of results through working agreements about how groups will work together in specific situations;

5) *Human Resources Planning*—Assure human resources to fill structure through programs for forecasting and providing requirements;

6) *Personnel Administration*—Assure that organization is staffed with people of high and improving performance through programs of selection, assessment, training and development and compensation;

7) *Managerial Arts*—Assure skills in the fundamentals of the process of management;

8) *Norms*—Enable people to fulfill own accountabilities and to help others attain theirs by encouraging favorable norms of behavior; and

9) *Operating Mechanisms*—Assure operating mechanisms that support accountability achievement, such as business planning, operating systems, control systems, office space planning and employee communications.

The "Wheel" also assumes the interdependence of the nine segments. That is, what happens in one segment affects all others. Thus, the overall assumption of the model is that the continuous "balancing" of the "Wheel" by line managers is required to create an organization climate which, in turn, will facilitate the accomplishment of the organization's objectives (note the center of the "Wheel"). These objectives are:

1) *Profitability*—Profit is defined as net profit after tax (NPAT) and return on assets (ROA);
2) Job satisfaction of employees;
3) External contributions to the community such as:
    (a) air and water pollution control
    (b) minority outreach, and
    (c) other contributions.

In summary, the "Wheel" defines OD at JJJ in terms of input variables (the nine focal points for action), a mediating variable (organization climate) and output variables (results in three areas). But it does something else. That something else is perhaps best described by the President who said, "The major contribution of the "OD Wheel" is not as a codification of an OD process. More importantly, it is a vehicle for inducing presidential commitment to change of an enormous magnitude." His statement leads to the third major requirement for an effective approach to OD.

### III. OD Must Be An Extension of the Chief Executive Officer

The CEO is the focal point for conceptualizing the theory, governing its implementation and evaluating its results. He is the catalytic agent for energizing the OD process throughout the organization. Operationally, he must devote a major proportion of his time to the OD function. Unless he does, the OD function is relegated or abdicated to the Personnel or OD department. If that happens:

1) The OD function is reduced to clerical status and OD Staff

Specialists are about as relevant as "putting air brakes on a turtle."*

2) OD is seen as a peripheral activity by the line organization. It is seen that way because, given the realities of power, it is peripheral.

At JJJ, the OD process is an extension of the CEO. For example, the President estimates that he allocates approximately 50% of his time to the OD effort.** Within that time allocation, he has been deeply involved:

1) In the conceptualization of the "Wheel" and therefore the "Wheel" accurately reflects his OD philosophy;

2) In implementing the "Wheel" through a process of delegation to all persons reporting to him;

3) In OD goal-setting sessions with key subordinates (these sessions are carried out within the framework of the "Wheel"); and

4) With key subordinates in planning their OD efforts, particularly in the area of organization structure, norm modification and working agreements.

In short, the chief executive officer is crucial to the success of OD. Unless he is committed to the theory, has the ability to operate consistently within its framework, is willing to allocate the necessary time required to do so, and is willing to "back up" that commitment with the "power" of his office, the process cannot succeed. Power is crucial to the process and is discussed in the following section.

### IV. For An OD Process to be Successful, It Must Be Supported by Clear, Authentic Power

By *power* we mean the ability to control and influence another person or persons in some way, such as through charisma or application of sanctions or expertise.

By *authentic* we mean the use of power by the individual manager in a manner congruent with his character structure or personality.

---

* Appreciation is expressed to Dr. Oron South for the metaphor.

** It should be noted that the individual who was President of JJJ for the first two years of this process has moved to the Presidency of another major corporation where he is actively applying the same concepts. The new President of JJJ is managing the company consistent with the governing concepts and time allocation, although his personal style is quite different.

As a simple and concrete example, an autocratic manager cannot be participative without being phony. Consequently, this orientation to power places a greater value on authenticity than participation, egalitarianism or collaboration.

Stated differently, we believe that the issue of autocratic vs. participative vs. permissive styles of management is less important than the issue of authenticity. All managers are ultimately autocratic in that they attempt to "influence" others to adapt to their preferred managerial styles. Thus a participative manager is no less autocratic or rigid in his encounters with autocratic subordinates than an autocratic manager is in encounters with participative subordinates. The participative manager generally tries to "force" subordinates to accept participation and the autocratic manager generally attempts to "force" subordinates to accept autocracy as a guiding managerial philosophy.

By *clear* we mean that the way in which power is exercised is clear to those over whom it is exercised. The assumption is that the greater the clarity with which power is exercised, the greater the clarity of choices people have in responding to it. Thus, if a manager is unsure whether his boss is autocratic, participative or permissive, he will be unclear about the alternatives he has for solving work related problems.

The orientation of implementing OD actions through the use of power is a requirement throughout the organization. In fact, a basic purpose of an OD process is to help people throughout the organization use their power—to act, to take risks, to solve problems, to make decisions, to "attack the environment"—and to learn to predict and accept the consequences of their actions.

We realize that a "power orientation" differs significantly from traditional OD approaches which value participation (Marrow, et. al, 1967 and Likert, 1967) and teamwork (Blake and Mouton, 1964) more highly than authenticity. However, we found that managers responded more positively to authentic management styles, whether authoritarian, participative or permissive, than to non-authentic approaches. Authenticity, which involves consistency of character structure and managerial style is viewed as less hypocritical and offers subordinates and superiors alike more clear-cut choices of action. Although we found we preferred a participative style, we also found that the manager's effectiveness was enhanced more by his being encouraged to manage authentically than by his being encouraged to change his style.

In summary, a line approach to OD recognizes and encourages managers to use power. It also encourages managers to act and to act with a managerial style consistent with who they are. And finally, it encourages managers to predict and accept the consequences, good or bad, of their actions.

At JJJ, the power orientation emanated from the Office of the President. For example, the President:

1) Set a variety of non-negotiable "givens" regarding the content and process of the OD effort (see this charge to the VPO as an example, page 5).

2) Indicated that participation in the OD process was not voluntary. The President made it clear that each manager reporting to him was accountable for implementing the "Wheel." Voluntarism, in fact, was not an issue since OD was a major part of the job, and not something "outside" the job in which managers participated if they had the time or inclination.

3) Assured that performance appraisal and consequent executive bonus compensation* would depend equally upon:
   (a) "bottom line" operating results (net profit after taxes); and
   (b) progress in the whichever of the nine "Wheel" areas were identified for "work" during the OD goal-setting sessions between the President and his VP's.

4) Encouraged subordinates to use the sanctions of their offices in a manner consistent with their authentic management styles.

### V. The OD Effort Must Be Supported by an OD Staff Competent to Provide Line Managers with Socratic Consultation in Implementing the OD Theory

The word "consultation" should be underlined for emphasis because the basic job of OD staff is to provide consultation assistance rather than to implement OD decisions, programs or actions. For example, at JJJ if a manager was faced with counter-productive competition between two of his divisions, the OD staff might meet with him and help *him* design a process for coping with the problem. The OD staff would not design and carry out a process for him. Or, if a manager was faced with a problem of reorganiza-

---

* At JJJ, bonus performance compensation provides a significant proportion of top management's total compensation.

tion, the OD staff might meet with him and help *him* design an off-site meeting with his subordinates as a means of carrying it out. But the manager himself would conduct the meeting and control the decision making process and accept the consequences. Or, a manager might ask for ideas regarding alternative organization structures. In response, the OD staff might produce a half dozen alternatives and make clear their preferences for structures with accompanying rationales. However, the manager himself would have to decide which, if any, *he* might use. This approach, which we term *Socratic Consultation* has the following elements:

1) A definition: A question-and-answer process to discover organization realities consistent with the manager's style and approach to problem solving.

2) An attitude: The attitude of the consultant is: "OD is not my job. It is the job of the line manager. My job is to help *him* get clear what *he* wants to do, help *him* decide how *he* wants to do it, help *him* become aware of the possible consequences of *his* doing it in the way *he* decides, and help *him* get committed to doing whatever he decides.* Alternatively, my job is *not* to tell him what to do, how to do it (that is, dictate his managerial style), or to implement (OD) for him. And finally, I am not responsible for his decisions and his actions, but I am responsible for mine."

3) A rationale: The rationale for the consultant's attitude is as follows: "If I get involved in implementation and succeed, the manager has failed because I have been able to do his job better than he. And furthermore, if I take responsibility for what he ultimately does, his actions have no meaning to him. They belong to me and not to him. So if I make and implement decisions for him and succeed, he has failed and his sense of competency is diminished.** Therefore, no manager with any "backbone" about him is going to let me succeed at the price of his failure. Either consciously or unconsciously, he will ensure that I fail because my success is his failure. As a result, whenever I get involved in doing his OD job, I inevitably

---

* This approach to consultation is similar to that advanced by Argyris (1970) in *Intervention Theory and Method: A Behavioral Science Approach.*
** The rationale is also similar to that described by Argyris (1968) in his article, "Conditions For Competence Acquisition and Therapy."

create the conditions for his failure, my failure and the organization's failure. Consequently, from any point of view my job as a consultant is to *assist* and *support* the manager in carrying out his OD responsibilities. My job is to help him succeed. If I want to implement OD, I shall get a job as a manager."

4) A problem-solving focus: Socratic Consultation, as we define it, always involves solving problems such as reorganizing a division, developing a coordinated budget, developing a business strategy or solving a production problem. Again, stated in the negative, Socratic Consultation does not involve T-Groups, team-building for the primary purpose of improving interpersonal relationships or intergroup meetings where perceptions, stereotypes and so on are exchanged without reference to solving a specific, substantive business problem. Perhaps the best way to describe this form of consultation is to summarize the process as it was typically employed at the VP level as a means of assisting VP's in structurally reorganizing their areas. In general, the process included the following steps:

a) The president recommended that the VP's work with the OD team in reorganizing their divisions. Although each VP technically extended the invitation, he was under considerable "pressure" from the President to "audition" OD staff resources. We are clear that such pressure violates the traditional OD concept of voluntarism as a condition for participation in OD efforts. We are equally clear that it facilitates authentic collaboration based upon the realities of power.

b) The OD staff team and the VP participated in a brief, "one hour" meeting. During the meeting, the OD team actively "sold" their services. In summary the OD staff said, "Here is our theory of OD and its underlying assumptions. We have found we can frequently be helpful to managers as they reorganize their divisions. Basically, here is what we can do. We can spend a day with you, off-site probably, and respond, question, make suggestions and think of alternatives as you describe any ideas you have about re-organization. As you make decisions we will record them on 'flip charts' and help you organize them into a time sequence so that, by the time you leave, you will have an initial plan for re-organization in hand.

In fact, we suggest having a secretary at the meeting so whatever is done can be in print shortly after the meeting concludes."

If the VP expressed interest, the OD staff would generally role-play a Socratic Consultation "event" with him so he could get a "feel" for the process. At that point, the OD group would ask the VP if he wanted their services and, from our point of view, he was *really* free to refuse. We found that most extended us an invitation to work with them and we believe it was because they really liked the concept of talking about their ideas to a group of respectful Socratic consultants who were not interested in dictating their decisions or determining their managerial styles.

If the answer to the "sales pitch" was affirmative; we arranged an off-site meeting with the VP. Whatever the subject of the meeting, we suggested that the VP bring a list of problems to the meeting as a starting point for work and agenda building. We never drafted an agenda before a meeting. The content of the agenda was his responsibility and was developed at the beginning of the meeting. We also suggested that either his secretary and an OD Staff Assistant attend the meeting to ensure that major decisions were recorded and necessary administrative details were completed at the meeting or shortly thereafter.

At the meeting itself, the OD staff would react to the VP's ideas, suggest alternatives, propose modifications and, in general, serve as Socratic stimuli for decision-making and action. The OD staff also recorded, on flip charts and in the VP's *exact* words his major ideas, action plans or decisions.

A typical Socratic exchange is as follows:

| | |
|---|---|
| VP: | I basically want to re-organize my division. (Consultant writes: "I basically want to re-organize my division", on a flip chart entitled "Agenda".) |
| Consultant: | Do you want to reorganize it or do you want to develop a process for reorganizing it with others? |
| VP: | I think I want to reorganize it myself. But what are you driving at? |
| Consultant: | There is a difference between your reorganizing it and your developing a process for involving others in the reorganization. I'm not sure which you mean. |

| | |
|---|---|
| VP: | What's the difference? |
| Consultant: | I think it deals with issues of commitment and getting people's "noses out of joint." |
| VP: | You mean if people get involved in it they are more likely to go along with it? |
| Consultant: | That's my experience. |
| VP: | I suppose what I mean is that I would like to develop a way to reorganize the division in such a way that people will go along with it. (Consultant writes that statement on Agenda sheet and marks out the previous statement.) |
| Consultant: | Do you have any ideas about how you would like to do it? |
| VP: | I would like to have the people who report to me involved in some way. (Consultant writes that statement on the flip chart.) |
| Consultant: | Is there anything you don't want them involved in? One way to start might be for you to get clear about what you aren't willing to negotiate with them. Do you have any "non-negotiable 'givens'?" |
| VP: | I can think of a couple — I am going to decide on who reports to me and what their basic job functions are. I'm not going to negotiate those issues with anyone. (Consultant writes that exact statement on flip chart.) |
| Consultant: | Anything else? |
| VP: | I'm going to go through the ceiling if you write everything I say on the flip chart. It makes me nervous. (Consultant writes that statement on newsprint amidst much laughter). |

The process of documentation is crucial to the Socratic approach. We found that capturing the manager's ideas and decisions in writing and in his own words not only stimulated discussion but also insured precision in thinking and execution. Seeing ideas, concepts, process and decisions in print lead to greater precision than if the same things were expressed orally and not recorded. Recording critical ideas, decisions and actions also produce a "work" as opposed to a "bull session" atmosphere. And finally, the flip chart records provided the basis for a written organization work plan completely describing the actions which would have to occur in each segment of the "Wheel" when the proposed changes in structure took place.

Subsequent meetings, based on the work plan, led to a broader and more detailed document which included the rationale for the changes, the specific human process which would be followed in implementing the changes, and the alterations which would be required in operating mechanisms, policy, and so forth, to provide administrative and technological support for the change.

We found the Socratic process greatly enhanced the credibility of the OD staff because:

1) The consultation was work oriented and directed toward solving substantive problems of importance to the manager. Interpersonal relationships were dealt with only if they had a direct bearing on the substantive issue.

2) The consultants maintained their integrity without being offensive. They made it clear when they didn't think an idea was sound or practical or workable or ethical, but made it equally clear that the final decision and responsibility for implementation was the managers.

### Results

Given that the five conditions for effective OD were met, what were the results? Did meeting the conditions result in effective OD?

On the basis of eighteen month's experience, we think the answer is, "yes", and we base our conclusion on three types of evidence — each of which is conceptualized within the framework of the "OD Wheel." That evidence includes:

1) The actions managers took in response to the "OD Wheel;"
2) Changes in organization climate; and
3) Operating results (net profit after taxes). These results are discussed below.

### Management Actions in the Nine Segments of the Wheel

At present, the following activities have been initiated since the start of the OD process by the President and key line managers (The list is illustrative, not comprehensive):

1) A strategic business process (Strategy and Policy). Specifically, the President and the eight managers reporting to him have completed four days of strategy and policy sessions. During

those sessions, they have developed a comprehensive, integrated business plan for the total company.

2) An active program of policy development (Strategy and Policy). Either on the initiative of line managers or managers from the Organization Division, policies are developed, written and approved by all affected managers. They are then distributed to the top fifty managers throughout the company for information and dissemination.

3) A personal goal-setting program (Accountability Management). Each manager develops, with his subordinates, written goals which relate to business targets, OD objectives and personal development objectives. The review of performance relative to goals is a major determinant of the manager's compensation.

4) A process for developing written working agreements, covering "gray" areas of responsibility and accountability between divisions (Working Agreements). Currently seventeen agreements have been written and five are in process. In keeping with the desire to increase communication throughout the organization, all agreements are distributed to the top fifty managers in the Company. Managerial participants in the sessions at which working agreements are developed have reported them to be excellent inter-unit team building experiences.

5) A formal system of human resources planning (Human Resources Planning). A General Manager of Human Resources Planning has been appointed. In consultation with line managers from several levels of the organization, he has developed a process which assures that the organization has adequate replacements for all important positions and functions. Within the framework of the process, he also helps individual managers plan their career paths and schedule their developmental activities.

6) An active program to hire and promote minorities and women (Human Resources Planning). Each major division has developed written goals relating to minorities and women at all organizational levels. For example, in 1973, one hundred three salaried jobs are anticipated. The goal is to fill twenty six of these positions with individuals from racial minorities. Also, it is anticipated that sixty two jobs above the clerical level will "open" during 1973. The goal is to place twenty women and fourteen minority persons in these positions.

7) A series of training programs dealing with fundamentals of management. Top management (The President and the Vice Presidents and General Managers who report to him), middle managers, and first line supervisors have participated, as teams, in a three-day seminar designed to insure that managers throughout the organization share the same managerial language.

8) A systematic approach for identifying counterproductive norms and altering them to meet organizational needs (Norms). The top management group plus six of the eight major divisions have worked with an outside consultant in a process designed to identify and change counterproductive norms.

9) A series of continuing education programs for all line managers regarding their OD accountabilities, with the "Wheel" serving as the governing concept (Managerial Arts). Thus, each manager periodically decides with (or for)* his subordinates:
   a) The potential managerial actions possible in each of the nine areas of the "Wheel";
   b) The specific action needs in each area; and
   c) Specific goals and deadlines for taking action to remedy whatever needs one identified.

10) The development of a performance appraisal system at the top management level which ties compensation of top management to OD actions (Accountability Management).

11) The restructuring of seven of the eight major divisions reporting to the President with systematic attention being given both to both technical and human concerns during the restruction process (Structure and Norms).

12) An "Overhead Value Analysis" program (Operating Mechanism). This involves a company wide process for helping managers identify unaffordable positions and eliminate them through staff reductions or attrition. If reductions are necessary, systematic managerial attention is given to coping with the human dilemmas which are inevitably created.

All of the above activities were initiated during the first eighteen months of the OD process. The question then arises as to whether the

---

* Depending upon his managerial style.

process, pursuant to the "Wheel Theory," had a significant impact on climate.

## Climate

According to the "Wheel Theory," climate is an intervening variable. It mediates actions and results. We have only two measures, neither of which might be persuasive from a "hard" scientific point of view. From a managerial point of view, however, they are sufficient to support the contention that changes in the "rim" of the "Wheel" did result in an overall change of climate in the organization.

First, we administered the Likert (1967) Profile of Organization Characteristics (POC) to the President and those reporting to him. The POC was administered approximately fifteen months after the OD effort began. In the perceptions of the top management group the character of the organization had shifted from System II (Benevolent Authoritative) to System III (Consultative) and without exception, they expressed satisfaction with the shift.

Second, the outside consultant of the staff OD team interviewed the President, all VP's and General Managers, and more than fifty third and fourth level line managers. The interviews were conducted under the guarantee that the anonymity of respondents would be maintained. They were done as part of the continuing process of organization diagnosis, but the data are equally relevant for evaluation purposes.

Three questions were asked each manager:

1) What is going well?
2) What blocks you from being effective in your job?
3) What would you change if you had the opportunity?

In responding to these questions, managers spontaneously reported changes in the organizational climate. For example, in one division eleven managers were interviewed approximately one year after the OD process started. Eight reported climate changes. Specifically, their responses were:

> There have been a lot of changes at the top. Life is now different and people are acting differently. People are being asked to take risks.

> It has been difficult for line people to imagine we have made such a large change. But some line people do not

understand the change—at least the ones reporting to me don't.

We have moved from autocracy to democracy and have become speedier and less cautious.

There have been changes at the top. Life is now different and people are acting differently. People are being asked to take risks and handle the broad aspects of the job.

There is a message that you can influence certain things regarding budget and manpower. The budget used to be set by edict. That has changed. There is less grumbling and people are coming forth with ideas. There is a trend toward a climate that makes this a good place to work.

People are used to being given information from a "directive" point of view. People are used to arbitrary edict but are now being asked to work by objectives. A lot of planning is required under the new system.

I'm not sure we understand the changes. There is a lack of comprehension on the part of people reporting to me.

We are having to relearn

There is more pressure on being a manager. We are now accountable for getting the job done within a given time instead of doing it as someone else says to do it. And there is much more emphasis on costs than previously.

Although some respondents clearly did not understand the nature of the change in climate, their responses did consistently indicate that the climate had changed. And similar responses were obtained from other divisions.

If climate has changed, the "Wheel" then raises the questions, "Did the change in climate affect the three target business objectives?" the answer to that question is the subject of the next section of the paper.

## Operating Results

In terms of the theory, operating results refer to three elements of the business. Results are reported at the end of eighteen months. *Profitability and growth*. The annual rate of profits more than doubled from the level being projected in July of 1970. (for the end of that fiscal year*).

In an attempt to measure the source of increased profits, the Controller "costed out" the estimated percentage of profit arising from technical and administrative actions such as improved logistics procedures, improved production processes, and improved inventory control procedures. The Controller's analysis indicated approximately two-thirds of the increased profits could be attributed to specific administrative and technological changes. The President, therefore, made the assumption that the remaining one-third of the unallocated increase in profits could be attributed to the more effective functioning of the people in the organization. In dollars and cents terms, more effective human functioning was worth approximately one million dollars.

*Job Satisfaction*: Two sources would indicate that job satisfaction increased. First, interview data clearly indicate that job satisfaction increased at the managerial level. Comments such as the following occurred after the reorganization of a major division.

I like my job, what I am doing, and the freedom I have.

Everyone is really committed to their jobs and enjoy them.

I am really with the managerial set up.

I like my job and the responsibility it has.

The best thing about my job is the freedom.

I respect it and hope no one takes it away.

---

* Preliminary figures indicate that at the end of three years profits have decreased somewhat. Specifically, profits for the third year are still double that of the first year but not increasing as fast as expected. Analysis indicates two factors have influenced the slowdown. Overhead costs have increased out of proportion to direct costs. Using the "Wheel" to guide actions, Operating Mechanisms have been devised to control costs. (All managers are eliminating positions and reducing staff. We now realize that if the conceptual guidance of the wheel had existed earlier, the need for such economics might have been identified early enough to take action *before* profits decreased.) Also, government actions "put pressure" on profits. The "Wheel" doesn't include "Outside Forces" as a "variable" and will have to be modified in the future if it is to be maximally used as a governing theory.

Although the comments above were more consistently "euphoric" than in other divisions because of a variety of circumstances, people throughout the organization expressed greater satisfaction with their jobs both in the interviews and in spontaneous comments to management and the OD staff.

Second, observational data indicated job satisfaction increased at the clerical level too. Specifically, during this period an attempt was made to unionize clerical personnel; but the union could not collect enough signature cards to hold an election. We assume that the failure of the organizing effort reflected an improved organization climate and an increased level of overall job satisfaction.

*External Contributions*: Several steps were taken to support JJJ's external contributions to the community. Some of these are:

1) A top management position was created to direct an active program for coping with plant environmental pollution.

2) Several programs were developed which allows JJJ employees to take part in a variety of community activities on company time.

   a) One of these enables black employees to engage in activities with black high school students to encourage them toward careers in business (Youth Motivation Taskforce, a segment of National Alliance of Businessmen).

   b) Another provides employees as advisors to the Junior Achievement program to teach high school students management and our economic system.

3) Heavy contributions of food and money have been made to victims of floods and other tragedies.

4) Heavy assistance has been given to drug rehabilitation centers.

5) A long range plan is being developed to assure promotion of minority employees and women to significant management positions. (This is far beyond the "regular" affirmative action programs the company has in compliance with legal requirements.)

In conclusion, we feel the results support the basic soundness of the theory and the overall approach to OD.

We also believe that this approach led to a number of generalizations which are relevant to the practice of the "OD art." In one sense, they are also results of the process and we feel that they provide an adequate summary of "where we are" in conceptualizing OD. They are summarized in terms of "Old Assumptions," "Our Experience" and "New Assumptions" and are presented below.

| OLD ASSUMPTION | OUR EXPERIENCE | NEW ASSUMPTIONS |
|---|---|---|
| 1. You have to get rid of a lot of "deadwood" to produce major organization change. | 1. We fired only two people. | 1. The quality of an organization's performance is not a function of the quality of individuals as much as the climate in which those individuals work. |
| 2. You cannot change an organization quickly and have the change be effective. | 2. In 18 months 7 out of 8 divisions were re-organized. 187 managers were promoted. 98% of the people in the first four levels changed jobs or had their jobs changed. Etc. | 2. Effectiveness of change is not a function of its speed but of the methodology employed (the "how"). |
| 3. Change is instinctively resisted by individuals. | 3. Virtually no problems of resistance were encountered. | 3. Change is desired and welcomed when it is *needed* and *properly managed.* |
| 4. To improve an organization, the focus of change should be on *structure.* | 4. In this case, we suspected the invalidity of this assumption and changed to the new assumption before starting our work. | 4. Effective change (improvement), in operational results required balanced, simultaneous efforts on many "fronts" (i.e. the nine areas of the "Wheel"). |
| 5. Organization development does not require a theoretical base. | 5. We encountered the real complexity of organizations — and found it unmanageable without a conceptual base. | 5. You *do* need a conceptual framework to guide organization development. |
| 6. Theory governing OD must be developed by outside specialists. | 6. Commitment to and relevance of the theory is increased if it is developed within the organization. | 6. There are tremendous advantages to developing theory within the organization. |

TABLE 1 *(continued on next page)*

| OLD ASSUMPTION | OUR EXPERIENCE | NEW ASSUMPTION |
| --- | --- | --- |
| 7. OD should be the primary responsibility of the personnel department. | 7. We found that the most capability for the design, development and implementation of OD lies within the line managers (if the personnel department can supply the necessary support and tools). | 7. The primary responsibility for OD lies with the CEO and his line managers. |
| 8. OD deals primarily with attitudes, norms, personal development, group development and other human aspects of organizations. | 8. We found that human factors are inextricably entangled with administrative and technological aspects of organization. | 8. The OD theory which governs the process must encompass such elements as strategy, policy, horizontal working agreements, etc. (the nine elements of the "Wheel"). |
| 9. The job of the manager is to motivate people. | 9. Motivation is always there — but frequently stiffled. | 9. The job of the managers is to keep from demotivating people; and the job of OD specialists is to keep from demotivating managers in accomplishing *their* OD accountabilities. |
| 10. Participative management styles produce the most positive results. | 10. Different management styles can accomplish positive results. | 10. Styles based on authenticity produce more positive results than inauthentic styles regardless of where the manager is on the autocratic participative-permissive spectrum. |

TABLE 1    *(continued on next page)*

| OLD ASSUMPTION | OUR EXPERIENCE | NEW ASSUMPTIONS |
|---|---|---|
| 11. Authoritarian power is required to change an organization. | 11. No type of power works well unless it is authentically applied. | 11. The exercise of power required for effective organization is most effective when it is:<br>- Based on substantive professionalism (which includes ability to manage change in all 9 different aspects of organization simultaneously).<br>- Articulated (clearly and unambivalently) in terms of limits and choices.<br>- Modeled by the CEO.<br>- Supported by organization resources which are also clearly articulated, i.e., staff support, compensation systems, administrative procedures, etc. |
| 12. You need a large staff of professional OD specialists to carry out OD. | 12. You do not need a large staff. We had three internal staff — none professionally trained and one external — professionally trained. | 12. You need a small staff who can assist line managers in carrying out OD responsibilities. In fact, a large staff is counter-productive in that it increases the probability that OD specialists will attempt to take over the management and implementation of the OD process. |
| 13. OD is a 3 - 6 year process. | 13. We produced substantial change within eighteen months — but new problems always arise. | 13. OD is a *perpetual* process. It is a major part of what managers *always* do in order to run an effective organization. |

*TABLE 1*
*Summary of Conclusions*

## REFERENCES

Argyris, C. "Conditions for competence acquisition and therapy." *The Journal of Applied Behavioral Science,* Vol. 4, #2, 1968. 147-177.

Argyris, C. *Intervention Theory and Method: A Behavioral Science Approach.* New York, John Wiley, 1970.

Bion, W. R. *Experiences in Groups,* New York, Basic Books, 1959.

Blake, R. R. & Mouton, J. S. *The Managerial Grid,* Houston, Texas, Gulf Publishing Co., 1964.

Likert, R. *The Human Organization.* New York, McGraw Hill, 1967.

Marrow, A. J., Bowers, D. G. & Seashore, S. E. *Management by Participation.* New York, Harper and Row, 1967.

# 9

# A Mixed Model for Medical Centers: Changing Structure and Behavior

## *MARVIN R. WEISBORD*

*Foreword*

There are two sets of theoretical issues in trying to improve organizations. One is an adequate "head map" of the way the parts fit together. This permits diagnosis of the gap between the way things are and the way they should be. The second is an adequate notion about how to close the gap. This means confronting resistance, anxiety and impatience (one's own and others') in face-to-face meetings, trying to redirect energy invested in maintaining the gap into excitement about new possibilities.

In this paper I have tried to address both issues. I see this as a first effort to tell how my colleagues and I have integrated theory making, research, application of new knowledge and education in such a way that all four activities are enhanced. As I write, it strikes me that this is precisely the problem facing medical schools. I hope no one will interpret this to mean I think we have discovered the ultimate way to manage such complex interdependencies, either for ourselves or for the schools.*

However, I do think we have created some valuable new notions about old problems. To have *some* conceptual handle on the "whole elephant" is for me essential to coping with it, more important, in fact, than any particular handle. I hope others will view this scheme, both for diagnosis and change, as a useful push in the right direction. Moreover, though I defend the utility of the "mixed model" for diagnosing present day medical center organizations, I make no claim that the change strategy based on it in one setting will be applicable everywhere. Quite to the contrary. What specific steps to

* This work represents a joint-venture of Dr. Paul R. Lawrence and myself. Dr. Martin P. Charns was and is our increasingly valued colleague. In addition, we have had the benefit of skills and support from Dr. Marvin S. Dunn, David L. Loomis, Dr. Robert S. Stone, and Dr. Allan B. Drexler. None are responsible for my opinions, though all have helped make possible this paper.

take will vary with every situation and require a look at many more variables than are discussed here.

The paper falls into two parts. First, it describes a "model" or conceptual scheme for thinking about how the parts of an academic medical center fit together. I have found this model useful in explaining why medical centers are so hard to organize. Others have found it useful in making decisions about which structural changes to support. The model is based on what *already* is happening in medical centers, and not on what I or my colleagues wish would happen. It is our belief that by putting a conceptual framework around some of the ways people in medicine cope with unprecedented problems, we can enlarge the awareness and choices of others. Our intent is to support and accelerate the continuing process of learning to organize better.

A word of warning. I strongly believe that the test of new knowledge is its utility. Even the best map will be useless to an organization unless people understand it, use the same vocabulary to talk about it, and derive from it common ground rules by which they order their relationships. Moreover, it is easier to map the way an organization "ought to be" than it is to figure out how to get it there. One responsibility for anybody trying to change things is establishing common concepts and language among people who must work together.

The second, but not secondary, purpose of this paper is to report a case study, still in progress, of one medical center's efforts to translate new knowledge into a new vocabulary and new management practices. This sometimes goes by the name of "change." It would be a shame to leave the reader with the impression that I see "mixed model" organizational changes, however needed, as the major products of this inquiry.

The major product, in my view, is a particular way of going about things. It is the process by which the mixed model emerged, is being tested, and will be changed. In OD jargon, this process is called "action research." It involves a belief in monitoring the environment, taking experimental action, reading the effects, acting again and learning all the while to tolerate conflict within oneself and with others, which many persons associated with this work in various medical centers have supported.

I have no data to prove to skeptics the worth of this process. One notion endemic in society (and, I should add, medicine) is that all problems have expert solutions, needing only the right technicians and/or technology independent of one's values or purposes. We cling to this belief like drowners to a liferaft, despite impressive evidence in our own lives that it is false. I think learning to do action research on one's own situation is the highest form of organizational accomplishment; valuable, in the words of an old radio commercial, "not for years, not for life, but forever." In my view, this process, upon which all scientific inquiry is based, is a good way to manage medical centers and also an appropriate way to live.

*How This Paper Is Organized*

I'm faced here with telling about several things at once: a critical social issue; a research project; various conceptual schemes; an organizational diagnosis; and a case study in change. Developing the relationship among these requires a step-by-step unfolding which is not true to the way things happen. To cope with my need to keep jumping back and forth between theory and practice I have organized the paper into seven sections. The first two introduce the problem and describe the theory and assumptions underlying our work on it. The third discusses practical issues involved in using research as an intervention strategy. The fourth is heavily theoretical, discussing research findings, the development of a conceptual scheme, and a general diagnosis of medical centers. The fifth is heavily practical, describing in narrative form what happened when we attempted to translate theory into practice. The two final sections deal with evaluating this effort, some values behind it, and conditions under which a similar strategy might be, as the doctors say, "contra-indicated."

## I - INTRODUCTION

"Both universities and health care delivery present complex unsolved organizational problems which limit their effectiveness and their ability to respond to changing circumstances."

—John R. Evans, M.D., Dean, Faculty
of Medicine, McMaster University[1]

A critical challenge to OD in the 70's is the coming reorganization of academic medical centers. Designed mainly to produce research and specialists, the centers are under tremendous pressure to turn out community minded doctors, and to give better care to more patients. How to change an organization structured around new knowledge into one which can produce an appropriate   mix of knowledge, education and service is not an easy task, even for "experts"—a fact supported by NTL's own stormy history.

In medicine, the academic center literally has become unmanageable in traditional ways. Deans once could count on 20 or more years of prestigious tenure. Today their average term is three years, many falling victim to heart attacks, ulcers or emotional problems. The strain on traditional academic departments is also severe. Community care programs requiring, say, pediatricians, obstetricians and psychiatrists to coordinate efforts, compete for funds with each of the specialities they need. Academic department chairmen, internationally famous as researchers, find themselves chiefs of service in large urban hospitals, an anamoly roughly like putting a man in charge of a manufacturing plant on the strength of his having found new uses for the product.

Indeed, the academic medical center is not one organization at all. It's a complex marriage of several:

1. A medical school and one or more teaching hospitals;
2. Other health professional schools, such as Nursing, Dentistry, Pharmacy, and so on; and
3. A university, with its various academic science departments.

The centers are tied into a patternless web of relationships with cities, states, counties, federal agencies, private foundations, local medical societies, accrediting boards, and other systems too numerous to mention. Finally, medical center administrative machinery is antiquated. Only recently have people begun working on computer applications to medical school problems—such as budgeting, scheduling, admissions and grants management. Until the 1960's, many of the largest schools, with budgets in the tens of millions, performed these functions using pre-World War II technology.

Even the administrative vocabulary makes it hard to talk about medical centers. In most places the chief executive officer still carries the title "Dean," an academic handle which makes him head of the school's faculty. The job has expanded beyond this narrow sphere. In many places Deans exert major, if not total control over one or more teaching hospitals, and may even have schools of nursing, dentistry, and pharmacy under their wings. In recognition of this fact, many a "Dean" is adding the title Vice President (for Health Affairs or Health Sciences), which complicates matters by making him his own boss. With his Vice President's hat on he has quite a different stake in many issues than the Dean does, a condition which often aggravates his sense of intolerable pressure.

Furthermore, colleges and hospitals both have governance structures, by which professional peers influence policy, monitor ethics and maintain standards. Nobody is clear about the relationship between management and governance.

Nevertheless, for better or worse, the Dean, overloaded with expectations, whipsawed between external and internal affairs, remains the single, widely-recognized legitimate authority for making center-wide decisions in most places. No one man can do it, and Deans increasingly have turned to each other and outsiders for help. Broadly speaking, the Deans need help with three kinds of problems:

1. Using business technology such as computer simulations, program budgets, long-range planning, and information systems;

2. Conceptualizing a new medical center structure; and

3. Initiating needed changes, when the use of new technology and new structure depends so heavily on new skills and behavior.

To help with these problems the Association of American Medical Colleges in 1972 started a major educational effort for medical deans in management systems and development, and OD. Independent of this work, Paul Lawrence, of the Harvard Business School, and I set out two years ago to find new answers to two of the above questions—what a better structure would look like, and how Deans might diagnose their present situations and initiate changes in a desired direction.

This paper describes one application of our work: an effort to adapt and test Lawrence-Lorsch organization theory in medical centers in such a way that our findings would generate momentum for change. The initial research was performed in four medical schools, including 13 associated hospitals, under grants to the schools from a branch of NIH. One of the four Deans involved contracted in advance for an "implementation" strategy in addition to the research. This paper, then, also constitutes a status report on the sequence of interventions which resulted, and the changes which his school has made between March and December 1972.

What makes our technology "new?"

1. We have drawn the first systematic conceptual framework based on quantitative and interview data which accounts for much of the disorganization in medical centers. The "mixed model:"

    a. legitimizes both functional departments and integrative programs, and provides a way to think about how they relate to each other;

    b. is a useful tool for diagnosing good and bad organizational arrangements; you can make reasonable predictions about certain organizational problems from the structure alone, and demonstrate where critical tasks, seen as "everybody's" job, in fact are nobody's; and

    c. enables each person to more clearly visualize how he fits in, where his accountabilities lie, and how he might change things for the better in dealing with others.

2. Our technology emphasizes structure as the priority area for change in medical organizations, rather than behavior, which has been the traditional focus of OD.

3. It creates an easily understandable relationship between structure and behavior—especially conflict management; thus it has provided an acceptable rationale for working on behavior—both interpersonal and organizational at deeper levels than doctors are accustomed to.

In short, our technology has opened doors to the use of more traditional OD interventions in a system which has strenuously resisted them. In the case described below, many people want to learn and practice new behavior because they need it:

    a. to change the structure and reorganize the system; and

    b. to make a reorganized system work.

4. Finally, our new technology provides some insight into a more general problem OD practitioners have: how to provide "expert" analysis and data about an organization which can be owned enough by people in the organization to build commitment for change. This is especially sticky when our *research* hats require us to advocate particular arrangements based on our findings, and our *practitioner* hats lead us to encourage our clients to confront us and each other over the issues and to preserve their freedom of choice.

## Some Definitions

Let me define some of my terms. By "academic center" I mean a medical school and the various hospitals and clinical programs centered around it. When I say "center" I'm *always* thinking of a complex wedding of at least two quite different organizations with three inseparable services: patient care, medical teaching and research.

By "structure" I mean job titles and functions, groups and individuals with special tasks, policies, procedures, systems, methods, coordinating mechanisms, and the like, which are orderly, systematic, can be written down and described by one person to another.

By "behavior" I mean how people act with each other, especially what they do when they disagree. In my view, disagreement and conflict are the appropriate handles for critical behavioral issues in medical centers.

Lawrence-Lorsch theory has a language of its own too. "Differentiation" means dividing up necessary tasks and organizing each differently depending on what the environment dictates is essential. "Integration" means coordinating different tasks. Because one can't teach medicine without caring for patients and (in medical center hospitals, at least) you can't care for patients without teaching medicine, the two tasks are interdependent. They are also in conflict some of the time. Integrating them requires mechanisms and procedures for legitimizing and managing unavoidable conflict.

"Mixed model" refers to a complex matrix-like conceptual scheme. It is an organizational model that makes legitimate *both* specialized departments, (for example, biochemistry, surgery, *and* integrative programs such as Undergraduate Medical Education; Methadone Maintenance), and demonstrates a structure which might enable both to maximize their performance. It resembles a matrix (such as TRW Systems, Inc.) in some ways, but is more complex. In a "mixed model," people may appear in four different places on the organization chart in a single day, and sometimes in several at once. If you doubt this, try to chart the organizational responsibilities of a (1) medical doctor, who is (2) recording data on the heart and lungs of a critically ill patient for research purposes, while (3) demonstrating to medical students some aspects for treating heart failure, (4) in a community general hospital over which the medical school has no direct control, in which (5) the doctor has a staff appointment only by virtue of his being on the medical school faculty. (Question: Who is the doctor's boss?)

## II - UNDERLYING THEORY AND ASSUMPTIONS

Our theory base is mixed. On the question of what's the right structure for a medical center, we're using Lawrence-Lorsch differentiation-integration (D-I) theory. This theory is the product of several years work by Paul Lawrence and his colleague Jay Lorsch at the Harvard Graduate School of Business Administration.[2] It was developed by looking at more and less productive businesses in the same industries with a fresh eye, developing some new ideas about how they differ and inventing new methods for testing the ideas. Lawrence and Lorsch found three critical differences between high and low performing businesses:

1. Tasks, such as sales and production, exist in different environments. People who do them need a different time sense, degree of structure, interpersonal capabilities and goal emphasis to do a good job. High performers recognize the need for these differences and try to preserve them when they organize.

2. However, the more different two units are from one another, the more likely they are to fight, *if* they also depend on one another for some things. In short, conflict is a symptom of the need for interdependence, which high performers acknowledge, recognize, and explicitly manage as a function of coordinating tasks.

3. Low performers might adequately differentiate tasks; they might also adequately coordinate departments by reducing differences, hence conflict, at the price of greatly reduced individual performance. High performers did both: they preserved differences and they integrated by managing conflict. In short they found ways to keep each department operating at maximum effectiveness *consistent with* overall performance of the organization. Effective integration was always carried forward in the name of the whole, and not any one of its parts.

These findings led Lawrence and Lorsch to a "contingency theory" of organization. There is no one best way to organize. Often units of the same enterprise needed different policies, procedures, and methods to contribute effectively to the whole, even at the expense of consistency. Business firms which somehow hit on the right mix for their environments and purposes consistently showed higher productivity and lower costs than those that didn't.

From this starting place, then, stems the central assumption on which this work is built:

> If a way existed to measure performance in patient care, education and research which everybody could agree on, it would be found that each of these tasks is performed better in those centers which are adequately differentiated and integrated than in those where (as is mostly the case now) these tasks are largely undifferentiated and

thus integrated mainly by individuals on their own behalf
and not on behalf of the system as a whole.

Following from this, several assumptions about medical centers,
and their critical need for structure:

1. A better differentiated structure would contribute to better
   performance of the whole system.
2. Doctors, who play key roles in medical centers, resist differentiated structures. They wear several hats by tradition and
   training. They are used to acting in their many roles as they see
   fit, and resist efforts of people in administrative and integrative
   roles to act in the name of the whole.[3]
3. However, health care in general tends to improve as doctors
   become more involved in an *organized* system.[4]
4. There is unavoidable conflict between personal autonomy and
   a medical center's need to organize and coordinate the many
   hats of a great many doctors in order to survive.
5. Education, research and patient care each have independent
   value in our society. All are essential to any reasonably
   complete medical center.
6. There is no one correct mix of research, education, and patient
   care. The mix, and thus the structure, varies with location,
   history and philosophy; which influence the mechanisms by
   which tasks become differentiated and coordinated.
7. Each task, properly done, requires *different* professional
   behavior. Hence, conflict between them is inevitable and
   legitimate.
8. Successful conflict management in medical centers requires
   that (a) the conflict be in the open and not suppressed, and (b)
   adequate means exist for working through conflicts to acceptable decisions.

Finally, I'm working from a set of assumptions about change. The
important ones are:[5]

1. Resistance is legitimate, inevitable and must be taken into
   account.
2. Data-based change strategies only work when people own the
   data—that is, feel strongly that it describes their reality.
3. Change can only take place when structures exist to encourage
   it.
4. Leadership counts heavily, especially in a system where
   management and governance are confused.

5. The "change" which improves organizational performance is not a set of new solutions to old problems. It is a change in the organization's way of life, of doing things, of handling problems. In short, processes must change, moreso than outcomes.

6. It is important for people in an organization to use new processes successfully early on, then receive periodic reinforcement. If there is no one best way to organize, there is also no one best way (or one-shot way) to change an organization.

7. Change takes twice as long as we think.

## III - RESEARCH AS AN INTERVENTION STRATEGY

The University of X School of Medicine (hereafter called UX) is a new medical school in a relatively poor, largely rural state. It controls its main teaching hospital, a large public facility managed under contract by the university, and has affiliations with a VA and other local hospitals. It also operates its own mental health center with in-patient facilities, located administratively in the Department of Psychiatry.

In the spring of 1971 the Dean, also the University's Vice President for Health Sciences, approached Paul Lawrence and me, having heard about our study already under way in two eastern medical centers. He believed his school needed reorganizing. He faced strong community pressures for better care and for the admission of minority students. He also was concerned about the complex college-hospital relationship, especially with a part-time medical director who doubled as chairman of a major clinical department. Moreover, he was inclined to split the Dean's job from the Vice President's, and wondered about the pros and cons of this move. He felt pressure from lack of money. His need as Vice President to be constantly on the go, steering budgets through the legislature or finding money in Washington conflicted with his need as Dean to stay home and support his academic department chairmen. They, like chairmen everywhere, were struggling with curriculum change. In short, he was looking for more realistic ways to divide up the work.

He saw our study as a means to initiate change. Indeed, he was less interested in the research, more in the use of the findings as a lever on change. As a result of his interest, our study was expanded to four schools, including his, and part of the budget was set aside for "implementation."

## Our Multiple Hats and Contracts

At this point we had several contracts, or working agreements, which it might be helpful to differentiate. In my view it's the explicitness of these agreements (or lack of) which determines the extent to which consultants and clients help each other.* In our study we found it useful to sort out the following working agreements:

1. An agreement with NIH to perform and document research valuable to them in their efforts to improve physician education.

2. An agreement among the research team to commit the required time, produce the necessary documents, and support each other in individual objectives (doctoral dissertation, future books and articles, and the like).

3. An agreement with each of four Deans to interview chairmen and administrators, observe meetings, administer a survey and discuss our findings (in terms of differentiation/integration and conflict management) with their faculties and staffs.

4. A further agreement with one Dean to collect the data and present it in such a way that (a) it would facilitate his making needed changes, and (b) would involve the faculty in organizational decisions relating to the center's future. For purposes of this agreement we needed to be clear that we would wear our research hats at first and would shift to our educational and consulting hats when, as, and if our findings provided an appropriate basis.

One important byproduct of this work has been my own growing awareness of the need to clarify which hat I'm wearing, and when. Lawrence and Lorsch have shown that different tasks require different behavior if each is to be done well. Practitioners of organization development, no less than those in medicine, need to make distinctions among research, education and consulting tasks, each of which has its own objectives. The continual redefinition of working agreements helps me focus attention on which attitudes and behavior are appropriate to whatever objectives I'm trying to achieve. In this paper I use the term "contract" to mean the various agreements mentioned above. I also use it to mean working agreements made explicit at the start of workshops and meetings in which my colleagues and I have been involved at UX, wearing one or more of our many hats. Finally, I use it to mean agreements between individuals and groups in the medical center about their mutual expectations.

* I also see this as an example of a mechanism for differentiating many hats and purposes.

*Faculty Support at UX*

The Dean's intent at UX was that our data be used as a lever for organizational improvements. For this to happen, it would be important that the faculty be told what we were doing and why. Their open-mindedness at this stage was critical to their giving our findings serious consideration later.

To build commitments for investing time in us and giving us good data, we did the following:

1. Paul and I met in August, 1971, with the faculty in an open meeting. We discussed the industrial findings and outlined what we hoped to test in medical centers, using detailed interviews, observations of meetings and other activities, and a questionnaire to a large sample of administrators, faculty, voluntary physicians and nurses. We ran the gaunlet of basic scientists questioning our methodology, and surgeons who wondered how somebody's perception can be a piece of factual data. We promised them a face-to-face data feedback meeting. The Dean said that he strongly supported the study and would use its findings.

2. In October, 1971, Martin P. Charns, our research associate, and I returned to UX to interview and distribute the questionnaire.* We met with department chairmen to discuss our methods and what would become of the data, and to enlist their support for the interviews. We also met with hospital administrators to solicit their help in distributing the survey to people on their payrolls.

3. Having interviewed 35 people in depth, we sent our survey to more than half the full-time faculty and many other key people. In a covering letter the Dean explained again what the survey meant to him. In our own letter we promised: (1) a summary of findings from four schools would be sent to every respondent; (2) meetings to discuss the data; and (3) follow-up consultation on uses of the data to promote change, if enough people wanted it.

Mainly, we wanted to test four things: (1) the required differentiation between tasks of patient care, research, education and administration; (2) the extent to which people perceived the required differences between their many hats; (3) the extent to which conflict

---

* This complex instrument was designed mainly by Marty Charns and pretested by him and David L. Loomis, a planning associate at Medical College of Pennsylvania and consultant to our project, on many medical people. Marty, now Dr. Charns, used some of the data for his dissertation at Harvard.

existed among people performing different tasks; and (4) the modes used to manage conflict. Moreover, we wanted to saturate ourselves in the system, trying to experience it the way people in it did, rather than through change agent categories like decision making, communications, control, openness and trust. Continually, we zeroed in on the influence of structure on behavior, which things helped to get the necessary work done, which things hindered it.

Most department chairmen and administrators talked frankly with us and expressed an interest in seeing the data. From this school we received a 51% response to our questionnaire. Pretty good returns, we thought, in a skeptical system for a complex instrument requiring 45 minutes. In addition, we had detailed verbatim notes of interviews with every chairman, many administrators and faculty members.

## IV - BUILDING A "MIXED MODEL"

We pooled our UX data with that from three other medical centers. Our data base now included more than 150 interviews and 1000 returned questionnaires in addition to many pages of notes on groups and individuals in action. From a relatively limited analysis of this material we built what we are calling a "mixed model."

Let me back off the case study for a moment to describe how this model evolved, using analogies from industry. The format below roughly follows that presented to the four medical school Deans in February 1972.

First, the main findings:[6]

1. Overall, people who wore more than one hat in medical centers (such as research, patient care, teaching and administration) tended to blur the distinctions between the task requirements of each hat compared to people who wore only one.

2. This tendency happened *least* in the center which had various explicit "task managers," such as a Director of Clinical Care, a Director of the Office of Education, and also written contracts between chairmen and Dean.

3. The better differentiated center also had the most *overt* or manifest conflict; in less differentiated centers, conflict tended to be latent, for few channels existed where it could be managed to closure.

The least differentiated center (more blurred task distinctions, fewer structural mechanisms for dividing up the work) *also* tended to be the most specialized, with strong functional departments and less emphasis on patient care goals compared to education and research.

By contrast, the most differentiated center showed more program organizations outside of traditional departments. This seemed to fit with a greater emphasis on patient care goals. Given its greater mix of purpose, the amount of open conflict within and between groups was greater too. (The Dean from this center supported our finding. "We're dealing with a bunch of switch-hitters," he commented, "and they're all batting about .150 from either side of the plate.")

One way to understand the significance of these data is through analogies with industry. There, Lawrence and Lorsch have shown a close correlation between productivity and good differentiation/integration. Industry, too, faces the dilemma of whether to organize by functions (departments) or product lines (programs). Many companies cope with this by reorganizing every few years. The organization builds strong functional specialties for a time (emphasis on differentiation), then compensates by reorganizing around products (integration).

Medical centers evolved as functional organizations, built around traditionally strong specialized departments. Departments, each in effect a small business, make excellent structures for producing specialists, but are structurally inadequate for delivering general community care requiring many specialities.

By contrast, a totally-integrated program organization could deliver excellent care. It would pay for this in reduced capability to recruit new members in each specialty and in-depth competence. At present, many centers organize mainly around departments, and none mainly around programs. Some are experimenting with the latter idea.

Figure 1 below, compares the strengths of special function and program organizations in both industry and medicine. Note that each pays a price for its capabilities. It lacks the structural capability to carry forward the other model's mission, no matter how strongly people wish it would.

In business, most people wear only one hat. Medicine, with its unique reliance on professionals who need to bat from both sides of the plate, and also play three positions at once, can't depend on either format; hence the tension between the departments and programs. Traditional departments stretch beyond their design capabilities when they seek to control integrative programs. Program organizations can't provide the stimulation, support and in-depth competence found only in specialized departments. Trying to force one structure to do something it was not designed for is like

|                          |                          |
|--------------------------|--------------------------|
| *Industry*               | *Medicine*               |

*Functional Organization*
- Functions as key units:

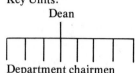

- Strong Focus on functional subgoals
  Products and projects fall fall behind

- Influence centered in functional heads

- Functional lines of promotion

- Budgeting by functions

*Specialized Organization*
- Specialty Departments as Key Units:

- Strong focus on specialization
  Program (mission) results (education, service, etc) suffer

- Influence centered in department chairmen

- Specialty lines of promotion

- Budgeting by departments

- - - - - - - - - - - - - - - - - - - - - - - - - - - - -

*Product Organization*
- Product organization as key unit:

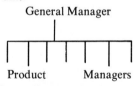

- Strong Focus on Product Results
  Technologies less well developed

- Influence centered in Product Heads

- Product Management as lines of promotion

- Budgeting by Product

*Program Organization*
- Program as key unit

- Strong focus on program results
  Specialties less well developed

- Influence centered in Program managers

- Lines of promotion through programs

- Budgeting through programs

—Neither organizational format is adequate to the many demands on complex medical centers.

FIGURE 1

*Comparison of Organizational Forms*

using an airplane on the highway. It can be done, but it creates more problems than it solves.

Consider the medical center dilemma in more detail. Each department is a miniature version of the entire center. It carries on research and education, has administrative tasks, and clinical departments also deliver services. Indeed, each person in each department does some mix of these things. Organizing around task similarities, and managing conflicts among the differences, is a medical administrator's toughest problem. Nobody who is (rightfully) pursuing his own special mix of tasks can possibly sort out the many tasks for the center as a whole. This is properly the job of people in integrative roles, on the Dean's staff, for example, or in charge of major hospitals.

Figure 2, below, shows why this is so. In the specialized system, an individual wearing many hats who also tries to sort out the many hats of his subordinates soon finds himself in conflict, with himself and with others. With his teaching hat on, it makes sense to budget one way. With his patient care hat on, he may be pressured to do it differently, while the research part of him has another set of priorities.

In the traditional format, a lack of program differentiation makes it very difficult to coordinate and integrate activities across departmental lines. Each person does it for himself, if it is done at

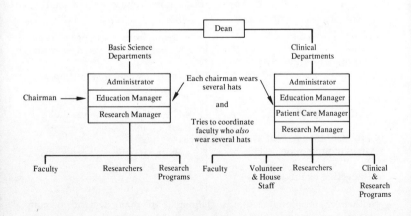

FIGURE 2

*SPECIALIZED SYSTEM (Traditional Model)*

all, thus losing one of the major purposes of organization. It is this tension between specialties and programs which has led on the one hand to departments jealously competing to control various programs, and to program managers zealously lobbying to give their pet projects departmental status. Others, disgusted with the whole business, have said, "Away with departments." In their view, interdisciplinary teams and core curricula organized around parts of the body, or new technologies, or human problems, are the wave of the future. Carried to its logical extreme such an organization might look like Exhibit 3, below.

However, this model also suffers from the weakness of its strengths. A lack of functional specialty differentiation cuts people off from critical sources of identity, professional growth and in-depth knowledge. We are convinced that medical centers cannot perform well without *both* the specialists and the integrative programs. How then organize for both?

In complex industries, like aerospace, which have analogous problems, the matrix has proved a useful way to sort functional from program hats. In the industrial matrix a man has two homes, one in the physics group, for instance, and another on the Project Y team. He also has two bosses. It takes a complex series of negotiations to set up and maintain his responsibilities to each boss. The analogy in medicine is the "mixed model," a form we see spontaneously taking root in many medical centers, where bits and pieces have emerged as the *only* reasonable way to get work done.

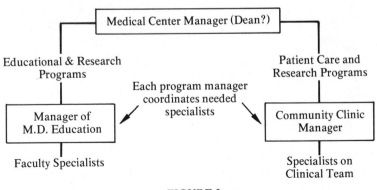

FIGURE 3

*PRIMARY SYSTEM (Prototype—Some systems are moving this way)*

However, even the most complex industries have fewer people wearing multiple hats than do the simplest medical centers. This is a major environmental difference between industry and medicine. In an industrial organization, *different* people tend to manage research, production and sales no matter how the company is organized. In medicine, many people manage several tasks *at the same time,* shifting back and forth all day between teaching, clinical care, research special programs, and governance tasks. This creates an unprecedented organizational problem.

A chairman (who wears four hats if you count administration) can't possibly coordinate the teaching, research and patient care hats of his many department members, who are working in different buildings, various programs, many hospitals, all over town. Neither can the various other medical center administrators. Indeed, most faculty professionals resist acknowledging any responsibility to non-physician managers unless explicitly ordered to do so by the Dean—something few, if any, Deans, would explicitly risk ordering.

Hospital administrators have recognized the problem for some time. As one wrote in 1964:[7]

> The role of the individual faculty member is inherently divisive, and his job has many facets. He is the key member of large complex enterprises and carries three different major enterprises. He is both a faculty member and a member of the hospital medical staff, and he is engaged in teaching, research, and patient care. Called upon to wear so many hats, he finds it simpler most of the time to wear his own. This is often necessary because he can't get anyone to recognize him in any of his other hats. . . .

This stance, at present the doctor's only defense against anarchy, puts an extraordinary burden on personal style. Indeed, in any medical center you find nearly every organizational problem being diagnosed by the people involved as one of "personalities." 'There are those you can get along with and those you can't.'

Thus the competition for money, for space, for power and influence, for time on the Dean's calendar, for choice committee appointments. The irony of this last is that everybody knows committees don't accomplish anything. They wrangle, report . . . and nothing happens. Indeed, in most medical centers no mechanism, widely recognized as legitimate, exists for translating committee recommendations into policy. Perhaps the Dean will act. Perhaps he won't. One of the great frustrations of the system is that committee output has no formal way of becoming input to the organization.

Committees serve a function, however. They provide a means by which the competitors tie each other in knots and prevent one another's hidden agendas from becoming policy.

In an attempt to create legitimate governing structures, academic centers have divorced management from governance. "Balanced" committees, on which all competing interests are represented, find themselves miniature politicized societies. As Warren Bennis, president of the University of Cincinnati, observed recently, "All this is supposed to add up to 'participatory democracy' but adds up, instead, to a cave of the winds where the most that can usually be agreed upon is to do nothing (like the bumper sticker 'My Vote Cancels Yours')."[8]

It's not that competition is a bad thing. It is necessary, and potentially useful. What is bad is that there are no boundaries to it, no legitimate ways to contain it. It's as if two highly skilled football teams are playing on a field with no yard markers and no sidelines. You never know where the locus of action really is. The game isn't much fun to watch, and even less fun to play. As one powerful department confided, "I've built a great empire here. I've manipulated and fought and undercut other people, and acted like the imperialist I am to build this strong department. And you know something, I don't like it. I wish to hell there were some other way to do it."

In this comment lies the clue to why interpersonal change strategies, which have revolutionized many businesses, fail in medical schools. There is no incentive to become more open, honest, and trusting in an environment of hungry wolves. Without ground rules, without structure, without recognized procedures for managing conflict, there is no way to get *anything* accomplished unless you make up your own rules as you go along.

This is a legitimate stance for a small entrepreneur, who carries his business in his hip pocket. Medical entrepreneurs have built excellent research organizations, and excellent production lines to turn out specialists in their own images. They cannot, in the traditional framework, also organize to produce enough general physicians and enough diagnostic and preventative services to meet new community demands.

Indeed, there is considerable disagreement among professionals in every center on the extent to which patient services should be a major focus of a medical school. One sign of missing structure is the fact few schools have any accepted mechanism for reviewing and altering mission and goals as conditions change. Hence, each professional believes *his* value about this is the correct one. One possible benefit of more explicit contracts could be to validate an organizational philosophy about what the right course of action is for this medical center at this moment in time.

A more precise exchange of expectations between Dean and chairmen and between chairmen and faculty, for example, would permit each professional to make more rational decisions about whether this organization is the right one for him.

From this analysis, then, comes the undergirding hypotheses for the mixed model:

1. To the extent that a medical center's environment and mission make feasible an emphasis on strong functional departments and specialties it will have *less* need for program structures, integrative organization units and administrators who wear only one hat; and

2. To the extent that a center's environment and mission push it in the direction of greater emphasis on service, it *must* create *more* program structures, have fewer professionals wearing multiple hats, especially in administrative roles, and seek new integrating mechanisms outside of the traditional departments.

3. However, academic medical centers cannot *replace* teaching and research with patient care, but need an appropriate mix of all three. To the extent that pressure for service becomes greater, conflict will increase:

— among multiple-task individuals, trying to wear many hats at once;

— between traditional departments and service programs;

— between department chairmen and administrators; and

— between individuals wearing single hats whose goals differ.

4. Thus, deliberate, explicit *conflict management* becomes a critical task in any academic center where the environment pushes towards greater differentiation *and* it is desirable to preserve specialized departments. However, conflict management costs something. The price is reduced autonomy for each department in return for a better functioning whole. In short, as open systems theorists have been saying, it is not *possible* to run patient care, research and teaching activities at maximum efficiency so long as

each is partly dependent on the others.[9] Nor is it effective to maximize one department's capability at the expense of another, if a center needs both. More people need to look out for the whole. To do this requires that program managers have power and influence equal to that traditionally enjoyed only by chairmen. Redistributing power in any center will heighten conflict and bring it more into the open.

A public declaration by the Dean that conflict is inevitable, legitimate and useful, and an attempt to create mechanisms by which it can be managed, are helpful steps in moving towards a mixed model. These steps cannot be taken unless the differences between departments and programs are recognized, encouraged and managed.

The mixed-model, Figure 4, suggests as best it can be done in two dimensions what such a recognition would look like. First, a few words about interpreting this chart. It is *not* an organization chart in the traditional sense. It is not intended to show all the many parts of the medical center and how they mesh. It *is* intended as a prototype map of the complex relationships between a medical center's chief executive, the specialized departments and the program organizations which require a variety of specialists to function well. The mixed model should be used to learn how to *think about* medical center relationships, and not as a literal guide to the way such relationships ought to be.

In this map, special departments are shown to the left and programs to the right. Diagonal lines indicate that (a) each department may have people located in any of the many programs, in addition to their departmental home; (b) each program is likely to include professionals from a variety of departments; and (c) program heads and department heads have a negotiating relationship with each other, rather than boss-subordinate. Each is responsible for a major set of tasks different from, and not subordinate to, what the other does.*

Using the mixed model, a professional, no matter how many hats he wears, can understand:

1. Where his organizational responsibilities lie when he is wearing each of his hats (he may be in six places on the chart), and how these differ as he switches hats;

---

* I'm struck by the similarities of this model and one arrived at independently by Dr. John R. Evans and described in his article cited as reference 1 at the end of this paper.

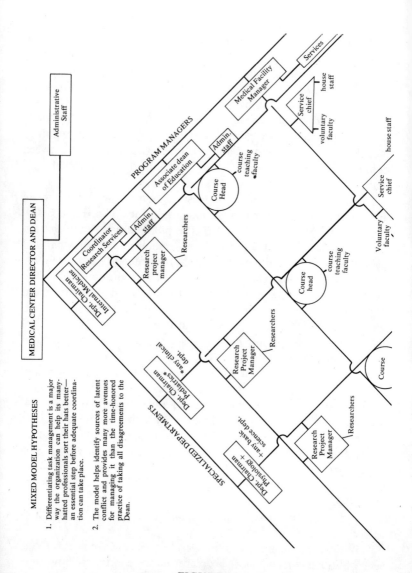

MIXED MODEL HYPOTHESES

1. Differentiating task management is a major way the organization can help its many-hatted professionals sort their hats better—an essential step before adequate coordination can take place.

2. The model helps identify sources of latent conflict and provides many more avenues for managing it than the time-honored practice of taking all disagreements to the Dean.

FIGURE 4

*Organization of a Mixed Medical System*

2. Which people he needs to talk with in order to establish the responsibilities for each hat; and

3. When he is trying to wear two incompatible hats. That is, trying to run a department, with its unique needs, and simultaneously administer a clinic or hospital (in practice, department chairmen with such diverse responsibilities either delegate one or both hats to others so that inherent conflicts can be managed openly or they experience paralyzing internal conflicts in their organizational lives, and their subordinates feel blocked and frustrated).

Properly understood, the mixed model helps professionals diagnose their existing organization for (a) missing structure, and (b) appropriate conflict management mechanisms and practices.

Carried to its logical extreme, a perfectly balanced mixed-model center would display;

1. Widely understood, and continually updated mission and goals which make possible, year to year, the inclusion of certain activities and the exclusion of others;

2. Explicit working agreements among the Center Director and each chairman, and the Director and each program head, including ground rules requiring chairmen and program heads to negotiate with one another for faculty services;

3. Explicit working agreements between each professional for each of his many hats, each agreement with the appropriate chairman, program director, project manager, course head, or whatever;

4. A budgeting system which reflects in individual salaries the mix of activities each person is doing *this* year; and

5. Widely understood procedures for handling conflicts between two hats, such as dealing with *each* of the task managers involved (or both together), in place of the time-honored practice, most functional in a highly-specialized center, of taking all disagreements to the Dean.

There are many other implications. The model, in this version, describes nothing about the relationship between management and governance. To display this requires a third dimension, in which committee hats would show up. An adequate model of management-governance relationships would also include the steps by which committee output becomes input to managers, and the procedures to be followed by management when committees are paralyzed by indecision. In the case study which follows we tried to help the Dean at UX create procedures for making organizational changes legitimate through the existing governance structure, thus creating a working model of the way such things might happen in other policy matters.

Those medical centers which need a mixed model are faced with a critical choice. They cannot both organize their many services and also cater to the tradition that professionals, no matter how many hats they wear, have only one line of responsibility to a chairman or Dean. Such a notion is unscientific and unworkable. Somebody has to say "The king has no clothes." The only person prestigious enough to say it and be heard is the Dean himself. As things stand, he is the repository for everybody's expectations, the one person looked upon, in the absence of adequate management structure, to be coach, referee, quarterback and ball-carrier. He also is the one person clearest about the impossibility of doing all the things others conceive he should.

How to change the game? The case study, in the next section, describes some things that happened as a result of one Dean's efforts to play it differently.

## V - INTERVENTION STRATEGY

In February 1972 Lawrence, Charns, Loomis and I had considerable data to support the above conclusions. In a two-day meeting with representatives of four schools we presented our data, and, with the Deans, built lists of existing (or potential) differentiating and integrating mechanisms. The Dean at UX, impatient to start changing things, asked us to offer our findings to his faculty at the earliest moment. Partly, it had to do with his personal time table. He was ready to trigger specific structural changes if enough faculty support could be mustered. On the other hand, once these changes were made, he wanted out.

Paul and I confronted him around how long change takes. We were reluctant to invest in an implementation strategy if the Dean didn't plan to see it through. This would take at least one to two years, we thought. The Dean didn't want to stay that long. Indeed, he'd already delayed his resignation awaiting the completion of our study. His leadership, he said, wasn't so crucial. If he could get the ball rolling, his faculty would do the right thing. We tried to differentiate having a good structural idea from implementing it: how perceptions, attitudes and behavior must change before a good idea becomes real. In confronting this issue, we had help from a department chairman and an assistant dean who confirmed repeatedly that unless the Dean stayed with it very little would happen.

After some hard bargaining, we reached a contract. The Dean would lead the change effort until (1) it became clear the faculty would *not* support it, or (2) new leadership emerged and it became self-supporting. In any event, he would not resign in less than six months. He then defined four objectives for his medical center:

1. Structure—Movement towards mixed model;
2. Resource Allocation—Program planning and budgeting;
3. Governance Structure—Collateral organization (described below); and
4. Role Behavior Clarified—Conflict management via contracting, and so on.

He agreed to present his change program to his faculty with two explicit messages:

1. "I believe in it and intend to lead it;" and
2. "You can and will have influence over and input into whatever happens."

We agreed to invest up to 28 consulting days between March and September 1972. The only objective we could not work on explicitly was resource allocation.

The Dean offered that, should the faculty not support change, we could pull out at any time and use the remaining budget for documenting the research. How our days would be used, indeed what interventions we might use, remained to be decided. The contract would depend on our capacity to continually redefine the "client" as more and more of the medical center, as we began to work with new people and new groups.

## Collateral Organization

Earlier, we had helped the Dean think through a conceptual framework for change strategy based largely on Dale Zand's work in setting up "collateral organizations"[10] In this notion we saw the chance to create an effective bridge between governance and management. The Dean needed a credible group of people whose task it would be to:

1. Collect and sort issues relevant to changing the medical center;
2. Traffic manage these issues onto the agendas of other groups, or create Task Forces to deal with them; and

3. Negotiate emerging changes with relevant groups in the center, creating a way in which all would have legitimate chances to influence change.

This organization would function in parallel to the existing administrative structure, and not in place of it. It was designed to handle tough problems, the ones not solved by issuing orders or making unilateral decisions. Indeed, it was a mechanism for taking "ill-structured" problems, where there is no clear view of which way to go, and turning them into "well-structured" recommendations, on which administrators, wearing their usual hats, could act with confidence.

The critical ingredient for success in this scheme is the method by which the collateral organizations output (its recommendations) become input to the formal organization. One method is to publicize in advance that recommendations from the collateral groups would be widely shared, discussed and open to influence before presentation to the Dean; that when finally presented he would respond in one of four ways:

a. Yes. We will do it. I assign____(person/group)____to act by ____(date)____.
b. No. Because_____.
c. Need more data____(kind)____from____(person/group)____ by____(date)____.
d. Need time. Will respond on____(date)____by ____(method)____.

Here, then, was a way to capitalize on the Dean's being seen as the major power figure in the medical center without reinforcing the fantasy of his omniscience.

*Faculty Feedback*

But first the faculty had to hear the data. In March, Paul and I met with UX medical faculty in an open meeting. We presented our findings. We suggested that should the faculty want to go forward, they take two steps:

1. Appoint a planning group to work with us in designing a workshop to examine the implications of our data in depth for *their* medical center.

2. Invite a representative group including all department chairmen to this workshop (40-50 people) with the explicit agreement that once the data were clear they could accept or reject further help from us.

The Dean agreed to abide by their decision. After a thorough airing of faculty skepticism the sense of the meeting was to proceed. The Dean quickly appointed a steering committee, including three department chairmen, to plan the next meeting. With this group we wrote the following contract:

| *Consultants* | *Steering Committee* |
|---|---|
| 1. Design a two-day meeting, in which data on the system would be presented and people would be encouraged to check it with their own experience; | 1. Develop list of 40-50 people (including all department chairmen) and administrative staff to invite to meeting; |
| 2. Provide a go/no-go choice point at the end of the first day; | 2. Find an off-site location for two days; |
| 3. If go, provide a method for choosing a more permanent committee to become coordinators of the change process and consult to them on next steps. | 3. Send out invitations and preliminary agenda; |
| | 4. Meet with us the night before to review the final design. |

It was explicitly agreed that the Steering Committee would metamorphose or be replaced with a group seen by the attendees as credible and legitimate to make recommendations to the Dean.

*Initial Meeting*

The initial meeting was held in March 1972. Paul and I acted as consultants, along with Marty Charns and Allan Drexler, an NTL Adjunct Staff Fellow whom I wanted to involve early should it develop, as we hoped, that a longer range effort would result. This was especially important because Paul and Marty, having academic duties, would have to limit their time during implementation, and the effort looked too big to me to carry alone.

Now we were faced with a critical test. Our objective was: (1) to present our findings and structural/behavioral ideas; (2) to have the participants test these against their own experience in the medical center; and (3) build enough face validity that those present would be moved to want to change things. But how to get the participants in touch with *all* the many problems? We decided on an "open systems appreciation" exercise as a way of getting people to experience together the pressures of the center's environment. Open systems technology forces attention to an organization's "core mission," and the various forces it must deal with.[11] It also provides a common vocabulary by which people can discuss their own experiences and conceptualize them in one framework. At the suggestion of an assistant dean, we wrote out a vocabulary list of words we intended to use (see Figure 5).

Our starting place, then, would not be the data we had collected. It would be a new data base, gathered quickly, on the spot, from the experiences of nearly 50 people with very diverse views of the medical center. Later, we would introduce our data and conceptual framework as an intervention to help people make sense of their experience.

The Dean opened the workshop with a strong statement of his hopes for initiating changes. He reaffirmed that the group assembled would control any decision to proceed. Next he introduced the staff, and we set a contract (we to provide methods, theory, data, they to provide open minds, data and frank expressions of personal view-points), noted the objectives and choice points, distributed vocabulary lists and asked people to meet in small groups and name the center's "core mission."

This resulted in various "motherhood" statements about the interdependence of education, research, and patient care. Next, we asked the small groups to list every environmental demand they could think of on the center. Soon the walls were papered with flip sheets listing demands by the score: from employees, patients, students, to local agencies, licensing boards and the mass media.

Finally, we asked each group to rate the adequacy of the medical center's response to each demand on a 1 to 5 scale. These exercises took most of the day. The data, and our feelings about it, seemed overwhelming. Toward the end of the day some clinical people confronted us that this was a waste of time. There were expert answers to these problems and we should simply supply them instead of doing Mickey Mouse small group exercises. "You call that data?" one doctor said, looking at the mass of flip sheets. "I say it's bullshit."

We countered that only they could decide whether the stuff on the walls was worth dealing with or not. As to time-wasting, we didn't know any other way, given the primitive state of this art, to build momentum for changing things. We pointed out that this probably

Below are some words we often use in talking about organizational problems and their solutions. Should we at any time become unintelligible, please help us by asking for clarification.

—Workshop Staff

1. Appreciation—To note and evaluate the characteristics of something. A combination of scientific observation and value judgment which helps people decide what to do.
2. Core Mission—An organization's purpose in the world, the reason it was created, the needs it is trying to fulfill.
3. Contract—A binding agreement between two parties. Contracts may be psychological as well as economic.
4. Domain—The areas, people, groups, etc. which supply and take from an organization, making demands, eliciting responses, and determining its character.
5. Values—Deeply held and felt beliefs not necessarily subject to scientific proof (a major source of organizational conflict).
6. Interdepndence—Situation in which parties or units need something from each other to do their work best.
7. Interface—Point of contact between units of an organization.
8. Goals—Long-range purposes (i.e. doubling size in 10 years).
9. Objectives—Short-range outcomes which support goals (i.e. 20% more space next year).
10. Ground Rules—Procedures agreed upon as rational means for handling "people problems," especially disagreements.
11. Differentiation—Dividing up and organizing work by sets of tasks which have similar characteristics. Adequate differentiation often leads to conflict.
12. Multiple-task professional—Person in medical organizations who performs two or more tasks (i.e. education, service, research, administration). We also say he "wears multiple hats."
13. Manifest Conflict—Open acknowledgment of differences and disagreements over purposes, values, resources, etc.
14. Latent Conflict—Conflicting purposes, not openly-recognized and/or openly acknowledged.
15. Integration—Coordinating differentiated tasks or, put another way, the constructive management of conflict, using ground rules, procedures, systems, etc.
16. Management—Process of coordinating and controlling a set of tasks to achieve certain outcomes.
17. Governance—Process of making and changing rules and policies which serve as guidelines to management.
18. Mixed Model—A suggested organization structure which provides for *both* strong specialized departments *and* various interdisciplinary and service-oriented programs, negotiating with each other on the basis of environmental demands.

FIGURE 5

*Some Vocabulary (our jargon)*

was the first time such a diverse group from one medical center had tried to develop a common view of the whole system. This led to a tense dialogue, with various participants heatedly speaking pro and con for continuing down this track. Finally, one doctor, who had fought us every step, said, "Whatever you call that stuff on the walls, the fact is we've got a lot of problems and we aren't dealing with them very well." Heads nodded in agreement. The hour was late. We decided to vote next morning on the decision to proceed. Two physicians left, one confiding that it was a bad use of his time to discuss medical center problems in small groups that included students and nurses. As I see it, this critical incident resulted in our contract being tested and made real.*

Next morning, the survivors voted almost unanimously to push on. We organized into small groups around interests: patient care, use of the mixed model to diagnose structure, problem census and conflict management. It was a productive day, marred periodically by skeptical observations that only 3 of the 14 department chairmen had come. Were they boycotting the meeting? As commitment rose to start changing things so did the anxiety that without chairman support nothing would happen. The Dean repeated his intention to support change.

He would like a "Continuity Committee," he said, "to evaluate the organization of the medical center and to consider an alternate organizational format" that would lead to better performance. He offered to let the group pick its own committee. They insisted that he name it himself. After some thought he named six physicians and a basic scientist, all of whom had been active (pro or con) in the meeting. It was a strong, able group of "middle management," united mainly by a commitment to better patient care in the hospitals. It included a chief of one major hospital service, an acting department chairman, chairman of the curriculum committee, directors of a pediatric clinic and student health service and respected members of surgery and medicine departments.

Carefully, the Dean, working alone, framed and wrote out their charge:

1. To educate themselves in OD language and ways of thinking;
2. Set priorities for dealing with the problems;

---

* I'm convinced that until people thoroughly air their resistances and anxieties about doing unprecedented things work on any task is largely fictional. Though I dislike tough confrontations, I watch for and encourage them when the commitment of an organization is at stake.

3. Recruit task forces to work on various issues;
4. Report progress to all periodically; and
5. Transmit "requests for action" to the Dean, who would respond promptly in one of four ways (i.e. Yes, no, need data, need time).

The plan had been to constitute task forces on the spot. Without the chairmen present, all were reluctant to do this. Instead, the newly formed committee decided to:

1. Draft a report of the meeting and distribute it throughout the medical center; and
2. Ask the Dean to convene a meeting with department chairmen to discuss their task, and what stance the chairmen would take towards them.

So enthusiastic was the newly-formed committee to get to work that all of us lost sight of the remaining 40 people. The meeting ended without any clarity about what, if any, future roles they would have. There was considerable grumbling. We urged the Dean to reconvene the meeting. People were already boarding the buses. Hurriedly, they were called back, and most came. From a discussion of the inept closure, we jumped to the dissatisfaction over the committee's composition. One hospital administrator openly confronted the Dean. Where, he asked, was administration represented? For an hour we worked various issues, reaching agreements between the new committee and the group that all would receive copies of the report and would have a chance to serve on subsequent Task Forces.

It was an open and a painful discussion, in which the Dean publicly raised the question of whether the game was worth it. He was for change, he said, but wondered whether they could afford very many tense sessions like this one as the price for it. Several remarked they were willing to try.

The last minute comments were enthusiasm mingled with doubt that anything would happen. At the end the spectre of the absent chairmen hung over all.

* * * * *

I have described this first event in some detail because it contains so many incidents critical to the success or failure of any long range change effort: setting a contract, leaving the client free choice, pushing for ownership of the data, testing the contract, acknowledging differences with resisters and taking them seriously, building a credible group to carry forward the process, planning strategy a step at a time, based on current information (rather than the need to use any particular intervention).

Indeed, we largely failed in our efforts to name a "core mission" in anything except cliches. We failed in our intent to build a full-blown collateral organization on the spot. We failed to involve a majority of department chairmen early on. The meeting's accomplishments, though, were considerable. For the first time nearly 50 people had come to some common perceptions about the medical center. A highly motivated group of respected (though not powerful) professionals had emerged who wanted change, and they had the Dean's support. The group had seen first hand what was meant by openly confronting conflict to make decisions and unclog previously blocked channels for action. Despite waves of enthusiasm mixed with despair, the Continuity Committee has continued since April 1972 to deal with increasingly deeper structural and behavioral issues; both its own and the medical center's. As consultants to this process, our objectives were (and are):

1. To force attention to missing structure and to encourage greater differentiation in management of tasks;

2. To legitimize conflict as inevitable, appropriate and useful in a system where task demands are so different;

3. To emphasize contract writing as one way to integrate activities and contain conflict within reasonable bounds;

4. To help people learn group skills so that they can:
   a. hold more productive meetings
   b. deal openly with conflict with less anxiety
   c. become better bargainers for the things they need;

5. To differentiate management from governance issues, and to set up ways of thinking about how each should be handled;

6. To create structures which lead to legitimate changes, even when some powerful people oppose change; and

7. To support the right of dissenters from change to dissent, and to confront the issues of legitimate processes for change; or, put another way, whether the right to dissent is also a license to block.

Underlying this strategy is an effort to build widespread support for decisions made by V.P., Dean, and (now) Medical Director, based on the ability of many people (not only chairmen) to influence such decisions. The commitment, willingness to invest time and energy and the accomplishments of the Continuity Committee continually validate for me the rightness of this strategy. Committee members held 7 a.m. meetings each week for months, fully accepting the responsibility for maintaining the pace of change, despite recurring bouts of self-doubt and pessimism. Their commitment was the more extraordinary in light of the Dean's decision in May 1972 to announce his resignation, retain his title as Vice President for Health Sciences while on sabbatical, and in June to appoint a Dean Pro-Tem who had not previously been involved in any of the intervention meetings.

### Carrying Forward Organizational Change

Let me summarize events between April and September 1972 by means of Figure 6. On the left are important events in the medical center (as documented by the Continuity Committee's minutes). On the right my comments re consulting interventions with them. (CC—means Continuity Committee; I am MW, Paul Lawrence is PL, Allan Drexler AD, Marty Charns MC.)

|                     *Clients*                     |                     *Consultants*                     |
| --- | --- |
| **APRIL** | |
| CC reports workshop outcomes to medical center, picks Addison-Wesley series as basic reading. | Phone calls back and forth around dates for a joint meeting between CC and department chairmen. |
| Dean calls general faculty meeting to report workshop outcomes. | We suggest CC ask chairmen what changes they want to see. |
| Clinical care in main teaching hospitals set as highest priorities. | |
| Meeting set between CC and department chairmen to get them on board, an "approach without antagonism." | |

FIGURE 6 *(continued on next page)*

*Clients*          *Consultants*

### MAY

| Clients | Consultants |
|---|---|
| 2 Day meeting between CC and Chairmen. Committee asked chairmen to list problems they'd like solved. Dean reiterated intention to support change. | PL and MW act as 3rd parties. |
| Both groups conclude contract specifying steps by which chairmen will influence recommendations to Dean. | We suggest intergroup contract, and work with both groups to clarify terms. |
| Dean tests with group impact of his impending resignation. Group agrees change will continue. | We accept Dean's contention that outcome of this meeting fulfills his contract with us. |
| CC sets up task forces for each major hospital plus the medical school to review problems, interview people, diagnose change priorities. | |
| CC meets individually with each Task Force, reviewing demands (both external and internal) as in original workshop. | Phone calls around ways to involve Service Chiefs |
| Meeting planned with Clinical Service Chiefs of main hospital around demands on each other. | Design meeting ground-rules, etc. worked out with CC. |
| CC assigns members to brief chiefs on "want lists" as preparation for meeting. | Plan: To demonstrate conflict management by negotiating selected "wants." |

### JUNE

| Clients | Consultants |
|---|---|
| Joint meeting of Chiefs, CC, and major hospital Task Force. | MW and AD as 3rd parties to display "want lists" and model negotiation. |
| Four pairs of Chiefs Negotiate selected issues. | |

FIGURE 6 *(continued on next page)*

| Clients | Consultants |
|---|---|
| CC meets to plan strategy for next day. | Next day, we domonstrate "styles of confrontation," using committee members and real issues between them. |
| Dean discusses process for selecting new Dean with committee. Disappointment at his leaving widespread. Fear that change process will stall. | |
| CC begins working on minority student issue at Dean's request. | We consult to process, around how to hold productive meetings. |
| Dean agrees to administrative assistant for CC to handle staff work. | |
| CC holds joint meeting with Department Chairmen and major hospital task force to discuss progress to date. | |

*JULY*

| Clients | Consultants |
|---|---|
| First recommendations ready: Full-time Medical Director, as peer of Dean, both reporting to V.P. for Health. Task Forces describe complex relationships between Dean, Medical Director, Hospital Administrator and Service Chiefs. | No direct involvement by us in these major structural changes. Assignments conceived and undertaken entirely by clients. |
| Chairmen agree to recommendations after joint meeting with CC. One clause sent back for reworking. | |
| Dean Pro Tem appointed (former Dean retains V.P. title while on sabbatical). | |
| V.P. appoints new full-time | We learn of changes and subse- |

FIGURE 6 *(continued on next page)*

| *Clients* | *Consultants* |
|---|---|
| Medical Director of main hospital. | quent confrontation after the fact. |
| CC confronts V.P. around process. Wanted more influence on decision. V.P. says administration must go on. | |
| Dean Pro Tem meets with committee to get contract between committee and former Dean transferred to him. Has hard time understanding process (he had not been involved in previous meetings). | MW consults to Committee and new Dean around relationship between them. |
| Surgery Department holds 2-day team building session (CC has two members from this department; chairman had been involved in contracting demonstration previous month; wanted better communication, clearer decisions, etc.). | MW conducts session after consultation with chairman. |
| Surgery department agrees to new procedures for communication between chairman and members; chairman delegates more tasks to others, including that of clinical service chief in major hospital. | MC interviews CC members and others around change process. Changes consistent with "mixed model." |
| Task Forces unclear about tasks. Bogged down in data. CC meets with one TF to clarify task. Agreements reached to change membership and focus on certain issues. | MW as 3rd party to two groups, working on ownership of task by Task Force. |

FIGURE 6 *(continued on next page)*

| *Clients* | *Consultants* |
|---|---|

## AUGUST

Mostly vacations. CC worried about absent former Dean, who has now moved to different part of country.

Phone calls to discuss work on:

1. Reviewing overall strategy and priorities.

CC feeling pressure of numerous tasks, uncertainty of relationships with new Dean Pro Tem and Medical Director.

2. Reviewing CC's relations to new Dean and Medical Director.

## SEPTEMBER

Meetings with Medical School Task Force, and with Dean Pro Tem and Medical Director.

AD and MW as 3rd parties. Help CC work through uncertainties of new administration and relations to it.

Working out role description for permanent Dean, along with School Task Force.

Consult to joint meetings between CC and School Task Force, focusing on how process issues block work on content.

CC works out independent contracts with Medical Director, and Dean Pro Tem. Joint decision to keep CC working made, after explicit discussion of pros and cons of continuing change effort.

Consult to CC in designing meeting with Dean and Medical Director, act as 3rd parties to that meeting.

Psychiatry department asks for help independent of CC efforts (largest department in school).

MW works out tentative contract with psychiatry Department to start diagnosis leading to possible reorganization.

CC asks for intensive change-agent training, begins to identify others in school who might be 3rd parties.

AD and MW agree to possible contract in coming year to:

1. Help CC plan strategy.
2. Build CC's skills around run-

FIGURE 6 *(continued on next page)*

| *Clients* | *Consultants* |
|---|---|
| CC applies for grant to continue OD work in current school year. | ning meetings, consulting to groups, contracting, etc.<br>3. Help people design individual change projects in own areas, or as consultants to each other. |

FIGURE 6

In short, the medical center has begun to make important structural changes consistent with a "mixed model." It is testing whether it is possible to have strong service programs without compromising the integrity of functional departments. Simultaneously, many people in the school are coming to see the open confrontation of conflict, and the working through to mutual agreements, as useful behavior, despite the pain involved.

Perhaps this sounds like a lot of consulting. In fact, days invested by the team between April and November 1972 numbered 30, of which 9 were given to the initial workshop. My point here is that significant change does not require massive consulting help, *when power and energy are supplied by clients*. A corollary to this is my belief that no amount of consulting help can make a difference in any organization in which a great many people, and especially the leadership, resist making commitments to each other.* Nobody can get out of trouble using the same behavior that got them into it.

## VI - EVALUATION

We have taken post-meeting reactions to some events. In July Marty Charns interviewed members of the Continuity Committee, the Dean, new administrators and a few chairmen. Some comments, both plus and minus, are recorded below to give the flavor of these interviews. I see these as "snapshots" frozen at one point in time, which need to be taken periodically if change is to be tracked and understood.

---

* I'm speaking of the voluntary, collaborative process I value most. Advocacy consulting can be very potent in getting resistant organizations to exhibit new behavior whether people want to or not.

*Positive Signs*

"It's not the same place it was 4 months ago. At first we spun our wheels over fear of the chairmen. Only a few were at the first workshop. Then we took the bull by the horns and met with them. They said, 'you're a valid force.' We formed a decent contract. They agreed to work with us and us with them."

(CC Member)

"We're starting to set up outlines of where people are. Several of us were turned off by the hassle with the Dean (V.P.) over appointing a new Dean and Medical Director before we finished the job descriptions. Our feelings were hurt. The positive thing is we were able to have a confrontation with him over it."

(CC Member)

"We have uncovered people, systems that are dysfunctional and we're getting a handle on why. We're going off on our own doing things. I'm in the process of learning more about being a third party and I've involved my staff. I find myself continually falling back into my old ways. The good part is I recognize they're old ways. We're getting to the point that we're damn free about telling things to each other."

(CC Member)

"Somebody's got to do the legwork and the chairmen don't have time. CC has done an excellent job. They've kept us informed. I don't feel threatened at all. I would be annoyed if we didn't have the opportunity to influence decision-making. If we don't, it's our fault."

(Department Chairman)

"We were pretty excited after the first workshop. We were very inept too. Each time one of the consultants came we got the feeling we knew how to do it, but when they left we couldn't make it work. Some felt we weren't accomplishing anything. I never did. I felt we were having better meetings than ever before."

(CC Member)

"I saw this crazy matrix thing with all the lines and I thought, 'this is bull.' I agreed with _____ that all you need is good men to do a good job well. By 10 p.m. Friday I was all for it. When I saw a guy with many jobs and several bosses, I saw that he couldn't hide behind one from all the others."

(CC Member)

"As a rank neophyte at the first workshop, I thought, 'These consultants are out of their minds.' The second day I decided two things bothered me: the lack of organizational structure, and the total lack of understanding the faculty had for the organization and particularly the role they played in it."

(Chief of Service, major hospital)

"CC took very seriously their responsibility to report to the faculty and deal with the absent chairmen. They knew they couldn't as a group develop a blueprint for the school and present it to the faculty. The _____meeting was highly significant. The chairmen came and gave validation to the CC. Having Marv sit with CC and Paul with chairmen in two separate rooms and then coming together, reassured the chairmen they would have an important role and told the CC that they would be listened to."

(V.P. and former Dean)

*And Some Doubts . . .*

"We're not doing a good job of specifying problems in problem terms. I think we slipped into this through the back door. I feel in retrospect that the survey developed a lot of irrelvant data and almost clouding what we wanted to find out about this organization."

(V.P. and former Dean)

"One of my frustrations is that I see people who haven't bought the contract and they're on the outside and we need them. I think they'll get trampled in the stampede."

(CC Member)

"I resent being by-passed all the time. The thing about a healthy organization is good communication. We haven't had a meeting between chairmen and Dean for 3 months. The CC is dealing with the Dean and we're not."

(Department Chairman)

"There are times when I wonder if it's worth it. A major feeling is that of uneasiness—that I'm reading a book about how to do it and that's not enough. I need professional help. Intellectually I know what developing skills means. Practically, it's hard to do."

(CC Member)

"We need to learn to do this ourselves. Consultants are a crutch. Does it hurt! Does it take my time! The way I learn to do is by teaching others. People need to be self-committed, and to do that they need to see a product come out. It's like a nuclear reactor. You guys (the consultants) have got the stuff together for us, and now we're doing it for ourselves."

(CC Member)

"People are enthusiastic just because there's change. I don't know if that's bad or good. The process is slow and inefficient. A lot of people are involved, and 90 percent of their time is spent in education. I don't know how long you can go without seeing anything concrete or enthusiasm will wane."

(Department Chairman)

"One of my concerns is that the development of all these mechanisms for change says nothing about the quality of what is done. No mechanism is built in for introducing values. I hope people don't feel that just having a good mechanism insures quality."

(Dean Pro Tem)

In addition to a second set of snapshots, we hope in 1973 to resurvey the school, using a random sample of faculty members who were *not* in the initial survey. The new data will tell us:

1. The extent to which people in the system now differentiate their various tasks, and what difference, if any this makes to them.

2. The extent to which conflict is confronted openly and worked through; changes, if any, in the quality of relationships between various departments.

By comparing these data with our initial survey, we expect to provide some quantitative evidence about the impact of the "mixed model" as a conceptual tool for change.

## VII - SUMMARY REMARKS

### Value Base

Some explicit values this intervention represents:

1. It's appropriate for science-based organizations to take a more scientific attitude towards their own organizations, even when the "science" is softer than they're accustomed to;

2. As practitioners we have a responsibility to confront clients with the limits the environment puts on their range of choices;

3. Health care delivery requires the organization of services in such a way that autonomous professionals must give up some autonomy or leave the system;

4. Conflict is necessary, inevitable, legitimate, and potentially useful;

5. In systems with multiple goals (that is, a "goal spectrum") it is not possible to achieve win-win solutions to every conflict. The cost is too high in good performance. Indeed, the appropriate stance is that each person should be free to pursue the goal he sees as important as vigorously as he knows how, subject only to the limitations of his contracts, and to reasonable ground rules about what to do when he disagrees with somebody else pursuing a contrary goal;

6. Most people would rather have a negotiated settlement than unrelieved covert warfare;

7. In an anarchic system credibility and legitimacy (that is, people seen as having responsible influence over change) are more useful for positive change than "representativeness" of all factions; and

8. Simultaneously supporting the clients' freedom of choice and confronting them with tough choices is a central goal of OD consultation.

### Applicability

This strategy is appropriate when:

1. People need a new conceptual handle to organize their thinking about the way they are organized;

2. Conflict is over personalized and people don't connect it to organizational realities;

3. The clients have it in their power to make structural changes which alter the nature of the system; that is, new task managers, policies, procedures, and so on;

4. People need to be clearer about "sorting their hats" when they perform many tasks, and make many decisions, each requiring different ways of confronting the world; and

5. Clients have a relatively small consulting budget, but considerable personal time and energy to invest.

## Limitations

This strategy probably is unworkable where:
1. People lack authority to change structure;
2. People don't have time for a sequence of interventions;
3. Too few influential people show commitment to changing their own behavior in addition to structure; and
4. It isn't needed; such as a system in which either functional or project organization is adequate to demands of the environment.

## My Doubts

1. I continue to be uncomfortable about the lack of performance measures. It is an act of faith to say that better differentiation and integration lead to better performance. It is proving much harder to define system effectiveness than we imagined it would be.

2. There is a tendency always for issues to proliferate. I worry that people not centrally involved in change meetings see outcomes (structural changes) as more critical than the process by which these outcomes are achieved (Task Forces, mutual influence procedures, validation of Dean's authority, collecting information before acting, reexamining and learning from mistakes).

How to balance successful outcomes (which are needed early on to reinforce commitment) with learning a new way of doing business? It *always* requires that some issues be explicitly ignored or placed low on the list, and those outside the process see this as failure.

3. It bothers me that I've missed opportunities to get better closure on certain critical interpersonal issues between key people; more so than with many clients where the focus of intervention is more heavily interpersonal. I accept this as an unfair and probably unavoidable price of other needed changes. Like my clients, I wish I didn't have to pay it.

# REFERENCES

1. Evans, John R., M.D., "Organizational Patterns for New Responsibilities," *Journal of Medical Education,* Vol. 45, December 1970, pp. 988-999.
2. Lawrence, Paul R. and Jay W. Lorsch, *Organization and environment: managing differentiation and integration.* Homewood, Illinois: Richard D. Irwin, Inc. 1969.
3. Freidson, Eliot. *Professional dominance: the social structure of medical care.* Chicago: Aldine Publishing Co., 1970.
4. Roemer, Milton I. and Jay W. Friedman, *Doctors in hospitals.* Baltimore: Johns Hopkins Press, 1971.
5. Bennis, Warren G., Kenneth D. Benne, Robert Chin.*The planning of change.* Holt, Rinehart and Winston, Inc., second edition, New York: 1969.
6. Charns, Martin P. *The organization of multiple task professionals:* A Study of Four Academic Medical Centers, (Unpublished Doctoral Thesis, Harvard Graduate School of Business Administration, 1972).
7. Brown, Ray E., "Dollars and Sense in Medical School—Teaching Hospital Relationships," *Report of the Second Administrative Institute, Medical School—Teaching Hospital Relations,* 1964, Ch. 6, p. 133.
8. Bennis, Warren. "The University Leader," *Saturday Review,* December 9, 1972, pp. 42-50.
9. Ackoff, Dr. Russell L., Wharton School of Finance and Commerce, University of Pennsylvania, "The Second Industrial Revolution." Unpublished address, 1972. The clearest summary of systems thinking and its relevance to organizations that I have seen.
10. Zand, D. E. "Collateral Organization: An Integrative Concept." (Unpublished paper presented to OD Network, October 1971.)
    Zand, D. E., Matthew B. Miles, William O. Lytle, Jr., "Enlarging Organizational Choice Through Use Of A Temporary Problem-Solving System." (Unpublished paper, 1970.)
11. Krone, Charles G., untitled address on Open Systems Appreciation and Planning, presented to National OD Network Meeting, October 6, 1971.

# 10

# MANAGING CONFLICT BETWEEN GROUPS

*W. WARNER BURKE*

When people work and/or live together, conflict is as inevitable as the chase that ensues when a cat sees a mouse. And, like the animals, we usually attempt to "manage" our conflicts by flight or fight. Since the 1950's, methods for managing conflicts more constructively have been developed by behavioral scientists, but such methods are used in a disproportionately small number of cases. Blake and Mouton (1961; 1962) have made a considerable contribution to the application of behavioral science to conflict resolution by taking the original research and theory of Sherif (Sherif, 1962; Sherif & Sherif, 1956) and applying it to organizations. A comprehensive explanation of this application has been published (Blake, Shepard, & Mouton, 1964) which provides strategies for improving headquarters-field relations, problem-solving in labor-management conflict and intergroup dynamics in mergers. Their discussion of the Scofield case, a headquarters-field conflict, clearly illustrates the usefulness of this kind of organization development intervention. Moreover, Blake and Mouton (1968) have devoted one phase of their comprehensive approach to OD to intergroup development.

Why are these strategies and others (for example, Beckhard, 1969; Walton, 1969) not used more often? There isn't any doubt that they are needed for improving organizational effectiveness. In my experience, team building is the OD intervention most commonly used by practitioners. But, as every practitioner knows, team building is not, of itself, OD. Of course, dealing with conflict is not easy even if one is a third party. Emotions are not only surfaced but are sometimes expressed in hurtful ways. The desire on the part of client and consultant alike to avoid these painful experiences no doubt provides one reason for the infrequent use of such interventions. Another reason may be our lack of knowledge about some specific procedures for managing an intergroup problem-solving meeting. Fordyce and Weil (1971) have provided some specific procedures (see for example, pp. 124-130), but their treatment of intergroup conflict is rather brief. Blake, Shepard, and Mouton's (1964) coverage of the Scofield headquarters-field conflict is comprehensive enough, but what if you do not have six days?

On the hunch that lack of knowledge about and experience with specific procedures for conducting an intergroup problem—solving meeting of a relatively short duration may account for what appears to be minimal use of an effective intervention, I have set for myself in this paper the objective of explaining in detail specific steps I take in conducting an "intergroup" when the time is limited to only two days. In providing the amount of detail that I do, I do not intend to present my procedure (which, after all, is a combination of many techniques I've learned from others) as *the way*. I simply want to explain what has worked for me and, as much as possible, provide the rationale for why I take certain steps.

I have used the procedure I shall describe with such groups as production and maintenance engineers from a company in the metals industry, medical technicians and physicians in a medical school-university hospital complex, and with manufacturing and engineering managers in an electrical products plant. This last intergroup is the one I shall use as a case example for my explanation of the procedure.

## Prior to Meeting

Some diagnostic work must be done before the meeting. This step is fundamental in practicing organization development (Burke & Hornstein, 1972). More specifically, the reasons in this case are not only to determine the need for such an intervention, but also (a) to give the consultant a "feel" for the situation, and (b) to determine the clients' motivation for and commitment to a problem-solving meeting. If you find low motivation and commitment, my suggestion is to consider strongly calling the meeting off or simply not hold it if one had not been presumed. Frequently managers assume that the purpose of a meeting such as this one, or a team building session for example, is for training and education. The consultant is going to "lay something on us." What must be made clear is that the objective of the meeting is to identify and work on real, nagging, and up to this point, unsolvable problems. Problem solving work is difficult and tedious. The client must understand that the meeting is for work. *Consultants in OD make mistakes at this beginning point by allowing the client to place them in a teacher or trainer role and not in a role of facilitator and catalyst.* The consultant must emphasize that he cannot identify the issues and problems much less solve them. The client must do this work, not the consultant. If the consultant determines that the objective for the meeting is not understood, then he must work to make it clear with a clear alternative being one of not holding the meeting, at least not the kind of meeting I describe in the article.

After determining that the diagnosis warrants an intergroup intervention, a general meeting of all concerned (the persons who will attend and do the work and those in the organizational hierarchy who are responsible for this client group), should be held on site prior to leaving for the meeting. This meeting should be called and conducted by the person (or persons) in the organizational hierarchy who is a common superior to the two groups. In the case example I am using, it was the Plant Manager to whom the heads of manufacturing and engineering reported. The purposes for the superior's calling this meeting are (a) "officially" to sanction the meeting; (b) for the boss (here, the plant manager) to present any mandates (what he hopes will be accomplished); and (c) to explain the "boundaries" or authority of the meeting. In other words, with this latter objective, the boss needs to say what decisions can be made, what actions can be taken, and what is "out of bounds." As the consultant, I follow the boss by then explaining, from my perspective, the purpose of the meeting, and what the design will be. With respect to the purpose, I explain that we will not attempt to change anyone's personality or character structure but that our objectives are to discover what the actual problems are in the *interface* between the two groups and to plan action steps for correcting these problems.

Incidentally, in my experience with this intervention, most people have *not* had laboratory training nor have they participated previously in any kind of team building process. I do not believe that either is a prerequisite for this intergroup design. These prior experiences would undoubtedly help but with the kind of structure I use for this two-day meeting neither is a necessity.

### The Off-Site Meeting

Although this meeting could be held on location, the advantages of going off-site are well known. Away from distractions, conditions are such that most energy can be directed toward the problem at hand and during breaks, meals and social time, the people usually

THEORY AND METHOD IN OD

remain together and continue working in some different ways than the work done during the "formal" sessions. These informal talks often facilitate the overall problem-solving process.

*Phase 1 — Image Exchange.* (Two hours) I like to begin a meeting of this kind with a brief description of other sessions I have conducted with other organizations. These examples (a) provide the client group with an overview of what they can expect and, therefore, reduce some of the ambiguity and anxiety, and (b) show that the consultant has done something like this before, again giving them some means of reducing counterproductive anxiety so that energy can be focused on the interface problems and not on the consultant and his design.

After my opening statement, usually no longer than 15 minutes, I divide the total group into their natural groupings. In this case there were six men in each group, Engineering and Manufacturing. Each of the two groups work separately for an hour and produce three lists on newsprint.*

1. How do we see ourselves?
   (It is frequently useful to include also a listing of how the group sees its responsibilities.)
2. How do we see the other group?
3. How do we think they see us?
   (In other words, each group is trying to predict the other group's second list.)

Their lists can be sentences, phrases, or one-word adjectives. Table 1 shows a sampling of what these two groups, Engineering and Manufacturing, produced. The rationale for conducting an image exchange is as follows:

> The meeting begins on a note of personal involvement and discovery and not that of wrestling with problems at the outset.

> Sharing perceptions usually takes care of some problems at the beginning. For example, the Engineering group believed that Manufacturing saw them as intruding on their (Manufacturing's) functions. (See Table 1, No. 3, item f.) The Manufacturing group didn't see them that way at all. This "perceived problem" was eliminated immediately.

---

* The tools of the trade in OD are three: (1) a flip chart or easel with a newsprint pad, (2) felt markers in a variety of colors, and (3) masking tape. With these tools, OD practitioners can perform miracles!

List 1. *How Do We See Ourselves?*

*Engineering*

a) Stabilizing influence in the plant
b) Flexible but uncompromising
c) Cooperative
d) Competent but fallible
e) Strategy formulators
f) Creative

*Manufacturing*

a) Competent
b) Inexperienced
c) Error prone
d) Not cohesive
e) Creative
f) Hard working
g) Sensitive to criticism
h) Second class citizens

List 2. *How Do We See Them?*

*Engineering* (describing Mfg.)

a) Unstable organization
b) Individually competent but not as a group
c) History oriented rather than forecast oriented
d) Unwilling to accept responsibility (they "call engineering")
e) Unwilling to compensate for others' errors
f) Not creative
g) Conscientious and industrious

*Manufacturing* (describing Eng.)

a) Error prone
b) Competent technically
c) Unaware of mfg. problems
e) Do not have a sense of urgency
f) More responsive to marketing than to us
g) Unified as a group and consistent

List 3. *How Do We Think They See Us?*

*Engineering*

a) Poor knowledge of their function
b) Engineers live in an ivory tower
c) Know technical end but not tuned to Mfg.'s needs.
d) Error prone
e) Don't feel pressure of end dates for product shipments
f) Intrude on other functions
g) Overly restrictive requirements and tolerances

*Manufacturing*

a) Constantly changing
b) Error prone
c) Not quality conscious
d) Reactors rather than planners
e) Crisis prone
f) Unwilling or unable to follow drawings
g) Inflexible

## TABLE 1

*Sampling of Image Exchange Lists Between the Engineering Department and the Manufacturing Group within a Plant*

The exchange helps to sharpen what the real issues in the interface are.

I like to conduct the exchange of perceptions in the following order:

*First*, Engineering (arbitrarily selected or they volunteer to go first) presents their List 1 (How do we see ourselves?)

*Second*, Manufacturing presents their List 2 (How do we see them?)

*Third*, Engineering presents their List 3 (How do we think they see us?)

*Fourth*, Manufacturing presents their List 1

*Fifth*, Engineering presents their List 2

*Sixth*, Manufacturing presents their List 3

The reason for this order is that it (a) maximizes *exchange*; one group presents followed by the other; and (b) provides for quick feedback; for example, Engineering reports on how they see themselves and this is followed with how they are seen. Engineering could present both their Lists 1 and 3 followed by Manufacturing's presentation of their List 2, and so forth for the remaining three steps in the procedure.

During this period of presentations, about an hour, the ground rule is that questions of *clarification only* can be discussed. This is not the time to debate differences or to take issue. The purpose of this phase is to present the data and to seek understanding.

*Phase 2 — Problem identification.* (Three hours.) This phase has four steps. Step one is to begin the task of identifying the problems that exist with the interface. To facilitate this step, I arrange for all six of the image exchange lists to be hung on the wall* so that the individuals can use the data for helping them to formulate their thoughts. This initial problem formulation is done by each person independently. About 30 minutes is required for this individual work. The rationale for this individual work at the outset of Phase 2 is to (a) legitimize and sanction independent thought; and (b) maximize conditions for comprehensive coverage of problems. Since group work predominates in this type of design, some individuals

---

* I refer to this particular step as "hanging up our dirty linens."

may be inhibited in a group and the opportunity for independent work may be the primary mode for their contribution.

The second step is for the two groups to meet again separately and consolidate their individual work into a group list. By consolidation I do not mean to imply that the final group list will necessarily be shorter than the total for the individuals' list. It may be that little overlap occurs although this is rare. It may also be that as a result of the group discussion other problems not previously thought of during the individual work become identified, a result that is common among groups that work effectively.

Step three consists of each group's presenting its problem list to the other. The purpose of this step is for each group to understand what the other group's perception is of the problems and what emphases each places on which issues. Again, only questions of clarification can be raised; debate is yet to come. In fact, I explain at the beginning of Phase 2 that a groundrule will be that we refrain from discussing any solutions to problems until we as thoroughly as possible identify and clarify what the problems are. The Engineering Department had a list of 16 problems and issues and, coincidentally, Manufacturing had 16 as well.

The fourth step is one of consolidating the two lists. At this point, I ask each group to select two of their members to meet together for the purpose of consolidating the two lists. I ask each of the two groups to select two of their members for this task because (a) I obviously cannot do the job as effectively as they since I'm not as familiar with the issues; (b) both groups' perceptions should influence the final problem list if accuracy of problem identification is to be achieved (people act according to their *perceptions* of issues not according to the reality of the issues); and (c) neither group holds a high degree of trust for the other at this point, and equal representation, as well as choice in selecting who will perform the work, contributes to an abatement of suspicion.

These four individuals (here, two from Engineering, and two from Manufacturing) take the two lists (32 statements in all), eliminate overlaps, and restate the problems in as clear a way as possible. This temporary group works in public view while the others either observe or take a break. The consolidating work, depending on the total list of statements, of course, takes about 30 minutes. In the case example, the final list contained 20 items (see Table 2 for a sampling of some of these 20).

— Engineering does not feel responsible for understanding and using procedures; a lack of concern for details.

— Organizational inconsistencies—Engineering is highly vertical and Manufacturing horizontal.

— Lack of participation by the Mfg. group at Engineering level on long-range planning.

— Both units tend to be overly bureaucratic and inflexible; not responsive to one another's requests.

— Drawings and "specs" full of errors.

— Instability of Mfg. organization; lack of depth and lack of experience.

— Frequent product and process changes; lack of advance communication on changes.

— Lack of mutual confidence.

— Engineering does not understand Mfg.'s problems with the union.

TABLE 2

*Sampling of Consolidated Problem List from the Engineering and Manufacturing Intergroup Problem-Solving Session*

*Phase 3 — Organizing for Problem Solving.* (30 minutes.) There are two steps in this third phase. First, each person selects from the total list of problems (20 in all) the ones he sees as the most important. In the case example, I told them to select the top six. I chose the number six based on how I wanted to organize the remainder of the session. I suggest that they select these top problems according to one or both of the following criteria: 1) those that affect you the most; and/or (b) those that you believe need the most immediate attention. After each person makes his selection, I ask him to rank these top problems from most important to least. These rankings from everyone are tallied and the top group of problems (again the number was 6 in the case example) is selected as a function of the sum of the tallies of the rankings and, of course, the group's judgment.

The second step in this brief phase is for each person to make a first and second choice of the problem he would like to work on. Following these choices as much as possible, problem-solving groups are formed with half of each problem-solving group's members being from one of the organizational groups and half from the other. In the case of the Engineering and Manufacturing example of 12 persons, three "cross" groups were formed of four members, two from

Engineering and two from Manufacturing. The rationale for this way of organizing is the same as the reasons I outlined for step four of Phase 2. Different perceptions influence the "shape" of the problems and both perceptions must contribute to the solving of the problems. Otherwise, the problems will remain, and no commitment to action steps on both parties' part will have been achieved. Moreover, the degree of misunderstanding and suspicion is reduced when the two groups have a chance to interact with one another toward a superordinate goal (Sherif & Sherif, 1956).

*Phase 4 — Problem Solving.* (4 hours.) This phase is begun with a brief lecture on steps in problem solving. The lecture includes an explanation of Force Field Analysis and how to use it in problem solving. I prefer to build the problem-solving steps around the Force Field Analysis because the technique is (a) easy to understand and use, (b) instrumental in establishing specific objectives for change, and (c) based on Lewin's theory of change which also provides the general theoretical frame of reference for organization development (Hornstein, Bunker, Burke, Gindes, and Lewicki, 1971). The seven steps I use are similar to others in use by applied behavioral scientists. Briefly, the steps* are as follows:

1. Problem identification.
2. Documentation — illustrations and examples of the problem.
3. Analysis of causes and establishing the objective for change: the Force Field Analysis.
4. Selection of appropriate restraining force(s) to reduce. This step is based on the Force Field Analysis conducted in the previous step. Selecting restraining forces for reduction is, of course, based on Lewin's principle of change, that is, reduction of restraining forces, as opposed to increasing driving forces, develops less tension in the system and therefore, less resistance to change.
5. Brainstorm ideas for reducing the restraining force(s).
6. Test brainstorming list for feasibility and make selections.
7. Plan action steps.

*Phase 5 — Problem-Solving Presentation.* (3 hours.) After completing the seven steps of problem solving for one of the problems selected, each group prepares a presentation of its work for the other groups. After each group's presentation, the other groups critique

---

* For a fuller explanation see Burke and Ellis (1969). The present list of seven steps has been modified slightly from this previous explanation.

the presenting group's work with feedback and suggestions. The rationale for this phase is to: (a) use each group as a *resource* to all others; (b) *practice* what they will probably need to do when they return to their job (often presentations need to be made back "at the shop" to peers, subordinates or to superiors); and (c) *enhance motivation* (shared ownership) since each group is presenting to its peers.

If time permits, each group can take a second problem, usually their second choice from the original list of most important problems, and begin the problem solving process (Phase 4) again.

As a conclusion to the meeting, I make a brief statement. It is usually something like, "Often when groups complete a meeting such as this, they take the attitude of 'we've done our work; now we'll go back to the shop to wait and see.' If your attitude is similar to this, then you'll wait and see nothing. Action must be taken by you if any change in the organization is to occur."

This statement is followed by a brief questionnaire of 4 items:

1. What are the advantages of following the kind of format (or design) we used during these two days?
2. The disadvantages?
3. To what extent do you believe anything will be different as a result of these two days? The question is answered via a seven-point scale ranging from 1, "no difference," to 7, "to a great extent."
4. What is your degree of optimism/pessimism about the "state" of your organization at this point in time? This question is also answered on a seven-point scale ranging from 1, "high pessimism" to 7, "high optimism."

The reason for asking the first two questions is to give me some feedback about the adequacy and relevance of the design. The purpose of asking the remaining two questions is quite another matter. I believe it is important to determine at this point in the meeting the "feeling state" of the client. People behave according to what they think *and feel*. If, for example, individuals believe that what they have done will amount to naught (a feeling of pessimism), then the problem-solving process will have been nothing more than an exercise. When I discover that pessimism is relatively high I then probe to try to discover why and if we can do anything about it.

For purposes of this paper typical responses to the first two questions are the most relevant. *Some quotes for question #1 have been*:

"Breaks down some barriers, may reveal feelings not previously known or understood."

"Working on real problems gives sense of purpose."

"Gets things going; gives you an idea of path to follow."

"Sets up actions and responsibilities for actions."

"It had the advantage of saving time and preventing disorganized discussion."

"Bringing things out in the open."

"Allows criticism without taking it personally."

"Helped to get problems down to 'bite size'."

"Helped to formulate most troublesome problems."

"Gave me more insight into other group."

"Opens the door to honest communication with each other."

"Reduces tension between the groups."

*Some quotes for question #2 have been:*

"The structure may keep some of the real issues hidden."

"Image exchange may have been unnecessary for groups who know each other as well as we already do."

"Aspects of total problem involving other management levels and other functions can't be covered adequately."

"Restricted some significant division problems from being presented."

"Some issues when discovered in the middle of the session may not be covered fully enough because backtracking is difficult."

"Could cause hurt feelings, widen gulfs."

"Can think of no disadvantages."

Naturally, groups' responses to questions 3 and 4 vary according to organization. Generally, people believe (but not strongly) that there will be a difference, the average is usually around 5 on the seven-point scale. Responses to the fourth question vary even more than those to the third question. This fourth question taps individual differences with respect to feelings more than the other questions.

To close the meeting, I report back to the groups their answers to the four questions and we discuss the implications. The primary purpose of this final process, as stated earlier, is to face the reality of people's feelings and that, in the final analysis, the extent to which action will actually be taken rests largely on individual emotion and motivation.

*Follow Up*

Follow up to an intervention such as this one may take a variety of forms. A must for the OD consultant, especially the internal practitioner, is to consult in whatever way appropriate with the problem-solving groups formed during the off-site meeting. For example, in the case reported above, a "progress report" meeting of the entire off-site group was planned for one day six weeks later. I met with the group to help design and facilitate the meeting for this day. I recommended that I return for this meeting to help with the design but also to insure that the meeting would indeed be held.

Another follow-up activity to an OD intervention is to plan yet another intervention. As the experienced OD practitioner knows, an OD intervention sets in motion new and different organizational dynamics that call for further diagnosis and possible intervention as a consequence. With respect to the case example described in this paper, two additional interventions were planned. One was a team building event for the head of Manufacturing and his staff, and another was an additional intergroup problem-solving session for the next lower levels of management in Engineering and Manufacturing.

In short, follow-up activities are planned and conducted as a function of the basic processes of OD, which is a continuous process of planned social interventions based on sound diagnoses.

*Summary*

So that the reader will not be lost in the details, I shall summarize this intervention for managing intergroup conflict by providing an outline of what I have described.

*Prior to the meeting*:   General meeting of both groups with the relevant person(s) in the organizational hierarchy to establish objectives, boundaries of authority and so on.

Phase 1:   Image exchange — The two groups share their perceptions of themselves and one another according to three questions. (1) How do we see ourselves and our organizational responsibilities? (2) How do we see the other group? (3) How do we think they see us?

Phase 2: Problem identification — State the problems individually, consolidate individual work in the organizational grouping, groups present their list to one another, and these two problem lists are consolidated into one working list.

Phase 3: Organizing for problem solving — Individuals rank order the problem list from most important problem to least, then make a first and second choice as to the problem they want to tackle, and, finally, "cross-function" problem-solving groups are formed.

Phase 4: Problem solving — The cross-function work groups follow the seven steps of problem solving.

Phase 5: Problem solving presentation — Each problem-solving group presents its work in terms of the content for each of the steps and their action plans.

Finally, it is important to obtain some assessment as to what the group thought about the meeting and their feelings about the future.

## Conclusions

With respect to the advantages or strengths of this design for intergroup intervention, the quotes above from previous clients speak for themselves. These quotes are fairly typical ones. The limitations of this design in my opinion, are primarily in the area of structure. The format is quite structured and paced. This structuring and pacing is deliberate on my part due to the brevity of time. What is sacrificed, however, is the opportunity for people to think inferentially as opposed to deductively; in other words, to "free wheel" and possibly discover issues and/or solutions that would not likely occur in this tight design. Moreover, people are not quite as free to express their emotions as would be the case in a less structured design. With follow-up support, however, there are certainly opportunities to think in these ways following the workshop.

With all things considered, especially time, I believe this design is the most productive one, at least for the kinds of groups I've consulted with. I also believe that this design has broader applicability to groups other than the ones with whom I've worked such as Blacks and Whites, headquarters-field, federal government and state government, school and community and many others. The design would undoubtedly require modification according to the kind of groups in conflict.

# REFERENCES

Beckhard, R. *Organization development: strategies and models.* Reading, Mass., Addison-Wesley, 1969.

Blake, R.R. & Mouton, J.S. *Group dynamics — Key to Decision Making.* Houston: Gulf Publishing Co., 1961.

Blake, R.R. & Mouton, J.S. "The intergroup dynamics of win-lose conflict and problem-solving collaboration in union-management relations". In M. Sherif (Ed.) *Intergroup Relations and Leadership*, New York; Wiley, 1962, pp. 94-140.

Blake, R.R. & Mouton, J.S. *Corporate Excellence Through Grid Organization Development.* Houston: Gulf Publishing Co., 1968.

Blake, R.R., Shepard, H.A., Mouton, J.S. *Managing Intergroup Conflict in Industry.* Houston: Gulf Publishing Co., 1964.

Burke, W.W., & Ellis, B.R. Designing a work conference on change and problem solving. *Adult Leadership*, 1969, 17, 410-412; 435-437.

Burke, W.W., & Hornstein, H.A. (Eds) *The Social Technology of Organization Development.* Washington, D.C.: NTL Learning Resources Corp., 1972.

Fordyce, J.K. & Weil, R. *Managing with People*, Reading Mass., Addison-Wesley, 1971.

Hornstein, H.A., Bunker, B.B., Burke, W.W., Gindes, M., & Lewicki, R.J. *Social Intervention: A Behavioral Science Approach.* New York: Free Press, 1971.

Sherif, M. (Ed.) *Intergroup Relations and Leadership.* New York, Wiley, 1962.

Sherif, M. & Sherif, C.W. *An Outline of Social Psychology.* (Rev. Ed.) New York; Harper, 1956.

Walton, R.E. *Interpersonal Peacemaking: Confrontations and Third Party Consultation.* Reading, Mass., Addison-Wesley, 1969.

# 11

# The Client as Theorist: an Approach to Individual and Organization Development*

## LEE BOLMAN

Most of us have heard more than once Kurt Lewin's venerable dictum that there is nothing so practical as a good theory. Yet, the power of Lewin's insight on this matter has been widely under-utilized. McGregor's use of "Theory X" and "Theory Y" is a notable example of a social scientist's recognition of the powerful interdependence between theories and behavior, but that fact is not widely emphasized in the applied behavioral sciences. This paper describes an approach to individual and organizational development which attempts to capitalize on Lewin's assertion, using a process in which clients are helped to become better theorists.

### Why Theories for Action?

To date, the evidence for the effectiveness of applied behavioral scientists, laboratory educators and organization development consultants is *under*whelming, particularly given the immense efforts of many very capable and dedicated professionals. Our interventions often seem to be all too impotent or temporary (much more temporary than the systems in which we make those interventions). In some cases in which enthusiastic claims of success are made (e.g., Blake et. al., 1964), the rhetoric is firmer than the evidence. In one sense, this merely reflects the difficulty of the undertaking. But the difficulty of any undertaking is closely related to the sophistication of our theories and technologies for dealing with it.

If our own theories as applied behavioral scientists are rudimentary, our clients' theories are more rudimentary still, and we have

* Many of the ideas presented in this paper evolved from discussions of the "clinical planning group" at the Center for Educational Leadership, and I am sure that I have borrowed many ideas from everyone involved in that group. I owe particular thanks to Chris Argyris, Charles E. Brown, Charles C. D. Hamilton, Daniel Munoz, Thomas P. O'Connor, Jim Rosenbaum, and Donald A. Schon.

provided them little help to develop better theories. Partly, this stems from the fact that many O.D. professionals do not have an explicit and consistent theory of their own. The lack of such a theory increases the likelihood that their behavior will depart from their espoused values and makes it very difficult for them to help clients develop cognitive clarity.

Such cognitive clarity—in both consultants and their clients—is critical because of the important functions which an effective theory of action can serve, functions which are not likely to be carried out effectively in the absence of such a theory.

First, the real world is impossibly complex, and cannot be negotiated without the use of concepts and theories. Man has no choice but to theorize—it is simply a question whether the concepts he uses, and the assumptions he makes, provide an optimal map of the world he needs to negotiate.

Second, a reasonably consistent and integrated theory provides guidance to an individual when he encounters significant choice-points. Such guidance makes it much more likely that his choices will form a coherent pattern which is validly linked to the individual's basic goals.

Third, an effective theory builds in tests of its own validity by being explicit about the predictions it makes at significant choice-points, and about the assumptions which underly those predictions. When experience proves inconsistent with prediction, the individual is clearly alerted to a problem either in the theory or in the consistency between theory and behavior. When a person is not explicit about his predictions at significant choice-points, then his theory is empty in the sense that it cannot be invalidated and he cannot learn.

Fourth, an effective theory is communicable to others. Communicability opens the theory to the possibility of dialogue, and increases the probability that the theorist can learn from others. For consultants, it is particularly important that their theory be communicable in a form that clients can understand since this is critical to the client's ability to make intelligent choices among consultants.

If we grant the importance of helping clients to develop better personal theories of action, several questions emerge: (1) What is a theory of action? (2) What differentiates effective and ineffective theories of action ? (3) What methods can be used to help people become better theorists? The remainder of this paper is addressed to those questions.

*Theories of Action*

Any behavior can be viewed as implying a theory of action, which includes at least the following elements:

1. *Goals*. A goal is simply an event or state of affairs which is preferred by the actor to other events or outcomes.
2. *Assumptions*. An assumption is a belief or hypothesis about the world—it may be a belief about oneself, about people, about situational contingencies, etc.
3. *Strategies*. A strategy is here defined as a recurrent pattern of behavior, as something which the actor does repeatedly or consistently.
4. *Outcomes*. Outcomes are simply consequences of an interaction.

A simple model of the relationship between goals, assumptions, strategies and outcomes is the following:

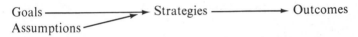

Goals ⟶ Strategies ⟶ Outcomes
Assumptions

In other words, an actor begins with a set of goals he hopes to achieve, and a set of beliefs which he holds. These goals and beliefs jointly determine the strategies he uses, and the strategies produce outcomes (which may or may not be congruent with the original goals).

Schon (1972) distinguishes three versions of the theory which underlies any action. The *espoused theory* represents the actor's own explanation of his behavior. It is the theory that is obtained when we ask an actor to explain why he behaves as he does. The *reconstructed theory* represents the theory that an observer might infer by watching the actor. The *theory-in-use* is the theory which validly predicts what the actor will do.

For example, consider an OD consultant attempting to deal with two departments which are engaged in unproductive conflict. The OD consultant might choose to arrange some kind of inter-departmental confrontation meeting. If we asked the consultant why he does this, he might respond with an espoused theory which states that his goal is to help the parties deal more effectively with conflict, and that the confrontation meeting is a likely means of achieving the goal. If we observed the consultant during the confrontation meeting, we might find that he avoided direct confrontations between the clients and himself, thereby modeling non-openness as a means of dealing with conflict. Such behavior is not predictable from the consultant's espoused theory. We might infer a reconstructed theory which includes the espoused theory, but also includes an additional goal of avoiding direct personal conflict with clients, and an associated strategy of non-openness about issues which threaten to produce such conflict. How well this reconstructed theory validly maps the theory-in-use could be tested by attempting to predict the consultant's behavior in subsequent situations.

The concept of "theory-in-use" is similar to what Vaill (1972) refers to as a "practice theory," which he defines as the personal theory guiding an OD consultant's practice. Vaill presents an illuminating discussion of many important characteristics of such theories. The primary area of disagreement between this paper and Vaill's argument centers around Vaill's "fallacy of misplaced coherence." He argues that, "it is a mistake to expect the practitioner to be able to give a satisfactory verbal account of the motives, content, and consequences of his practice." I believe that it is essential to expect the practitioner to provide such an account, even though that account can never be complete.

It is essential because an individual's espoused theory is commonly a poor map of his theory-in-use. A person's own explanation of his behavior is usually incomplete in the sense that many of the things he does are not mentioned in his espoused theory. Worse, the espoused theory is often irrelevant to or inconsistent with the theory-in-use. This occurs whenever a person's beliefs and behavior are poorly synchronized. Under these circumstances, the individual is unaware of important elements of his behavior and is unreliable as a predictor of his behavior.

Everyone who has worked in human relations laboratories is well aware of the phenomenon of low self-awareness, and of the fact that low self-awareness is often costly. Reconceptualizing low self-awareness to represent a lack of fit between espoused theory and theory-in-use makes it easier to see certain significant consequences. Experience in working with individuals around their theories-in-use indicates that all of the following tend to occur when the espoused theory is a poor map of the theory-in-use: (1) the theory-in-use can be shown to contain assumptions which are untested or are obviously invalid; (2) the theory-in-use is internally inconsistent; (3) the theory is so constructed that it minimizes tests of its own validity and tends to generate self-fulfilling prophesies.

*Effective and Ineffective Theories of Interaction*

The Peter Principle (Peter and Hull, 1969) is only one of a number of plausible but misleading hypotheses which have been offered to explain "why things always go wrong." Actually, things do not always go wrong, but they go wrong often enough in most organizations. A fundamental reason for this is a widely-shared, pervasive theory of effective human interaction which is, unfortunately, an ineffective theory.

This theory of effective interaction has emerged as the predominant theory-in-use for every population with which I have worked in the past year—including graduate students (in education and business), helping professionals (psychiatrists, psychologists, social workers), clergymen and company presidents. There are, of course, substantial individual differences in interaction style, yet there seems to be little variation around certain basic assumptions.

This pervasive theory, as I have inferred it from more than 100 "personal case papers" (which I will describe in detail in the next section of the paper) has the following elements:

A. *Goals for interaction*

In most interactions, each actor has some substantive goal that he can specify to a reasonable degree. In addition, most actors seem to pursue the following interactional goals:

1. Unilateral influence and/or unilateral management of the interaction;
2. Achievement of own goal as initially defined, without testing that goal against new information or against the goals of others;
3. Protection of self;
4. Winning, or avoidance of losing;
5. Suppression of emotion.

B. *Assumptions*

The following are the most common assumptions, in approximate order of frequency:

1. "I am right, the other person is wrong;"
2. It is too risky or harmful to be open about one's own feelings;
3. People are most effectively influenced through persuasion and logical argument;
4. Other people's emotions are most effectively influenced through logical, rational appeals;

5. When people resist influence, it helps to intensify the persuasion and logical argument;
6. Others can easily use and respond positively to advice.

C. *Strategies*

Given the goals and assumptions outlined above, it is not
surprising to find that the following are the most common strategies:

1. Present logical arguments, try to persuade and "sell;"
2. Punish others, tell them they are wrong, threaten them;
3. Withhold one's own feelings, remain calm and rational;
4. Ask for additional substantive information (but not for feedback);
5. Meet resistance with additional persuasion, increased pressure;
6. Avoid the exploration of other people's feelings and perceptions (particularly when they disagree);
7. Give advice;
8. Defend self against criticism;
9. Compliment others, start with the "bright side;"
10. Lean on authority, give orders, make demands.

D. *Outcomes*

The following are the most common outcomes from the cases I
have worked with:

1. Case-writer accomplishes own initial goal (occurs in about 50%
   of cases);
2. Relationship deteriorates or stays poor;
3. No learning or minimal learning (case-writer's assumptions are
   not tested, no feedback about his behavior);
4. Other's commitment to outcome is external (because case-
   writer managed process, influenced unilaterally);
5. Reinforcement of norms for non-openness, manipulation,
   mistrust;
6. Self-esteem of participants to interaction declines.

For simplicity, I shall refer to the above cluster of goals,
assumptions and strategies as the "competition theory" of human
interaction. It is based on the assumption that interpersonal relations
are inherently competitive, and tends to guarantee that they will be.
Kelley (1972) has shown that competitive theories of interaction tend
to drive out cooperative ones, even in settings where, objectively, a
cooperative relationship would produce more optimal outcomes for
all parties concerned. That is one reason that the competition theory

persists, despite the fact that it rests on a number of shaky assumptions and is a recipe for human ineffectiveness.

There are other reasons that it persists: (1) it is an effective theory in many routine interactions; (2) in more complex situations the theory is partially reinforcing, since people accomplish their initial goals about half the time; (3) the theory creates self-fulfilling prophesies, and minimizes the likelihood of having to learn an alternative theory.

It is possible to create educational experiences which enable people to choose whether to retain or move away from the competition theory, but this does not happen easily. My experience in working with individuals who have experienced basic human relations laboratories suggests that only a small percentage (less than 10%) have moved away the basic elements of the competition theory, even though most laboratory graduates feel that the experience helped them to be more sensitive and open. One reason for the minimal impact of laboratories on the basic theories-in-use is that laboratories usually do not focus on the participants' theories for action (partly because of an anti-cognitive bias which is characteristic of many laboratory trainers).

It is possible to combine laboratory methodologies with educational experiences that do enable an individual to explore systematically his theory of interpersonal effectiveness. Use of such a combination makes it much more likely that an individual will choose to move away from the basic competition theory. Methods for creating such a process are discussed in the next section.

### Methods for Training the Client as Theorist

Everyone has theories about all sorts of things, but few people view themselves as theorists. For this reason, most people cannot respond directly to a question of the form, "What is your theory of $X$?" (Where $X$ might be "organization development," "management," "watching television," or whatever). It does not help that the concept of theory is popularly associated with such adjectives as "abstract," "impractical," "intellectual" and "hard to understand."

Two influential theoretical approaches in social psychology converge to suggest a route. Self-perception theory (Bem, 1967) suggests that persons determine their beliefs and attitudes as least in part by making inferences from their own behavior ("I must enjoy television because I watch it a lot"), while attribution theory suggests that each of us makes inferences about the beliefs and attitudes of others by watching their behavior. This suggests the possibility that an individual can be helped to explicate his own theories-in-use through a dialogue between himself and others which centers on trying to make inferences from his behavior.

To provide a starting point for such a dialogue, it is helpful to ask the client to write a paper which can be called a "micro-theory paper" or an "intervention case paper." The client is asked to write this paper under a set of instructions like the following.*

1. Select a situation in which you attempt to influence, educate or change another person or persons. The situation should be one which you see as genuinely challenging for you and of significant relevance for your professional functioning. It might be one that you have already experienced, are currently facing or that you anticipate facing in the future.
2. Present a brief description of the case situation (in a few paragraphs sufficient to allow someone unfamiliar with the situation to understand its basic elements).
3. Indicate your goals or objectives in the situation. In other words, indicate what you consider to be a successful outcome.
4. In the following format, present one or two pages of dialogue between you and the other person(s) in the situation.

| Dialogue | Underlying thoughts, feelings |
|---|---|
| ME: | |
| OTHER: | |
| ME: | |
| OTHER: | |

The left side of the page should contain an actual script for a conversation between you and the other person(s) in the situation. The right side should indicate the underlying thoughts, feelings, inferences, and so on, that you would be having during the course of the dialogue. Please try to write a dialogue which is representative of the important issues you see yourself facing in the situation. As an alternative to the written dialogue, you may also

* The idea for the split-page dialogue outlined in instruction 4 was borrowed from Chris Argyris.

submit a tape recording, transcript, or video tape of an actual conversation.
5. Review the dialogue, and try to specify what you think were your basic strategies for achieving your objectives.
6. What assumptions underly your strategies?
7. Finally, how would you evaluate your intervention? Where did you succeed and why? Where were you unable to achieve your goals and why?

Over the years, behavioral scientists have had discouraging experiences with the validity of self-report measures, and that raises questions about the usefulness of such a case paper. Does it really reflect anything significant and valid about the individual? Conclusive evidence on this question is difficult to obtain, but experience so far suggests that the answer is very definitely yes. Rosenbaum (1972) compared group predictions based on individual case papers with the individual's behavior in discussions of that paper. He concluded that the case paper frequently represented an accurate preview of the individual's interpersonal style. In my own experience, the following cases are illustrative.

> *Case A:* "A" wrote a paper centering around the difficulties he had with a co-worker, which he tended to blame on the hostile and rigid attitudes of that co-worker. A's description of his own behavior clearly suggested that he dealt with conflict primarily by avoiding it. Two weeks later, a situation involving serious conflict between A and another individual arose. A reacted by physically withdrawing from the program for several days.

> *Case B:* "B" wrote a case paper depicting a situation in which he tried to persuade an organizational superior to save a project from extinction. B's behavior, as he described it, consisted of a sales pitch about the merits of the project, which he intensified in response to any signs of resistance from the superior. In a residential program, he consistently received feedback from others indicating that they saw him as manipulative and resistant to input from others.

Such cases rest on "clinical judgment," and do not constitute conclusive evidence of the validity of the approach. But experience with such papers so far suggests two things: (1) it is relatively easy for individuals to "misrepresent" (often unintentionally) what they do when they describe it in relatively global and inferential terms; (2) it is much less likely that the person can actually write a script with himself in it which is equally misleading. For example, a person may write that: "My basic strategy is to communicate to the other person that I want to hear his views and give him a chance to have a say in the decision," yet write a script in which his behavior is unilateral and non-listening. Experience with such papers suggests that the reader is well-advised to suspect the rhetoric and trust the script.

## A Case Example

A university-based consulting team was working with a small school system. One member of that team wrote an intervention case paper describing the team's approach, and, in lieu of the written dialogue, submitted a tape recording of a meeting between the consulting team and the Superintendent of Schools. The paper indicated three major objectives for the consulting project: (1) helping the staff direct its energies and commitment to system-wide problems more effectively and systematically; (2) develop new problem-solving structures in the system and help them work cooperatively on manageable objectives; (3) assist the system to use existing resources more effectively and to seek needed additional resources from outside.

The team's espoused strategy included the following elements: (1) increase the effectiveness of the superintendent in his role; (2) involve teachers in the renewal of the system; (3) help the system make linkages to other institutions which could provide needed resources. The team diagnosed the system as suffering from serious conflicts which were rarely discussed openly. The superintendent was felt to encourage the non-openness by continually asking for "dialogue" and "sharing of opinions" but behaving in ways that did not encourage such openness.

The writer of the paper submitted a tape recording of a meeting between the consulting team and the superintendent. He indicated that the team was not satisfied with its handling of several parts of the meeting, although they did not have a clear sense of what had gone wrong.

At the beginning of the meeting, the superintendent discussed visits he had made earlier in the day to two of the schools. He indicated that he was upset by some of the things he had seen happening (for example, teachers who sat in their lounge after the bell had rung). He received the following reply from a consultant:

> Consultant A: Certainly one of the keys now will be the method and the technique of your intervention. At one extreme you might intervene in such a way that there will be less communication, less structure for action, and therefore a situation which will be a greater problem. What we really want to see—and when I say we I mean all of us because there's certainly no doubt that what you want, and what we want, and what all educators should want, is precisely the same, and this is an immediate remedy for problems that can't be immediately remedied. So if we can discuss this a little bit—the possibilities of intervention in the schools, emphasizing a positive entry, and perhaps the specific techniques so that there can be a very profitable use of the next few minutes.

If the superintendent were to learn from the consultant's behavior, he would presumably conclude that a "positive entry" consists of lecturing to others, and telling other people what their goals are. Perhaps the superintendent was confused by the apparent inconsistency between the substance and the process of the consultant's intervention. At any rate, the intervention was followed by a half-minute of silence, which was broken by a second member of the team, who turned to the superintendent and asked him if he wished to say more about the schools he had visited. The first consultant cut this off by saying, "Well, I don't know if we should be moving to specific schools. If we're talking about the specific problems of schools, these are things that should be brought out already." This consultant went on to provide additional human relations advice to the superintendent, of which the following is an example:

> Consultant A: I wonder if it might be more profitable if we discussed a structure beginning on Monday for attempting specifically to attack the problems so that by Tuesday someone is acting. Such as you meeting with the principals, again in a *positive* context, without just inviting them in and saying, "Your school is in miserable shape and these are the problems." That alienates these men and puts them in a bad light with the others. If somehow this can be put in the context of the strength

that exists and the desire of the chief executive to do all in
his power to help.

The consultant implies that the superintendent has minimal interpersonal skill and sensitivity (why else would the superintendent need
such simplistic advice?), but does not say so directly, and provides no
evidence to support such a contention. Without testing the
superintendent's reactions to this message, the consulting team then
decided that the superintendent would be helped by role-playing a
situation in which he was interviewing an under-qualified job
applicant. The superintendent indicated that he would be open in
expressing his feelings that the applicant was underqualified. One
consultant apparently felt this was a breach of good human relations
principles and punished the superintendent for behaving in this way.
Another consultant then asked the superintendent if he felt helped by
the experience, and he indicated that he felt it had been useful.

During the meeting, a considerable part of the consultant's
behavior was controlling, advice-giving and occasionally punitive,
even though the substance of their statements continually urged
cooperative and open communications between the superintendent
and his subordinates. Some members of the consulting team felt
uncomfortable with this consultant dominance, but none of them
said anything in the meeting about their discomfort. The consulting .
team thereby provided an unintended model of the system's
problems (non-openness in dealing with conflict), and managed to
extract from the superintendent a statement that he felt helped by
such consultation.

In preparing to work with the case-writer around the theory
underlying the intervention, I prepared a "reconstructed" theory (see
Figure 1). I included in the model the goals, assumptions and
strategies which the consultants stated for themselves, and these
appear in the top half of each of the three boxes labeled "goals,"
"assumptions," and "strategies." Then, when I felt that the consultants' behavior implied assumptions or goals which were not
explicitly stated, I made inferences as to what these might be.

As one example, the consulting team's rhetoric emphasized staff
commitment, involvement and cooperative problem-solving. This
implies a consulting process with the same qualities; yet the tape
recording showed a process which was dominated by the consultants,
in which there was little communication and feedback to the
consultants and in which the consultants were willing to confront the
superintendent but not one another. From this behavior, I inferred

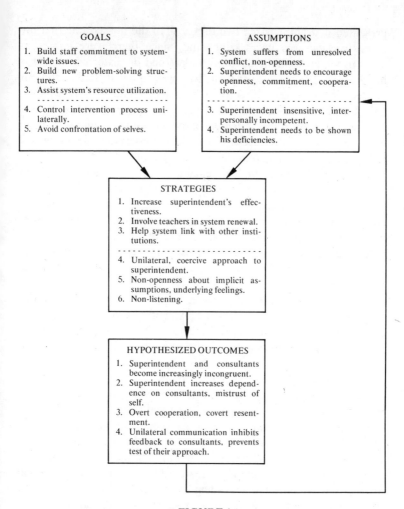

FIGURE 1

*Reconstructed Theory: Case Example*

latent goals of controlling the intervention process and avoiding confrontation of self. Similarly, the consultants did not explicitly state that they viewed the superintendent as interpersonally naive, but they treated him as if they were making such an assumption, and I added this to the list of consultant assumptions.

In subsequent discussions with the case-writer, I presented my version of the reconstructed theory underlying the intervention. As I presented it, I emphasized two things: (1) I did not assume that my reconstruction was necessarily valid, since there were numerous ways in which I might have misunderstood or distorted what was happening; (2) I believed that the best way to test differences in our inferences was to refer directly to the original data—the case paper, and the behavior in the meeting. The ensuing dialogue was characterized by a high degree of openness and mutuality from which both I and the case-writer derived considerable learning. He indicated, for example, that the consulting group had been concerned for some time about undue dependence in the client-consultant relationship, and were aware that the superintendent tended, at least overtly, to buy "whole hog" whatever the consultants presented. The consultants had never confronted this issue because they were unsure how to do it without making both themselves and the superintendent defensive. At the case-writer's request, time was spent role-playing alternative ways to try to confront this issue with the superintendent.

The strongest evidence for the case-writer's learning from this process was a subsequent case paper he wrote, in which he was able to present his theory much more explicitly, and to behave more consistently with it. Equally important, he showed considerable insight into gaps between his espoused theory and his behavior, and was able to discuss the latent goals and assumptions which caused him to depart from his desired behavior.

In this situation, I chose to work with the case-writer client by presenting a reconstructed theory that I had developed independently. This has the advantage of providing a coherent and specific model to which the client can react, and also helps the client to get a sense of what is meant by a "theory of action." On the other hand, some clients are overawed or unduly threatened by such a presentation and are likely to become too dependent or too rejecting in responding to the model. An alternative is to work jointly with the client in using the case to develop a model from scratch. This is often a difficult and frustrating process in its initial stages, but is likely to help the client develop a clearer sense of how to get from behavior to the underlying theory, thereby making him less dependent on someone else to do this task for him.

In either case, I try to work with the client until we can arrive at a model which he and others can agree is a reasonable approximation of the theory underlying his behavior in the case. Where agreement cannot be reached, I try to make certain that each of us clearly understands the nature of the disagreement, and the position of the other. Because the case is brief and written, problems of perceptual distortion or faulty memory are considerably less troublesome than in discussions of here-and-now behavior, and this makes it considerably easier to reach agreement.

Once agreement is reached, two things are usually apparent: (1) the reconstructed theory differs markedly from the client's espoused theories, usually in ways which the client finds distressing; (2) the disparity between the two theories frequently results from self-defensive strategies and from deficiencies in the interpersonal skills of the client. At this point, the client can begin work on the twin objectives of developing a theory which is more consonant with his personal values and goals, and developing the behavioral skills which will enable him to implement the improved theory.

The objective of increasing the behavioral capabilities of the client can be attacked through a number of available techniques in individual and organizational development. The objective of helping the client develop a more adequate theory is one about which relatively little is known. We have used three primary methods: (1) presenting the client with an example of an "ideal" theory of action (developed by the consultant), in order to provide at least one model of what a better theory might look like; (2) presenting a conceptual framework to help the client understand some of the properties of a good theory and criteria for evaluating a theory; (3) asking the client to write a second case paper in which he tries to incorporate learnings from discussion of the previous case. However, when deficiencies in the original theory stem from defense reactions or lack of skill in the client, the client needs to learn to deal with these before he is able to write a better theory. For example, if a client's only known way to influence others is through covert manipulation, he will be unable to write a consistent non-manipulative theory, much as he might like to develop one.

## Individual or Organization Development?

The methods discussed in the previous section were developed originally within the context of professional education, with a focus on the individual professional and his own theories for intervention. In this form, it is particularly relevant in the education of organization development consultants, managers, and laboratory educators.

I am convinced the goal of working around theories for action is equally relevant as a technique for organization development. Just as the patterns in an individual's behavior imply a theory-in-use, the regularities in behavior in any social unit imply a theory-in-use for that unit. Experience in working with organizational units is still in a very early stage, and the methods which are appropriate to individual development may not be equally effective with organizational units.

For example, the "intervention case paper" has been found extremely helpful as a starting point for inferring an individual's theory-in-use, but this method is much less applicable to larger social systems. In working with a larger system, it is possible to develop the espoused theory from written materials and from interviews with key decision-makers. The theory-in-use can be determined by looking at the structure and behavioral norms of the organization: its control systems, its interpersonal norms and its personnel policies.

In working with a hospital-based drug treatment unit, I have developed an espoused theory from their verbal descriptions of their approach and from the one written statement which they have produced. I have also reconstructed a theory from the staff's interactions with one another, and this theory departs in several respects from the espoused theory. As one example, the espoused theory emphasizes open expression of feelings by both patients and staff, but the staff often has difficulty being open with one another. In working with the staff I have asked them to become more explicit about their espoused theory, and to explore gaps between what they espouse and what they do. I am using progress on these tasks as an index of the success of the consultation: we will terminate when the staff feels satisfied with its theory and with its ability to implement it, or when the consultation is no longer providing significant help on the task.

## Conclusion

I have argued that human relations and organization development professionals can become substantially more effective by developing better personal theories of action for themselves, and by helping themselves to develop such theories. Currently, most clients adhere to a "competition theory of interaction" which emphasizes unilateral influence and self-protection. The prevalence of this theory is an important cause of the organizational ills which created the need for organization development. My experience suggests that consultation and educational process which do not focus explicitly on those theories usually have little effect on them, and, therefore, on the ways that people behave.

The effectiveness of action cannot be separated from the effectiveness of the theories underlying that action. We can and will develop better theories, and we can certainly help our clients to become better theorists. In this paper, I have outlined some approaches to the problem of more effective theory and action. The approaches are admittedly formative and rudimentary. But I hope that the paper is sufficiently clear that its shortcomings can be seen by readers, who can then begin the process of dialogue through which the theory underlying this paper can develop.

## REFERENCES

Bem, Daryl J. "Self-perception: an alternative interpretation of cognitive dissonance phenomena." *Psychological review,* 1967, *74,* 183-200.
Blake, Robert R., Mouton, Jane S., Barnes, Louis B., and Greiner, Larry E. "Breakthrough in organization development." *Harvard Business Review,* 1964, *42,* No. 6, 37-59.
Kelley, Harold H. and Stahelski, Anthony J. "Social interaction base of cooperators' and competitors' beliefs about others." *Journal of personality and social psychology,* 1970, *16,* pp. 66-91.
Peter, Laurance J. and Hully, Raymond. *The Peter Principle.* New York: Bantam, 1969.
Rosenbaum, J. "Report of results of 'evaluation of intervention' questionnaire." Unpublished manuscript, Harvard University, 1972.
Schon, Donald A. Seminar discussion, Summer clinical program in educational administration, Center for Educational Leadership, 1972.
Vaill, Peter B. "Practice theories in organization development." Paper presented at NTL Conference on New Technology in Organization Development, Washington, D.C., December, 1972.

# 12

# OD In A Large System

*BILL CROCKETT*

*BOB GAERTNER*

*MARGE DUFUR*

*D. CHARLES WHITE*

How does a company measure the results of a program which it sponsors for the purpose of improving the condition of its human relationships? What are the values of such things as leveling, trust, care, freedom and influence? And if values are ascribed, what are they and how might they be measured? Should the worth of such values be measured in tangible things such as turnover, profits, productivity, overhead and costs?

These and other questions were considered pro and con when Saga commissioned the Drossler Research Corporation of San Francisco, California to survey management attitudes in the spring of 1971.* The survey was designed also to produce data about Saga's Organization Development Program. This research group, familiar with dealing with hard data—facts, figures, correlations and statistics, were intrigued with the challenge Saga presented with the request to measure the results of Saga's OD effort—and to do so in harmony with the stated basic purpose: "To make Saga a better place for people." The process they used and the results they came up with are the purpose of this paper.

Saga is a twenty-four year old food service company that has until recently specialized in contract feeding at colleges, hospitals and businesses. In 1971, the company entered the restaurant business and at this time operates both fast food and full service restaurants. The company was started by three college students at Hobart College,

---

* Drossler Research Corporation is a national marketing consulting and opinion research company whose San Francisco Headquarters have been in operation since 1962. The principal people from Drossler involved in the Saga Survey were Richard A. Drossler, President, D. Charles White, Vice President, and Duane Kime, Research Analyst.

Geneva, New York, when they secured from the college a contract to
run the cafeteria.** The venture was a success from the beginning,
and Saga has prided itself with the fact that the qualities which led to
early success are still the company's foundation stones: ethical
conduct to all (customers, suppliers and employees); a passion for
customers' interests (their needs, their problems and their
preferences); a spirit of innovation, entrepreneurship and fun; and a
large amount of very hard work. The atmosphere of Saga has always
been open, informal and humanistically-oriented. It's a "people"
business with its people providing a basic need, food, to others. It is
also a low profit margin, people intensive, highly competitive and
easily entered market.

The company has grown rapidly and for the past eight years has
had earnings growth of about 20% compounded. In fiscal year 1972,
the net income increase was 26%. There are about 1100 management
personnel and some 25,000 full and part-time employees. But rapid
growth in profits has meant corresponding growth in numbers of new
people, new managers, new systems, new practices, new policies and
new bureaucracy. Questions arose: "How do we preserve the old
value system of Saga? How can we pass on that spirit of care and
concern we used to have for each other and for the customer? How
can we ensure that people will feel free to be innovative and act like
Saga 'owners'?" By a process of asking such questions and seeking
answers, Saga management developed and enunciated a statement of
ethics known within the company as "The Saga Way" (see Exhibit
1). This statement expresses the basic value system of Saga and lays
out, at all levels, the way the people of Saga want the company to
operate.

In 1967 management asked themselves the question, "How well
are we achieving these goals?" and commissioned the University of
Chicago to conduct a Management Attitude Survey to find out. The
survey showed that the Saga managers did have a model of a

** In November, 1948, three college seniors, Harry W. Anderson, W. P.
Laughlin, and William F. Scandling were awarded the opportunity to re-
open and run the Hobart College student dining hall. The only previous
business experience the three had was publishing and selling class notes and
desk blotters. With the G.I. Bill being their only source of income, their
economic motive was to supplement that income. Currently, Bill Laughlin
is Chairman of the Board, Bill Scandling is President, and "Hunk"
Anderson is Vice Chairman of the Board and Senior Vice President. All
three are directors of Saga Administrative Corporation.

TO PROVIDE MAXIMUM SATISFACTION FOR OUR CUSTOMERS through quality performance, thoughtful personalized service, and efficient and effective operations.

TO MAINTAIN THE HIGHEST ETHICAL RELATIONSHIPS WITH OUR CUSTOMERS, employees, suppliers and competitors.

TO EARN SATISFACTORY LONG-RUN PROFITS so as to maintain the health of the company and assure the availability of the necessary capital for continuing growth.

TO DEVELOP AND MAINTAIN A SUPERIOR MANAGEMENT TEAM dedicated to the objectives of the firm.

TO ASSURE OUR EMPLOYEES OF FAIR AND EQUITABLE COMPENSATION and the opportunity for individual self-expression and continuous personal growth.

TO ANTICIPATE THE FUTURE NEEDS OF OUR CUSTOMERS and develop the plans necessary to meet these needs and ensure growth.

TO FULFILL OUR OBLIGATIONS TO OUR FREE COMPETITIVE SOCIETY by constantly developing new and improved techniques, methods and procedures which will assure our progress and growth.

BY CONSISTENTLY STRIVING TOWARD THESE GOALS, BY SEEKING ALWAYS TO PERFORM MORE EFFECTIVELY, THE "SAGA WAY" WILL SERVE THE INTERESTS OF ITS CUSTOMERS, EMPLOYEES AND STOCKHOLDERS — ALWAYS GUIDED BY ETHICAL PRINCIPLES AND HELPING TO MAINTAIN OUR AMERICAN WAY OF LIFE.

EXHIBIT 1

*The Saga Way*

management style in their minds which had its roots in the values expressed in the "Saga Way." But they also felt that the model wasn't being fulfilled and expressed such feelings as: "We have lost influence. We feel smaller in a big environment. The company has become impersonal and bureaucratic. My boss doesn't care for me any more. Communications are bad. Headquarters people aren't responsive to my needs. Work isn't as much fun as it used to be. We have lost the old team spirit, etc., etc."

## The OD Decision

This survey provided the data upon which Saga management made its decision to embark upon an Organization Development effort. Long before that, however, when Saga management had developed "The Saga Way," they had answered the first question, "What kind of company do we want Saga to be?" Now, in 1968, they needed an answer to the question, "How can we work with our people in restoring the climate to what it had been when the company was much smaller and people felt more personally involved?" Once a model for an organization's management style has been stated, it is fairly easy to determine whether or not the values expressed by the model are being achieved. In Saga's case, the survey data in 1967 showed that they were not being achieved. The question then was, "why not?" In order to find out and to develop a continuing effort to insure the existance of the values the company held to be important, a formal Organization Development Program was started in 1968.

Early in 1968, the new OD change agent held meetings with Saga managers at all levels to try to understand the survey data, to gain insight into the issues that lay behind the data and to get some ideas for the kinds of things that might be done in order to achieve the values expressed by the Saga managers and enunciated by the Saga Way.

## The Diagnosis

The discussions in those early meetings convinced us that the primary problems to be dealt with were the feelings of impersonalization and isolation in the growing organization. The typical Saga manager in the institutional divisions is in the field, working autonomously in a food service operation in a college, hospital or business and industry setting.

A second problem was that of developing a pattern of managerial behavior that would start building the human and organizational climate the people said they believed in and wanted to achieve. As Kurt Lewin observed, "There is nothing as practical as a good theory." Our theory for changing the organizational climate was to change the attitudes, feelings and behavior of its people in quite a massive scale. The dilemma was not "what" but "how." How should we intervene in the human processes that now exist which result in the situation we say we don't like, so that we can re-direct and re-program them?

We decided our primary intervention strategy would be "Team Building." This decision was made for several reasons:

- Saga had always used the concept of "team" in its management style and its communications, and the word has meaning and substance in Saga;

- We believed that the basic building block to organizational change must involve the natural work groups (teams) as well as their individual members;

- We believed that only as the work team achieved a life of its own would people in Saga regain their feeling of closeness, influence and belonging, for it is only the team, in a large (and growing) organization, that can respond to the basic security needs of human beings;

- We believed the only way we could change the climate fast enough to make any impact would be to reach a critical mass of management during the first phase. In our opinion, the only way we could achieve this objective was through the team;

- We believed that the most effective learning unit, in so far as changing behavioral norms were concerned (influencing peoples' behavior as well as their theories), was the team.

### The Intervention Process

Once having come to the conclusions as to the results we wanted, we designed a program that would achieve those goals. We would start the OD process with the top team—the President, Vice Presidents and other members of that team. We hoped each team member would in turn elect to hold a Team Building Meeting with his own subordinates and so on until every management team in Saga had had such a meeting.

Our two-year goal was three-fold:

- To have had at least one team building meeting with each management group down to the hourly workers;

- To involve every manager in at least two such meetings; his attendance with his peers at the meeting held by his boss and then his own meeting as a boss with his subordinates.*

- To have created enough of a critical OD mass in all parts of the company so that people would actually start the process of change by *behaving* differently.

This strategy worked, with some minor exceptions, as we had

---

* Today the word "Boss" often elicits negative connotations. The word is used in Saga as "a person whose job it is to help each defined subordinate working for him meet their own unique and individual needs while at the same time successfully accomplishing organizational goals."

anticipated and at the time of the Drossler survey the program had been active in Saga for about four years. Virtually every management team in Saga had held one or more Team Building Meetings.

## Planning The Survey

In planning the OD portion of the survey, we had several secondary objectives we hoped to serve as well as fulfilling the primary objective of determining the impact of OD upon Saga Managers.

- To share the results of the survey with other institutions that have an interest in OD theories and applications;
- To involve a number of OD practitioners in the design of the survey in order to improve its quality and to enhance its credibility;
- To develop data that might be used for case studies and further research into the processes and meanings of OD for an organization;
- To discover new uses, avenues and directions for Saga's OD program;
- To explore and innovate new ways for measuring the impact of OD.

The first request we made of the Drossler people was that they acquaint themselves with the concept of OD and how its impact might be most creditably measured. They did this by conducting interviews with some of the well known practitioners in the field.*

## The Consensus of the Experts

Our objective in these interviews was to determine if we should undertake a measurement of this type and if so how could we best determine what change had taken place. The general consensus of those interviewed was:

- The research program is desirable and feasible;

* Dr. Chris Argyris, Harvard University, Cambridge, Mass.; Mr. Sheldon Davis, TRW, Redondo Beach, Calif.; Dr. Charles Ferguson, University of California, Los Angeles, Calif.; Dr. George F. J. Lehner, Los Angeles, Calif.; Dr. Warren Schmidt, University of California, Los Angeles, Calif.; Dr. Herbert Shepard, Stamford, Conn.; Dr. Robert Tannenbaum, University of Calif., Los Angeles, Calif.

- Saga should have modest expectations as to the precision of the results;
- Saga managers at all levels should be involved.

From these conclusions, along with discussions with Saga's management, the following objectives were decided upon for the survey itself:

- To furnish feedback on OD and the Saga Way.
- To chart *new directions* for the OD program and uncover unmet needs that could be met through the OD program.
- To determine the impact that the OD program has had on the effectiveness of management's style and relationships.
- To furnish benchmarks for tracking the continued impact of the Saga Way and OD in the future.
- To generate and publicize findings concerning the results of the *Saga Way* of management to the world outside Saga.

### The Approach*

The next step was a meeting between Drossler and Saga's OD staff and Personnel management to agree upon techniques. A two stage interviewing approach was decided upon:

1. Interviews.

A series of two-hour interviews and one-day group discussions with a cross section of over 100 managers were conducted by two outside consultants to gather inputs for quantification. An interesting and important aspect of this step in the research was Saga's contracting with an additional consultant with a different perspective than Drossler to contribute to the questionnaire. Mr. Sam Farry, an OD professional with prior experience at TRW, contributed the external viewpoint to the public opinion approach of Drossler's Mr. D. C. White. A further beneficial contrast that emerged from pairing these two objective outsiders was that while Farry's career has been in OD none of the Drossler group had heard of OD prior to being asked to make a critical evaluation of its impact.

* This technical section of the report was prepared by Drossler. Questions about the data, the analysis, or the correlations may be addressed to: Drossler Research Corp., 570 Pacific Avenue, San Francisco, Calif. 94133.

## 2. Questionnaires.

A self-administered questionnaire survey among all managers was conducted in December-January, 1971-72. It was decided that the survey design would take the form of an overall management attitude study covering many topics for three reasons:

- We found that an investigation of opinions about all aspects of the company would be most responsive to the desires of the prime audience for the study (management). Top management was also interested in specific information in other areas (such as compensation).

- It was concluded from interviews that the most valuable comments about OD emerge when it is included as one of a number of corporate activities.

- Drossler wanted to have answers to questions on corporate performance issues independent of OD queries in order to provide an analytical framework for measuring the impact of OD.

The questionnaire combined numerous rating questions and open ended opportunities to comment on issues of interest. Thus, for example, ten questions were asked about the future of the company; following which, space was provided to volunteer personal comments.

### The Sample

Of the total compliment of 1,100 Saga managers, 627 questionnaires (57%) were returned. Although not precisely a random sample, for analytical purposes, projections about the population can be made at the 95% confidence level.

### The Analysis

The report concentrates upon numerical tables generated from the managers' opinion ratings. The Drossler analysis is based upon their prior non-quantitative knowledge about the sample and population resulting from their extensive personal exposure to over 10% of Saga's managers and use of the open-ended answers obtained in the survey. Since the approach utilized here does not follow the rigors of Bayes' formulae, the Drossler analysis should be qualified in its reliance on inference (based on observation) and interpretation (based on respondents' written comments).

Among the factors that are judged to somewhat dilute interrelationships between OD and other corporate issues are the following:

- Number of OD sessions attended increases as grade increases.
- Number of OD sessions attended increases as performance ratings increase.
- Number of OD sessions attended increases with tenure in the company.
- Opinions about OD is higher based on exposure (number of sessions attended).
- 60% of Saga managers are grade 6 and below and average 1.5 sessions attended.
- 50% of Saga managers have been employed by Saga for three years or less and have averaged attendance at 1.2 sessions.
- Twenty-five percent of the sample has never attended an OD session.

Therefore, analysis by regression or other multiple correlative technique or mathematical cross matrix was impractical and uninformative.

The tables that follow are from Drossler's analysis of cross matrices produced on the scaled questions in the survey. The cross matrices shown in this paper are those which indicated a relationship with OD. Tables regarding issues that did not show mutuality with OD (for example, "the way top management is planning for the future") are not summarized here.

The approach led to two tables per issue:

- First, a table relating questions about OD ("I think OD is . . . "POOR or NOT SO GOOD or ACCEPTABLE or GOOD or GREAT) to attitudes toward some other aspect of Saga using the same rating scale (for example "My relationships with my boss are . . . POOR/NOT SO GOOD/ACCEPTABLE/GOOD/GREAT).
- Second, a table relating the *numbers of OD sessions attended* with the ratings of the issue.

To evaluate whether a true relationship between OD and an issue exists, Drossler conducted a cross matrix analysis. To establish such a relationship, the "a" table must satisfy conditions under (a) below and the "b" table must meet the criterion stated under (b) below.

(a) To first establish commonality of an issue with OD, there must be high figures in the lower right hand corner (of "I think" tables such as Tables 2a-7a and 8-16). The criterion of relationship applied called for over 70% of the respondents who think OD is GOOD/GREAT to also state that the level of performance on the issue is GOOD/GREAT. *Low* figures in the upper left corner of the "a" tables (OD thought of as POOR/NOT SO GOOD) also support an issue being related to OD.

(b) To establish *correlation* of an issue with OD, we must next look to table "b." Increase in respondents from 0 sessions attended to one session attended, and an either flat or positive general trend line reflects a positive effect of OD on the issue. Further support is given if we have a declining trend line in categories POOR and NOT SO GOOD. A declining trend line in POOR or NOT SO GOOD is sufficient to indicate but does not necessarily indicate a relationship to OD.

Coincidental, uncorrelated relationships are possible because most of Saga's manager problems improve with tenure and grade promotions. Since number of OD sessions attended and opinions about OD also improve with tenure and grade, we find issues and facts moving in the same direction not because of any relationships between the two. We call these NC (not clear or no correlation).

Correlations were established for some of the issues covered in the survey, reported here in Tables 2b-7b. Other issues where correlations of more impact from more OD could not be firmly established but where the levels of OD/issue performance were high were numerous; some are reported in tables 8-16.

## The Results

The results of the survey are reported in eight major categories as follows:

I.     The internal image of the OD program. The program has high acceptance among Saga Managers and the acceptance grows with increased exposure to OD.

II.    The impact OD has had upon people. The self-perceived impact has been high and the impact increases with increased exposure to OD.

III.    The impact OD has had upon the role of the Boss. One of the results of OD is the positive impact it has had upon this role.

IV.    The impact OD has had upon the role of the subordinate. This impact has been positive but not to the degree of its impact upon bosses.

V.    The impact OD has had upon job effectiveness. In this important area the impact has been of dramatic scale.

VI.    The changes OD has brought about. The OD program over time has had a positive impact upon such issues as boss-subordinate relationships and job effectiveness.

VII.    Here and now data about other aspects of the Saga people climate. Although there are not direct correlations of such things as leveling, trust, care, team spirit, confidence, freedom and motivation, the state of such issues is high.

VIII.    Some conclusions about OD.

## I. The Internal Image of the OD Program

Perhaps the most powerful single finding of this study is not the interrelationships between OD and other issues, but is simply the strongly favorable light in which OD is viewed by Saga's management. Over *half* of Saga's executives think OD is GOOD/GREAT (52%) and (28% think OD is ACCEPTABLE),*while only one in five thinks OD is POOR or NOT SO GOOD. (These numbers appear as the base in the "a" tables that follow.)

The two key measures used with other issues are what "I think of OD" and the "number of OD sessions attended." Looking at these two indicators together also presents a favorable reading on the internal image of OD at Saga.

1. Saga managers, even those who have not attended an Organization Development session, consider the OD program at least acceptable.

2. The more exposure Saga managers have to OD sessions, the better they think of the program.

3. There appears to be no peaking of manager enthusiasm with attendance of four or more OD sessions (no saturation with OD). We cannot tell where this incremental increase drops off.

Drossler Table 1 shows three important things: First that the

---

* The ACCEPTABLE percentages (difference between 100% and the combined totals of POOR/NOT SO GOOD/GOOD/GREAT in the left hand column of the tables) are omitted to make the tables easier to read.

NUMBER OF OD SESSIONS ATTENDED

|  | None | One | Two | Three | Four+ |
|---|---|---|---|---|---|
| I THINK THE SAGA OD PROGRAM IS . . . | | | | | |
| Poor/Not So Good | 23% | 23% | 21% | 21% | 10% |
| Good/Great | 40 | 51 | 50 | 56 | 65 |
| Base: | 127 (100.0) | 135 (100.0) | 119 (100.0) | 81 (100.0) | 95 (100.0) |

TABLE 1

program has wide acceptance in Saga. For example, of the 127 managers who have never been exposed to OD directly, 40% of them (Col. #1) say that they believe the program is Good and Great. And for the managers who have had OD, an increasing percentage say OD is Good/Great.

The most interesting thing about this is the effect OD has had upon the attitudes and climate of Saga that makes new people coming into Saga feel comfortable and positive about the program. This means that the informal communication systems support the concept as well as the fact that the behaviors of people on the job support it. A second finding from this table is that favorable feelings people hold for OD increase with more OD exposures (and unfavorable feelings about OD decrease with more OD exposure). The 40% (Col. #1) who have never had an OD expereince but who consider OD to be Good-Great increase to 65% (Col. #4) upon exposure to four or more OD sessions. In like manner, the 23% who have never had OD and who consider OD to be Poor (Col. #1) reduces to 10% (Col. #4) with four or more OD exposures. There is no "peaking" of the OD effect.

## II. The Impact of the OD Program Upon People

90% of those who think OD is Good/Great also think the impact of OD upon them as a person is Good/Great (Table 2a). In Table 2b, 80% of those who have had four or more OD exposures say the impact of OD upon them as a person has also been Good/Great. We also see that the 26% who rate OD as being Poor and Not So Good

I THINK OD IS . . .

| THE IMPACT OD HAS ON ME AS A PERSON IS . . . | Poor | Not So Good | Accept | Good/ Great |
|---|---|---|---|---|
| Poor/Not So Good | 77% | 49% | 5% | 3% |
| Good/Great | 9 | 19 | 41 | 90 |
| Base: | 44 (100.0) | 47 (100.0) | 130 (100.0) | 278 (100.0) |

TABLE 2a

NUMBER OF SESSIONS ATTENDED

| THE IMPACT OD HAS ON ME AS A PERSON IS . . . | None | One | Two | Three | Four+ |
|---|---|---|---|---|---|
| Poor/Not So Good | 26% | 18% | 14% | 14% | 4% |
| Good/Great | 36 | 63 | 63 | 63 | 80 |
| Base: | 58 (100.0) | 131 (100.0) | 115 (100.0) | 81 (100.0) | 91 (100.0) |

TABLE 2b

(Table 2b) decline with additional meetings. The Good/Great ratings increase with exposure from 36% to 80%

These data are among the most dramatic in the whole survey in that they show the favorable impact there is with increased exposure to OD. Some of the OD comments of the Good/Great groups bring this out.

"OD helps you to understand yourself, supervisors, subordinates, co-workers, family."

"OD opens up communications and develops honesty."

"OD initiates changes and awareness."

### III. The Impact OD Has Had Upon Me As A Boss

The most important single force in shaping the climate of any organization is the attitude and the behavior of its power group—the bosses. Regulations, policies, theories, meetings, awards and training will not change the reality of "what is" until the on the job behavior of the boss is changed. It is the way that he deals in every aspect of his job and his relationships with others that set the climate. If OD is to succeed in changing the climate of any organization it must succeed in changing the behavior of the power group. Not only must their behavior change, but they must be aware of the change and its meanings. Their subordinates must also perceive the change and like what they see.

Drossler Tables 3a and 3b show the impact the OD program has had upon peoples' self-perceived leadership roles. The OD program in this case is seen as an effective management development program because bosses say that it has had positive impact upon them.

I THINK OD IS . . .

| | Poor | Not So Good | Accept | Good/Great |
|---|---|---|---|---|
| THE IMPACT OD HAS HAD ON ME AS A BOSS . . . | | | | |
| Poor/Not So Good | 60% | 50% | 3% | 2% |
| Good/Great | 18 | 22 | 50 | 90 |
| Base: | 40 (100.0) | 46 (100.0) | 124 (100.0) | 265 (100.0) |

TABLE 3a

NUMBER OF SESSIONS ATTENDED

| | None | One | Two | Three | Four |
|---|---|---|---|---|---|
| THE IMPACT OF HAS HAD ON ME AS A BOSS . . . | | | | | |
| Poor/Not So Good | 30% | 9% | 12% | 12% | 2% |
| Good/Great | 43 | 67 | 60 | 74 | 86 |
| Base: | 53 (100.0) | 124 (100.0) | 109 (100.0) | .76 (100.00) | 90 (100.0) |

TABLE 3b

The question arises as to the reality of this self-perceived change for the better on the part of the boss, between him and his subordinates. Other questions were asked to determine how well bosses performed. Examples which reflect favorable boss behavior, are given later in Tables 6, 10, 16 and 18. These tables reflect the perception of subordinates *about* their bosses and would thus tend to corroborate the boss' perception about their own effectiveness.

### IV. The Impact of the OD Program Upon Managers In Their Roles as Subordinates

Drossler Tables 4a and 4b show the OD impact upon the subordinates' role.

### I THINK OD IS . . .

|  | Poor | Not So Good | Accept | Good/ Great |
|---|---|---|---|---|
| THE IMPACT ON ME AS A SUBORDINATE IS . . . |  |  |  |  |
| Poor/Not So Good | 71% | 47% | 9% | 4% |
| Good/Great | 10 | 14 | 36 | 83 |
| Base: | 41 (100.0) | 49 (100.0) | 127 (100.0) | 276 (100.0) |

TABLE 4a

### NUMBER OF SESSIONS ATTENDED

|  | None | One | Two | Three | Four+ |
|---|---|---|---|---|---|
| THE IMPACT OD HAS HAD ON ME AS A SUBORDINATE IS . . . |  |  |  |  |  |
| Poor/Not So Good | 23% | 14% | 16% | 17% | 10% |
| Good/Great | 43 | 62 | 59 | 50 | 64 |
| Base: | 61 (100.0) | 129 (100.0) | 113 (100.0) | 78 (100.00) | 90 (100.0) |

TABLE 4b

It can be seen from these tables that OD does have a positive impact upon subordinate roles. There has been a lesser OD impact upon the subordinates' role (4b) than upon the Boss' role (3b) *as a result of more OD exposure*. The direct impact (Table 4a) shows about the same percentage of difference in the Good/Great columns as for the boss (3a).

Comparing Tables 4a and 4b with 3a and 3b, it appears that OD has impact (effect) as a "manager development" tool, and its value increases with increased exposure. This value increase is demonstrated in Table 3b (last line) in the jump from One Session Attended to Four Sessions Attended.

## V. The Impact of OD Upon Job Effectiveness

Since involvement in OD is seen as helping to improve the working roles (boss and subordinate), do people see OD as improving their job effectiveness? The Drossler Survey addresses this issue in their Tables 5a and 5b:

From Table 5b, it can be seen that there is a 21% increase in self-percieved effectiveness from the group with no OD experience to the group with one OD experience; but there seems to be less improvement for multiple OD sessions.

The most dramatic change in attitude (Table 5b) is among those who have had no OD to those who have had four sessions.

### I THINK OD IS . . .

| | Poor | Not So Good | Accept | Good/ Great |
|---|---|---|---|---|
| THE IMPACT ON MY JOB EFFECTIVENESS IS . . . | | | | |
| Poor/Not So Good | 64% | 47% | 2% | 3% |
| Good/Great | 10 | 24 | 35 | 87 |
| Base: | 41 (100.0) | 45 (100.0) | 124 (100.0) | 277 (100.0) |

TABLE 5a

### NUMBER OF SESSIONS ATTENDED

|  | None | One | Two | Three | Four+ |
|---|---|---|---|---|---|
| **THE IMPACT OD HAS HAD ON MY JOB EFFECTIVENESS IS . . .** |  |  |  |  |  |
| Poor/Not So Good | 23% | 14% | 7% | 15% | 3% |
| Good/Great | 40 | 61 | 62 | 63 | 71 |
| Base: | 57 | 129 | 111 | 78 | 88 |
|  | (100.0) | (100.0) | (100.0) | (100.00) | (100.0) |

TABLE 5b

## VI. Changes Over Time

Some readings on the impact of OD over the three years since its inception were built into the survey. The results of these measurements parallel the favorable responses uncovered in questions regarding the "impact of OD" discussed so far. Two examples of the approach of directly asking about change follow. Note the change from the rating scale we have been discussing so far.

*Relationships Over Time*

Paralleling other results on the impact of OD on people in various roles, here we see that management role relationships in Saga over the past three years have moved, on the whole, for the better (6a); although increased exposure to OD *does not* make them consistently better(6b).

### I THINK OD IS . . .

|  | Poor | Not So Good | Accept | Good/Great |
|---|---|---|---|---|
| **MY RELATIONSHIPS WITH MY BOSS OVER A THREE YEAR PERIOD ARE . . .** |  |  |  |  |
| Much worse/somewhat worse | 22% | 23% | 15% | 8% |
| Somewhat better/much better | 48 | 44 | 48 | 67 |
| Base: | 54 | 62 | 162 | 303 |
|  | (100.0) | (100.0) | (100.0) | (100.0) |

TABLE 6a

### NUMBER OF SESSIONS ATTENDED

|  | None | One | Two | Three | Four+ |
|---|---|---|---|---|---|
| **MY RELATIONSHIPS WITH MY BOSS OVER A THREE YEAR PERIOD . . .** | | | | | |
| Much worse/somewhat worse | 16% | 11% | 15% | 19% | 11% |
| Somewhat better/much better | 51 | 64 | 50 | 52 | 68 |
| Base: | 155 (100.) | 134 (100.0) | 117 (100.0) | 81 (100.0) | 95 (100.0) |

TABLE 6b

A "current status" question similar to the above question was also asked. This information is shown on both Tables 7a and 7b below. Since the present situation answers were on the poor/not so good—good/great scale, the answers are somewhat different from above.

### I THINK O.D. IS . . .

|  | Poor | Not So Good | Accept | Good/Great |
|---|---|---|---|---|
| **MY RELATIONSHIPS WITH MY BOSS ARE . . .** | | | | |
| Poor/Not So Good | 25% | 19% | 11% | 6% |
| Good/Great | 53 | 53 | 63 | 80 |
| Base: | 55 (100.0) | 62 (100.0) | 162 (100.0) | 304 (100.0) |

TABLE 7a

### NUMBER OF SESSIONS ATTENDED

|  | None | One | Two | Three | Four+ |
|---|---|---|---|---|---|
| **MY RELATIONSHIPS WITH MY BOSS ARE . . .** | | | | | |
| Poor/Not So Good | 12% | 10% | 10% | 19% | 11% |
| Good/Great | 69 | 74 | 66 | 62 | 76 |
| Base: | 157 (100.0) | 135 (100.0) | 119 (100.0) | 81 (100.0) | 94 (100.0) |

TABLE 7b

*Job Effectiveness*

Another question which was asked both in terms of change and current status was each manager's evaluation of his job performance over the period that OD has been in development. Again, the differences in ratings make comparisons difficult. Portions of these findings follow:

I THINK OD IS . . .

|  | Poor | Not So Good | Accept | Good/ Great |
|---|---|---|---|---|
| MY EFFECTIVENESS IN MY JOB THE PAST THREE YEARS WAS . . . | | | | |
| Much worse/somewhat worse | 6% | 11% | 3% | 2% |
| Somewhat better/much better | 63 | 66 | 66 | 80 |
| Base: | 54 (100.0) | 62 (100.0) | 162 (100.0) | 301 (100.0) |

TABLE 8

I THINK OD IS . . .

|  | Poor | Not So Good | Accept | Good/ Great |
|---|---|---|---|---|
| MY EFFECTIVENESS IN MY JOB THE PAST THREE YEARS WAS . . . | | | | |
| Poor/not so good | 7% | 3% | 2% | 2% |
| Good/great | 73 | 76 | 80 | 84 |
| Base: | 55 (100.0) | 62 (100.0) | 162 (100.0) | 304 (100.0) |

TABLE 9

## VII. Data on the Saga Climate

The direct correlation of the OD impact upon the climate and values of Saga is hard to establish. The things that occur in an organization's climate, as a result of any intervention, are like the insertion of yeast into flour and water. The results are evolutionary in nature and hard to trace to any cause and effect relationship. The Drossler people have explicitly stated that some areas of potential OD impact such as trust, leveling or influence cannot be directly tied to their data. Thus, the "b" versions of the tables that follow are omitted since no increase in performance is reflected across the number of OD sessions attended.

In the items that follow, we do not claim that these conditions have improved as a direct result of an OD session: but several factors should be borne in mind:

when these factors (values) are high in an organization, then the climate of the organization is better for people than when they are low.

they are the critical norms (values) by which we measure the quality of organizational climate.

they result from (are built upon) the behavior of the people in the organizations.

they are quite high in Saga at this time.

*Leveling*

Leveling implies the degree of interpersonal honesty in the system, especially between bosses and subordinates. While the following table does not show that OD increases leveling, it does show the high degree that leveling is perceived as taking place in the organization

I THINK OD IS . . .

|  | Poor | Not So Good | Accept | Good/ Great |
|---|---|---|---|---|
| THE DEGREE MY SUBORDINATES FEEL I LEVEL WITH THEM IS . . . |  |  |  |  |
| Poor/Not So Good | 0% | 0% | 3% | 3% |
| Good/Great | 69 | 60 | 73 | 81 |
| Base: | 94 (100.0) | 63 (100.0) | 161 (100.0) | 303 (100.0) |

TABLE 10

*Trust*

Trust·in a team or an organization is one of the basic factors that must exist before other things can happen. It is one basis for effective delegation, for two-level communication, for giving and receiving feedback and for team spirit. It does not come by regulation or by order, but is the result of many painstaking efforts over a long period of time and develops in a team when the behavior of those on the team base their own relationships upon it.

Drossler Table II which follows reveals a fairly high degree of trust existing in the relationships.

I THINK OD IS . . .

|  | Poor | Not So Good | Accept | Good/ Great |
|---|---|---|---|---|
| THE WILLINGNESS OF MY BOSS TO RECEIVE FEEDBACK FROM ME TO HIM IS . . . |  |  |  |  |
| Poor/Not So Good | 20% | 26% | 14% | 8% |
| Good/Great | 44 | 44 | 58 | 73 |
| Base: | 55 (100.0) | 62 (100.0) | 159 (100.0) | 303 (100.0) |

TABLE 11

*Care*

In our team meetings, we have tried to build the concept that our involvement with each other must stem from our mutual caring about each other. We believe care is the basis for which feedback is given and received. We believe that it is feedback that is the basis of our personal growth and development, and try to establish the norm, "I will give you feedback because I care enough about you to take the risk of offending you, of hurting you or of making you angry at me." Table 12 shows the degree bosses are perceived as caring.

*Team Spirit*

In our OD interventions, we have used the Team as the basic building block of our change effort. We have tried to make the "team" the "safe haven" where people can share deeply, learn about themselves, create new norms and develop action plans for achieving them. This is the place where they "belong," can influence the

I THINK OD IS . . .

| | Poor | Not So Good | Accept | Good/ Great |
|---|---|---|---|---|
| **THE LEVEL OF INTEREST AND CONCERN BY MY BOSS IS . . .** | | | | |
| Poor/Not So Good | 31% | 19% | 17% | 8% |
| Good/Great | 46 | 56 | 56 | 76 |
| Base: | 55 (100.0) | 63 (100.0) | 162 (100.0) | 305 (100.0) |

TABLE 12

system and feel that they "are" Saga. This is the place where they can try out new patterns of behavior and hopefully become more effective managers. Table 13 illustrates the high degree of spirit that exists in Saga.

*Security and Self Esteem*

Our OD effort attempts to bring emotional security to people in their teams and in the work situation, so that they can be mentally honest and build their self-respect. It is our belief that much of our present management style, particularly our concept of "management by exception," tends to emphasize the negatives at the expense of the positive. People get the feeling that they are never right, and that they can never win. We have deliberately tried to set into motion

I THINK OD IS . . .

| | Poor | Not So Good | Accept | Good/ Great |
|---|---|---|---|---|
| **THE TEAM SPIRIT THAT EXISTS IN THE GROUP REPORTING TO ME IS . . .** | | | | |
| Poor/Not So Good | 13% | 8% | 5% | 6% |
| Good/Great | 64 | 63 | 69 | 72 |
| Base: | 53 (100.0) | 62 (100.0) | 160 (100.0) | 299 (100.00) |

TABLE 13

positive attitudes towards self within the framework of the team. We
think that these positive attitudes about self are important to one's
attempt to develop improved skills and understanding of human
relationships. They are an important ingredient (motivation) for
change and they help to develop a self reliance and self confidence
that in time improve the self image and set the cycle of self
improvement in motion.

Table 14 reflects the level of personal security that exists within
the Saga Management Group.

## Freedom

One of the basic cornerstones of Saga's management philosophy is
the concept of entrepreneurism; the ownership that a Saga manager
feels about his own job. This attitude says "I'll fulfill the requirements of the regulations regardless of your need." This only
comes about if there are secure and firm boss-subordinate
relationships, and if people feel secure enough to innovate and free
enough to relate to customers in a need fulfilling manner. Table 15
reflects the high state of this condition in Saga.

## Motivation and Satisfaction

When people feel they belong, and that they have influence and
freedom, it follows that they have a high level of satisfaction and
motivation. Table 16 reflects Saga's high degree of performance in
this area.

## I THINK OD IS . . .

|  | Poor | Not So Good | Accept | Good/ Great |
|---|---|---|---|---|
| MY BOSS'S CONFIDENCE THAT SAGA WILL KEEP AND IMPROVE PROFITS ON ACTIVITIES I MANAGE IS . . . |  |  |  |  |
| Poor/Not So Good | 4% | 16% | 6% | 4% |
| Good/Great | 54 | 70 | 74 | 75 |
| Base: | 54 | 63 | 159 | 301 |
|  | (100.0) | (100.0) | (100.0) | (100.0) |

TABLE 14

I THINK OD IS . . .

| | Poor | Not So Good | Accept | Good/Great |
|---|---|---|---|---|
| THE INFLUENCE AND IMPACT I FEEL I CAN HAVE OVER MY OWN JOB IS . . . | | | | |
| Poor/Not So Good | 24% | 14% | 9% | 3% |
| Good/Great | 47 | 67 | 68 | 83 |
| Base: | 55 (100.0) | 63 (100.0) | 162 (100.0) | 302 (100.0) |

TABLE 15

I THINK OD IS . . .

| | Poor | Not So Good | Accept | Good/Great |
|---|---|---|---|---|
| THE MOTIVATION MY BOSS FEELS I HAVE IS . . . | | | | |
| Poor/Not So Good | 13% | 3% | 5% | 3% |
| Good/Great | 55 | 67 | 70 | 79 |
| Base: | 55 (100.0) | 63 (100.0) | 162 (100.0) | 304 (100.0) |

TABLE 16

## VIII. Conclusions on Saga's OD Program

Perhaps the most telling conclusion about the OD program is that expressed by Saga's management team in their 1972-73 plans: "Every management team in Saga will have at least one Team Building meeting during the work year." The Drossler data may not be sufficient to prove to a skeptical management that it should embark upon such a program, but we believe that the data do validate the positive feelings of Saga Management "That the program is indeed worth both its effort and its cost." But why is it worth its effort and its cost? Simply, because OD has been instrumental in creating the management behavior that has made real the norms and values of "The Saga Way." In the perception of the Saga managers, "It has worked!"

## Some New Directions for OD

The OD program in Saga is taking several new directions for the year ahead. As the result of the extensive experimentation reported here, we have determined that Team Building is an excellent vehicle for developing and improving the relationships of unit level teams of hourly people (cooks, salad ladies, pot washers, and so on) and their supervisors. The survey did not gather data from this group, but we have conducted some twenty meetings among these teams and without exception, the people attending have expressed pride in working for a company that will recognize their feelings as being important and needed in the total picture.

This level has a history of high turnover and it is too early to predict the effectiveness of the meetings in this regard. We do know from feedback received that after holding Team Building meetings, the teams are showing more innovativeness and pride in their jobs as well as having better interpersonal communications with each other, their bosses and our customers.

Our management people are discovering in the meetings that these people are just like themselves in the ways they feel and in what they like; that by having the opportunity to express these feelings, they too can fulfill their need for a sense of self worth and the right to human dignity.

Secondly, we have initiated a series of "Black/White Labs" to enable Saga's white managers to better understand and facilitate the successful growth and development of Black human resources in the Company. This may prove to be one of the most dynamic OD programs we have launched.

Thirdly, we have recently linked our OD staff directly into the negotiation channel with prospective acquisitions. We have had good results. If acquisitions go on the rocks because of the human misunderstanding that occurs at the time the deal is negotiated, then OD may be one means of insuring that these problems are minimized with the resultant minimization of anguish that accompanies such experiences.

Fourth, we are using OD in helping management at all levels integrate newly acquired businesses (their processes and their people) into Saga. The sharpened human awaremess that OD brings to our management teams, as well as OD skills and techniques, are making our new acquisitions much easier for all concerned (The acquiree as well as the acquired).

Fifth, we also believe that the OD program has some secondary applications in family lives based on comments expressed by people, and we believe our business clients are interested, as evidenced by requests to help them develop OD programs of their own. Additionally, a new thrust for Saga's OD program is in developing effective relationships with suppliers by working through false assumptions held by both parties which in turn generate ineffective behavior and possibly an unneeded dollar cost to all concerned.

### The Essence of OD

Finally, OD has become the behavioral norm as well as the technique for achieving good personal relationships within the company. People frequently use the term "In the spirit of OD" to get at knotty human issues. But more importantly, its value system of care, oppenness, honesty, trust, directness and awareness have become the basis for the way Saga people work on business issues with each other. OD has become the essence of "The Saga Way."

In a larger sense, OD seems to be the means whereby people can risk changing their old, traditional social norms (hidden feelings and rationalized behavior) to more open ways of relating to each other. It seems to be a breakthrough for people to see their behavior as something they can change for the better if they desire. It seems to be a means for creating deeper and more caring relationships between members of a team. It seems to be a force that sets in motion an increasing sense of self worth, freedom and personal dignity. It seems to be the key for developing a climate in an organization that is good for people.

The data suggest that Saga has responded to peoples' needs for finding meaning in their lives. Their need to believe in what they are doing and their need for a personal commitment to a course that is of Saga but which is also ideally much larger than Saga; a new way of life and a new way of relating to and dealing with people.

# Section IV

# Macro Systems and the
# Interfaces Between Organizations

This final section represents an area for the application of applied behavioral science theories and methods which has become of great importance very rapidly—the issues of very large systems and multiple systems. The generic term "Macro-Systems" has emerged recently to include these areas. It increasingly has become clear that, if the applied behavioral sciences are to have a major impact on our complex society, practitioners must focus more of their attention upon large systems and upon the social problems which can be solved only through the collaboration of major institutions.

In Chapter 15, Cy Mill describes the efforts to date to change the roles and images of the entire U.S. Army's chaplaincy. In addition to feeling pressures to take more initiative in dealing with social issues as they impact on army life, the chaplains also are dispersed widely and must respond to civilian society, their denominations, the army and the chief of chaplains as well as to their own posts—truly a macro system undertaking! Mill describes the three year history of this massive training and professional development effort and discusses the overall project from within the framework of basic OD tenets.

On another front, Lee Vansina's chapter deals with the increasingly complex world of the multinational organization. Based on his experience of working with internationally composed management groups, Vansina describes the factors which hamper learning from and about international organizations and their development. Using case material to illustrate, he reviews the contributions of OD to international organizations through a sequence of steps which work through the cross-cultural issues which are inherent. He also points out some of the limitations of OD as it currently exists to cope effectively with problems of this magnitude. One of his major points is that OD must learn to transcend the fields of individual and social psychology and borrow more from the contributions of other social and political sciences and from existing theories of organization and management. Only then, Vansina feels, will OD be able to make a meaningful contribution to the development of organizations as learning systems.

Open systems planning represents a relatively new technology which may well take some of the steps which will be necessary to move beyond the limitations of current OD technologies in dealing with Macro-system level interventions. In the final chapter, Charles Krone describes some of his latest efforts to advance the open system planning concept. In his search for an organizational form which will be effective in a complex changing world and which also will promote human growth, he compares traditional, socio-technical and open systems theories of organization and describes the factors which must be considered within an open system redesign format.

# 13

# OD In A Macrosystem:
# A Three-Year Progress Report

*CYRIL R. MILL*

OD is often performed in a macrosystem but usually it concerns itself only with systems elements to the neglect of intersystem dynamics. A consultant who works in a major corporation or with a community agency may consider his arena to represent a macrosystem because of its size. A macrosystem is not simply a very large organization, however, although that may be an important dimension. The term as used here applies to a system of systems. Each system has its own culture with independent structure and function; the various systems are interrelated through patterns of influence, control and power; the systems are interdependent and the loss of any one of them would significantly reduce the effectiveness of all. Community development represents a good example of macrosystem work because of the complex, interdependent relationships between organizations. Too often, however, community development focuses exclusively on just one organization such as the school, the police, or the mental health center, in which case the OD effort remains at the system level.

I wish to report on a macrosystem project where there has been some opportunity to work not only at the system level of a large and widely dispersed organization, but also to begin to work on intersystem relationships. This project has provided us with a chance to test out some of the well-established principles of OD for their applicability to macrosystems, to call some of them into question, and to reaffirm others.*

* The size of this project has required the use of many consultants. The ideas presented in this paper have been distilled from many discussions with them. While these conclusions are the result of a group effort, their specificity as reported here is the responsibility of the writer alone. Nevertheless, I find it difficult to claim sole ownership by the use of the personal pronoun. When I occasionally revert to the use of "we" I am including some of the consultants who have worked continuously on the project as "Lead Trainers." This group includes Bill Latta, Otto Kroeger, Harry Frankiel, and Len Morgan. Special appreciation is given to the inside consultant, Chaplain (Lt. Col.) Wendell Wright.

The project I wish to describe is that of the U.S. Army Chaplains. For the past several years they have been undertaking a change in regard to their role in the military. NTL Institute has been assisting them to promote this change and to manage the process. Thus, we have been engaged in an OD project slightly different from those usually reported in the literature. We have not been initiating change—the change was in process when we came on the scene and what we have done is to manage it and accelerate the rate. We have not been acting directly on organizational decision making, communication, and planning, but our presence in the system has influenced these factors to some degree.

What we have been doing is to work on the culture of the organization by attempting to change the self concept of chaplains to social technologies which many are now applying in their regular duty assignments (for example, adopting group methods in teaching, consulting with line officers and managing drug abuse programs).

The macrosystem aspects of this project apply in the cluster of systems which impinge on the Chaplain Branch, itself. Any change in the traditional style of behavior on the part of chaplains will have both positive and negative reverberations in some of the other systems. The chaplains provide a service in the military environment and therefore resemble staff, not line, personnel. Yet they report to and are evaluated by line officers, who are similar to line personnel in industry. The Chaplain Branch as embodied in the Office of the Chief of Chaplains is responsible for training, duty assignments, and for setting objectives, but commanders of the units to which chaplains are assigned influence how the objectives are carried out.

Chaplains generally work in isolation. That is, they are separated from other chaplains. On a major post, however, there may be from 10 to 20 chaplains, each reporting not only to the commander of his *unit* but also to the Post Chaplain who has responsibility for their technical supervision, local assignment, training and the promotion of the objectives of the Chief of Chaplains.

Each chaplain, of course, is a member of a civilian church denomination, which holds its own expectations for what its men will do. Some of these denominations maintain fairly close contact through annual or semi-annual visits to the men at their duty posts.

The cluster of systems is roughly depicted in figure 1.

Our emphasis with the chaplains has been only partially on the introduction of social technologies such as organizational diagnosis and team building. While the use of these methods will become more

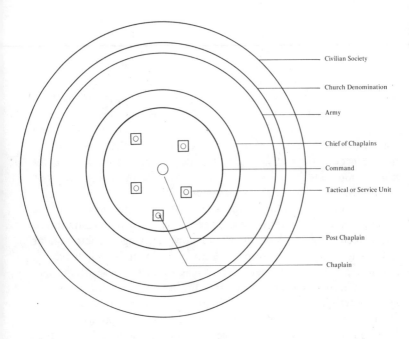

Civilian Society

Church Denomination

Army

Chief of Chaplains

Command

Tactical or Service Unit

Post Chaplain

Chaplain

FIGURE 1

valuable and necessary as time goes by, the primary need has been to enlarge the scope of behaviors of chaplains on the job. A goal that was mutually agreed upon between the NTL consultants and the Office of the Chief was that chaplains needed to re-examine their shared assumptions about the norms which govern their behavior with a view towards engaging in a more active, socially conscious ministry in the military community. We needed to work on the culture of the organization as it affected their work with the "parishioners." We were equally concerned with their internal working relationships, but not at the level of first priority. As their on-the-job behaviors become more proactive, it is expected that their image will change in the eyes of command, from the point of view of the enlisted men, and as seen by the civilian church.

A chaplain in a training session discussing this cultural change in the concept of the chaplaincy sketched out the following dichotomies which economically and usefully reflected the trends we see:

| *The Former Chaplain* | *The New Chaplain* |
|---|---|
| Chapel-oriented | Field-oriented |
| Preacher | Counsellor |
| Sunday School | Activist in social ministry |
| Big choir, big service | Small-group oriented |
| Religious man | Secular man |
| Denomination-oriented | Ecumenical |
| Establishment-oriented | Establishment questioner |
| Serving the establishment | Conscience tickler |

Only when the new image has been established over time through solid achievements of many individual chaplains, can this organizational change program be regarded as a *fait accompli*. It is too much to expect that every chaplain will be able to make this change in his self concept and in his work. But, according to Alinsky (Peabody, 1971, p. 346), a small percentage, say from two to four percent, of a group can be effective in establishing new norms, particularly if the general mass is not against the change. We are confident that a much higher percentage than this is ready and moving to effect the change we are working for.

The central questions, then, have been how to promote an expanded ministry where individual chaplains become more proactive in attending to social issues as well as fulfilling their traditional role of providing individual spiritual guidance, and, secondly, how to establish a climate of receptivity and collaboration in adjacent systems, particularly Army Command and the civilian church denominations. We believe that solid progress has been made in the last few years. Let us review how this has been achieved.

*Project Activities, 1970-1972*

The project began as a training program to bring as many chaplains as possible into a greater awareness of their own attitudes on race and motivate them to expand their ministry into such social issues as race problems, problems of drug usage, and problems of youthful dissent. They first had to become aware of their own prejudices and then determine, each for himself, the extent to which work in those areas could legitimately and rationally become a part of their job as they defined it.

The stimulus for this effort came from a request by the Secretary of Defense early in 1970 that all commands report on their efforts to improve communications between the races. A group of chaplains from the Office of the Chief of Chaplains decided that they would launch a training program that would make a difference not only in the way chaplains felt in working with racial minority groups but also in their priorities of work and in their definition of the proper role of the chaplain in the Army.

Another impetus was provided by the *Objectives for the '70's* published by the Chief of Chaplains. These objectives stated in part that chaplains would be expected to "encourage individual and social change within the military community in order that people may more fully express their individual identity, achieve group cohesiveness and be a witness to God." We interpreted the phrase "encourage individual and social change" to mean that chaplains would be increasingly rewarded as they worked toward the development of human potential and social justice in the military community. They must become more aware of social issues and develop change agent skills in order to effect change where needed.

The following activities were planned and carried out during the first year:

1. One hundred Career Chaplains in training at the U.S. Army Chaplain School in Ft. Hamilton, New York, went through a three-day workshop in human relations, focusing on their attitudes toward minority groups such as blacks, drug users and members of the younger generation.

2. Three-day workshops of a similar nature were conducted at 19 army posts throughout the U.S. Each workshop accomodated 24 participants and was designed on the spot by the NTL trainers who worked with local project officers who briefed them on problems of concern at that particular post. About 500 chaplains received this training during 1971.

3. Twenty-four chaplains from the career officers' course at Ft. Hamilton were selected for a three-week "training of trainers" program as a start at developing in-house capability for laboratory education.

4. A research project was conducted to help us better understand the population we were working with. With the use of the Dogmatism Scale we found that chaplains as a group were more conservative than a typical population in a human relations training program such as NTL conducts in Bethel, Maine, but were no more conservative than a cross

section of middle management drawn from business and industry.

5. A conference for evaluation at the end of the first year recommended a change to more emphasis on self-awareness for the following year. Chaplains would be brought to search for answers to questions of identity and role, such as "Who am I?" and "What can I do, or should I be doing in my ministry?" Race issues and especially institutional racism would continue to be included as part of the content.

The conference also recommended that the laboratories be extended to four days from three and that more non-chaplains be invited to attend. Training laboratories also were to be held in Germany. Wherever possible, the alumni of the training of trainers program would be used as co-trainers, and an expanded research program was designed.

The recommendations from this conference were all carried out during 1972. The Chief of Chaplains took an additional step which the conference recommended. He created a new position in his office to be called something like "Director of Organization Development" and selected a chaplain to pursue 18 months of graduate study to further prepare him for the responsibilities of that position. We began to have assurance of continuity of the OD program, even after we leave.

By the end of the second year approximately 900 chaplains out of a total of approximately 1,300 had been in an NTL human relations training program, along with about 350 non-chaplain personnel including enlisted men, WAC's and line officers. A start had been made in developing professional competence among chaplains in the use of experiential learning techniques and numerous chaplains were venturing into new areas of ministry. An opening move toward the institutionalization of the use of social science technology had taken place through the establishment of a new position at a high level.

We began to receive word through letters, telephone calls and "after-action reports" submitted to the Office of the Chief that indicated a significant shift in norms regarding the way chaplains were viewing the scope and potential of their role. Some were consulting with line officers on human and social issues, some were creating new types of chapel activities designed especially for blacks, and others were introducing new teaching methods using small group activities in their work with the troops.

*Activities during 1972-1973*

It became evident that awareness training in three and four-day programs needed to be supplemented with skill training, and that we must reach more of the higher echelons with an emphasis upon management and administration. We also needed to bring chaplains and line officers together in a more concentrated way to work on intergroup issues. Therefore, during the third year 96 chaplains attended regularly scheduled NTL laboratories and conferences. These included Human Interaction Laboratories, Laboratories on Institutional Racism and Higher Education, Management Work Conferences and Key Executive Conferences. The Chief of Chaplains is currently trying to schedule his attendance at a Presidents' Conference. Twenty chaplains entered the Training Theory and Practice Laboratories and the Professional Development Learning Community programs offered by NTL.

In order to assure that laboratory learnings would be transferred to their jobs, these laboratories were followed by a three-day Learning Utilization Conference which, in turn, was followed by individual consultation for any who wanted technical assistance in getting started on a new project at their post. Figure 2 presents a schema illustrating the manner in which general, broad range training moved to ever more specific training until it reached the point of individual consultation so that a chaplain could then move out to broader-based activities of his own.

Ten workshops conducted in Germany were specifically designed to work on the interface between chaplains and command officers. During the second year, 86 chaplains were assigned to interdisciplinary teams to work full time in drug abuse programs. This step was taken independently of our program by the Office of the Chief. Other chaplains are part of OD teams that have been organized on some of the larger army posts in the U.S.

Issues deriving from civilian church affiliation have been worked on by developing special designs, in some of the training programs, on ecumenism among chaplains. More work must be done on this interface. It is not so crucial, however, as the interfaces within the military branches. I have met with the Methodist selection and visitation staff where we discussed their selection and communication procedures. My impression is that for most denominations, the change we are working toward will not only be accepted, but welcomed, since this parallels some of the changes that are taking

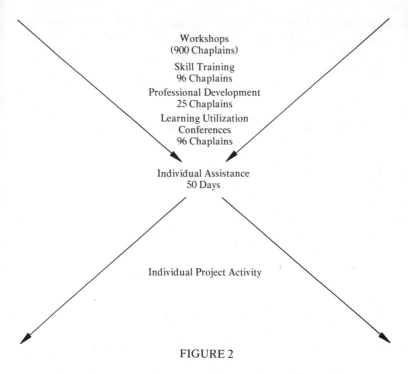

Workshops
(900 Chaplains)

Skill Training
96 Chaplains

Professional Development
25 Chaplains

Learning Utilization
Conferences
96 Chaplains

Individual Assistance
50 Days

Individual Project Activity

FIGURE 2

*Schema for moving from general focus to the specific, and from
mass-training to the individual*

place in the civilian church. Moreover, the push is not strong for
parochialism among the chaplains. Ecumenism is desired, and is
perhaps achieved to a greater extent in the military than anywhere
else. Civilian churches agree that the chaplain's first priority is to be
a pastor for every soldier regardless of his denominational affiliation. The civilian church, viewed as a system, is more likely to assist
the chaplains with their change program than to resist it.

Finally, a continuing research program is underway to determine
some of the effects of military life on attitudes toward self and
others.

In summary, let me mention that the Army Chaplain Branch is at
this time, one of the few units of the Department of Defense making
use of behavioral science technology as a means of achieving its
organizational goals (The Office of the Surgeon General is another,

as well as the Navy Chaplains to a small degree). Only a few of the techniques of OD typically employed in work with large organizations have been applied thus far. The Chaplain Model has included:

(a) a massive training program;
(b) training of "inside" trainers and OD consultants;
(c) training in management and human relations in civilian courses for selected chaplains;
(d) intergroup problem solving within and between systems;
(e) organizing for new positions and assignment of personnel to interdisciplinary teams;
(f) research, evaluation and conferences for feedback with recommendations for follow-through, and
(g) consultation on training programs and design, on research, and on varieties of other issues.

The massive training program has served several purposes. It has changed the attitudes of many chaplains toward their role in the military, enlarging their horizons and giving them a glimpse of possible new, exciting areas in which they could work. It has created a desire on the part of some to seek further training opportunities in order to develop their skills as a change agent. And it has introduced a new language, which permits conceptualization regarding human relations, change, social policy in the military, and collaboration for organization development.

OD typically includes other types of interventions which have thus far been minimally employed with the chaplains, such as team building and data collection-feedback sessions. It is expected that these will become useful as we work with smaller units within the organization in the future.

*Operational Principles for Macro-System Development*

Burke (in Hornstein, et al, 1971, pp. 3-6), defines OD as "a process of cultural change that attempts to institutionalize the use of various social technologies which are designed to regulate subsequent cultural and technological change." His emphasis is upon introducing social technologies in such a way that there results an increasing expectation and use of democratic decision-making, open communication and sharing in responsibility for planning.

While this definition provides us, in my opinion, with the currently most complete summation of what OD is, it cannot be transferred *in toto* to macrosystem work. It is conceivable that sets of systems could improve their interaction by first engaging in extensive intrasystem OD, followed by intersystem confrontation and problem solving, but to my knowledge this has rarely been done. (An approximation occurred in Jamaica where we first conducted some role-clarification and goal-setting sessions with the top management teams of the Ministry of Health and the National Family Planning Board, followed by a two-day inter-group problem solving session. Work that had been done within the Ministry, however, was minimal, while extensive OD operations had been carried on within the National Family Planning Board.)

Intersystem work usually finds its most fruitful application at the interface. Walton (1970) relied heavily upon intergroup designs in his effort to bring rapprochement among participants from Somalia, Ethiopia, and Kenya in a search for solutions to border disputes. Wedge (1971), after intensive consultation in the Dominican Republic ingeniously used an invited luncheon affair and a cocktail party as the setting for bringing University and Embassy officials together after 15 months of conflict. Just as intrasystem OD reduces in practice to work with small units and even individuals, so does macrosystem work reduce largely to intergroup activities. The consultant assists members from different systems to understand the effects of intersystem stereotyping, competition, communication and eventually he assists in building collaboration based upon new images held by each system of the other. Without these clarifications in regard to goals and intentions, a superordinate system could well inhibit efforts of a subordinate system to modify its procedures, for example, line officers holding an image of the "old" chaplain could continue to expect behaviors of that type and withhold rewards for behaviors of the "new" chaplain.

We need to know more than we do at present about power, as we venture into macrosystem work. Timothy Costello, deputy mayor and city administrator, New York City, calls our attention to this as he says, "Unfortunately, in recent years behavioral scientists have written more about the process of power equalization than they have about the acquisition and effective use of power. For that, we have to go back almost to Machiavelli" (1971, p. 132).

A description of macrosystem OD as currently practiced is that it is *the use of social science interventions both within and between systems which clarify intersystem perceptions and relationships so that subsequent collaboration will be facilitated.* A requisite for macrosystem OD is that the consultant be constantly aware that his primary client system does not exist in isolation. He focuses on both internal system dynamics and intersystem dynamics and calls attention to those that need to be worked on in order that the various systems can accomplish their objectives without interference.

With these introductory comments in mind, let us return to the Chaplain Project to identify some principles for consultation that may have general applicability to macrosystem work:

A. *Start with the felt need and at the level of system readiness.*
Some OD consultants refuse to begin with a client organization unless they can start at the top, and usually with a diagnostic-feedback procedure. There are excellent and well known reasons for this, chief of which is to gain high level support so that the work will not be scrubbed when the going gets rough. The initial diagnostic measures also make sense—one wants to have the problems defined before going to work.

In macrosystem work, however, this principle may have to bend a little. Among sets of systems it may not be readily ascertained as to which constitutes the "top." More important may be the understanding of how influence is exerted to win on a specific issue, or the ways in which coalitions are formed to achieve common goals.

In the Chaplain Project, training was asked for and it was with training that the project began. With this entree, we were able to introduce also some other OD activities such as consultation, developing internal capabilities and research. The execution of entry is more important than its level or form.

B. *Macrosystem diagnosis is not so much a procedure as it is an emerging process.* As one works with the focal organization in a macrosystem, issues with neighboring systems begin to take form. One only belatedly learns that one can, or cannot, do certain things according to permission granted by neighboring systems. A consultant rarely (never?) has equally free movement throughout a macrosystem, and therefore an adequate diagnosis of interlocking relationships may not be possible. Examples: Even though we know that chaplains are evaluated by their unit commanders, there is no way at present that we, as consultants, can influence command officers to look for and reward those behaviors which accord with the newer model we are working to bring into being. Nor can we readily learn from line officers and enlisted men which behaviors of chaplains they like or dislike so that these can be fed back to chaplains. Line officers and enlisted men constitute separate systems to which we have limited access.

C. *Move slowly, capitalizing on observable progress and working always at newly exposed points of felt need*. Work in extended systems is frequently like using an emergent design in a laboratory. One constantly evaluates, looking for cues which point to newly exposed needs. For instance, the human relations workshops moved from racial orientation to a focus on self-awareness. This led to a need to reach higher ranking officers. The training of trainers program led to placing people in the more organized sequence of the NTL Learning Communities for professional development. Experience with basic T-groups led, by request from former participants, to intergroup problem solving. Requests are now beginning to come in for team building sessions at various locations, starting with interdisciplinary teams assigned to drug abuse programs.

In this way the overall effort has reached out into neighboring systems, particularly command units, at a time when they are ready. It has taken two years to get to this point. In retrospect, it is doubtful that intersystem work could have been seen as relevant any earlier.

Costello (op. cit. p. 141) uses the term "chain-type change" to describe this phenomenon. "In this type of change the distance between the original problem and the final solution is connected by a chain of events, with each event forging the next decision, which then becomes an event for a subsequent link, and so on from beginning problem to completely unanticipated final result."

D. *Inside consultants are a necessity in macrosystem work*. The outside consultant in macrosystem work is at a disadvantage due to his lack of knowledge about the intricacies of the organizational culture and the intersystem relationships.

Those on the inside are aware of the structure, points of stress and feelings of the personnel. They are continually informed of structural changes and newly developed organizational thrusts which may not come to the attention of the outsider.

In the course of our work the structure of CONARC, the Continental Army Command, has changed twice, the war in Vietnam has changed from land to air, and there have been changes in the higher echelons of command in the Pentagon. All of these have had an influence on the system which is our central concern. Our inside consultants, being so much a part of this total culture, did not always think to report some of these changes to us; they came to light as we evaluated and planned together. Without this information we would sometimes have been structuring our project toward persons or groups who were no longer there, or we would have missed opportunities to move in significant new directions.

We have learned to be alert to many sources of information in addition to the formally designated inside consultants. As more and more chaplains have obtained advanced training, there are more who conceptualize problems in ways responsive to OD types of interventions. We hope to have similar resources located within other systems soon. Our primary inside consultants, however, are invaluable in helping us to use the proper channels for communication, in assisting with long range planning, handling management problems and checking with top command for occasional guidance and support.

E. *Build a base of support, both horizontally and vertically.* By horizontal support, I refer to within the system, or in the Chaplain Branch. Vertical support refers to outside of the focal organization. The Chief of Chaplains has supported this program from the beginning and has continually provided assistance when requested. We have learned to make sparing use of his power; wide recognition of its existence and potential has usually been all that was necessary. The change program is seen as his program, not that of the outside consultants. A large majority of the participants in the workshops have been supportive, particularly after their initial experience with laboratory training. Those who have gone through professional development training programs have added to the internal base of support.

Vertical support outside of the Chaplain Branch is another matter. We have little access to the top command echelons in the Pentagon although currently the climate for the use of behavioral science in the military is favorable. The Chaplain Project has been instrumental in setting this climate, since it is being carefully watched by other service units. In a hierarchical organization like the military, however, and this is perhaps characteristic of macrosystem work, the climate of receptivity in adjoining systems must be continuously monitored.

All organizations in a macrosystem do not have equal power and prestige. If one has a choice, it would be hard to decide whether to move with power or go for the organization with prestige. Prestigious organizations can sometimes experiment more freely, and frequently are smaller than those whose power stems from mere size, money and brute strength. We have been pleased to be working with the chaplains since we see them as deriving their influence through moral strength more than through official sources such as is implied in "Command." We have long felt that the chaplains possess more potential for influence than they recognize or use. They have the power of the church behind them; power of their position as representatives of right and justice; power of their individual personalities; and to some extent, they can limit the degree to which they will accede to the restrictions which bind other branches of the service.

Macrosystem work calls for fostering and nurturing support sources in many organizations which can then be called upon when the time is right for intersystem problem solving. Behavioral scientists may find it distasteful to make friends with a view that they may some day come in handy. On the other hand, behavioral scientists tend to become inbred in thinking, in values and even in the problems they consider worthy of their time and efforts, partially as a result of not sufficiently associating with persons in other walks of life. To quote Costello once again, "the proper cultivation or reaching out to men in power to gain understanding and personal acceptance," is a legitimate form of developing an entry point. "Strong personal relationships are a prime vehicle for mutual influence. Good friends affect each other's values and courses of action," (op. cit. p. 144).

F. *Expect resistance and be prepared to meet it.* The corollary to this principle is that volunteerism can be requested but cannot be assured in macrosystem work. I suspect that is usually the case in OD work with industry although it is rarely acknowledged. During laboratory education's early years voluntary attendance was stressed, and this is still true for training programs offered to the public. As soon as you enter an organization to work on the inside, however, implicit coercion becomes unavoidable. Persons in positions of power decide that the OD program will go into effect and, willy nilly, others must go along.

The larger the system, the more probable it is that there will be a number of people present for any specific intervention who do not understand why they are there and who, if they did understand, would prefer not to be. It is likely that in the early stages few of the managers will grasp the whole concept of OD outside of a select body of inside consultants and top level executives.

This has been the case with the chaplains. Typically, a chaplain will attend several conferences, training programs or workshops a year dealing with internal administrative matters, family counseling, race and drug issues, and the like. To many chaplains the NTL workshops were just another in a long line of workshops. In spite of our request that only volunteers attend, we regularly discovered that our groups were composed only partially of men who knew what they were there for. Our methods wore strange, our appearance did not conform to their stereotypes of "experts," and the thrust of our programs, particularly as we dealt at the feeling level, was often repugnant. We learned to deal with hostility on the firing line, so to speak, and have learned a great deal about how to work with antagonistic groups.

More important were the ethical issues involved. We have

spent some uncomfortable days examining this issue. Given that we have confidence in the rightness of the goal we are seeking to attain, where does one draw the line between the prerogatives of the consultant and the right to undisturbed privacy of a participant? Our broad-spectrum solution has been to maintain complete openness regarding our goals, and to offer participants the option of abstaining from participation if they chose. A few did choose to sit aside for the three or four days of the workshops, but we do not know how many others participated still feeling that they had been seduced or coerced by the pressure of group and organizational norms.

With increasing support, as described above, the hostility has reduced, but marked resistance still exists on the part of some. Four sources of resistance to the change program, that is, change in the role and function of the chaplain, have been identified.

1. Comfort and security with routine and the *status quo*.

2. Ignorance and misunderstanding about the larger OD program, seeing it only as another series of workshops.

3. Lack of enabling skills for carrying out new forms of ministry.

4. Fear of reprisal from superiors within the Chaplain Branch or from command officers if experiments with new behaviors fail.

Steps have been taken to counter each of these resistance sources. For instance, it is becoming increasingly evident that the former *status quo* is no longer satisfactory, so security is found in conforming to the new standard and in meeting new expectancies. Ignorance and misunderstanding can less easily be used as an excuse since all members of the Chaplain Branch have been informed of the OD program through command conferences, personal communications from the Office of the Chief, and through publications (Mill 1972). New skills acquired through training are helping many to try out new ideas, and wide publicity is given to the fact that certain chaplains who took risks are being promoted or given interesting job assignments.

## Summation

Few persons are so grandiose as to deliberately set out to effect changes in systems of systems. Most of us, if we really take a self-assessment, subscribe to the old adage that "you can't fight city hall," and are not swayed by exceptions like Ralph Nader, Martin Luther King and Sol Alinsky. As I think of the exciting work we have been doing with the Army Chaplains, the picture that comes into my mind is that we slipped into it by the side door labelled "race relations training," backed into OD as we saw an opportunity for effecting change in the nature of the Chaplaincy, itself, and are now peering out the front door at the larger systems which make up the Army. Since the Chaplains touch many of these systems, perhaps we can touch them through the chaplains. OD technology has helped; true macrosystems technology is yet to come.

## REFERENCES

Costello, Timothy W., "Change in municipal government: view from the inside." *Journal of Applied Behavioral Science,* Volume 7, Number 2, pp. 131-145, 1971.

Hornstein, H. A., Bunker, B. B., Burke, W. W., Gindes, M., and Lewicki, R. J., *Social Intervention, A Behavioral Science Approach,* New York, The Free Press, 1971.

Mill, Cyril R. "A new concept of the chaplaincy." *The Military Chaplain,* 1972.

Peabody, George L., "Power, Alinsky, and Other Thoughts," in Hornstein, H. A., *Social Intervention, A Behavioral Science Approach,* New York: The Free Press, 1971.

Walton, Richard E., "A problem solving workshop on border conflicts in Eastern Africa." *Journal of Applied Behavioral Science,* Volume 6, Number 4, pp. 453-489, 1970.

Wedge, Bryant, "A psychiatric model for intercession in intergroup conflict." *Journal of Applied Behavioral Science,* Volume 7, Number 6, pp. 733-761, 1971.

# 14

# Improving International Relations and Effectiveness Within Multinational Organizations

*DR. LEOPOLD S. VANSINA*

The second half of the 20th century is giving a new outlook to the organizational structure of the world. National and cultural boundaries are being crossed by the development of international and multinational organizations. There is no need to impress you with data on the billions of dollars, pounds, Deutsche Marken or yen that are being invested abroad. The international or multinational enterprise exists and continues to grow. Along with them, one observes the development of international union associations, international economic and/or political institutions such as the European Common Market, the European Free Trade Association and the United Nations and the "mushrooming" of international institutes for research, education, consulting or training. Some authors go so far as to say that the existing nation states and state nations* are outdated and overtaken by international financial, economical and political institutions. The nation states are no longer capable of optimizing their economic and human resources. On the contrary, their efforts to maintain their sovereignty lead to stagnation and dissipation.

Not all international organizations reflect in their action a common view on the future development of the world. Some hold an almost utopian idea that eventually historical and cultural differences will be transcended by a new worldwide manhood or pan-culture. Others reflect the belief that despite the technological

---

* Nation-state is a political unit characterized primarily by a community of feeling and tradition shared by its citizens and only secondarily by the presence of a unifying public administration. In a State-nation the unity is more maintained by the public administration, rather than by ethnicity (E. Glenn, R. Johnson, P. Kimmel and B. Wedge, 1971).

similarities, important cultural and political differences will continue to divide the world. Still others strive to build institutions in which cultural and political differences are being bridged by the pursuit of worldwide objectives and concerns.

At present, however, the world and even the international organizations are still struggling with differences in culture and interests, while searching for common objectives and ultimate models that will allow them to live and work together. Quite a few social scientists and international managers are working together to build international institutions that meet the *socio-technical realities* of the international organization and its environment. Yet, the end of their search and struggles is not in sight. Most probably it will never be.

Improving international relations and the effectiveness of international organizations, is *not a simple psychological* assignment. It is an organizational process whereby psychological, as well as sociological and political elements are blended for the sake of *building* international institutions. It is, in other words, a "social-architectural" assignment like H. Perlmutter (1965) so nicely conceptualized.

The building and development of international institutions presupposes a deep understanding of the essential properties and functioning of the system. Although one can learn about the functioning of a system while trying to change it; more often than not planned change without an understanding of the functioning of a particular organization leads to arbitrary or superficial modifications.

In the first part of this paper, I will briefly discuss the various factors which hamper the learning from and about international organizations and their development. In the second part, I'll discuss the possible contribution of organization development to the international organization. This discussion includes a set of principles and procedures to improve the international relations and the effectiveness of inter or multinational organizations. I will also mention some of the difficulties and limitations of this OD approach.

Since my professional work has almost exclusively been with industrial international organizations, I will restrict myself to the issues of, and our approach to, the international enterprise. I believe however that some of the ideas and principles have validity for the international organization in general.

Part one: OBSTACLES TO LEARNING FROM AND ABOUT
         THE INTERNATIONAL FIRM AND ITS
         DEVELOPMENT

I. The absence of a generally accepted "ultimate model" of the
multinational organization.

International organizations differ from one another in their
structure, policies and views of the "ultimate model." These
differences are reflected in H. Perlmutter's (1955) typology of the
international organization and the absence of generally accepted
definitions, which go beyond the operational level.

The ultimate model is seldom made explicit, but it can be derived
from their organizational and management activities. At one
extreme, one has the international organization with the apparent
ultimate model to exploit the economic and/or technological
advantages—developed in the parent company (most often a
national company)—on an international or worldwide scale. Other
nations provide the lacking natural resources and/or supporting
personnel in return for some employment and possible know-how.
The major part of the benefits are however kept within the
organization which is controlled and managed by the parent
company.

At the other extreme, one has the international organization which
pulls together, on an international level, the necessary capital,
technological and human resources. The economic and technological
gains are shared and controlled by the contributing parties. Apparently its ultimate model is to become a multinational organization, namely an international organization that is genuinely internationally managed and owned, psychologically as well as financially.

Between these two extremes one finds a variety of implicit
ultimate models which vary not only from one organization to the
other but also within the international organization. Consequently
one does not have one ultimate model or *mediating structure,* that is
"a system of ideas—a partial cognitive structure—either actually or
potentially shared by the parties" (E. Glenn et al, 1971, p. 37), that
legitimizes actions and decisions, and facilitates conflict resolution.

Furthermore, it is very difficult to grasp the total system. The
mere size, and the geographic distances between operating companies and headquarters make it difficult to gain intellectual and
psychological understanding of the functioning of the total system.

The environment  of the international organization is a complex pattern of nation states and state nations, which affect differentially, the various parts of the organization. Legally imposed product specifications may affect the production units in Switzerland while the Swedish state  legislation on social benefit plans create distinctive and additional demands on personnel policies.

Some managers and social scientists continue to explain the organizational issues rigidly in terms of rivalry between nationality groups or cultural differences, where the problems are in fact more complex and require a more refined set of concepts. Some of these persons have fallen in the trap set up by conflicting parties, which use the nationality group as a label, either to strengthen their positions, or to cover up more basic sources of disagreement. Others are simply projecting their own nationality consciousness onto the organization.

But a greater number of managers and professionals have not yet gained a sufficient understanding of the functioning of the international organization. They try to manage the international firm as if it were a large national enterprise, applying old solutions to new or different problems. A proper conceptual framework is not only a prerequisite for understanding, effective diagnoses and problem solving; it is also a must for guiding the building and integration processes.

II. The lack of a conceptual framework for understanding and diagnosing socio-psychological issues in international organizations.

The first concepts that come to mind when we talk about international organizations are nationality, cultural and ethnic groups. Although these concepts are likely to cover real entities they are often too broad and consequently cloud the understanding and blur the diagnosis. Therefore, I suggest that we use the "reference group" as the basic concept.

Indeed, the nationality group is more often than not a mix of cultural, ethnic, political, religious and professional groups. Therefore, another concept is needed which includes more adequately the complexities of the various, often interrelated groups, and which explains more accurately the behavior of international organizations. The "reference group" is such a concept.

A. The reference group

I like to define a reference group as: ". . . that group whose outlook is used by the actor as a frame of reference in the organization of his perceptual field" (T. Shibuteri, 1955). All groups tend to develop a particular orientation to the world which is more or less rigidly shared by the group members.* The individual who has incorporated this frame of reference uses it, often without awareness, to structure his perceptions of new situations. Therefore the reference group can be the nationality or the cultural group, or the outlook can have its source in the ethnic or work group. In the international organization one has a number of overlapping and interacting reference groups. Their development is facilitated by geographic isolation, distinctive work and selected bits of information. Consequently, it is natural that headquarters and subsidiaries have a distinctive way of looking at the business. The outlook, the aims and priorities of these groups operating in different environments, must be expected to diverge.

The work group can, and often does, become a stronger reference group than the nationality, cultural or ethnic group. In our correspondence, Chris Argyris raised the following hypothesis about the relative importance of the workgroup over other groups:

The more cohesive or interdependent the multinational organization is among its parts, the more critical will be the variables associated with work, and the more critical will be work groups as reference groups. The less cohesive (or the more defensive), the more nationality, cultural or ethnic groups will become reference groups.

This hypothesis, as any other hypothesis specified in this part, needs further testing. It is, however, an explicit formulation of an assumption upon which part II is largely based.

## B. The nationality groups

The nationality groups may introduce nationalism and nationalistic feelings into the organization. They create or at least increase the potential for intergroup conflicts (e.g. inter-departmental, or conflicts between headquarters and subsidiaries).

Otto Klineberg (1964) defines nationalism as: ". . . an attitude subject to the same kind of developmental history as other attitudes, with a similar interpenetration of rational and irrational factors, it has the special quality that it is not only *for* something but is almost always at the same time *against* something else" (p. 54).

Nationalism as an attitude is always accompanied by nationalistic

---

* An individual does not necessarily need to be a formal accepted member to adhere to a particular reference group. It is sufficient that one psychologically feels a member or that one aspires membership.

feelings. These feelings can be related as much to the defense of the nation and its interests as to the members of the nation state and their interests. Nationalism and nationalistic feelings are almost always directed *against* something, (other nations or their members), that threaten the survival and/or prestige of the nation. Even rationally founded differences such as salary differences or un-equal promotion possibilities, stemming from basic differences in qualifications, tend to unite the members of the same nation and to generate feelings of injustice and discrimination against their respective nation states or their members. *In an international setting particularly, people tend to interpret real or imagined differential treatment in terms of national (or ethnic) discrimination.*

Not all nationality groups express the same strength of nationalism. One may hypothesize that the members of state-nations, which do not satisfy reasonably well the needs of their members, will experience less nationalistic feelings. In these instances where the nation, due to institutional weakness and cultural or ethnic heterogeneity, has little or no instrumental value to its members, members will tend to search group loyalty, prestige and even security in other, often less secular groups, like ethnic, cultural, work or professional groups.

The nationality group is often a powerful group, feared by other nationality groups and by the international organization. The reasons for this are: (a) that the nationality group—as distinct from most other groups—has powerful institutions behind it which have the capacity to retaliate legally or by force. Nationalization of foreign enterprises, imposed partnerships, tariff barriers, restriction on capital flow and manpower are among steps which have been taken to protect the nation, to circumvent real or feared losses or to retaliate; (b) the nationality group brings intergroup conflict and competition into the organization. Peaceful coexistence is still an ideal. Strong competitive feelings prevail. Members of poorer nations, for example, tend to resent members of richer nations. They may, however, attract investments from richer, more developed countries, but only for as long as they can benefit or learn from them. Furthermore, historically developed frictions may become linked to economic rivalry and blur or reinforce the primary reasons for resentment. The whole set of negative feelings may lead to a refusal to accept foreign assignments in that particular country. In the same vein, members of one nation may not be willing to work under a boss from a rival nation. For example, some Danes bluntly refuse to work in Sweden. The Flemings, in one international organization, objected to the replacement of their American boss by a Frenchman (a felt substitute for a Walloon) because they were said to doubt his objectivity.

I cannot conclude this discussion of nationality groups and nationalistic feelings without a clear warning to the OD practitioner or social scientist active in the field of international organizations. Nationality groups and in particular nationalistic feelings in the form of care for one's nation and its people, are often used as a *cover* to defend other interests or to *depersonalize* interpersonal or intergroup conflicts (conflicts between subsidiaries, operating units and headquarters). The seductive quality of "caring for one's people" is a nobel shield to fight for personal or local interests. In most instances the interests of the nationality group and the local manager(s) are indeed interrelated, but if one focuses only on the nationality group or the feelings for one's country and for one's people, the issues and conflicts under discussion never find a genuine solution.

## C. The Cultural group

Nationality groups are often, but not necessarily always, *cultural groups*. Most human beings are born and raised in families, groups and institutions (schools, hospitals, universities, churches) which are products of the nation-state or the cultural group. Consequently, the individual becomes rather completely embedded in the culture of the nation or the community in which he was raised. Later, as an adult, it becomes very difficult to get rid of one's culture, or "those conventional understandings, manifest in act and artifact that characterize societies" as Redfield (1941) states it. The culture has become so much part of himself that he is no longer aware to what extent he is accepting or influenced by these cultural habits of action and of thought. Cultural habits of action are readily identified through observation of his models of behavior. But etiquette, ceremonial and daily ways of behaving do not create major obstacles for cross-national or intercultural collaboration. Real difficulties, especially in problem solving and decision making, stem from the habits of thought, ways of thinking and reasoning (global vs. a more articulated cognitive style, (H. Witkin, 1967), associative or abstract, case oriented vs. associative or abstract, universal oriented thought processes (E. Glenn et al, 1971)), which are not readily observable but must be inferred from the cognitive activities or products.

The assumption that no major cultural differences exist may initially facilitate cross cultural decision making or negotiations, but as behavioral differences become apparent, it often results in distrust and suspicion. Through the internationalization of education, training and work assignments, one can develop more skills in understanding cultural habits of thought, while increasing identification with one's own cultural or national group. This was at least the case with Scandinavian students, who studied at American universities (H. Kelman and L. Bailyn, 1962). If their findings may be generalized to other cultural groups, we foresee an improvement in decision making and trust—due to a better understanding of one another—along with an increase of negotiation-time over basic cultural differences and interests.

Although in some instances the nationality group is a cultural group, the members can at the same time belong to other cultural or ethnic groups existing within or across national boundaries.

Organizational issues involving nationality, cultural or ethnic groups are difficult to clarify, mainly because every individual brings his own membership into the situation. Even when one's actual behavior does not reflect one's group identity, nor any prejudice or ethnocentricity, his environment will role cast him as, for example, an American or a Jew. In other words, psychological processes hamper the understanding of the functioning of international organizations.

III. Some psychological processes hindering the understanding and clarification of social issues in international organizations

A. Ethnocentricity

Each group, but in particular nationality, cultural and ethnic groups, are prone to enthnocentricity and ethnocentric perceptions, especially when they see themselves as successful (or powerful) in one or another area of activities such as economy, philosophy, arts or technology.

The American sociologist, W. Sumner (1906), was the first to define the concept of ethnocentrism as a " . . . view of things in which one's own group is the centre of everything, and all others are scaled and rated with reference to it" (p. 13).

Otto Klineberg (1964) speaks about ethnocentric perception, which he defines as " . . . the tendency to see and judge external occurrences in terms of one's particular ethnic or national identification, that is to say, in terms of the values, wishes and expectations acquired as a member of a particular community" (p. 95).

Ethnocentrism and ethnocentric perceptions include a *judgmental* aspect. They hinder the understanding of an international organization because the person becomes preoccupied with the *evaluation* of a system in terms of his *own criteria,* and he consequently *distorts reality.*

## B. Prejudice

Ethnocentrism has been linked to prejudice and personality factors by T. Adorno, et. al. (1950), and H. Smith and Rosen (1958). The results of the latter authors' investigation indicate that world mindedness is closely and inversely related to the dimension of authoritarianism.

Prejudices apparently reflect cultural norms. They are not only embedded in the character structure of the individual, but also in the total social-economic system (G. Allport, 1958). "Essentially, prejudice is an intergroup phenomenon that involves a negative attitude, a prejudgment, regarding other individuals in terms of perceived group affiliations" (E. Hollander and R. Hunt, 1967, p. 590).

Prejudices are more likely to arise when management practices maintain or even accentuate distinctiveness and inequality of nationality, cultural or ethnic groups through clearcut geographic separation, differential job-assignments, promotion and compensation. The latter situation occurs frequently when companies move into developing countries where the human resources required to manage the local operations are difficult to find. The expatriates filling the gap enjoy a much higher standard of living, due to the companies' expatriation plan or international salary system, than the local employees, while occupying at the same time the most interesting positions.

## C. Stereotyping

Stereotyping refers to the process by which attributes, traits and behavior are ascribed to individuals because of their particular group-membership. The product of this is a more or less accurate or inaccurate stereotype.

Too favorable stereotypes may eventually lead to distrust when one gradually becomes confronted with the actual behavior of the persons or groups concerned. Too unfavorable stereotypes lead to avoidance, and it takes time to realize what human resources one has neglected. The inaccuracy of stereotypes are therefore difficult to identify. They are also difficult to correct once they have developed (Gilbert, 1951).

The less one knows about a particular person, the more one relies on the stereotype one has about the nation, ethnic, cultural or the professional group. Furthermore, it appears that the more salient the nationality is in the mind of the judge, through the presence of other nationalities in the group for example, the more his stereotype of the nationality will influence his judgment of the person (J. Bruner & H. Perlmutter, 1957).

Stereotyping, like ethnocentrism and prejudice, *distorts reality* and attributes *different meanings* to even quite local distinctions between groups.

These three psychological processes are still easy to detect, but most international organizations are coping with deeply rooted, new forms of alienation. Because they are often carefully hidden it is harder to gain awareness of them, but they seem to hinder the development of the international organization.

IV. Forms of alienation which hinder the development of international organizations.

A. Alienation from the results of one's efforts

As international organizations grow and diversify, they tend to develop structures based on world-wide product divisions, geographic divisions, or a combination of the two (L. Fouraker & J. Stafford, 1968). Clear cut profit responsibilities are taken away from the operating units and located higher up in the hierarchy to the product division manager or area manager. Task-forces, often operating above the head of the operating units, are more frequently used to decide where units should be located and what their role is to be.

Transfer pricing and other international management practices displace secretly the achieved results from one nation to another. These developments reduce a sense of proprietorship, group or individual ownership—at least partial ownership—of their successes and failures. Proprietorship implies that: (a) individuals or groups have some freedom or meaningful influence upon "what to do" and/or "how to do it;" (b) that the given freedom or influence can be brought to bear on issues which, *a priori*, will have an impact on their own successes or failures; (c) that the individuals or groups are able to confront themselves with the results of their efforts and are recognized accordingly; and (d) that the countries, in which the operating units are located, can benefit from the resulting increase in economical and technological value.

B. Alienation from cultural and meaningful social interaction

The increasing demand that international managers or key people help in directing foreign activities toward achieving standards or goals, which may differ from those which local cultural or political influences would prefer,* put a heavy psychological burden on these people. They are trained to become international, but once they have given up cultural or national membership, they often discover that they belong nowhere. As J. Gardner (1964) writes: "Most human beings *are* capable of achieving the measure of autonomy and mature individuality required by our conceptions of individual dignity and worth. But certain kinds of separation of the *self* from *all that is beyond the self* are inherently *destructive* and *intolerable to human beings*."

The international manager and the foreign assignee need a social base which is bigger than arid egocentrism or individualism. Although the work team may provide such a base for the manager or assignee (D. Northern, 1972), his family and himself—once he leaves the organization—may be adrift in the community. The problem of belongingness, therefore, is difficult to solve since it goes beyond the boundaries of the organization into the community.

The alienation from significant others is not restricted to foreign employees. In a foreign subsidiary, national managers, executives and even regular white and blue collar workers can become estranged from their own folks in their own country. This phenomena is frequently noticed in underdeveloped and in developing countries. Often, so-called "well Europeanized" African managers start suddenly complaining about psychosomatic disturbances. Some even request to be transferred to Europe in order to

---

* This managerial component, rather than the technical or specialized one, is seen by Lee to be the essence of the role of the Multinational Executive (R. Lee, 1968).

escape the loyalty conflict between the foreign subsidiary and the tribe. In a foreign subsidiary in Spain, the Spanish managers felt that they were not accepted by headquarters and by their international colleagues because their local business practices and philosophies were incongruent with those of the international corporation. At the same time, they were looked down upon (even ridiculed) by their Spanish colleagues from the neighboring national companies, because they could not make the foreign subsidiary that profitable with the imposed "no cheating," "no tax evading" policies of the international organization. A lack of success which, in turn, reduced their prestige in the eyes of the headquarters. In general, we hypothesize that the danger of alienation from significant others will be higher, the greater the difference in culture, management philosophy and practice of the host country and the international organization.

While proprietorship defends the human being from alienation of his results, belongingness protects him from alienation from cultural, national and meaningful social interaction. Both forms of alienation could be curbed through the development of a genuine multinational organization.

## Part two: AN OD APPROACH TO THE BUILDING AND DEVELOPMENT OF MULTINATIONAL ORGANIZATIONS

Organization development is a learning strategy, aimed at the development of an organization, or parts thereof, in relation to its (or their) environment(s), with the ultimate goal of making this learning about one's own organization functioning and development a characteristic of the organization (L. Vansina, 1972). In other words, OD is a learning strategy to help an organization become more an organization that is more integrated. In an international organization, the learning strategy will consequently and inevitably aim at helping the organization to become more of a *multinational organization*.

Therefore, improving international relations and effectiveness within international organizations means the integration of the various parts and resources. The actual integration of individuals, groups and other resources can only be achieved within the concrete and changing realities of the organization.

Since the building and development of a multinational organization is more than a psychological assignment, it requires *knowledge* from sociology, and the political sciences, as well as *the right* and the *commitment* for managerial decision making. I postulate that *the improvement of international relations or the integration of nationality groups can only be achieved through the development of an international top management team, which is the representation in micro format of a truly multinational organization.*

The development of an international top management team is necessary because (1) the top management team is willingly or unwillingly taken as a model; and (2) because they have the *right* and the *power* to make decisions on policy and large structural changes—decisions which can either facilitate or hinder the multinational developments.

I. The OD model and its principles

A. Our OD approach is based on the confrontation model in which various subsystems (operating companies or subsidiaries, headquarters, nationality, cultural and functional groups), are brought together in a temporary face-to-face situation, to study actual issues (projects, problems, and strategies) of their own organization.

The resulting understanding of the functioning of the system may or may not lead to change. Only when one has acquired this understanding is one able to answer the four basic questions which precede planned change. Namely: (1) Change for what purposes? (2) For whose purposes? (3) With which means? and (4) What consequences? Without clear answers to these questions the OD practitioner (and even the client system) may become the victim of political manipulations or social pressures.

The confrontation can be with (a) valid information about the organization, or theoretical input (concepts that allow people *to grasp the realities* and to understand the difference between realities and *the way they are being used or exploited*). The confrontation can further be with (b) the actual physical situation and (c) oneself, one's own thought processes and behavior.

B. The principles upon which the OD intervention is based

Principle I.  A temporary system is created in which the key people, who are supposed to work as a team or a system are brought together in a face-to-face situation.*

---

* The temporary system created in this context and in organization development work in general, is of a particular type. In contrast with most temporary systems, the members are taken from enduring groups or form more or less stable subsystems to which they will return after completion of a specific assignment.

A special workshop or a four-day business meeting which is primarily designed to facilitate the integration of nationality groups is generally required to start the process.

1. Central and connecting subsystems and their key members

The total client system, or the total system to be understood and possibly changed, is seen as being composed of a central sybsystem and connected subsystems. A particular subsystem becomes central when it is the focus of change. While the connected subsystems are seen as conditions which facilitate or hinder this change, a connected subsystem can in turn become a central subsystem when the focus of change has been shifted to that particular subsystem.

In terms of these subsystems, one distinguishes two categories of key persons. First, those persons who are members of the system in need of integration are called the *central subsystem*. They are, *in casu,* the formal members of the very top management group. Secondly, those persons whose *collaboration is required* for the integration of the central subsystem, or persons who *can make a meaningful* contribution to the integration because of their position in the *connected subsystem.* The last category of key persons are there to facilitate the integration of the different nationality groups, represented in the central subsystem. Indeed, the central subsystem can only achieve a meaningful and realistic integration when the disintegration issues are worked *within the context of the total organization.* In general, it means that the temporary system or conference is composed of key persons from at least three different hierarchical levels. For example, the president, his headquarters staff and the country general managers.

The collaboration of key persons from outside the central subsystem is needed for two purposes. Firstly, to provide *first hand information* about the business operations in various countries or geographic areas. This information should include the views and opinions of the local people in these areas. In other words, one allows the information about the business operations to be influenced by national or cultural factors. Secondly, by their presence they allow the central subsystem *to define its role and responsibilities,* to develop a coding and decoding system, in relation to themselves, or in other words, to the other parts of the organization.

2. The interfaces

Indeed, roles and responsibilities become real when one succeeds in bridging the "interfaces" between the different organizational parts. The role of headquarters can only become clarified in relation to and with the help of national management and vice versa. Likewise, the clarification of coding and decoding systems, on the communication level, requires a joint effort from the organizational units involved.

The coding system, according to D. Katz and R. Kahn (1966) determines "...the amount and type of information they receive from the external world and the transformation of it according to their systematic properties" (p. 228). Someone who is outside that system tends to see things differently, and may experience great difficulties in understanding the information generated by that system.

Bridging the interfaces between systems (e.g. headquarters and national management), gains additional importance in the international organization because of geographic distances, cultural and language differences. Therefore, a serious analysis is required to identify those key persons.

The number of key persons which can be brought together in a face-to-face situation is not unlimited. When the group exceeds about 30 persons, it becomes very difficult to manage the intersystem interactions and overall team-building. In such instances, one may be forced to collect the information from the key persons in the connected subsystems and feed it back directly to the central subsystem. In this way, one breaks down, temporarily, the existing information channels, to provide the central subsystem with (unfiltered) data from further down the hierarchy. Principle I can therefore be supplemented as follows.

Principle I. a. In the temporary system designed to integrate different nationalities, the existing communication lines of the connected subsystems are replaced by direct information channels to the central subsystem.

In some cases, the connected subsystems need to sort out their own internal differences before they can seriously inform the central subsystem, or send a representative. In those instances, a development plan of two phases is recommended. For example, in one big international organization, we decided to bring together, in the first phase, all key persons of the country management team (as one subsystem) and the general managers of the various operating units in that particular country (as another subsystem). This procedure was repeated for the two other countries involved. Still in another large international organization, all the country general managers, the management staff of area-headquarters, and the headquarter staff, were brought together.

Where one has to proceed gradually, because of group size and the realities of the organizational context, the first phase is already designed to develop a (international) team, a frame of reference and interpersonal ties which are solid enough to allow them to work as a subsystem with the other groups in phase two.

In these two examples, the second phase took the following form. In the first international organization, the general managers of the operating units in the three countries concerned, their respective national management staffs and the person from headquarters, directly responsible for that area, were brought together in a work-conference. In view of the particular task (see Principle II) the groupings were changed. The total membership was divided into four groups: an area headquarter group composed of the three national management groups plus the person from headquarters, and three product groups in which the general managers of the operating units, per product group (thus internationally composed) were assembled.*

In the second international organization, representatives (always more than 3 persons) of the country management group and of the area-headquarters were brought together with the headquarters group and the president. In this organization the groupings were not changed.

The groupings in the two given examples, during the two phases, can be graphically represented as follows in figures 1 and 2. The oval and the straight lines designate respectively the groupings in phase 1 and phase 2.

Phase two is, in other words, designed to build an overall international management team, which takes into account the various opinions and inputs of the composing central and connecting subsystems, which have functional meaning to the organization.

The nature of composition of the temporary system creates, however, conditions for the depth and scope of problem solving and

* One could question the necessity or even desirability of the first phase in our first example. After consideration, however, we decided to embark with a preliminary phase because: (a) one country (subpart) was motivated to face up to its issues; (b) there was a reasonable chance that the two other countries would follow after having heard about the successfulness of the intervention; and (c) product groups, across national boundaries, can only be effectively installed after a serious hearing of the thoughts and feelings of the managers of the operating units. This last consideration could only be dealt with through phase one, which brought them together nationally.

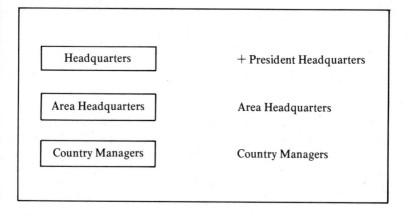

FIGURE 1

*International Organization One*

FIGURE 2

*International Organization Two*

learning. The less geocentric the organization, the smaller the probabilities that one can learn from all these different key persons.

I explained in the first part of this paper that it is very difficult to distinguish nationality and cultural differences from those which result from one's particular organizational position. The following table shows how the *composition* of the temporary system facilitates or hinders learning in particular areas.

| Organizational position of key-persons: | Nationality or Cultural background of key-persons: | |
| | shared | different |
| Similar | individual or personality differences<br><br>PERSON-LEARNING | nationality, cultural and personality differences<br><br>CULTURE-LEARNING |
| Dissimilar | differences in frame of reference, coding and decoding systems; personality differences<br><br>ORGANIATION-LEARNING | differences in personality, culture frame or reference, coding and decoding systems are mixed<br><br>INTERNATIONAL ORGANIZATION - LEARNING |

TABLE 1

*Areas of Learning or Conflict Resolution*

The ideal mix of the temporary system includes persons with different national backgrounds occupying the same organizational position, and persons with shared backgrounds in different organizational positions. If, however, nationality and organizational positions are simultaneously at variance, but these differences are crystalized, in each case, in one person, learning is generally poor because of lack of check or reference points.

Principle I. b.   In the temporary system, everyone is encouraged to share his information from the position he occupies, without foreclosing problem solving with decision making.

This principle dictates an abolition of authority based on rational-legal principles during the problem solving phase, to make room for authority based on expertise and first hand information directly related to the issue under discussion. The original structure, however, becomes reestablished at the decision making stage, if the learnings call for changes in the organization or its structure.

3. The face-to-face meeting

The face-to-face meeting with all the key persons, is an essential aspect of principle I. It fulfills various functions.

First, it opens up a variety of blocked or filtered communication channels. Organizations, especially large ones like most international companies with their crossings of product and functional lines, suffer from communication deficiencies. Communications are not only slow, less clear than they should be because of language and semantic difficulties, but they also tend to be channelled. Different members of the organization receive different bits of information. And as J. March and H. Simon (1958, p. 128) observed, the channelling of information increases the differentiation of perception within the organization, and consequently the probability of conflict, since one has different perceptions of the same reality. The free information flow and the direct contact with key sources of information are basic conditions for the development of a *shared frame of reference.*

Secondly, the face-to-face situation facilitates more *accurate perception* of other people and a better understanding of their *decisions.*

The gradually developing frame of reference precedes a change in attitude. We do not hold the naive assumption that getting to know the people of the other country will lead to liking them. But there is ample research evidence that first-hand experience reduces extreme *stereotypes and prejudices.* One acquires a more *realistic* view of the other. The perceptions of other nationality or cultural groups become more qualified. The individual members become recognized as individuals with certain personality traits, competences and shortcomings and also with different frames of reference.* While one learns about the others, one also gains insight into one's own attitudes and outlook, one's own reference groups and loyalty conflicts.

Thirdly, but no less important, the face-to-face meeting for an extended period (of four to five days) allows *professional and personal relations to grow.* Something that cannot be achieved by quick random meetings or visits.

* Chadwick F. Alger (1965) reported similar observations in his study "Personal contact in intergovernmental organizations" undertaken in the United States.

Principle II. The various subsystems are given a common task, which is real in the organizational context, and which can only be accomplished through the acceptance of a superordinate goal.

1. Common task

A common task, relevant to and imbedded in the realities of the particular international organization, is given to all the key persons from the various sybsystems concerned. Such a task could be the development of a five year plan, or the identification of the major obstacles or opportunities for organizational survival or development. Each individual or subsystem is encouraged to study this task from his organizational position.

2. A superordinate goal

From the start, together with the diagnostic preparation of the common task, a set of superordinate goals are given. The importance of superordinate goals have been demonstrated in the well known experiments of M. Sherif (1958, p. 349) on the reduction of intergroup conflict. He defines them as " . . . goals which are compelling and highly appealing to members of two or more groups in conflict but which cannot be attained by the resources and energies of the groups separately."

Such a set of superordinate goals is, for example, the survival, growth and profitability of the international organization. They are generally accepted by managers as goals that can only be attained when the various groups of the organization pull together and cooperate. They replace, initially the lack of a generally acceptable mediating structure.

The first principle, the face-to-face meeting, created the necessary conditions for open communications and the reduction of prejudices and inaccurate stereotypes. The second principle provides opportunities to confront views, clarify roles and responsibilities, and to build *a reference group*. Indeed, the reports are presented in the work conference as the points of view of the various groupings (e.g. country general managers, area-headquarters, and so on) to facilitate the needed confrontation. Divergence of opinion and priorities and unclarity of roles and responsibilities thereby come to the surface.

As I said earlier, the work, the daily problems and the bits of information which people in headquarters and subsidiaries receive, make them develop their *own way of looking at the work*. The aims and priorities of these groups, located in different environments, cannot help but differ. Headquarters, national management and operating units each have their established practices and a life of their own, which they seek to preserve, often at the expense of the interests of the international organization as a whole. These different perceptions, aims and priorities must be discussed, understood, completed or corrected where ever they are partial or false to become integrated. This is far from being an easy task. It requires a lot of social skill and wit, to weigh accurately the extent to which these views and goals are defended in the pursuit of local interests, or the extent to which they are founded on a deeper understanding of the local situation. "Realities" are often used knowingly or unknowingly to *defend* acquired positions or to *protect* interests and priorities. The question, therefore, is how valid are these arguments and how are these "realities" used? In most cases, it is not a question of either one or the other. Treating problems as such from the start is foolish. Careful evaluation is needed before they can be rejected or integrated in the total organizational framework. It is also a delicate work. In the process of the discussion, ideas are, or at least tend to become, "part of" the group or the individual. A rejection of them is easily *felt* as a rejection of the group or person who owns it. Furthermore, the position of certain individuals or groups may be changed to the extent that they were based on the exclusive possession of information, or on the existing competitive feelings against another group. The expected outcome, however, is a more realistic insight and understanding of the various points of view, as well as a more valid appreciation of the different individual resources. In order to arrive at this positive outcome and to create optimal conditions for a basic learning experience for the international executive, we need a proper set of rules which facilitate problem solving.

Principle III.   International teams can only be built in adherence to a set of norms of openness, trust and reality testing, which guarantee effective problem solving.

While the first two principles create possibilities to communicate on relevant shared issues, the third one guarantees the *meaningfulness* of the verbal interchange.

## 1. Trust

It is most unlikely that the above stated norms, especially openness and trust, are sufficiently present at the outset of the conferences. Indeed, Chris Argyris (1969) was unable to observe any trust interactions in the 112 task sessions studied in enduring groups. The lack of trust in international organizations is almost a general phenomenon. "Mountains do not meet, but people do!" is a common but informal explanation why the meeting went in a particular way. Pockets full of hidden agenda's color and steer the discussions. Although a sharp observer, or someone who is *in* that particular group is able to identify them. It is often outside the formal meetings, in the cozy atmosphere of the bar that they become fully revealed.

The importance of trust in international relations is clearly underlined by M. Deutsch (1967) in his paper "Some considerations relevant to national policy," and by D. Zand (1972) in "Trust and Managerial Problem Solving." Our views concur with Deutsch's statements, that one cannot expect rational behavior as long as one does not trust another. Mutual trust is most likely to occur when one discovers a superordinate goal (M. Deutsch, *op. cit.*). Therefore, it is of crucial importance that the superordinate goal and these norms are made clear at the beginning of the discussions and kept salient throughout the conference. An *explicit* statement about the norms which will guide the discussions is not a full guarantee of their adherence. One may openly agree "to speak one's mind" but it often becomes qualified by counteracting *implicit norms* like "one says what one thinks as long as it is not going to offend the boss!" The norm of reality testing, namely the freedom to check information and to question opinions, is therefore an essential rule.

## 2. Reality testing

The reality testing norm legitimizes *process analysis,* or in other words the analysis of the psychological processes that take place, when people work together. Implicit assumptions or norms, stereotyped views, feelings, interpersonal relations and hidden agendas *which interfere* with the problem-solving and decision making can thereby be opened up for discussion.

Reality testing facilitates *confrontation* between personal views and between the standpoints of different groups represented or present at the conference, without an unnecessary increase in tension. People often use these norms to introduce their attempts to further explore issues or to reveal thus far hidden information about facts or feelings. "We were told to be open; well I would like to check this opinion . . . " is, for example, an opening statement to new issues or to a release of pent-up feelings. Painful experiences of the past with other nationality groups or more personal experiences and misunderstandings like the feeling of being put on a dead end road by a particular foreign assignment can consequently be brought up. As long as they remain concealed, they not only continue to influence one's thoughts and feelings, but they can never be looked at, checked and brought into proper perspective. International organizations often operate with unclear or overlapping areas of responsibility. The rapid changes of managers from one function to another does not make it easy to know who is responsible for what in the organization. The unclarity can easily be exploited either by a manager to duck his responsibilities or to take on others. In any case, unclarity of roles and problems of the interfaces between groups are a source of misunderstandings and possible apprehension. The set of norms legitimizes their clarification. And this is possible because all key people are present, face-to-face.

Process analysis and reality testing help to make sure that *all resources available are fully used,* and that everyone involved in the debated issue is heard. It safeguards against hasty or "hand-clasp" decisions, and against agreements based on convenience or tradition. Just because one always used to think or run the business in a particular way, does not necessarily mean that it is the right way. Attention needs to be given to agreements " . . . repeated for their immediate value in reducing the costs involved in face-to-face influence and in smoothing out the course of the interaction" (J. Thibaut & H. Kelley, 1959, p. 128). This is especially true when one is building something new, such as an integrated international management team.

Reality testing implies a systematic *analysis of the consequences* of action proposals and decisions. Although managers are accustomed to examining carefully the estimated monetary costs and gains of their actions, they often hesitate to deal with the human and social consequences, namely, the ensuing sacrifices in terms of reconsidering personal aspirations, or abdication—partially or totally—of particular group interests. Everyone involved needs to be fully aware of the implications of the decisions before one can expect to get *internal commitment.* The human or social sacrifices are as much a part of reality as the expected economic gains. They need to be worked through before one can expect that the achieved commitment *will be maintained* when the individuals return to their jobs. Working through does not mean that all implications should be deplored publicly, but that they become acknowledged cognitively and emotionally by the parties involved. One cannot allow them to be repressed in the mild euphoria which accompanies the achievement of a different solution.

Adherence to this set of norms is difficult. These norms cannot be imposed. They gradually become internationalized as the group gains confidence in their usefulness in dealing with the issues at hand. A clear statement of the rules of the game at the outset makes it possible to bring them back to mind whenever the work requires it.

Principle IV. The work conference should be held at a location which does not give psychological advantages to any of the groups involved.

A neutral place, away from the daily business life facilitates the building process. It is only in this type of work conference that one realizes the potency of the primitive, territorial instinct and the interwoveness of cultural behavioral patterns in the local environment settings.

Language is often a critical issue, since it inevitably gives one langauge group an advantage over the others. Most international organizations have, however, accepted one as the official company language. Whenever the persons at the workshop cannot agree on a language in which everyone can communicate with ease, they have to stick to the official company language. The resulting communication problems must be handled in the light of the available resources. In our experience, however, language is often a concern not so much because of lack of fluency as for the feared advantage native speakers may take. The fears may be related either to the chance that non-native speakers will hide themselves behind language difficulties, or that fluent speakers will hide themselves behind language difficulties, or that fluent speakers will drown the others in a flood of sophisticated words.

In general, these four principles make it possible that an aggregate of individuals and various nationality, cultural and reference groups become an integrated team. One problem remains: to build continuity in the newly achieved integration, so that it survives the temporary system and continues to steer the daily management practices of its members.

Principle V. Near the end of the temporary system, one jointly explores or creates international settings that facilitate the continuation of the learning and integrating processes within the business practice.

The implementation of this principle can take basically two forms. Firstly, the identification of those business practices that can easily be turned into a learning situation about one's own international functioning, such as the development of a five year plan, or the revision or development of the corporate strategy.

Secondly, the international management team may make decisions with implications that reach *beyond* the temporary system. These decisions, bearing on policy issues or concrete problems, must reflect the realized international integration. In a positive way, one may say that they need to include moves to increase the international characteristics of the organizational objectives, the sense of proprietorship, belongingness and identity of its members. More specifically, they may include action plans to open up all organizational positions for all employees regardless of their nationality, or indicate ways of sharing financial ownership, knowledge or influence in the company. They may also include plans to provide the employees with the opportunity to accomplish, as individuals, something over which they have at least a modicum of control. Or they may provide some structures that permit them to consider themselves part of the organization (M. Brown, 1969, p. 354).

In a negative way, these decisions include concrete steps to reduce the impermeability of key organizational or financially rewarding positions in the company, or to define clear paths toward progress within the organization.

C. An OD procedure for the improvement of international relations and effectiveness within international organizations

It would be presumptuous to assume that the following procedures are the only ones that integrate the above five principles. There may be many variations which can be equally effective. The ones described below have been tested and proven effective in more than ten international organizations.

1. The role of the OD practitioner

Although many teams have been built without outside help, I feel that the integration of international management teams is accompanied by a number of intergroup issues whose constructive solution is facilitated by the presence of a *neutral outside consultant*. Furthermore, a few organizational building principles particular to the multinational enterprise are not yet generally recognized. They could be most usefully be introduced when the problem solving attempts bring the discussion to focus on issues of organizational structure. Indeed, and I must emphasize again, that nationality groups, or any other kind of groups, cannot remain integrated without support of an appropriate organizational structure.

The OD practitioner will most likely be asked to intervene in four major areas:

1. The development of appropriate confrontation *procedures* which meet the client's needs;
2. Analysis of the *socio-psychological processes* of the group to improve their problem solving and decision making;
3. *Theoretical and conceptual input*—often empirical data—*on the structure* of international organizations which might facilitate the understanding of the functioning of the system and the formulation of action plans;
4. Jointly explore the business practices which can be used to continue the learning and organizational development processes.

Consequently, the social scientist-consultant takes various roles. At one moment he may be a helpful diagnostician and expert-advisor on procedures instrumental to confrontation, learning and problem-solving, a neutral process-observer or at another time a teacher on building principles and organizational structure (L. Vansina, 1970, 1971).

The particular roles of the OD practitioner will be further described in the following discussion of the team building procedure.

Step 1.  Identification of problem area and client system

In close collaboration with the client, a diagnosis is made of the problem area, the possible sources of conflict, the developmental possibilities and the future plans or ultimate model for the organization. On the basis of these deliberations, a more refined analysis is made of the particular state of the various sub-systems and their key persons. Careful attention must be given to keep the client system alive by keeping the essential central and connecting subsystems together.

In this first step, the role of the OD practitioner is predominantly one of helping the client system: to make a preliminary diagnosis, develop a working relationship and a contract. The expected gains, difficulties, expectations and areas of uncertainty need to be discussed before a contract can be made. Such a contract specifies (a) the right and the possibilities to collect valid information which allows the client or client system to (b) make conscious and informed decisions with (c) internal commitment (C. Argyris, 1970).

Step. 2.  Preparation for the common task

The invitees (key persons) to the work conference need to be informed about the task and the aims of the conference well beforehand. An outline of the task can be formulated by the OD practitioner and sent to everyone by the president or the manager in charge of the client system. Every manager or senior staff member invited is asked to make a force-field analysis (K. Lewin) of the organization. In other words, everyone is asked to *diagnose* the *driving forces* (opportunities, resources, and so on) and the *restraining forces* (obstacles, weaknesses) in the *external* environment and *within* the organization that affect the survival, growth and profitability of the international organization. These reports are either written and directly sent to the OD consultant, or the data are collected through personal interviews. In some cases, where one may assume rightfully that a lot of valuable information is not available to the key persons, the consultant has to collect this additional information himself (through individual or group interviews), for example, in situations where most *local* managers have not yet been promoted to positions which would legitimize their participation in the team building project. This is often the case when an international organization has operations in developing countries, or when plants have recently been built by a group of predominantly foreign managers.

The outline also guarantees the confidentiality of the reports or interviews, and an explanation about the way in which the data will be analyzed and presented at the conference. Accompanying the outline  is the letter of the president or manager in charge, endorsing the outline and explaining the aims and practical arrangements of the workshop.

The role of the OD consultant is characterized here by technical preparation of the conference, writing instructions, interviewing invitees or other relevant persons and making a content analysis of the collected information. The data are analyzed per relevant subsystems (e.g. national management and general management of operating units in our first example) for presentation at the conference.

Step. 3.  First work conference (with the teams separate)*

The top manager present opens the meeting restating the aims and encouraging the participants to be open and frank in the discussion. The role of the consultant here is more complex. He structures, at times, the discussions through questions and procedures; or he may give short lecturettes on particular organizational issues or concepts. Mostly, however, he behaves as a process consultant, building trust, clarifying the psychological processes of the group at work and reality testing.

1.  Immediately after the opening of the conference by the top manager, the consultant restates the task and the superordinate goals. Before he introduces the norms and procedures of the work conference he may feel it desirable to develop a proper working climate by a lecturette on, for example, communication difficulties in international organizations. In any case, he attempts to establish a positive relationship with the total group *in plenum* before presenting the diagnostic data.

2.  He then reviews the collective findings on the present situation of the organization, while encouraging the individuals or subsystems to sharpen their diagnosis, to elaborate on particularly unclear or opposing driving or restraining forces and to own up to their statements. In the following discussions, he behaves more as a catalyst, stimulating reality testing and making process observations where needed to improve the quality of the group's work. He is not only a catalyst of opinions and remarks, which are later-on channeled back to the group for confrontation but he is also a catalyst of *tension*. Because of his tension absorbing effect, the group can deal with more stressful issues and can devote more energy to rational problem solving.

The total group is then asked to identify:

a. the *most important* external and internal driving and restraining forces, namely those forces which have the most impact on the survival, growth and profitability of the international organization;

---

* In our first example the three countries separately. In the second example headquarters, area headquarters and country general managers separately.

b. those forces over which the present group has *control,* which they can manipulate or change in a meaningful way. These forces are called "we" forces, because the group has authority and ability to do something about them. All the other forces are called "they" forces. They are then asked to name those persons, groups or subsystems that have responsibility and control over the "they" forces.*

3. The real life groups meet (separately if there are more than one) to set priorities. They decide which are the most important "we" forces on which the conference should be working to improve the chances of survival, growth and profitability. If there is more than one real life group, the priorities need to be compared and agreement needs to be sought.

4. The most important "we" forces on which there is general agreement are to be put on the agenda first, the others are set aside for later work. Indeed, whenever interpersonal or intergroup tensions arise, it is advisable to develop further the agreement basis they have in common. Later on, after a successful experience of working together on these issues, one can turn back to those for which there was no agreement.

5. The issues on the agenda then become the basis for the composition of problem solving groups. Persons are asked to join the various groups because of their interest in the issue under discussion, and their ability to contribute to the formulation of constructive proposals. Different groups are, however, allowed to work on the same issues.

6. At regular intervals, the different problem solving groups come together, *in plenum,* to report on their deliberations. Consequently, everyone is kept informed about the lines along which one should proceed and the consequences for themselves personally, for their group (nationality, cultural or other reference group) and for their own problem-solving attempts. On these occasions, short theoretical inputs can be given to clarify possible consequences of their action proposals. The major consequences are explored and worked through, before commitment is sought. This may require further

---

* This procedure allows the participants in the conference to clarify roles and responsibilities. Later on, in step 4, when all key persons will be present, a direct confrontation and clarification of responsibilities and roles are made possible.

work in the problem solving groups and *in plenum*. The working through of the economic, human and social consequences, and the search for internal commitment contribute meaningfully to the final integration of the team.

7. If the conference ends at this stage, procedures for follow-up, continuity and evaluation must be defined and decided upon. In its simplest form such evaluation consists of comparing the action proposals with the initial diagnosis. Issues which are not covered need to be dealt with later on.

If, on the other hand, step 3 is only a preparation for the final conference with other teams, then the diagnosis is kept together with the identification of the "we" and "they" forces. Evaluation and follow-up procedures for their own solutions and action proposals can, however, be formulated.

Step 4.  Second work-conference with all teams included.

The development and procedures of this conference are identical to step 3. Here, however, one always has more than one group present. The intergroup issues are therefore unavoidable. Differences in organizational diagnosis, unclarity of roles and areas of responsibility must be fully discussed. The working through of the consequences and the search for real commitment gain crucial importance here for the eventual integration of the international management team.

A conference like this, lasting three or five days, is a firm start of building a multinational organization. Such processes never end. Roles, responsibilities and individuals change, as well as the environment. Consequently, the team needs not only to be maintained, but is expected to adjust itself and to redefine its relationships in view of the developments.

Step 5.  Building continuity for learning and organization development

The OD consultant and the client system explore jointly which of the normal business practices could be transformed into opportunities for learning and development for themselves and for the other subsystems. For example, headquarters may visit area headquarters as a group rather than as a sequence of individual short in-and-out visits. Or existing meetings of the relevant subsystems are, at regular times, extended to look at functioning as an international organization.

After a review of the various factors which hinder learning and development of the international organization, a particular OD approach was described.

The improvement of international relations can only be achieved through the building or development of a truly multinational organization. A first and essential step is the building of an international top management team. Characteristic for such an integrated team is that the group of various nationalities becomes a new and additional reference group. In this group, role and loyalty conflicts can be openly discussed and worked through, while providing identity and meaning to its members.

The development of the team is based on five major principles. A temporary system is created around a common task, which can only be accomplished through the acceptance of a superordinate goal. The various members work together in a face-to-face-situation eventually characterized by a work-climate of openness, trust and reality testing. The team building itself takes place in a neutral location and in a language that does not give real advantages to some of the parties involved.

The chances that the resulting international integration will survive the temporary system are better to the extent that the team is able to make decisions that reflect the international integration and have organizational implications with bearings beyond the temporary systems.

The international integration can be developed further through regular international meetings on major business issues and a continuous reflection on how the international management team operates.

## REFERENCES

Adorno, T. W., Frenkel Brunswick, E., Levinson, D. J., and Sanford, R. N., *The Authoritarian Personality,* New York, Wiley, 1950.

Alger, C. F., Personal contacts in intergovernmental organizations, in: M. C. Kelman, (Ed.), *International Behavior: A Social-Psychological Analysis,* New York, Holt, Rinehart and Winston, 1965, 521-47.

Allport, G. W., *The Nature of Prejudice,* Garden City, Doubleday Anchor, 1958.

Argyris, C. The incompleteness of social psychological theory: Examples from small group, cognitive consistency and attribution theory. *Am. Psychologist,* 1969, XXIV, 10, p. 893-908.

Argyris, C., *Intervention Theory and Method—A Behavioral Science View*, Reading, Mass., Addison-Wesley Publ. Company, 1970.

Brown, M. E., Identification and some conditions of organizational involvement, *Adm. Sc. Quart.*, 1969, 14, p. 347.

Bruner, J. S., & Perlmutter, V. H., Compatriot and foreigner: a study of impression formation in three countries. *J. Abnorm. Soc. Psychol.*, 1957, 55, 253-60.

Deutsch, M., Some Considerations relevant to National Policy. In: Hollander, E. P., & Hunt, R. G., (eds.), *Current Perspectives in Social Psychology*, New York, Oxford University Press, 1967.

Fouraker, L. B. & Stafford, J. M., Organizational structure and multinational strategy, *Adm. Sc. Quart.*, 1968, 13, 47-64.

Gardner, J. W., Individuality commitment and meaning. In: Hollander, E. P., & Hunt, R. G. (eds.), *Current Perspectives in Social Psychology*, New York, Oxford University Press, 1967, p. 86.

Gilbert, G. M., Stereotype persistence and change among college students, *J. Abnorm. Soc. Psychol.*, 1951, 46, 245-254.

Glenn, E. S., Johnson, R. H., Kimmel, P. R. and Wedge, B., A cognitive interaction model to analyze culture conflict in international relations, *J. Conflict Resolution*, 1971, XIV, I, 35-48.

Hollander, E. P. & Hunt, R. G. (eds.), *Current Perspectives in Social Psychology*, New York, Oxford University Press, 1967, second edition.

Katz, D. & Kahn, R. L., *The Social Psychology of Organizations*, New York, Wiley & Sons, 1966.

Kelman, H. C. & Bailyn, L., Effects of cross-cultural experience on national images: A study of scandinavian students in America, *J. Conflict Resolution*, 1962, 5, 319-34.

Klineberg, O., *The Human Dimension in International Relations*, London, Holt, Rinehart & Winston, 1964.

Lee, R. J., Multinational Executive, paper presented at the Graduate School of Business, Columbia University, November 11, 1968.

Lewin, K., *Field Theory in Social Science*, Harper, New York, 1951.

March, J. E. & Simon, H. A., *Organizations*, New York, Wiley & Sons, 1958.

Northern, D. M., *Satisfaction in International Assignments: The American Manager in Belgium and Italy*, University of Louvain, Department of Applied Economics, M.B.A. thesis, 1972.

Perlmutter, H. V., L'entreprise internationale: trois conceptions, *Revue Economique et Sociale*, mai 1955, Université de Lausanne.

Perlmutter, H. V., *Towards a Theory and Practice of Social Architecture. The Building of Indispensable Institutions*, London, Tavistock Pamphlet N° 12, 1965.

Redfield, R., *The Folk Culture of Yucatan*, Chicago, University of Chicago Press, 1941.

Sherif, M., Superordinate goals in the reduction of intergroup conflict, *Am. J. Sociol.*, 1958, 63, 349-58.

Shibuteri, T., Reference groups as perspectives, *Am. J. Sociol.*, 1955, 60, 562-70.

Smith, H. P. & Rosen, E. W., Some psychological correlates of world mindedness and authoritarianism, *J. Pers.,* 1958, 26, 170-83.

Sumner, W. G., *Folkways,* New York, Ginn, 1906.

Thibaut, J. W., & Kelley, H. H., *The Social Psychology of Groups,* New York, J. Wiley, 1959.

Vansina, L. S., Die Psychologie der Beratung, *Gruppendynamik,* 1971, 1, 12-21.

Vansina, L. S., Sensitiviteitstraining voor organisatie-adviseurs: *Kroniek Ambacht, Klein en Middenbedrijf,* 1972, 26, 259-269.

Vansina, L. S., Enkele psychologische beschouwingen bij de adviesverlening, *Nederl. Tijdschrift Psychol.,* 1970, 133-143.

Witkin, H. A., A cognitive style approach to cross-cultural research, *Intern. J. of Psychology,* 1967, II, 233-50.

Zand, D. E., Trust and Managerial Problem Solving, *Adm. Sc. Quart.,* 1972, 17, 2.

# 15

# Open Systems Redesign

*Charles G. Krone*

As I sit down to write about changing a complex social system, I am filled with ambivalence. On the one hand, I feel the work is worthy of writing about both because of my need to present those concepts which I feel might contribute to others who are engaged in the field of change; and as some level of expression to my many friends who have worked and dreamed towards a more meaningful existence. On the other hand, I am filled with concern about being able to adequately portray something so complex and to convey the essential living and breathing character which exemplifies it.

Perhaps the place to start is with the thoughts that were passing through my mind some years ago. I had strong feelings (perhaps more adequately expressed as a "passion") that man could find more for himself, if he had the chance, than he was finding in the social forms and processes presented by existing organizations. These feelings of mine were based on the sense I had of myself and of my own potential to actualize as well as the growth potentialities I had experienced in others in groups of which I had been a part.

The literature and knowledge available to awaken this growth process for the person seemed an adequate foundation to accept and work with, but what seemed to be grossly lacking was any broad scale framework by means of which to describe the organization which promotes growthful human behavior. The closest I could come to this was the efforts by those working with socio-technical systems design. Although I would be the last to cast aspersions on the contribution people engaged in this work have made, a real sense of dynamics seemed to be missing. An organization acting against an ever changing environment is a dynamic thing. An individual is dynamic in the sense that he has a need to search out for new behavior and new skills as well as have a platform of certainty from which to launch himself. My search for answers carried me through most of the literature on General Systems Theory and to many far flung writings which deal with concepts of organic and growthful behavior. At the time of this writing, there is on my part no sense of completion; however, the concepts which I refer to as "open systems organizations" have provided me and my colleagues a useful framework within which to operate. The successes we have had in their application, both in developing new systems and changing ongoing ones, heartens us.

In order to provide some basic insight into open systems organizations a brief exposé of a traditional supervisory system, a socio-technical work group, and an open systems group is in order.

In a traditional system, each worker occupies an individually delimited space called a job (See Figure 1). These jobs normally turn out to be highly compartmentalized spaces which are protected by the workers. The supervisor, through directing and controlling, is supposed to see that all the blocks fit together to meet some productive purpose. When mismatches occur, they are resolved by grievances and arbitration against a previously described set of rules.

The autonomous work group of a socio-technically designed system (Figure 2) provides semi-autonomous space for a group which, within identified and rather fixed boundaries, workers have the freedom to make decisions. Typically, these boundaries allot to the workers freedom in the details of task organization, scheduling, quality control, training, employee evaluation, vacation scheduling, discipline and the like. The contact with the encompassing organization is through a boundary manager who has as his primary responsibilities the assurance of resources in the nature of utilities, machinery and new employees, as well as regulating the input flow of such things as materials, changes in product, changes in equipment design, wages and so on.

The open system "flowering" design (Figure 3) provides an autonomous system which provides the employee the opportunity to learn the fundamental operating requirements of the core technology with which his task group is associated. As he/she develops

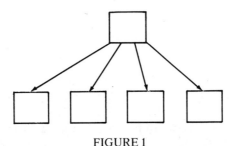

FIGURE 1

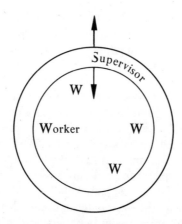

FIGURE 2

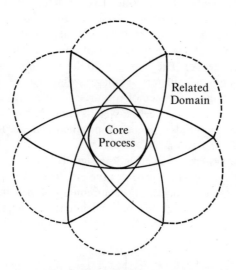

FIGURE 3

competence in the basic skills he gains "access to totality" and the opportunity to engage in every domain related to the core process and its supporting functions. That is, his growth potential is enhanced by the freedom to proactively integrate with his system's environment to the extent that his training and competence allow.

The flower connects with the organization as it needs resources—experts to train and help decide on technical issues, and so on. Managers become technical experts and consultants to teams. Boundaries are implicit in the limits of team competence and are "worked" in conjunction with those who have held responsibilities by reason of priority, legal definition or expertise.

The open systems mode of relating to one's work and co-workers does not suit everyone equally in either worker or manager roles. People who display high dependency needs find the lack of a highly delineated role and the absence of directive supervision discomforting. People with high needs for independence also find difficulty with the needs of the team for interdependent support. For many, however, opportunity for growth, freedom from structural limitations and absence of directive supervision are adequate rewards.

My experience to date is that open systems designs do not have to be justified on humanitarian grounds. The economic, personal and extra-work effects are highly positive. The most frequently experienced dilemma is keeping space free for the outward seeking of growth. As the work force becomes competent in operating their transformation processes, maintaining their social system and transacting with their environment, they continue to solve problems in broader areas. They push outward against management personnel, not to obstruct work but to take it over. Management is placed in the position of resisting, searching for problem solving voids, assuming task responsibilities of their hierarchy or getting literally squeezed out of a meaningful role in the organization.

At the present time, I feel I can say for myself and my colleagues, that we have the proven capacity to help develop open systems work environments in new work sites which have proven to be psychically, socially and productively healthy. The frontier, for the present, exists in those institutions which have lived in the traditional or "scientific management" mode for some period of time. It is here where we confront issues of deep seated alienation, mistrust, indirect resolution of differences and the like.

The first subject I would like to talk about in the change of ongoing systems is that of who the change agents are. More often than not, I find them not to be those who are formally designated by the organization as consultants or OD specialists. They are instead emergent personalities of two different types, both of which I feel are essential to creating system change. The first type is the manager or

union officer who either through make-up or through development
sets up tight but workable boundaries. My stereotype is that those
people are oftentimes characterized as enemies or resistors of
change. In my own mind they serve the essential function of
maintaining boundaries until effective competence within them is
developed and, secondly, when those boundaries are transcended, the
breakthrough becomes a meaningful or an "aha expereince" for
them. The second type of personality which I feel is equally essential
is the person who develops a deep seated passion for a more
meaningful existence. Nothing is more personally gratifying to me
than to see these passionate allies emerge from the system. On the
other hand, nothing can be so terrifying as to work with a designated
group of change agents lacking in this ingredient which I call
passion. Although I have talked about change agents out of context
or sequence, as a practitioner I always have an eye out for them and
try to cultivate their emergence in any processes with which I am
engaged.

One of the first targets in the change of a system is the
establishment and maintenance of what has come to be known
(Figure 4) as an "envelope group" or sometimes as a total systems
"Core Group." The membership of this group consists of those

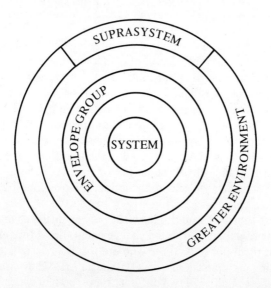

FIGURE 4

people who occupy power roles for the entire system (union and management) and the change agents for the system. Sometimes members of the suprasystem are also members of the envelope group, especially when the performance of their roles is inter-related with the total system.

The functions of an envelope group consist of:

1. Maintaining a context for the total system through "open systems planning;"
2. Integrating change efforts within the system with the suprasystem and the greater environment;
3. Maintaining a sense of balance and thrust within the total systems;
4. Providing a many faceted body for reflecting the change efforts and proposals of product streams and plant "core groups;"
5. Providing the nucleus for core groups to develop from; and
6. Sanctioning and maintaining a compatible environment for test cells within the system.

These functions in all likelihood require a great deal more elaboration than I have given them; however, in the interest of trying to provide an overview, I shall refrain from doing so at the present.

Members of the envelope group form the genesis of a core group for a product system selected as a potential site for a test cell (Figure 5). Additional members of the core group are most often selected by people within the product system after interaction with the envelope group members about the purpose and need to form a core group. The eventual core group membership consists of members of each sociometric group within the work force. The core group becomes responsible for creating and maintaining an open system within the larger organization. In my experience with change efforts without the development of a core group, the eagerness to develop open values becomes a double binding nightmare of permissiveness and authoritarian demands.

Task forces oftentimes eminate from core groups in much the same way that core groups are spawned from envelope groups. Task forces are temporary problem solving bodies who work on problems defined by the core group (Figure 6.)

One of the first processes we engage in with a core group is normally an open systems planning exercise around the core processes and task environment of that particular product stream. The purpose of this exercise is to depict for themselves and to

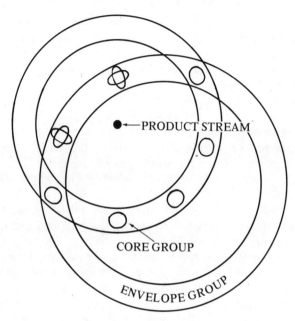

FIGURE 5

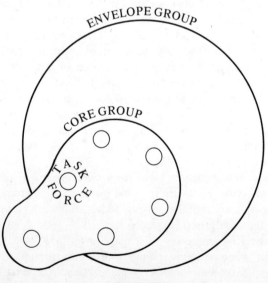

FIGURE 6

communicate to the product system members answers to the questions 'why change?' and 'change what?'

The following example was developed by a core group of which I was a member and represents the totality of the stresses they felt from their different areas of membership within the system.

## Why Change?

The response to why change has no simple answer. We are confronted on all sides by a series of stresses which are both internal and external to our system. The more appropriately we transact with the totality of the stresses, and the more adaptable we remain, the healthier and more viable we become. The following diagram (Figure 7) and descriptions describe at least a portion of the stresses of the internal and external environments.

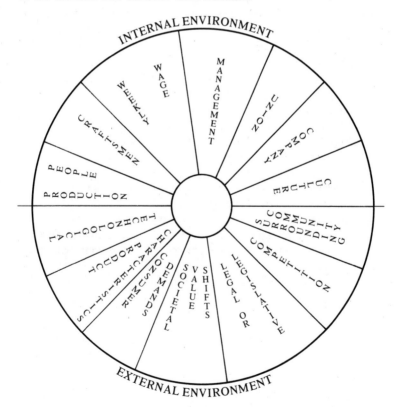

FIGURE 7

Internal Environment

— Present pay system is not adaptable to our more complex jobs.
— Incentive systems based on machine efficiency measures put a ceiling on production rates.
— People are motivated for monetary purposes to move to the lower skill manual jobs.
— People are not encouraged to make their potential contribution to the overall effectiveness of the business by the present definition of jobs and our current methods of operation.
— Craftsmen, because of geographical and social separation from product streams, are hindered from developing ownership in these streams.
— Craftsmen are provided skill areas or crafts within which to work which they must protect from the standpoint of economic rewards, and for reasons of personal security, identity and safety.
— The automation and elimination of tasks threatens the job security of many people in some categories.
— The directive style of management creates an aggressive interface between management and employees.
— Proposed changes in the management role and style creates a concern within the present system of how change will be dealt with.
— Incentive systems sometimes encourage contradictory goals and encourage directive management approach.
— The culture we have developed is accustomed to physical change but devoid of planned social change. Consequently, the development of social change produces considerable anxiety in the system.
— The present function and structure of the system inhibits growthful behavior and decision making process by people.
— People are concerned that management will force changes and that this will adversely affect their level of earnings and their job security.
— Although there are elements of all of the above within our culture there is an overall sense of a need and desire to change and improve the social and technological effectiveness of the system.
— A pilot system is viewed with some level of suspicion with

the fear that it may become an unwanted continuing part of the system.
— The representative body for the employees has taken a very responsible posture that change within the area is healthy and necessary.
— The union is appropriately concerned that change be undertaken with the full involvement and participation of the employees so any change will best answer the employee's needs and desires to make a more beneficial and meaningful place to work.
— The company has a strong loyalty to the people because of the long-term supportive relationships.
— There is an increasing concern on the company's part about the technological and social effectiveness of the plant as contrasted to some of its newer operations.
— The company has shown a willingness to risk large-scale capital investments with the expectation that they will facilitate both social and technological rejuvenation.

### External Stresses

*Technological*

— The capital cost of equipment is growing at an increasing rate, therefore increasing the number of shifts the equipment must be operated and increasing the cost of downtime.
— Pieces of equipment and operations are increasingly linked together requiring integrated responses and knowledge of social units.
— The replacement of people as a power source by mechanization is increasing at an accelerating rate.
— There is an increasing integration of various fields of knowledge within a specific unit of equipment requiring a broader span of knowledge of the people operating, maintaining and improving it. (For example, a case packer must integrate the fields of mechanics, electricity, electronics, pneumatics, and piping.)
— The above also indicates the need to develop a social organization which has more depth in various fields of knowledge.
— The increasing sophistication and inter-linkage of equipment increase both the importance and difficulty of appropriate problem diagnosis and solution.

— The increasing rate of range in technology indicates the need for more closely coupled efforts between the people who are directly responsible for the equipment and the people who are knowledgeable resources for technological change.

*Products Characteristics*

— Societal needs and values are changing. This causes more rapid change in the character of our products and reduces the time period when any product is the appropriate answer. This means more product changes, a shorter life for each, and a social system that is adaptive.
— The increasing production rates and the consequent increasing effects of deviations from quality limits dictate a closer coupling of quality control with operations and more rapid feedback loops.
— Product formulas are changing more rapidly, requiring quicker solutions, indicating the need for closer information links between product streams, process development and technical services.

*Consumer Demands*

— The consumer and marketing needs are demanding a broader range in sizes and a more rapid change in character of products. This dictates a closer and more responsive coupling of our product streams and the readings taken in the activity of the market place to prevent excessive inventories and the appropriate availability of the right products at the right times.

*Societal Value Shifts*

— The society of which we are all a part is undergoing a multitude of strong value shifts which exert pervasive influence on us all. Those shifts which we can identify as strong and persistent enough to be taken into consideration are:
  - A desire for everyone to have an equal opportunity to be heard and to participate in deciding about things that are affecting them.
  - The increasing right to question and to be given more free will and become more responsibly autonomous.

- The desire for a greater sense of community and caring for one another and the ability to find more meaning in relationships and less in things.
- The desire to have a greater outlet for creative expression.
- A need to develop the capacity to cope with the rapidly changing world about them.
- The desire to make life more meaningful at a personal level.
- The right to be different and to be able to differ and yet be accepted.

— Societies need to find more productive solutions to the question of minorities.
— The need and desire for equality for women.
— A rising concern for the long-term effects on the ecology of the things we produce and the processes we use to produce them.

## Legal or Legislative Demands

— That we employ the same number of minorities in the work force that appear in the community from which we hire.
— That we employ proportionally the same number of women in the work force as there are seeking employment in the community from which we hire.
— An increasing concern that women and minorities appear in these same percentages at all employment levels.

## Competition

— New plants with more modern technology and more effective social organizations are able to produce products at approximately half the manufacturing cost of the same products.
— The key to competition is faster responses to changing demands and circumstances with the requirement of greater flexibilities to different situations on the part of the producing systems.

## Surrounding Community

— As a part of a greater community, we have the responsibility of remaining a responsible community member.

Completion of environmental scanning and its dynamic trends provides core group members with an imprint of their environmental totality. It becomes evident which present modes of operation do not allow for effective transactions with the environment.

The next portion of the process for a core group is the articulation of their quest. The process effect of this is hard for me to capture in words. It often becomes for core group members a deeply meaningful process. Figure 8 is a symbolic attempt to capture the meaning of this experience coupled with that of open systems planning.

The circle on the left developed by open systems planning represents the ground of being people find in the on-going system. The star at the right represents the luminence of the defined quest. The quest takes the form of defining life giving processes and behavior for the system and all of its members. Examples of this definition for two different groups follow. I would like to suggest that the words are rather simple but for the members involved in their development, the essence of their meaning is beyond the words.

The two general objectives to be worked toward at the plant are:

1. Create a culture in which there are no artificial barriers which could prevent any individual from making his maximum contribution toward achieving the objective of the enterprise.
2. Provide an atmosphere in which each individual is properly

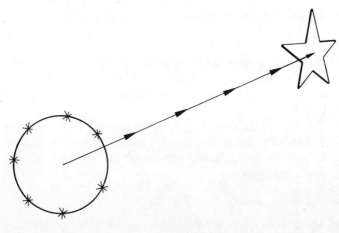

FIGURE 8

trained, motivated and rewarded to attain maximum success in achieving the objectives of the enterprise.

The more specific objectives felt to be needed in today's situation are:

1. Broad, flexible job design should be used, without restrictive job titles or job boundaries.
2. Maximum flexibility should be used in accomplishing tasks and solving problems. This does not mean that "everyone is to be able to do everything." Team members should learn to do those jobs for which need, aptitude and interest exist.
3. Team orientation should be toward the total operation rather than individual jobs.
   a. The effectiveness of team effort is greater than the sum of individual efforts.
   b. Team membership for problem solving must be carefully defined. Members without input or a stake in the solution should not be involved in most cases.
4. Mutual trust is a building block of work effectiveness.
5. Hygiene factors must be satisfied on a continuing basis in such areas as pay, employee benefits, work rules and facilities.
6. Solving problems and establishing relationships should be accomplished through an open exchange of thoughts and feelings, aimed at satisfying both individual and company needs.
7. A dynamic organization is maintained by encouraging exposure to the environment that requires change and by providing freedom to respond to those signals.
8. Mature people are proactive in assuming increasing responsibility, given appropriate timing, input and freedom.
9. Decisions are best made close to the source of input, implementation, effect and accountability.
10. Teams gain unity and direction in a large part through goals which they have participated in setting.
11. Long term organizational health needs must be considered in situations where short term production goals threaten to become overriding.

## Behavioral Beliefs

The basis of our effort to develop concepts for a proposed new wage and social structure rests upon certain behavioral beliefs. These behavioral beliefs are not based upon what currently happens, but what it is we feel that people would want to happen if they were provided the choice. In our efforts to develop wage and social structure concepts, we have attempted to allow for the development of these beliefs. In the final analysis we cannot create the desire for, nor the carrying out of these beliefs. We are dependent upon the people directly involved to breathe life into them and sustain them through time. We can only expect this if those people find them personally meaningful and worth the effort.

*Behavioral Beliefs*

1. People want to belong to a stable group of friends who share a common productive purpose in order to be helpful and supportive toward one another.
2. People like an equal opportunity for growth and development and seek to be responsible.
3. People enjoy applying imagination, ingenuity and creativity.
4. People like to be part of a group which has self-direction and control
5. People gain a great deal of benefit and satisfaction from being part of a group which engages in an open expression of feelings and needs.
6. People like a comfortable amount of stress toward their own development and team achievements, and gain a good deal of satisfaction by being able to set and achieve new horizons.
7. People have a need for recognition and respect for what it is they are as persons and gain satisfaction from the growth and application of new skills.
8. People want the right to question what's going on and participate in changing it if it needs changing in order to develop a caring, effective and healthy system.

The next stage of evolution most often undertaken by a core group is the description of the social forms and social process that are seen as necessary in the development from the "ground" toward the "star" (Figure 8). Most of the system changes I have been involved with have also included fairly extensive physical or technical changes along with social change processes. In undertaking these physical changes, an organization is developed with the same sort of social concepts, forms and processes as are visualized for the on-going operation of the changing system. The following social systems concepts were developed by a core group I have recently been working with.

## Social System Concepts

The organizing principle underlying the concepts for social structure is that of creating identification with a product stream. A conceptual view of a *product stream* includes at its center a core process, an open area which represents the boundary of the system, and space outside the circle which represents the environment of the system (figure 9).

The proposal is built upon the following definition of *core process* for any product stream. The core process of any product stream is defined as the optimal integration of three sub-processes (figure 10).

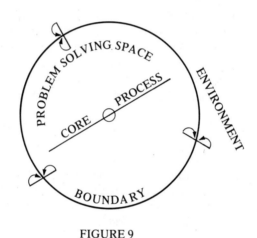

FIGURE 9

FIGURE 10

These separate processes are identified as relating to the individual, the group and the creative producing thrust. Each of these is identified as a process because they are seen as evolving through time.

The *individual process* has the goal of allowing each individual to grow and develop in ways that lead to a more meaningful contribution to organizational purposes to the full extent of his personal potentiality.

The *group process* has the goal of developing both the process and problem solving capabilities to bring together in a reinforcing way the development of the individual and the creative producing thrust of the product stream.

The *creative producing thrust* is not just a cumbersome way of saying the need to produce something in the most effective way possible. Instead, these words are used to indicate that nothing in the conversion process is static. The technology, supplies, quality, scheduling, repairing and product change methods, if viewed in a non-static way, continually lend themselves to creative improvement.

The overall core process for a product stream is developing these sub-processes so they come together in mutually reinforcing ways to create the healthiest and most productive system possible.

The open area in figure 11 between the dot in the circle (which represents the core process) and the circle (which represents the boundary) is the problem solving space occupied by the people. People occupying this space need to look both inward toward the

FIGURE 11

core process and outward toward their environment in order to create a healthy, viable system. Schematically this is represented in figure 12.

The outward view is almost universally left out of most work situations. The cost of leaving this out is the creation of static non-changing product streams. This is seen as inappropriate with the increasing rates of change that the future holds.

The outer circle, or *boundary,* represents the divisions between what is inside the system and what is outside the system. What is inside is determined by conditions of space, time, and capacity for problem resolution. The boundary of an open system allows for transactions and feedback in terms of material, energy and information flow essential to the system.

The *environment* of a system is what is on the outside of the system with which it must engage or transact. The effect of the environment is better grasped and understood if we classify this environment into domains. An example (not totally inclusive) of the environment for a product packing system classified into domains is portrayed in figure 13.

The environment is described as largely containing information because the behavior or action of a system first takes place on the basis of information that it receives. This is then followed by the flow of energy, then material, and finally by internal incorporation into the system. An example would perhaps better illustrate this.

An engineer discovers that a new model case packer exists which he thinks would be of benefit if purchased. He approaches a resource

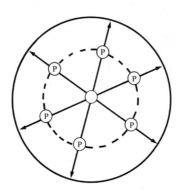

FIGURE 12

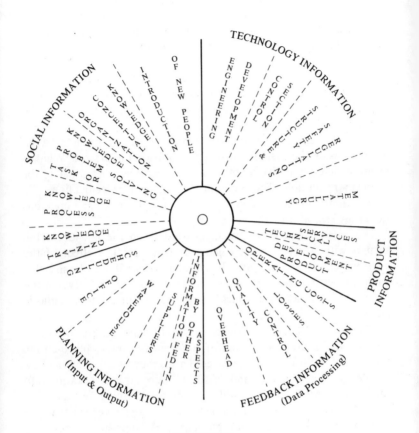

FIGURE 13

inside the system and they exchange (1) *information* leading to the decision to purchase the case packer. The next step is that the case packer is purchased and (2) *energy* flows in the form of money from our system to theirs. The case packer arrives and (3) new *material* flows into the system. Finally, the new case packer is effectively (4) *incorporated* into the system.

The reason for describing this incident or process is that from an organizational or conceptual point of view this total process can take place most effectively if the same person or persons are involved in all stages.

A further organizing concept of the proposed social system is that of teams which are semi-autonomous groups of the total product stream. Certain principles are involved in determining the appropriate definition of a team.

1. Responsibility for a particular technological unit.
   Example 1. A packaging line together with its inputs and outputs.
   Example 2. A making system which needs to operate as an integrated whole.
2. A stable group of people which rotates in shifts together.
3. Be relatively self-sufficient in technical skills necessary for quality control, maintenance and operating adjustments.
4. Consist ideally of membership not exceeding ten to twelve persons.
5. Share or be located within a common geographical area (best within sight of one another).
6. Quality control functions which provide feedback information to the operation should be included as an operating team function.
7. The operating unit should provide the team clearly definable and easily measurable results in the form of quality and quantity of product.
8. The team should operate on the basis of joint ownership and responsibility for the total task or problem solving space without exclusive ownership by any member of a particular task or problem solving responsibility.

In product streams containing multiple teams, a member from each team (elected stewards, management and OD resources) will form as the *Core Group* for the product stream. The *purpose* of the core group is to provide linkage and autonomy within the product stream. In order to do this, the core group engages in the following activities:

1. Diagnoses the product stream and its environmental relations;
2. Initiates and develops task forces to propose solutions to particular problems which affect the total product stream;
3. Maintains a healthy and open communication to the total product stream, management and the union;
4. Is responsible for the growth and development needs of the people within the product stream;
5. Plans for the future to maintain a healthy and viable system.

Task forces are temporary problem solving bodies which develop proposed solutions to specific problems. They are:

1. Made up of people relevant to the problem in question;
2. Responsible to generate proposed solutions to problems defined by the core group;
3. Responsible to the core group and communicate their proposed solution to it;
4. Take into consideration the boundary concerns identified by the core group.

Management is viewed more as a process than a role filled by a particular group of people. This process is defined as having the following facets:

1. Providing able technical resources;
2. Providing effective process skills to allow for optimum realization of individuals and groups;
3. Facilitating linkage between the product stream and its external environment;
4. Enabling the development of decisions which optimize the long term development of the product stream.

The reward structure for the individual in an open systems design is based upon the amount of skill and knowledge the individual has available to the needs of the system. This will perhaps be better understood if we take a look at the following wage structure developed by a core group. These proposals are then sanctioned as an experimental basis by both the company and the union.

## Wage Structure Concepts

1. Everybody will have an equal opportunity to develop the skill necessary to progress through the wage structure. Progression through the wage structure will depend upon the capability and desire of the individual to progress and the needs of the business for the additional skills.
2. Every person within a product stream is a part of the same wage structure. The system should remain flexible based upon the changing needs of individuals and of the business.
3. The basis of payment for the wage structure is dependent upon the amount of applied problem solving skills the individual has. Sufficient resources must be made available within each product stream so that the training needs of the individuals within the product stream are adequately met.
4. The wage structure will be a combined hourly and weekly salary system. All people within a product stream will be hired or originally employed at an hourly rate. This hourly rate will

continue so long as they remain non-guaranteed employees. All people within the unit will convert to a weekly salary system of payment to signify they are permanent members of the system.

5. The concept of indexing for establishment of wages will be maintained.

6. The aim of the wage structure is not to create generalists with diffuse skills, but is developed with the aim that depth of skills and training be maintained and built upon.

7. The wage structure was developed with the potential for application to any product stream.

8. Each individual will be able, by his own free choice, to develop and exercise the skills to move through the wage structure.

9. Progression through the structure will be on the basis of percentage assessments of skill elements people learn and employ.

10. Individual wage adjustments will take place on the basis of the percentage movement they have achieved toward the next level of the wage structure.

## PROPOSED WAGE STRUCTURE

### Explanation

The dot (Figure 14) in the center and the first level of the wage structure represent a new employee entering the system. The employee designated by this part of the wage structure will continue to be hourly paid as long as they remain discretionary. This will not prohibit their advancement through the wage structure.

The second level of the wage structure represents a weekly salary potential.

The second level of the proposed wage structure represents a measuring point for the predominance of technologies within the system. Progression to this level of the wage structure is dependent upon the individual developing and applying the following problem solving capabilities.

*Fully functioning operating team members.*
The individual has and appropriately applies the capacity to perform all of the operating functions of the team. Included in the

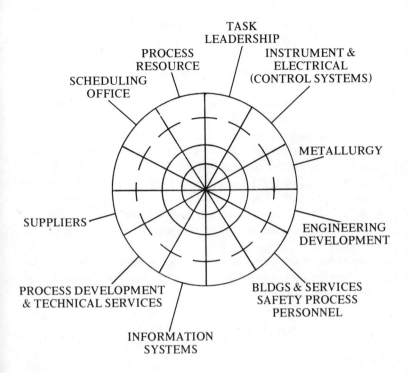

FIGURE 14

*Proposed Wage Structure*

operating team are quality control functions which support the particular technology.

*Technological problem solving.*

Technological problem solving involves a team member having sufficient knowledge of his team's technology to effectively diagnose problems and contribute to their solution.

*Operational problem solving.*

Operational problem solving involves a team member having sufficient operating knowledge of his own and adjacent team's input or output technologies so that he is able to and does contribute effectively to operational solutions; that is, a team member of packing operation should not only possess operating knowledge of his own system but also have sufficient understanding of making, supplier and warehousing operations so he can more creatively and inclusively contribute to the solution of operational problem solving within his own team.

*Boundary or feedback problem solving.*
Boundary problem solving involves a team member acquiring and using skills which deal with the effectiveness or regulation of the product stream of his team; i.e., examples of such aspects are:

1. Loss problem solving
2. Quality problem solving
3. Scheduling problem solving
4. Unit cost problem solving
5. Methods or improvements problem solving

The third level of the wage structure represents a weekly salary potential for the concepts in the more sophisticated operation which exists within the system.

The outer level represents the potential earnings in the wage structure for individuals who are able to develop and apply and mediate the knowledge of a scientific description in the environment relevant to the technology of the product stream.

An instrument man who has progressed to the outer level of the wage structure would be knowledgeable about and able to apply the following types of skills:

1. Those of a fully qualified instrument man;
2. Electrical skills;
3. Operating skills for the product stream;
4. Planning skills for that scientific description;
5. Purchasing skills for that scientific description;
6. Necessary engineering and project skills;

7. Be able to develop solutions with instrument and control section as appropriate to that product stream;

8. This list is not meant to be limiting or complete and would finally be determined by the present future needs of a product stream.

Schematically, the problem solving space he would cover would be as portrayed in figure 15.

A packing operator who has progressed to the fourth level of the wage structure would be knowledgeable about and apply the following skills:

1. First be a fully competent operator:

2. All those skills relevant to that product stream;

3. Machine adjusting skills;

4. Machining skills;

5. Planning skills;

6. Purchasing and inventory skills;

7. Engineering and project skills;

8. Develop solutions with the engineering development section relevant to that product stream;

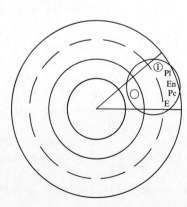

I  = Instrument
E  = Electrical
En = Engineering &
       Project
O  = Operations
Pl  Planning
Pc = Purchasing &
       Inventory

Instrument &
Electrical = Mediation
of information from
Instrument & Electrical
Section

INSTRUMENT
&
ELECTRICAL

FIGURE 15

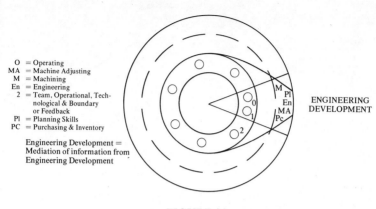

O = Operating
MA = Machine Adjusting
M = Machining
En = Engineering
2 = Team, Operational, Tech-
      nological & Boundary
      or Feedback
Pl = Planning Skills
PC = Purchasing & Inventory

Engineering Development =
Mediation of information from
Engineering Development

ENGINEERING
DEVELOPMENT

**FIGURE 16**

9. This list is not meant to be limiting or complete and would finally be determined by the present and future needs of a product stream.

Schematically, the problem solving space he would occupy may be portrayed as in figure 16.

A laboratory analyst who has progressed to the fourth level of the wage structure would be knowledgeable about and apply the following skills:

1. First be a fully qualified analyst;
2. All those skills relevant to that product stream;
3. Planning skills relevant to the laboratory function and product characteristics;
4. Purchasing skills relevant to the laboratory function and product characteristics;
5. Laboratory management skills;
6. Develop solutions for that product stream with technical services and product development.

Schematically, the problem solving space he would occupy would look like this (figure 17).

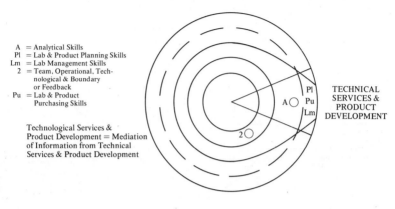

A   = Analytical Skills
Pl  = Lab & Product Planning Skills
Lm  = Lab Management Skills
2   = Team, Operational, Tech-
       nological & Boundary
       or Feedback
Pu  = Lab & Product
       Purchasing Skills

Technological Services &
Product Development = Mediation
of Information from Technical
Services & Product Development

TECHNICAL
SERVICES &
PRODUCT
DEVELOPMENT

FIGURE 17

The use of sanctioned experiments has been a methodology used by those systems with which I have been engaged. This procedure bounds off a segment of the total system for a definitive period of time to provide for evaluation of the forms and processes of the redesign. It provides both sanction and security for the population of the experimental area. This concept evolved from the Norwegian work of Thorsrud and Emery except that their sanctioning documents were a great deal more formal than the following example:

## Test Cell Concepts

1. The primary emphasis during the test cell period would be on establishing a culture consistent to the behavioral beliefs enumerated above.
2. Participants in the test cell would be guaranteed no loss of earnings for the test period. This means providing people a base of their present hourly earnings and existing bonus percentage.
3. The length of the test cell period will be determined on an individual basis for each product stream.
4. Changes in existing practices will be voluntary by each individual.
5. Acceptance or continuance of test cell applications for any product stream is contingent upon the agreement of both the union and the company.
6. Members entering into a test cell would continue to have the same rights and benefits provided by the contract and company plans.

7. If the test cell is discontinued either on the part of the union or the company, practices which are consistent within the area will be introduced.

8. Individuals will move into product streams on the basis of a particular team's need for a role function.

In reality, the material I have covered is the prelude to change and not about the change itself. The design or redesign of an open system, however, is never a completed work. They continue to change and evolve as a result of the growth of their membership and the dynamics of their environment.